The Cocoa Plantations
America's CHOCOLATE Secret
Forced Child Labor, Rape, Sodomy, Abuse of Children Child Sex Trafficking, Child Organ Trafficking, Child Sex Slaves

The Chocolate Industries Well Kept Secret
Harkin-Engel Protocol

Raymond C. Christian

authorHOUSE®

AuthorHouse™
1663 Liberty Drive
Bloomington, IN 47403
www.authorhouse.com
Phone: 1 (800) 839-8640

Published by AuthorHouse 08/13/2015

ISBN: 978-1-5049-2624-9 (sc)
ISBN: 978-1-5049-2625-6 (hc)
ISBN: 978-1-5049-2623-2 (e)

Contents

When you speak about laws needing to be passed and bills that need to be ratified in order to make adequate changes for the wrongs being done to children? My thinking is this should not take a long time for our judicial system to incorporate laws, rules and regulations needed to bring about a change for children unable to make decisions. I have uncovered many laws of which you shall be reading throughout this book which reveal, violation, after violation after violation. Concerning the rights of these children who are working on the Cocoa Plantations on the Ivory Coast of Africa and Ghana, little girls and boys five years of age working over 100 hours a week to get the cocoa bean or cocoa pod to America in order for the Chocolate Industries will be able to produce chocolate. United States Former Senator Thomas Richard "Tom Harkin and United States Congressman Eliot Engel along with Susan Smith and the Chocolate Industry as a whole are all named in this book to make you aware of what is not being done to help innocent children on the Cocoa Plantations.. A promise was made in 2001 to make changes to the Cocoa Plantations it is now 2015 and children are still suffering. The Harkin-Engel Protocol is what they named the law that was to bring into abolishment the raping, sodomizing, beating, sex trafficking, organ trafficking and murdering of these innocent children on the Cocoa Plantations. Laws were being set as far back as 1973 Convention 138 of which you will read about later in the book. The Convention on the Rights of the Child (CRC), International Labor Organization (ILO), and the ratified Conventions will be listed later in this book but just to give you a little insight on the wrong being done to these children on the Cocoa Plantation in Africa and Ghana I present to you Convention 182. I am doing this in order that you have an understanding that meetings in high places are taking place but nothing is being done to give these children on the Ivory Coast of Africa and Ghana any relief.

"Although the apple may fall from its branch and roll a little further from the tree. It is still a part of the tree it has fallen from. My concern and question to you is just because it has rolled a little further from

the tree than the rest of the apples that fell. Should I show more or less concern that the worms will have a greater chance of infecting the one apple that rolled away from the tree?

In my expression of concern what is being said here is that although these children on the Cocoa Plantations are not my biological children. Although they do not have the privileges other children in America have they are still considered to be children. Unable to take care and feed their self or live a life style other children in America are able to live. It should not only be my concern but the concerns of all those in politics, government officials, child protective screening agencies, child monitoring sites, the National Confectioners Association, and other organization involved in the protection of children to bring the abusers of these children to justice. **So the question here is not how did the apple get eaten by the worms? The question is who allowed the apple to be eaten by the worms? Who allowed this situation on the Cocoa Plantations to get so far out of hand that maggots are now wiggling all over the world?** *Convention 182 begins to inform us about the rights of which I will present to you Articles within Convention 182 to help give you a better understanding much later in the book. I am delaying the majority of the laws that apply to these children on the Cocoa Plantations because I did not want you to become too consumed in reading the book and forget about the laws you have read that does apply. You will have a much better understanding of what is taking place with the children on the Ivory Coast of Africa and Ghana as you read this book. For the purpose of laws and conventions I now present you with other laws that apply will be mentions in the middle and end of this book:*

Convention 182

Convention 182 concerning the prohibition and immediate action for the elimination of the worst forms of child labor, adopted by the conference at its eighty-seventh session, Geneva, 17 June 1999.

The General Conference of the International Labor Organization having been convened at Geneva by the governing body of the International Labor Office, and having met in its 87th Session on 1 June 1999.

Considering the need to adopt new instruments for the prohibition of elimination of the worst forms of child labour, as the main priority for national and international action, including international cooperation and assistance, to complement the Convention and the Recommendation concerning minimum age for admission to employment 1973, which remain fundamental instruments on child labor?

Considering that the effective elimination of the worst forms of child labour requires immediate and comprehensive action. Taking into account the importance of free basic education and the need to remove the children concerned from all such work and to provide for their rehabilitation and social integration while addressing the needs of their families?

Recalling the resolution concerning the elimination of child labour adopted by the International Labour Conference at its 83rd Session in 1996, recognizing that child labour is to a great extent caused by poverty and that the long term solution lies in sustained economic growth leading to social progress, in particular poverty alleviation and universal education.

Recalling the Convention on the Rights of the Child adopted by the United Nations General Assembly on 20 November 1989 and recalling the International Labor Organization Declaration on Fundamental Principles and Rights at Work and its follow-up adopted by the International Labour Conference at its 86th Session in 1998.

Recalling that some of the worst forms of child labour are covered by other international instruments in particular the Forced Labour Convention, 1930 and the United Nations Supplementary Convention on the Abolition of Slavery, the Slave Trade and institutions and Practices Similar to Slavery, 1956.

Having decided upon the adoption of certain proposals with regard to child labour, which is the fourth item on the agenda of the session and having determined that these proposals shall take the form of an international Convention: adopts this seventeenth day of June of the year one hundred and ninety-nine the following Convention, which may be cited as the **WORST FORMS OF CHILD LABOUR** CONVENTION,1999.

Article 1 of the Conventions
Summarization by the Author

Makes each member of the Convention responsible to take action and to do everything possible to eliminate the worst forms of child labor immediately

Article 2 of the Convention
Summarization by the Author

Clearly states that all persons under the age of 18 are to be referred to in Convention terminology as considered to be a "Child"

Article 3 of the Convention
Summarization by the Author

It is duly noted the Convention is stating "The Worst forms of child labor consist of:

1. Any form of slavery in practice which is a part of the selling and or child trafficking, a child cannot be used for debt bondage, a child cannot be forced to be used in illegal or war activities:
2. Children cannot be used to participate in prostitution or any sexual and obscene activities:

3. International treaties dictate that children cannot be used in abnormal activities, such as drug trafficking:
4. The child's safety for any reason should not be jeopardized under any circumstance that may have a conflict concerning the child's health or safety:

The further you read into this book the more you will see the horrible, insensitive and non-moralistic situations taking place with these five year old children sold to the Cocoa Plantation owners, destined to never see their parents again and to work as slaves for the rest of their life. What the International Labor Organization and Conventions call for is a cease to all child abuse immediately. There should be sanctions places on the owners not only of the Cocoa Plantations but also on the Chocolate Industries throughout the world. The laws I have read are distinct and enforceable without question and should bare the weight of such judgment as stipulated. When those who are in position to help such as senators, congressmen and congresswomen, government officials, chocolate associations, chocolate industries, the National Confectioners Association, political leaders and politicians act as though such a crime as raping, sodomizing, the sale of children into slavery, sex trafficking of children, false adoption papers of these children, organ trafficking of these children which is nothing more than murdering them for their organs. The abuse of these children does not have a place in a civil society such are the United States of America but the United States stands back knowing what is taking place on the Ivory Coast of Africa and Ghana allowing such behavior to exists. I have listed Convention 182 which clearly shows the violations of these innocent children and nothing is being done about it. Article 1, Article 2, and Article 3 are concise and clear as to what should and should not be taking place with these children on the Cocoa Plantations. But still the urgent need to make the corrections has not occurred. You will find laws and Conventions mentioned throughout this book. I will give you more of Convention 182, as it relates to Article 4, Article 5, Article 6 and

Article 7 later in the book to gault your memory in order that you are able to refer back to the cruelty of these children.

Although there is an ending to this book I must state I have already started book Two (sequel) on The Cocoa Plantations

Introduction

The scorching heat of the sun is something five year old American children will never feel. The hot penetrating rays of the sun beaming down on their unblemished skin will never be the concern of an American child. A five year old child in America would not be able to begin to understand how five year old girls and boys in Africa have to live. These children are working 100 hundred hours a week on the Cocoa Plantations on the Ivory Coast of Africa and Ghana.

Before I began this horrifying true story based on what is taking place on the Cocoa Plantations and the disheartening and disgusting facts taking place on the Ivory Coast of Africa. It is important that I first enlighten you as to where cocoa comes from.

Cocoa comes mainly from the Ivory Coast of Africa and Ghana there are five other areas, Indonesia, Nigeria, Cameroon, Brazil and Ecuador. Only the Ivory Coast of Africa and Ghana are the largest of the overall global cocoa production. Many of you think cocoa is the powder you put in your milk to make hot chocolate which is true but there is a process. The cocoa bean is what is first picked from the cocoa trees and then shipped to the United States of America and other parts of the world. The production of the cocoa starts when the cocoa bean or pod which reaches the cocoa factories in America. America is where it is produced. When the cocoa bean or pod reaches America it is then combined with other products before it becomes cocoa, chocolate ice cream, candy bars, chocolate kisses, chocolate candies, chocolate cake, and all the products chocolate is combined with which also includes the chocolate candy many schools sponsor for fun raisers. Before it is produced into chocolate, cocoa originates from cocoa beans or pods that grow on trees on the Ivory Coast of African and Ghana. These trees are as high as 40 feet tall. Just recently Cocoa Plantations have also been discovered in the United States of America. So far in two states Hawaii and Florida. For most of you who are already aware as to what product comes from cocoa just think about all of that delicious chocolate you see in just about every store you go to shop. Just think about it chocolate is a heavy market and high in demand throughout the world. It's in every candy store, convenient story, grocery store, food mart, corner store, gas station, supermarket, Walmart, Target, K-Mart, shopping centers, let's just face it chocolate is all over the world. Chocolate in American stores can be found in the everyday quick stop at the nearby Dollar Store to the most eloquent of stores, Tiffany's.

There are a few company's making big money in the Chocolate Industry one of the major leading company's makes a whopping 60 billion dollars a year, and the second leading company makes a whopping 30 billion dollars a year put the two together and you've got 90 million dollars in assets a year. Just between the monies made from the top two chocolate company's I am certain a more in-depth investigation could be done to correct things on the Cocoa Plantations.

Unfortunately due to the insensitive nature and working conditions of how cocoa is prepared before it is imported to America leaves a distasteful taste in my mouth.

The horror stories have been validated over and over again through CNN, magazine articles and others who have researched the abuse there. Many of the issues taking place on the Ivory Coast of Africa and Ghana in order for America and other countries to have chocolate will leave you with your mouth wide open. I am quite certain you will say the same thing I did when I first learned about the Cocoa Plantations, and that was, "Oh my God these children need my help." It was not like they ever received any fair treatment when it came to care, health, education, food, shelter, dental care, etc.

I would like for you to slowly draw a picture in your mind of five year old boys and girls in slavery working over 100 hours a week on the Cocoa Plantations. Five year old babies (boys and girls) trained to climb 40 feet high trees. They are taught at the age of 5 years old how to swing a machete. What civilized Industry is going to put children to work? These Cocoa Plantations hire these under aged five year old boys and girls without any pay or benefits to cut the cocoa pods from the trees. America is number one on the list when it comes to the top ten countries heavily invested in chocolate. America just like any other country does not have an excuse that legally allows the abuse taking place with these children on the Ivory Coast of Africa and Ghana. I will list the top ten countries later in this book. Many issues can be bought to closure with a joint effort by every country involved if they would do their part to end this nightmare of chocolate for 2,000,000 children enslaved on the Cocoa Plantations on the Ivory Coast of Africa and Ghana. You will find much more intensifying concerns throughout the book. Keep in mind these changes that must take place does not just involve the abuse of children on the Cocoa Plantations but it also involves sex trafficking of these minor children when they are no longer useful to work at the Cocoa Plantations. What character of men or women would actually work in these hidden remote areas throughout African and Ghana that enslave children? What kind of mind set do individuals that, beat rape and sodomize children have? I don't like being repetitive but I am prayerful you will realize that buying children, kidnapping children and enslaving children, and putting children who are under age to work is against the law. And working five year old boys and girls 100 hours a week is unheard of. The ages of these children are considered to be underaged and are in violation of International Labor Organization laws. When it sinks into your mind that these helpless children need relief you will find that the Calvary arrived too late, the damage done to these children will be irreparable. What's even worse is that political officials in Washington, DC did not see fit to immediately rescue these children after acknowledging the Cocoa Plantations is the worst form of forced child labor and slavery in the world. Instead they gave the

Chocolate Industries until the year 2020 to adhere to the laws of illegal child labor and child abuse. Although it is possible that change may occur in the year 2020 the question is to what degree will change occur? Please keep in mind the bill was passed in 2001 which means it will be nineteen more years of abuse these children have to endure. How many people in Washington, DC are in position to do something to implement immediate change but nothing has been done? How are these politicians able at the end of the day to go home to their family and have dinner with their wife and children and not have any remorse as to what is taking place with these children on the Cocoa Plantations? What low minded individual sits back and allows these hateful acts to happen to children. What kind of person indulges in abusive activities against defenseless children? To be frank and to the point the answer is someone who does not have a conscience.

Is chocolate detrimental to the existence of America, it is a trillion dollar industry? Why aren't American politicians pro-active when it comes to these African children? Why are they sitting on their hands and twiddling their fingers knowingly accepting the abuse these children are going through. Why are these politicians turning their head and looking the other way? We must do something to implement change with the abuse taking place against these children. It is only for the sake of their survival that these five year old children working on the Cocoa Plantations ask no questions. They do try to escape and are reminded daily through continual beatings and abuse that they do not have anyone willing to speak up for them. An eye opening tragedy and quite obvious problems concerning these children is that nobody knows of their existence. Who has the birth certificate of these children? Who has the records showing from what parent the child was taken or purchased from? What record is there to show of the child ever being taken to the Cocoa Plantation? What record is there to show if the child ever left the Cocoa Plantations? An even bigger question concerning what I have not found in my research is when a child falls from a 40 foot tree and breaks his or her neck in the process of trying to cut a cocoa pod or accidentally slips from the tree and falls to his or her death is the death reported and how is the body disposed of? Is there a marked grave with the child's name and date of birth on it that is a good question? Are there any records of the child's existence? Or since there is no record of the child ever existing and there is no one there to ask questions of the child's whereabouts is the child given a proper burial or is it just fed to the alligators or disposed of in other ways?

What are the odds of a 5 year old American child having to live under such conditions of having to work 100 hours a week or be trained to work with a machete?

The answer is zero percent; it's just not going to happen? I am by no means trying to negate the problems we have here in America with missing children and runaways there is a lot of kidnapping taking place right here in America. Many police officers give up looking because the child cannot be found in America, could these missing children be in other countries? We have our problems in America as stated earlier but nothing compares to the abuse and forced child labor and slavery taking place on the Ivory Coast of Africa and Ghana.

A five year old American child will never have to worry about working a fifteen to twenty hour work day. A five year old American child's skin will never be burned from the intense heat of the sun because a five year old would not be allowed to work. A five year old American child is considered to be a baby and dependent on the parents. They will never be forced to work anywhere it would be considered to be inhumane and child neglect in America. But take the five year old African child on the Cocoa Plantations and the adverse conditions they work under there is nothing humane about the treatment they receive and there is nothing legal, moral or ethical by which these children are existing.

American children five years old will never have to worry about how to survive in the blistering heat of the sun. It is unlikely that a five year old baby in American will ever have to endure such conditions.

America has child labor laws which are enforced immediately and by the time the White House, Senate and Congress are flooded with complaints from the children's parents you can bet that situation would be cleared up quickly, that is if the child was American. American children will never have burns and welts on their backs because the perspiration on their skin has dried up from working outside in the elements. The only hot sun a five year old American child will feel is the heat from the sun while out on a family gathering or maybe playing outside during school recess. An American child five years old would not be in question today concerning forced child labor. But as for the five year old children on the Ivory Coast of Africa and Ghana working on the Cocoa Plantations sun up to sun down American politicians turn their head as though forced child labor and child abuse is acceptable. These children moans and cries for relief go unheard, empty and void of nothing. They have no one to complain to in the isolated areas of the Cocoa Plantations were some of these children were sold into slavery for as little as fourteen dollars. They are forced to work a life time in slavery for the purchase of their blood. Their little bodies are made to endure the abuse that takes place on the Cocoa Plantations. They teach themselves to adjust to the needs of the overseers by watching others learned behavior, it is important for their survival. These children (babies) are not old enough to understand this kind of cruelty taking place in their life. To a five year old child (baby) there is no right or wrong way of life. The mind conditioning they are being taught on the Cocoa Plantations will become their doctrine for life on how to survive. Whether it is to rob still or kill it becomes a learned behavior for these five year old children (babies) and their existence. Children working under intense heat, fed (corn mush) for a meal and living under guard in abnormal living conditions. What are these little ones to do? What are the odds of this kind of treatment that is taking place on the Cocoa Plantations with five year old African boys and girls will ever happen to an American child? Let me answer that for you quickly, the odds are zero percent. It would not be heard of because there is no five year old child in America who will be forced to work one hundred hours a week. Let me be even more realistic a five year old in America will never understand such extreme measures and would not be subjected to such cruelty. Did you say AMBER ALERT yes we send out an AMBER ALERT if we think a child of ours is in trouble I guess the five year old children on the Cocoa Plantations are not worthy of statewide concern. Did you get the memo AMBER ALERT for what? The politicians are not concerned and neither is the people running the chocolate industries in America. These five year old children are in Africa not America so what government official cares about what happens to them?

Double Edged Sword

Let me introduce you to a scenario of the doubled edged sword. A doubled edged sword cuts both ways and if you pay close attention you will find it to be sarcastically quite hilarious. What I am referring to here is the so-called pretentious attempts the politicians in America have made to make corrections on ending the forced child labor and child abuse on the Cocoa Plantations, are you laughing yet? With laws already passed the violations taking place concerning these under aged children on the Cocoa Plantations are clear and concise. There is nothing facetious about five year old children being sold or five year old African boys and girls working over one hundred hours a week. These bogus attempts of pretending to make things better for these children are only presented to pacify those in the hierarchy involving the trillion dollar chocolate business. The profit in the chocolate industry is just as valuable and just as big as the drug cartel, big business. Trillions of dollars have already been made off the backs of these five year old children, slaves if you may have it. These political open forums of debate is a show front window designed to overt and neglect making things look to appear to be trying to get corrected. It is all a delusion of fixtures designed to put political figures in position of servicing more propaganda, more delays and more appeals. They say let's amend this law and change that law to make themselves look concerned but the real motive is to…Delay! Delay! Delay! I wonder whose overseas bank accounts are getting fat. In all actuality these politicians intentions are to do nothing other than to stall for another twenty years, while the rapes and abuse of these children continue. The diorama is all laid out before you there is no other side to search for. America has been turning its head for quite some time now.

Everyone is familiar with the old cliché "If it is not broken don't fix it." There are International laws of which I will disclose in the body of this book which gives American politicians the right to help these children once again they know the laws exist but nothing has been done. Now that American people have heard the truth about how cocoa is brought to America from the blood and sweat of children do you still want to continue buying chocolate? The truth about this book concerning the Cocoa Plantations is quite graphic when you think about the five year old children and the horror they live with daily. There is a need for open forums to discuss the changes that need to be implemented to help these children. Issues concerning the lack of support of these children and why need to be brought to the green carpet. The brutality and abuse of these five year old boys and girls need to stop. American's can help with that change by merely doing what is right. As for me I just don't buy chocolate.

This is a book that everyone in AMERICA and those with children should read. You should want to know how five year old boys and girls are sold into slavery for as little as $14.00 dollars on the Cocoa Plantations. Just because the chocolate industry is a big money maker and everyone wants chocolate. America and other countries want their chocolate regardless of the cost. And it doesn't make a difference as to what five year old child in Africa pays the price with their life as long as Americans and American children can have their chocolate. I will try not to be too graphic concerning what is taking place with these five year old boys and girls on the Cocoa Plantations. If I am able to go another route I will try to not be so vague in my description of what is happening to them without any parents around to protect them. I will try to spare you the mental picture but I will not hide the facts.

A scab has been opened in the United States of America and if something is not done about the Cocoa Plantations it which will implicate many people, Politicians, CEO's and Founders in America and other countries, nationally and internationally. This will open up the doors as to why very little has been done to destroy this beast of burden, slavery, rape, murder and abuse on the Cocoa Plantations.

What have the politicians done to inforce the laws being violated to bring about a change on the Cocoa Plantations? Change that would involve the conditions under which these children are living, nutritional conditions concerning their diet, their healthcare, their lack of education and lack of wages these children are not receiving? American politicians have put policies and laws in place that are not being adhered to so who's at fault? Americans have done more in foreign countries to protect countries not able to protect themselves yet American politicians sit back and watch the abuse of these innocent children and do nothing that would show some form of concern by at least trying to make some form of significant changes on the Cocoa Plantations yet nothing is done.

Let me revert back to history for a brief moment and take a look at what American soldiers throughout history have been sent out to do all over the world. American soldiers go to other countries, on what is called (Peace Keeping Missions). We have sent soldiers out in some of the worst of wars, Vietnam being one of the worst wars ever. In the Vietnam War 58,220 soldiers were not able to return home they were either (KIA or MIA). It is now 2014 and there is still a very strong probability that (MIA's) are still captive in the concentration camps of Vietnam. The 58,220 soldiers killed in Vietnam were shocking and to this day we still mourn for the lives that were lost. I will not compare the 2 million children in slavery on the Cocoa Plantations to soldiers who have returned home from fighting a war but the numbers do not lie. The not so funny thing about these lives lost is that these children did not volunteer to go to war but they are being treated worse than (POW's) or should I say (MIA's) on the Ivory Coast of Africa and Ghana.

I do believe I mentioned the year 2014 there is not too much more that need to be said concerning slavery. The Emancipation Proclamation was signed in 1862 implemented in 1863 and slavery continued in Texas until 1865 this is how Juneteenth came about in America. The abolishment of slavery, although slavery was considered to be inhumane was never totally abolished. Though slavery was supposedly abolished in America with the connection of African Americans being taken from Africa, the connection of slavery continues to be persistent with the Ivory Coast of Africa being the location of which the original slaves were taken. In fact slavery was never abolished and has been well in practice through the years. The 13th Amendment confirms it yes, slavery "It Still Exists Today". Is America adopting the Pontius Pilate syndrome that is a good question if you follow me carefully? You know when something is not right and you should do something about it but all you do is relieve yourself by washing your hands or turning your head the other way as though you did not see it. Has America Turned its head because American's would much rather have chocolate, then save an innocent five year old child's life? The problem is not going anywhere just because you turned away, as you can see it is just getting worst. How do you turn your head on five year old children or should I say five year old babies and expect to have a quiet and peaceful life? The horrifying treatment of children is happening right in our face America on our watch and we are not doing anything about it. Turning your face away is not going to make the problem non-existent neither does it negate the fact of these children needing our help?

Guilty by association, is a legal term I will discuss later within the chapters of this book. Make no mistake if you are not a part of the solution to help change this issue then you are a part of the problem. Many times I have put forth this question, "What would you do if these where your children"? Well believe it or not they are all of our children. We live in the United States of America, the greatest country on earth, a country that stands for justice. There is a solution to the abuse these children are suffering from. The question is how much longer it will take for everyone to get from point A to point B so the abuse of these children can stop? These five year old boys and girls are being whipped like slaves, beaten, sodomized and raped.

Their blood cries out from the ground "Where is thy brother, where is thy sister" are you not your brothers and your sisters keeper? Why, my dear Lord why, would a country you have blessed with so many resources stand back and watch not just the captivity of the physical body of these children but also the captivity of their mind? What progress can be made if everything remains stagnated? We already know what is documented by other researchers and writers concerning the Cocoa Plantations it stated over and over again these children on the Cocoa Plantations are a part of the worst form of slavery since human existence. Do you want chocolate in America so bad that you are willing to allow a child's life to be taken? *(Matthew 6: 22-23) "The lamp of the body is the eye. If therefore our eye is good, your whole body will be full of light. But if your eye is bad, your whole body will be full of darkness. If therefore the light that is in you is darkness, how great is that darkness!* Historians and theorist have searched many years trying to find a solution to hatred. Not just abroad but also in the United States. There is no need to dig any further this is one memo that has circulated quickly and it goes like this "as long as it is not our children suffering in America continue to turn your head as though nothing happened or nothing is wrong."

When you turn your head and look the other way things began to happen. Situations which are not of the norm had begun to develop into what is considered to be an oversight. What is an oversight when unusual events present themselves? Just because the good old United States of America government refuses to step in and do something about this matter on the Cocoa Plantations. I am certain and I do not want to sound like some biblical nerd but the Holy Bible does speak of diverse happenings throughout the world and yes that does include America. The bible speaks of things happening in areas you never dreamed of such tragedies happening. Here is the NEWS HEADLINER, tragedies taking place throughout the United States, children killing children. It wasn't too long ago that one of the worst massacres in U.S. history that hit a quiet town in Littleton, Colorado. It was in April of 1999 when Columbine High School was under attack by a disarrayed student who killed 13 other students and one teacher. In Newton, Connecticut on Dec 14, 2012 twenty elementary children and six adult staff were fatally shot to death while in class. It was really sad to hear.

Americans stepped up to the plate as usual to find a different solution to see what could be done different in order that this kind of tragedy does not happy again. The same could be done for the little five year old boys and girls on the Cocoa Plantations. Step in and do something, oh well I guess the little African children don't count? I can remember hosting my radio show during the time this tragedy happened. The outbreak of cries, coverage and support that sweep through the United States was not something unexpected. In America we fight for the rights of our children, I was proud to see that but what happened to the rights of these five year old children on the Cocoa Plantations. I must admit that other countries are extremely poor and do not have the power of political diplomacy as America. I was in shock and so was everyone else as we all watched in wonder as to what would cause someone to lose their mind and go into a classroom and murder 20 children and 8 adult teachers? Once again babies who did not have the slightest inkling on how to defend their self or even cry out for help. This was such a cowardly act and what was even worse was this massacre took place on December 14th, ten days before Christmas. What heartless person could go out and intentionally destroy families, people's lives for no reason at all? I couldn't help but think about the presents parents had already went out and purchased. Along with all of the shopping they had done with their child not realizing when their child went to school they would never see it alive again. Travel plans being made for the holidays to visit with grandparents, going to the mall to get a picture with Santa Clause. I am certain many families already had their Christmas trees up. Only by the days end of December 14, 2012 there would be no joy, no laughter of children being greeted by their parents. No stops at Mac Donald's or Burger King on the way home. America would be held in awe and at a standstill concerning this tragedy, this massacre. Twenty children in elementary school would not survive this nightmare; there was no mother or father to protect them from the reality of what was getting ready to take place. Their innocent blood would be wasted inside of the very same classroom that was to begin their life. Unbeknownst to the children when they left home that morning to go to school they would never see their parents again. And the parents would never hold their five year old babies in their arms again. These are tragedies that continue to sweep the nation with no real explanation as to why these shooters at different times snapped and went on a killing spree taking innocent lives. Let me remind you there are 2,000,000 children on the Ivory Coast of Africa whose blood is being spilled daily. There is no national media there to cover the pain these African children's parents are feeling. There aren't any mourning sessions or candlelight community prayer vigils set up to ease their parent's pain. I have said this before and I will say it again pain is pain in all languages pain hurts and everybody wants some form of relief, stop the hurt, stop the abuse. We feel pain when we lose a loved one. It is even more devastating and hard to phantom the loss of a child particularly your own. In America we miss our children when they are going to a slumber party and we know they are right next door. How are these parents on the Ivory Coast of Africa supposed to feel when their child is picked up at five years old and never seen again? How are they supposed to feel when a child is sold for no more than $14.00 and taken away to work on the Cocoa Plantations for the rest of his or her life? When you combine the two I would say God is not pleased at all. This is America; this is the country where we believe that all men are created equal.

I am going to close out my Introduction and say to you all there is much work to be done. But there is no time for more delays if things are to change for the betterment of all humanity.

Child abuse is really putting it mild there aren't enough adjectives to describe what is taking place on the Cocoa Plantations with these children. Exactly what do we expect five year old babies to do on the Cocoa Plantation? The word of God says, in Luke 17 v 2 "It were better for him that a millstone were hung about his neck and he cast into the sea, than that he should offend one of these little ones." This is the word of God and it shall come to pass. There is no exception to the rule when it comes to children. God has already said to keep your hands off of them.

I will leave you with this: "A kindling fire remains small and in control as long as it is being watched but oh what a blazing roar it will turn into once a little fuel is secretly added." I pray to God this story touches your heart so you can share this knowledge about the Cocoa Plantations. And America can be the first on the list to make the changes necessary in order that these five year old children can be given some form of an opportunity in life. God Bless you all and with all my heart I say God bless the greatest country on earth America.

If you are not reaching out to call your senator, congressman or the President of the United States of America after reading the first few chapters of this book then you are not doing your part. Dr. Martin Luther King Junior once said, "An Injustice to one is an injustice to us all." Now I am certain you can see where I am going with this story. Get a real big box of handkerchiefs I am certain you will need it.

A Servant of Obedience, for it is better than Sacrifice

My duty as a Christian is to give honor and edify my Father in heaven. To be chosen by God to carry out a mission and to serve him in whatever purpose he would have me to labor in for the benefit of his glory. So let it be the will of the Father because it is written in:

Isaiah 55v 8-9

"For my thoughts are not your thoughts, neither are your ways my ways, saith the Lord. (9) For as the heavens are higher than the earth, so are my ways higher than your ways, and my thoughts than your thoughts."

Because we all have purpose in life there is a reason for everyone's existence. It is just the path in which each of us as individuals chose to approach the task we are given. Whether it is in a sense of serving God or serving Satan the choice is truly yours but you must understand you cannot serve both. So as an obedient servant of my Father in heaven I will leave you with this scripture to make it even more personal for me.

1 Peter 3:14

"But and if ye suffer for righteousness sake, happy are ye: and be not afraid of their terror, neither be troubled."

A Dedication to the Highest of all, My God, My Father in Heaven An Unshakable Faith,

a dedication to the Father in Heaven

God Almighty is the author and finisher of my faith. Without God you can do nothing, with him you can do everything. I am one man who believes God is all I need in my life to complete the mission I was put here to do.

As you begin to advance through this book you will find out that being picked by the Father to carry out his mission does not come with a sense of fear. It is a mission that does not come with a question of whether I want to complete it. God already knows he has chosen a willing vessel. Someone who is willing to do the work of the Lord regardless of the cost, whether it is going to be a profit or a loss it is a purpose that must be filled a mission that must be accomplished. This book about "The Cocoa Plantations" I am prayerful will help bring even more awareness to politicians, government officials, the National Confectioners Association and Chocolate Industries all over the world, people in high places who are able to show compassion. Although the changes needed to be made by those in charge of the Cocoa Plantations may seem impossible to mankind. I can wholeheartedly say through my own personal struggles experiences of what God has delivered me out of and has stepped in to be an advocate for me. My belief of his love and mercy for his children is unlimited which means that my faith is unshakable, I believe in God and I confess Jesus Christ was raised from the dead. Like the three Hebrew boys, Shadrach, Mushach and Abednego, I know without a doubt and believe in my heart that God is able to deliver. This is why this book is dedicated to the way maker, the only true God I follow; he is my way maker God Almighty, the Father of Abraham, Isaac and Jacob. I pray that you enjoy and entrust in your heart what this book will challenge you to do. The questions this book will present and bring to your mental thinking and your emotional feelings as you become deeper and deeper involved with the purpose and many reasons as to why it was written. It was just time to question this free world that I live in, you know the good old U.S. of A. In doing so I not only put my mind to the test but I also would like for you the reader to stop and think to yourself and just say is chocolate worth all of the raping, sex trafficking, organ trafficking, sodomizing and abuse and murdering of these children to get the cocoa seed to America so that you can have your chocolate? Please try to understand my dedication to help you to become better informed of what is taking place on the Ivory Coast of Africa and Ghana... the next page is my prose titled "The Cocoa Plantations."

The Cocoa Plantations

No civilization there to enforce the laws
mankind has set before them;
Their laws are hidden deep within the grounds unseen by many;
Out in the wilderness where you can hear
the drums roar, signals being sent;
The enemy is about us grab your children
so they will not be sold.

They are coming to our homes to bargain
once again no laws to stop them;
Laws are set and rules are made to balance the scales of justice;
The International Labor Organization says
there are legal Conventions to follow;
There are Convention 138,182 and child labor
rights covered in Convention 29;
These five year old children lives are being
violated and that is a crime.

There are many who know about the
Cocoa Plantations slave trade;
The truth about this matter is the children
are not even getting paid;
Little girls and boys are getting raped and beaten all day;
While the Senate and Congress say that help is on the way.

Over 100 years have passed no help for
these children no, not any relief;
Children working 100 hours a week and
climbing forty-foot trees;
Trained at the age of five to swing a machete;
They eat corn mush during the day for
fun they are raped for play.

Those in Washington are aware of what's
going on but they don't care;
On the Cocoa Plantations you can do what
you want with the children there;
Use them for labor, for trade, for sex or
for a slave the child has no rights;
Politicians, government officials in American
they know and refuse to fight.

They have a law called the Harkin-Engel
Protocol; I have really heard it all;
A store front law that looks good on
paper I am putting it quite mild;
Unfortunately this is not service with a
smile but a death notice for a child;
Brought to you by animals have no rights
neither does children without names;
The Cocoa Plantation, The Cocoa
Plantations, my God what a shame
Children sold for as little as fourteen dollars
and beaten with bike chains;
Their organs are sold and transported to the United States;

They do not have a long time to wait
to save some rich child's life;
Murder in all languages still spells out the same;
You took an innocent child's life and guess
what no one gets the blame.

Written by Author/Hall of Fame Poet
Raymond C. Christian

Many Children in a Pool of Blood

"Blood Covered in Chocolate"

So not only are Senators and Congressman involved we also have hospitals, surgeons, doctors and nurses involved with the organ implant, the surgical procedure. Chocolate is a trillion dollar I want to open your minds so you can see this horrific, hideous, monstrosity taking place on the Cocoa Plantations. When you think about the sex trafficking of 2 million children on the Ivory Coast of Africa and Ghana, five year old boys and girls being raped, sodomized abused, beaten and murdered they are not just murdered trying to escape. They are also murdered for their body organs.

You really have to think if someone in the United States or other parts of the world needs an organ such as a heart, liver, kidney etc.

Now you can see why it is so important for Senator Thomas Richard Harkin and Congressman Eliot Engel to correct the problems on the Cocoa Plantations.

Just think about the organs the heart, liver and pancreas in the human body you only have one. In order for these organs to be taken out the African child it must first be murdered. Because these organs can only stay out of the body for a few hours the child must be transported close to where the recipient of the organ is located. So not only are there Senators and Congressmen involved we also have hospitals, surgeons, doctors and nurses involved with the organ implant, the surgical procedure. Chocolate is a trillion dollar business. Organ trafficking also brings in billions of dollars a year. Due to the monies involved concerning the cost of implants and the surgeons and medical team needed to do the surgery I do not have a clue as to who is being paid what but their pockets are lined deep with money from the blood of these children on the Ivory Coast of Africa and Ghana. A little girl or boy who has been taken away from the Cocoa Plantations, murdered, and their organs used to save someone else's life.

You have a duty as children of God to remain in prayer. In the shedding of innocent blood you will remember the vengeance of the Lord and it shall be upon you. Even in darkness God still sees you and he shall repay you for your works. You cannot take a life and give life to another thinking it is okay. God told King David his hands had blood on them. You surgeons, doctors and nurse involved, your hands have blood on them as well no matter how many times you wash them know that God is watching.

I am Elder Christian in Jesus name.

The Cocoa Plantations is a smoke screen as you can see with many hidden secrets. But the eyes of the Lord are everywhere

Special Dedication of this book

To the Children on the Cocoa Plantations

First let me say to all of the children on the Ivory Coast of Africa and Ghana, children who are forced into the WORST FORMS of FORCED CHILD LABOR, ABUSE and CHILD SLAVERY in the history of the world. And to the children in all the other nations who are suffering from abuse and forced child labor. I am prayerful that people who will be reading this book will understand there is a need for everyone's voice to be heard where something can be done expeditiously. These children need our help. I ask everyone to please stand up and let their voice be heard. "Silence only respects what is said and nothing being said supports everything a nation of people is against, Child Abuse, of which is child abuse of any kind, of any race creed, color or ethnic background.

This Special Dedication goes out to these abused children all over the world who haven't a voice to defend themselves. They have nothing and no one to give them hope. Five year old boys and girls sold into slavery to work on the Cocoa Plantations of Africa and Ghana to get the cocoa bean so you in America can have chocolate. Little boys and girls five years of age are worked 100 hours a week, every week from sun up to sun down. They haven't a father or mother to speak up or pray for them. The parents of these children do not have a clue as to where their child is being transported to or even if the child is alive.

I have shed many tears trying to complete this book in a timely fashion so that nothing is overlooked in the process of trying to bring awareness to the attention of those capable of making changes on the Cocoa Plantations.

An Honorable Mention
For the Men I Respect

It is not easy to write a book such as this without giving the respect due to those who took the time out of their very busy schedules to show concern in a manner in which I never had to ask:

Honorary Mention

To my father Robert Christian who worked tiring hours most of his life as time went on before his death. My dad and I learned to get to know each other. Many times a person does not have to teach you how to be strong in life. You can be strong just knowing they are there.

Honorary Mention

To my uncle James M. Jones who many times kept my dreams alive just by saying, "It's going to be alright pal." I often would look at my uncle and see in him hope and fortitude. Although he did not have much materialistic stuff he embellished and implemented all of the characteristics of a great uncle.

Honorary Mention

To my grandfather A.C Jones a remarkable hard working man who had a loving heart and believed in family. I remember our walks together and how you would always talk about family members you had helped; there was never a limit to what you were able to accomplish. Everyone loved being around you and listening to you talk and tell jokes. Great men never die and our walks together will never be forgotten. Thank you for telling everyone I was your grandson. And thanks for believing I had a special gift. Thank you "Grand Dad" bka "Daddy".

Honorary Mention

To my mentor Dr. Albert L. Powell Sr. I use to enjoy the stories of your telling me about how you knew Maynard Jackson (Mayor of Atlanta), Thurgood Marshall (First Black Supreme Court Justice), Ralph Abernathy (Best friend of Dr. King and President of the NAACP) and George Washington Carver (Discovered the peanut). It was always interesting to listen to you Dr. Powell Sr. I remember when you gave me the pin Boaz to wear after I learned the prose of Boaz. I was so proud when you pinned it on my lapel. I asked you why you chose the pin (Boaz) for me because you had several you had created that you could have made me earn. You later told me because you saw me as your Boaz (your right arm of strength). I always pictured you as a very modest man; you never talked about your accomplishments and you remained very humble and taught me the way of obedience and patience.

Honorary Mention

My friend Chuck Atkins was amongst the intellectuals. A strong educated man (Alpha) who stood for what he believed to be true. Chuck was a connoisseur of philosophy; he was very inspirational in sharing his experiences in life? He always said to me, "Ray, you are the type of man who will stand out wherever you go, it's just in you." He would say, "I just want to be around to see the end of your story, I am certain it is going to be awesome."

Honorary Mention

He always kept me inspired Dr. Eddie LaShea had a way of teaching and would never discourage my thoughts of what I wanted to do. He remains to this day to be the thought of me doing what is righteous. In his teachings Doc. LaShea was never one to criticize but only used his insight and intellectual abilities to build, construct and enhance my thoughts for a better future. A brilliant man and mentor in every sense of the word. "Learning is a tool we must all indulge in using. And once you have accomplished the challenge and mastered the gift of it make sure you pass it on to the others who are waiting."

Honorary Mention

To my longtime military buddy Danny Butler (Aka Dangerous Dan) Omega Psi Phi, graduate of Howard University are there any Q Dogs in the house? Your friendship as a fellow Marine meant the world to me. You have served the United States of America with honor and dignity. I know you are up there in heaven asking the Lord to watch over me. God bless you and may God keep you…Semper Fidelis

An Honorary Mention to everyone who has been significant in my life and did not get your name personally mentioned in this book. I do not want you to feel you were forgotten just know that I appreciate you for all you may have done in my behalf… please consider this your Honorary Mention…..

A Special Dedication and Thank You

To **Danette Hayes,** it has been a grueling and very sensitive journey for me. When I think about the long days and nights just working and typing, researching and putting my ideas of concern on paper then later reviewing my work all over again? I feel you have been quite patient in waiting on the completion of this book and very respectful of the time I have dedicated in completing this project. I remember discussing with you the lack of material for the Cocoa Plantations and how information was so scarce and minimal to the point when many times I had to ask God to intercede for me to be my eyes so I could complete this task put before me. This has been an untiring journey for me, my back was against the wall many days, hurt from what I was finding out through my research concerning these children. Never thinking politicians in America or people in corporate level positions and organization today could be so bitter and hateful toward children. Many times while writing I wondered how the world would receive this book on the Cocoa Plantations. Sometimes I would venture out through the day when I needed a break or just to go out of the house and grab a quick bite to eat. I often spoke to strangers and told them about this mess America had created for itself, as it relates to the Chocolate Industries and five year old children working the Cocoa Plantations. Many times during my conversations they would just say "I did not know that." You have shown great concern in listening to my work and the many prose and poems written throughout the book so I say thank you for your attentive ear, your warm loving heart and your unselfish nature. Which showed me you had a greater concern of wanting the children to receive the help they are in desperate need of. I thank you for your support.

A SPECIAL THANK YOU

Now begins the creation of my **Special Thank You** pages. It is a big part of my book. I created it because I felt the need to let all of my family and friends realize just how much they are appreciated. No one likes being forgotten so I figured out a way to add those I love and care about so I could show my heartfelt thanks openly. I called it my **Special Thank You** for those who have supported my work.

A Special Thank You

To my dear sweet and loving, **Caroline Clark,** better known as (**Big Mama**) not every family had a Big Mama but you were most certainly mine. Although you have moved on to a better place I want you to know you are not forgotten. You are and will always be so special in my life. I thank you for the long and endearing talks you had shared with me and all of the wonderful things you taught me as a child. It is nice to have grown up in a household under four generations of women. I remember so many wonderful things by just being around you as a child. I wish every child could have had a childhood just like mine. Thank you for being there for me and for always coming to my defense. I love you and miss you so much...RIP

A Special Thank You

My dear friend, **Millicent A. Bess**, You have sat through many recitations of this book with me and you have listened to my ideas for change concerning these children on the Cocoa Plantations. It has been a long journey with this book on the Cocoa Plantations. I thank you for having an attentive ear and for showing your patience and concern. I appreciate your consistency. I was committed to write this book to let the world know how these children on the Ivory Coast of Africa and Ghana are suffering. The Tobacco Farms is included in the chapters of this book. Child abuse is child abuse no matter what country these children are in. You've been very supportive and of course the timing of this book is all in God's hands, meaning it is time for a change concerning these helpless children. Yes! The Cocoa Plantations is a story the world needs to know about. What I have found out is Americans know about what is taking place with the children but are afraid to voice their feelings. I am looking forward to getting the word out even more this is book one there will be a sequel. All I can say is stay turned, "there is a quiet before the storm." You've been closer to me than a mother guiding her own son throughout the years and always quite inspirational, this was a journey for me. Thank you for being so understanding of my love for God and the sacrifices I made when I made my decision to write this book. Thank you for your support. I will end with as always in Jesus name.

A Special Thank You

To Judge **Donald Davis,** my Brother in Christ Jesus and dear friend, I most certainly thank you for all the sound advice you have given and all the time you have invested in listening to me discuss the many different angles I was going to take while working on this book about the Cocoa Plantations. I enjoy our great debates and the different views and concepts you would bring to my attention in order to make me think about my next move. You are truly a great debater and quite witty with your intellectual finesse of knowing the law and legal terminology continues to keep me on toes when conversing with you. You are a man of the highest integrity who stands strong and continues to carry the torch for justice. Let your flame continue to burn bright in the eyes of those who cannot see the truth, let your light continue to shine in your representation of justice and all you have endured through the years. Thank you for being a man of valiance, I am honored Sir and I thank you for your support.

A Special Thank You

To my little precious one, **LaTesia A. Christian,** what I have found in life is that it takes you through many obstacles, it is usually for lessons to be learned and not repeated. Love is priceless; I thank you for understanding my feelings and concerns as to why I wrote this book and my reasoning for wanting to do something to help these little boys and girls who are being raped daily. I thank you for the Birthday cards and the Father's Day cards throughout the years, they mean so very much. I pray your strength in Christ Jesus. I love you regardless of any condition, that would be unconditionally. I thank you for your support. Love Dad.

A Special Thank You

To my mother, **Christine Tolbert,** life always has a way of working out for the best for those who love and trust in Jesus. I never thought that your reciting "Little Orphan Annie" to me when I was a child would have such a big impact on my life; it was exciting just listening to you. I must say life has been great and I thank you for sharing with me how you thought I was great writer. One more thing I appreciate is the church song you use to sing around the house when I was a little boy. (That's Enough) hear are a few of the lyrics to the song "There's always somebody talking about me but really I don't mind. They try block and stop my progress a most of the time. The mean things you say don't make me feel bad because I can't miss a friend that I never had I've got Jesus and that's enough." That is one song I will never forget mainly because it is so true...Thank you for your support (Mama) with all that is said I must say thank you...No Charge when I think back I can certainly smile and say... Paid In Full.

A Special Thank You

So many thanks are due to **Freddie Ewing,** I call Freddie my big brother because he stepped in when my difficult days were about me just like a big brother would and came through for me over and over again. When funds were low you were an understanding big brother and friend. Although my challenges were great and nobody knew I could count on you big brother to be fair and understanding. Many times we don't get the opportunity to tell our friends thanks you but I must say you have been more than an friend Freddie and I will always call you my big brother. God bless you for all you have done for me. Thank you for your support.

A Special Thank You

To my friend of many years, **Veronica McFadden-Jones,** life for me has been uplifting since I first met you during my first book publication. It's always a pleasure to share the positive things taking place in our life whenever we talk. I cherish our friendship and your professionalism you have been there to help in my time of need. Your expertise has always been on point. Thank you for your support.

A Special Thank You

To one of my longest living and dearest of friends, **Carolyn Meadows-Dixon**, time is of the essence and waits for no one. Through the years you would think someone would have written about this horrific situation on the Cocoa Plantations. Every child is on a special treatment list and should be given a chance at life. I was happy to hear you felt the same. You really touched my heart when you said, "God picked the right warrior." Thank you for your support in Jesus name.

A Special Thank You

Growing up as children, Bobbie Jean Robinson, I will never forget the love you showed in the passing of my grandmother. I know we are always just a telephone call away. Thank you for your support.

A Special Thank You

What can I say about your support through the years **Dee Dee**, you have shown your dedication toward my work and you have stepped in during some crucial moments and I appreciate all of the concern you have shown. Thank you so much and may God continue to bless your business in Jesus name.

A Special Thank You

To **Doctor Carl Strauch,** the pleasure is truly all mine, your dedication to the medical profession and people you have helped makes me more than gracious to know such a man of your caliber. The giving of yourself encompasses the meekness of your personality. If more medical doctors were as understanding and compassionate as you there would be less people in pain. I appreciate you telling me that my fifth book "My Book of Poems for the World" has been an inspiration to you and how you take it with you wherever you go. I thank you for the personal concern you have shown regarding my health. Your support remains untiring and I thank you for the encouragement.

A Special Thank You

To **Katherine Rhodes,** there is nothing like good old Holy Ghost power. Because of your dedication to God I understand the many battles you have fought to remain the kind and considerate person you are. Through your continual prayers and support you have shown the love of God in you and because of the spirit that dwells from within God is not short of his blessings. It is not by coincidence, or neither is it accidental that our paths have crossed. I was tickled to find out that you had taken my books across country with you and you became an overnight sensation everyone made you their personal celebrity. May God continue to be a shield around you Ms. Rhodes and keep you safe always? I thank you for all of the support you have given me.

A Special Thank You

To **1LGT,** as usual another unique cover for this book coming from your special design team which motivates because you are in tone and your work is so passionate. The effort conveyed in the cover says much before the book is opened. The cover conveys a profound sense of pain with these children working in the hot scorching sun, the man with the whip as an overseer watching the children makes one's mind wonder. We do not know who the abusers are; we do not know what they look like, where they live. In the shadows of the Cocoa Plantations small children lurk about in fear of being beaten. Children who are being abused remain hidden because there are so many hurting. I thank **1LGT** for your dedicated work to making this project go. I look forward to working with you all in the future. From my heart I say thank you for all of your support and may God continue to bless all of your creative talents in Jesus name.

A Special Thank You

Hello my friend, Swayzene **Douglas,** life is great with friends who are intellectually sound. It is always nice to know good friends from childhood days still care. You have always been a professional woman and of course I appreciate you. I am happy to know you are one of many who have decided to stop eating chocolate by embracing the importance of this journey as it relates to the children on the Cocoa Plantations. As I reviewed some of my material in the book with you, you said to me, "You made me see everything as you described it, I felt like I was there." I thank you for your support your friendship and professional opinion of which I know you will not deviate from. Thank you.

A Special Thank You

It has truly been a pleasure, **Dwayne Jasper,** I am happy to know that you also have deep concerns when it comes to the safety of all children. Thank you for your support.

A Special Thank You

In Honor of **Pamela E. Veal,** you have given your life in service to humanity. Your dedication in weighing the scales of justice equally as it relates to the laws of the land left no stones unturned. The honor and respect you diligently showed toward all who entered into your chambers of justice reassured everyone that the due process of law would work. It truly has been a pleasure and of course I thank you for your support.

A Special Thank You

I was once told by **Judith Eagle** I was brilliant because I did not have a law degree. She explained that she was a genius because she was a lawyer. Since then I have written six books. I will soon be finished with books seven and eight. Thank you for your encouragement. I never forgot that conversation.

A Special Thank You

I must say to my cousin **Jiles Pugh,** for all of the times you have texted me concerning my morning devotional word. It has been a really fun time with you being critical of my work. I will never forget your badgering me to make the appropriate corrections at times. You kept me laughing and I will never forget you for that. I know you were a Christian and you will most certainly be missed. (Jiles passed before the publishing of this book.)

Preface

Based on a true story "The Cocoa Plantations" was a challenging project for me. Simply because after researching what was taking place on the Ivory Coast of Africa and Ghana it began to become very personal as it should be to everyone who will be reading this book. And for paying attention to what is taking place in America in relations to what it takes to make chocolate. The Cocoa Plantations use hard working five year old children to work 100 hours a week in order to get the cocoa pods or cocoa beans to America so the chocolate industries could manufacture and produce all of your flavors of chocolate. I have had long grueling days and sleepless nights gathering material of which was very scarce. The interest of the American public was just not there but there were a few articles by journalist of which some quotes are made in this book due their research. There is some news coverage by CNN and even Pope Francis talked in a few of his speeches about the Cocoa Plantations. But the material remained scarce I received it in only parts and pieces. There is so much light that needs to be shed on this horrific situation concerning the two million children who work the Cocoa Plantations. It is so horrific the journalist who gave this story life. And the voice of Pope Francis speaking out gave me even more hope in completing this much needed book. Because of the treatment of these five year old children, the rape, sodomy, abuse, murder, sex trafficking and organ trafficking the Cocoa Plantations has been called, "the worst forms of child slave labor" in the history of the world. This is the preface to the story...The Cocoa Plantations.

I could not help but to be drawn into the giving of my time due to my love for not just my children but children all over the world.

In my wanting to keep everything real I had to ask myself this question, "what would I want done or what would I do if my child was subjected to such cruelty". I mean this is one time that it does not take a rocket scientist to figure out something needs to be done on the Ivory Coast of Africa and Ghana to help these innocent children. Five year old boys and girls being used as sex slaves; they are raped repeatedly, sodomized, abused, worked 100 hours a week every week. They are used for sex trafficking and of course this is the killer they are set up for false adoption and the child's organs are sold. All of this is taking place with these little boys and girls on the Cocoa Plantations and those who are aware like Former Senator Thomas Richard "Tom Harkin and Congressman Eliot Engel of which the law related to the Harkin-Engel Protocol named for the Cocoa Plantations has not budged since it became law in 2001 we are now in 2015 he is now retired. Oh I forgot to mention these children are beaten with whips and bike chains. They are guarded by an armed guard and if they try to escape these children are probably used as example for others to not to attempt an escape and shot, just call it murder. This is what is taking place on the Cocoa Plantations but not for all the world to see because of course you wouldn't care about little African boys and girls being murdered, would you?

With America being the number one producer and manufacturer of chocolate it would seem like the politicians and government officials involved with the Harkin-Engel Protocol would step in to make immediate changes in order to stop the abuse of the children and to change the horrific conditions under which they had to work. There is also the National Confectioners Association (NCA) who happens to be representatives of the chocolate industry. The (NCA) have been in existence since 1884. With their sole purpose being to handle all policies and issues as it relates to the chocolate industry. I am going to be a bit facetious at this point and assume that just because there are two million African children who are being raped, murdered and their organ parts sold that it's not a big deal just another dead African child who no one is going to miss. It is not an important issue because it is not an American child is that how it really works, these are defenseless children regardless of their color. But the Senate and Congress can take their time because to them it is not a matter of urgency. Let me review this carefully once again so you the reader can understand my view point when it comes to the protection of innocent children.

With chocolate being a well-kept secret, not chocolate as a product but the brains behind the operation that made it work. A trillion dollar industry that spread out across the world and was welcomed in everyone's home only its taste has begun to become a bitter sweet mess. What further reviews are needed to come to the aide of five year old boys and girls? Children who are raped, children who are sodomized, children who are beaten with bike chains, children who are abused physically, emotionally, verbally and mentally, children are murdered for their body organs. Children who are forced to participate in sex trafficking. Children, who are told they are being adopted, purchased in Africa with false adoption papers. Remember the child does not know its name of its name was changed. So the child is given a name for adoption purposes taken to a remote place in America and held there until the child's organs are needed, (of course, I am only giving you a vivid picture of the possibilities of what could be taking place) and by all means it is a very strong probability. Murder is against the law isn't it? Well let me correct that and say murder is against the law if the person murdered is considered to be human and not animal. Remember slaves are considered to be property and a product hasn't any feasible rights to defend. Therefore it becomes subjected to the will and mercy of its owner. Without further delay I bring to you the world's chocolate mess unveiled before the world in its raw nakedness. Based on a true story of about what is taking place on the Ivory Coast of Africa and Ghana welcome to:

"The Cocoa Plantations"

"They Loved the World and Hated Him"

They hated Jesus without cause and did all manners of things to him. Because God loved us so he gave us his only begotten son Jesus. Jesus was able to give those who did not believe a chance to believe.

How can a man who has nothing be feared by those who apparently had everything? Those in power sought after Jesus from city to city because of the good he was doing. Who was this man Jesus? A man who had no physical riches or wealth but had a treasurer, a man who had no physical property but owned everything, a man who was not given a physical army but was given legions of angels at his beckoning call his name is Jesus. What was there to fear when there wasn't any evidence of anything he had done wrong. He was not clothed in a robe aligned with rubies, diamonds, pearls, topaz, tanzanite, turquoise or other precious gems as the President's, Governor's, Senators, Congressmen, Mayors and other government officials of status were. He did not have to expose what was already his; all power was given to him.

Jesus was a meek man in a common every day robe who rode into town on a donkey. A man who said, foxes have holes and the birds of the air have nests but the son of man has no place to lay his head. Harmless yet feared for caring, loving and taking care of those who did not have those who did not know he was the Son of God. Telling them to seek the kingdom of God and its righteousness and all things shall be added unto you.

A man who had nothing feared by the most powerful men on earth, what would you like to be adorned in for the suffering you have intentionally caused to a people who have nothing? They are nothing more than entertainment for you to look upon. What pleasure do you get from those who are helpless in your ploy to channel their movement through planned manipulations? My final question is what pleasure do you get out of murdering, raping and incarcerating a people God has created?

I am Elder Christian in Jesus name.
Amandla!!!

How can the world be so blind to the treatment of so many little children? The laws and regulations that apply to these children are not being enforced. Where are the law enforcement officials when it comes to the protection of these children in foreign countries? Just close your eyes for a brief moment and think about all of the laughter you were able to enjoy with your parents. Think about the zoo's you visited, the underground aquariums, family outings and beaches. Don't let me leave out the barbeques, Christmas Day opening gifts that Santa Clause left for you and New Year's Eve with the family. What about the memories of taking pictures from kindergarten. Making new friends in high school and how about commencement night? Children on the Ivory Coast of Africa and Ghana will never have the opportunity to live such a life. Will you please speak up in their behalf, please say something? Do something to help these children, they deserve so much more, and they deserve the opportunity to have the same chance as you and I. I have enclosed the contact information on how to reach the Senators, Congressmen and the National Confectioners Association. Please do not forget to contact them.

The COCOA PLANTATIONS
Chocolate for AMERICANS

So many times Americans never see the downside of life in other countries. Unless you have traveled, self-learned or either formally educated many of the hardships others countries suffer with will never cross our borders. Being a nation of people who are justified by being in the land of milk and honey a land where many benefits are taken for granted, abused and forgotten about. Maybe I should have said forgotten about until the next free-bee comes along. Everyone wants to come to America; yes the great land of opportunity, where dreams are made to come true no matter how big or small. Americans have a way of making things happen, changing things for the betterment of all humanity. A nation where love, hope and charity extends to other parts of the world with charity being the greatest attribute of all unfortunately America's arms have not reached out to help the children on the Ivory Coast of Africa and Ghana concerning the Cocoa Plantations.

There is a different side to every story which gives those who understand and have experienced life a different view point, an outlook that defines within their heart why situations in other countries are structured a certain way. Make a note in your heart that every story is not based on success. As I began to unravel the Cocoa Plantations for you please do not take this as a metaphor but this is a bitter story a story that originates from your favorite chocolates but in all actuality drenched in five year old boys and girls blood.

The daily fighting within oneself to get up and go and the struggles to live a decent life is a daily journey for each of us. The majority of American's will never come close to the struggles of those in third and fourth world countries. On the average most American's struggle with making decisions as to whether they want to further their education, take a trip into some foreign country, search for a better paying job. Where they might want to have lunch or if they will eat out at some restaurant and have their favorite shake or dealing with the bigger problem of just paying their bills. You see Americans do not have a need to worry about their five year old children being sold into slavery. And if you read the introduction to this book you will notice that I did mention (AMBER ALERT). Of course in Africa they are saying what's an Amber Alert? The decisions and choices afforded to our children and our children's, children are all a part of the American dream. It is a part of what is instilled in our children in America through laws that protect them. Laws that assure them some form of freedom in their life to make decisions, laws that say they will have an education that will prepare them for the outside world. The opposite end of the spectrum for these children on the Cocoa Plantations, they do not have the freedom of choice, they have laws that are not being enforced and as far as education is concerned they haven't a clue.

These children on the Cocoa Plantations are not given the privilege to be children first. They are not allowed to be children before they become adults. These children work 100 hours a week every week from sun up to sun down their life becomes the Cocoa Plantations, work with no pay.

With the Wagner and Wages act in full affect knowing that children in America at the age of sixteen are only allowed to work 20 hours a week. The good thing about it is there is a minimum wage they will be paid. On the other hand how does American politicians explain five year old children working over 100 hours a week and receiving no wagers and of course no education. From the age of five until they are no longer useful to the plantation owners these children are put

2

on the streets without ever receiving any of the four basic essentials skills of life. They have not received any form of educational skills for survival, they are not taught math, science, reading or writing, and how are they to survive? It is even questionable as to whether they are even taught their own native language.

Cocoa Plantations- Americans (Are Not Aware)

What makes this Cocoa Plantation dilemma even more scrupulous is when these children after working the majority of their life on the plantations and later become young men and young women are released? Put out on the streets without a clue as to who their father, mother or their siblings are. Remember they were sold at the age of five years old. They have no American dream of being successful they are not blessed with being a part of a nation of people who will allow their dreams to come true. In America we have "mom's apple pie, three meals a day and a motivational cry of endearment which says to all American's **"No Pain No Gain."** A cry out that tells all Americans this fight is worth it and whatever it is that you are striving for there is no mountain high enough for you to climb to get it. This is the hope and comfort we give in support of one another. Being able to afford yourself the chance to at least have a slice of the pie, being able to taste the whip cream of life, being able to rise to the top this is what America is all about. My question is how will these five year old children be given any form of hope if they have no support and they only feel the thrash of a whip on their backs all day? Has Americans lost focus of what we as a nation stand for, have we lost consciousness concerning the protection of our children and enforcing laws in other countries involved in child abuse. Has common sense gone out of the window? Or is it the greed of the politicians Americans have put in office. Politician who are in elected positions, politicians who are supposed to make the right decisions for the people of America and not make it appear as though this great nation of people are in agreement with slavery or forced child labor just so America can continue to produce its chocolate. There are so many people not only in America but all over the world who are not aware of the abuse these children are going through daily on the Cocoa Plantations.

If you were to go back and review the Constitution of America what you will find is that it was written for a reason. Of which we could all live in a nation and be in agreement with one another and also disagree with one another without being hung, beaten or sold. The American way of life was designed for everyone born in the "Free World" to live without the vices of others ignorance, unfortunately things happen and situations occur. To this day America has issues of hatred, racial discrimination, and injustices including law makers violating the due process of law. Some things can be overlooked but how is it at all possible to overlook five year old children. Boys and girls on the Ivory Coast of Africa are being beaten, raped, sodomized and possibly murdered. How do we close our eyes or turn our head to such horrific treatment of five year old children. Children are working on these Cocoa Plantations on the Ivory Coast of Africa and Ghana which are described as being the worse forms of child abuse and child slavery ever. Playing favorites as to what American's will and will not do only puts America in bed with other nations who are guilty of such crimes. Have Americans become so desensitized with the old adage of "If it is not my problem them why should I worry about it"? Are Americans now so preoccupied with such negativity they no longer feel secure in allowing others to have a piece of the American dream. Using pretentious ideologies that harbor biased feelings of hate which would hide behind the truth of what others looking on would consider nothing more than hypocrisy? If Americans wanted to do you think we could stop this system of injustice? Could Americans have a sit-in until what is speculated concerning justice and a balanced scale of laws in the courtroom really is justice for all? Or is made into law by finally making what should be right and binding for all right. For the most part it seems like we are all created equal when in actuality its not just the Cocoa Plantations that's re-introducing slavery to the world but right here in America, Black Americans are suffering slow dearth of the

African American race due to imprisonment, Mass Incarceration. I would openly describe it as embalming an entire race of people prematurely with formaldehyde before death has been announced. Sabotaging an entire race of people to save its own beliefs and making it quite obvious that this great nation still struggles with the fear of African American leadership. Of which their own fear would lead them to the annihilation of those in leadership as it is today. Look how freedom in America is no longer focused on taking care of its own but has now turned to "Mass Incarceration" of its citizens. Yes, prisons are now being built instead of Factories and Mills jobs that were once created for those who wanted to earn an honest day's wages are no longer available. Let me correct that and say they are available they just are not available to Blacks in America. The American system that once worked for everyone is being gutted open.

My poor, poor America, the lamb set out before the world for mockery, humiliation, and slaughter. Because America has desensitized itself concerning the pains of other nations the "Free World" as we have it now looks upon investments in prisons. Not schools to enhance learning, not programs to promote skills and trades. Not institutions to entice the younger generation for a future of growth but prisons to cease all progress of those who are less fortunate. (Please read this website)(www.prisonlegalnews. org 11/13/2013) Prison Profiteers invest by using **"private prison companies, investment banks, churches, guard unions, medical corporations, and other industries and individuals that benefit from this country's experiment with mass imprisonment."** What you will find out is so many organizations are investing in the prison system of which there is a whopping $185 billion dollars being invested in the prison system a year. Because of the investments being made in the prison system to ensure a return on the billions of dollars invested one out of every 137 Americans will be incarcerated. While we stand and watch school programs, housing for the needed, food stamp and welfare programs set up for those in need are being slowly wiped out. (Please read this website) www.huffingtonpost.

com 2013/09/19/ food-stamps) what you will find is quite shocking. **"The House of Representatives on Thursday approved sweeping reforms to the nation's food stamp program that would cut some 40 billion in nutrition aid over 10 years and deny benefits to millions starting in 2014."** Sifting monies away from the needed has never been the American way of life. Of which has already affected the hot lunch programs in the public school system, free hot lunches has been abolished, along with teaching band in middle schools and many other programs in the public school system. Is there some kind of recycled meaning as to why Americans can care less about the less fortunate I must say the proof is before you and the statistic do not lie?

I did not mean to deter your train of thought from the main topic of this book but isn't it amazing how certain issues have a way of rising to the surface and being exposed. Let me get back to the issues concerning the Cocoa Plantations with aide being given to assist other allies in order to stay in good grace with them. I have not heard anyone say, let's just take some of the funding we are using to invest in building prisons and assist with the renovations needed on the Cocoa Plantations. Let's invest about 2.5 billion dollars so they can stop murdering and abusing these 5 year old boys and girls. I have not heard anyone say, let's take some of the moneys from the programs we have shut down in America and help the 2,000,000 million children on the Ivory Coast of Africa and Ghana. I do believe that most Americans want to do the right thing and now would be a good time to follow "Nike's" slogan "Just Do It". Americans want to sing with pride "God Bless America my home sweet home, but can other countries sing with the same passion while in question as to whether the shores of their home front are protected? There are so many people hurting and so many wrongs being done that a numbing affect has started to set into the minds of those who could help but the feelings of doing what is right is no longer there. The sad part about the numbing affect is what affects one leaves a trickling effect on others not just the United States of America but countries all over the world. It may sound a bit facetious but when the finger pointing starts will there be anyone able to sit up at the table or shall it all be called to order underneath the table? Whose hand is in whose pocket? I am quite certain the American people are not aware of the trillion dollar business the Chocolate Corporations are worth throughout the world, not just America. The last I researched those who were profiting in the Chocolate Industry out of the top two the first was making **60 billion dollars** a year and the second was making **30 billion dollars** a year, I have not checked on other chocolate companies to see how many billions they were making per year in reference to the top two. I do not want to get too far ahead of myself before I complete my introduction so please allow me to divert from this topic for a second and return to it later. With the information I have just given you should know why nothing has been done to correct the problems on the Cocoa Plantations. The child abuse taking place on the Cocoa Plantations would be hard for anyone to stomach but it exists. The government officials in Washington, DC who are literally sitting on the Cocoa Protocol bill have forgotten it was the citizens of the United States of America that put them in office to do the right and moral things. No matter how many trees in the forest wherever the tree falls the noise all sounds the same. Where the tree falls is a myth to everyone because guess what no one heard it fall. When these government officials and others in high places begin to fall officials who are over the legal legislature are in question as to why noted accounts of child abuse on the Cocoa Plantations are not in question or being investigate yet the Cocoa Plantations are still in operation. American's now look away from the truth instead of standing for the truth in which it once took pride in. The excitement on the climb up usually gives everyone involved a positive rush. The finish line winner gets the most attention. So many politicians have forgotten they started from the ground up or should I say they have forgotten their struggle of fighting to get the votes to be elected to a position and do nothing about the obvious wrongs taking place on the Cocoa Plantations. They have forgotten they are voted in office to protect the wrongs of foreign and domestic matters as it relates to the law. A reminder always helps as the old cliché goes "The same folks you see on the way up are the same ones you will see on your way down." Might I add sin is only good for a season however long that season exists for you just remember change is inevitable and will occur?

As Americans we see a plane flying in the sky and think, wow! Modern technology is great? People in other countries say for what it takes to fuel that plane they can feed their entire country for ten years. Americans look at the new model cars we drive and say," next year I want to upgrade to a newer model car." Those in other countries just want to have the opportunity sit or ride in any car. A change of mindset involving cultural differences portrayed in many grievous needs and wants many of which are catastrophic.

Americans are adamant in wanting to sing, "The Star Spangled Banner" Oh say can you see by the stars early light. Well there are questions that need to be answered because there aren't any stars in the pitch black darkness of the night where only gloom and torment moves about concerning the Cocoa Plantations. Unfortunately Americans concerning this matter of the Cocoa Plantations are not sitting in darkness. We are fully aware of the legislation call Cocoa Protocol of which Senator Tom Harkin and Congressman Eliot Engel have touched and agree to represent. Americans are not blind to injustice aboard or in international waters as long as the Statue of Liberty continues to hold the eternal flame of life. A flame that promotes freedom, equality and justice for all, America is not blind to the so-called mishaps taking place with these children on the Ivory Coast of Africa. The United States of America government has bought into the chocolate industries and has become bed partners with those in power. Which makes the chocolate industries less vulnerable to the laws and regulations that govern change and as long as the United States is bed partners with the chocolate industries not any significant changes will occur. The name of the government and chocolate industry game is "Delay, delay, delay. Yes! "Delay" for more time in renovations, delay for investigations of rape, sodomy, child abuse and questionable murder. Does greed over power the need to expose what is taking place on the Ivory Coast of Africa and

Ghana or is it that the United States of America who's the number one producer and manufacturer of chocolate in the world honestly just did not know these things were taking place. The legislation set forth to make the changes on the Cocoa Plantations is not being acted upon which negatively affects the policies already passed and disillusions further progress. To make it even clearer concerning the delays is that I would have to say because these are not American children suffering they are only Africa children, five year old boys and girls working 100 hours a week so there is not a need to rush so America politicians will just play the old game called, (Hurry Up and Wait). Justice concerning the Cocoa Plantations is justice long, long overdue. Hidden secrets and agendas prompted these words by the late and first black Supreme Court Justice Thurgood Marshall, "Don't look for justice because there isn't any." Is America ever going to live up to its promise of "Freedom and justice for all" when the very same words spewing from its lips makes government and the justice system in America quite the hypocrite? There is nothing that can validate what is currently taking place on the Ivory Coast of Africa in the year 2015 that would enhance a need for further delay but due to the poor living conditions, the rapes and abuse of five year old boys and girls taking place. There is a need for an immediate evacuation of the entire Cocoa Plantation operation until these issues of which I will continually mention are rectified.

Laws have not been outdated where it is now legal for boys and girls at the age of 5 to be sold into slavery while America and other nations just stand by and watch as though it is okay? If you will allow me to ask this question, "Why are we in the year 2015 and still talking about slavery"? Well pay very close attention to Amendment XIII and you will get an even better understanding: **Amendment XIII** the proposed amendment was sent to the states Feb. 1, 1865, by the Thirty-eighth Congress. It was ratified Dec. 6, 1865.)

Amendment XIII Section 1
[Slavery prohibited]

Neither slavery nor involuntary servitude, except as a punishment for crime whereof the party shall have been duly convicted, shall exist within the United States, or any place subject to their jurisdiction.

If you read Amendment XIII carefully what you read was: as long as you are not incarcerated you are considered to be free. Once you are incarcerated you haven't any rights and can be treated as a slave in accordance to the crime you may have committed. Amendment XIII does broaden the spectrum of any legal ramifications one might want to look into and is most definitely not in conjunction with what is stipulated in the Emancipation Proclamation concerning the abolishment of slavery. Of which appears to be quite contradictory as it relates to Amendment XIII. What also lies in question here is the act of rehabilitation concerning inmates in order that their obstructive behavior is corrected. Only how does one correct obstructive behavior when a slave is not even considered to be trainable enough to understand the behavior that needs to be corrected. A slave is not even considered to be human or treated as such as it relates to past law classifications of what is considered to be a slave.

Slave definition
A person who is the legal property of
another and is forced to obey them.

synonyms: *historical* serf, vassal, thrall; More
This is why we are still talking about slaves and slavery today because it was never completely abolished. Just keep reverting back to the Ivory Coast of Africa and the Cocoa Plantations you might begin to see the bigger picture.

Blue States/Red States

The bitterness of the southern states in support of slavery carried over into future generations of what we look at today as the infamous Red States. My personal experience with that kind of racial hatred happened in 1985. True story, I worked with the Department of Transportation for the state of Oklahoma. I worked in Edmond, Oklahoma on the surveying team. I remember this incident as if it were happening as I speak. The surveying team was returning back from a job and one of the older white men on the crew started talking about confederate money. He said he had a whole chest full of confederate money and he could not wait to spend it. Well my response to that was he should go ahead and burn the chest because it will never be worth anything in the United States ever. That confederate currency will never have any value and should not have had any when it was created. What he did not realize is although I was a young man I was upon my history. What he was telling me is that he was hoping to be able to spend his confederate money but in order for his confederate red state money to be worth anything the south would first have to be successful in invoking slavery back into existence once again. That is why I told him to go ahead and burn his chest because it slavery would never be again. This kind of thinking is one of the reasons why in the year 2015 the United States of America, this great nation still battles with such hypocrisy because of what is seen on many of these types of fake smiles and grins is a different kind of demon contained in their heart.

When we talk about being constructive and wearing out the barriers of bondage for everyone many changes for the better of all humanity would have to come into play. I personally think back on the many **obstacles (I want you to remember the word obstacles, you will see it again)** of hate Black Americans were once subjected to in an extreme way is now more moderate and appears to many whites today to be fair. Today we look at a divided nation of people, a divided nation of states, a divided nation of color. When I say a divided nation of color I am not talking about race or ethnicity. I am talking about once again this Blue State, Red State division the color of one's spirit that remains unnoticeable. Yes! Color can be involved if you really want to see color. If you want to see the physical person you know the skin color yes that kind of discrimination does exist. But the color I am discussing covers one of the major problems in life we face today the Democratic Party and the Republican Party, the Blue States verses the Red States. The political sides of this mutual inner hatred are the issues where there is no right or wrong but there is a happy medium. If the United (divided) States Blue and Red of America will ever find a happy medium remains questionable to me?

Let me get back to what I was saying earlier about the many **obstacles** intentionally set before Black Americans to impede their progress in the social status, climbing the ladder to the top. Obstacles which later became noted as diverse, undignified and inhumane but are still being practiced today but in different ways? America will have to take an in-depth look historically to see what's been consistently reoccurring in a system that frowns on its own causations. The American government should at some point have a moral desire to stop covering up its little intentional mishaps which will later turn out to be big disasters. The more important issues at hand can receive the proper attention needed to be resolved the better chance the United States will have the opportunity to make a full recovery. Turn the tables back for a minute and look at the way Blacks of today and slaves of the past were intentionally demoralized. These are issues that are not talked about today but exploited in many motion pictures and plays where Blacks were never good enough to have the leading roles. Black women were used as nothing more than bed warmers to white leading actors. There are also the old plantation movies such as "Roots" and many others where the owners of the plantation often referred to as (master) has his pick over the plantation female slaves no matter how young or old, the (master) of the planation slept with whatever slave he wanted. Although the female slave was not giving the (master) consensual sex he would never be charged with rape since she was his property and a slave hadn't anyone to report too. She was made to feel obligated to give the (master) of the plantation whatever he wanted, to not disappoint him. She also did not want to be tied to a tree and stripped naked in front of everyone and whipped. This is the kind of south the Red States want slavery in full effect and this is what the fight against racism in America is all about. Red States set limitations to non-whites. These individuals who are not of the white persuasion will only be allowed to go so far up the social ladder but never reach the top. No matter how smart, how loyal or dedicated to their job or position their skin color would be the stigma to keep them from attaining anything higher than what whites wanted to give them but never reaching the top. Other situations that occurred on the plantation against the slaves may be a bit graphic for you today. There were also times when the (master) would decide he wanted to have sex with one of the married female slaves. Of course, this was done to humiliate the male slave and strip him of his pride and dignity. The sexual contact with his wife was not done in private but right in front of her husband. The male slave was at times made to stay by the bedside and watch his wife being raped by the (master). A failure to comply by either the female or male slave could lead to them being whipped or an even greater possibility hung for not complying with what the (master) wanted. This is the kind of good old day's treatment those in the Red States want back. If you want to add a little Jim Crow please do. This and so much more concerning the Red States hatred is why Blue Sates fight so hard for equality and due process. This routine went on until the (master) got tired of raping the female slave and he found another he was fund of. The (master) would also find him another female slave if the one he was raping got pregnant. She would then be sold to another plantation or kept on the plantation until the babe was born and then sold. To this day of 2015 African American women have been known to date prominent white males and are stigmatized as nothing more than bed warmers. Let me clear this up and say this is not how I think but this is how things are viewed at least for those who are red in color. *Black women are often classified as being good in bed but never good enough to take home to mama or marry.*

History does not have to repeat itself. There is no obligation involving a time frame as to what is to take place in this world but many feel a need to captivate or should I say recycle what they want slavery back so badly "the good old days", "slavery". Staying focused on the Cocoa Plantations in combination with what is taking place in America today with the mass incarceration of Blacks filling the prison cells has been consistent throughout the their existence.

Legal Black Genocide a Match for the Cocoa Plantations

I call it intentional legal Black genocide which is now being looked upon by whites and other investors as an opportunity to legally reintroduce slavery to the world. I must give them credit for trying to do it diplomatically by legally taking away the majority of the jobs out of America so Blacks and other minorities will not have any recourse to find a means of supporting themselves. How do you feed your family when you haven't any means of finding employment? Prisons are growing in numbers as well as the incarceration ratio. We are looking at a system geared toward locking people up. A system intentionally making a weaker generation of people right before our eyes along with colonization of the infrastructure combined with mass incarceration of minorities in prison. What we are and have been looking at over the years right here in America is the overt operation of cause and effect. Making things appear to be what they really are not but having an hidden agenda of race genocide, particularly of the Black race. At one time there was a focus on wiping out Black males. Now it is the entire race since prisons are now being built for black women as well and their incarceration ratio is just as high. I will give you the numbers later in the book and of course I am certain they will astound you, at least most of you who are paying attention.

Let me interject for a few precious seconds and say just from what I have briefly revealed to you about what took place on the old cotton plantations in the south during slavery and for many years after slavery. It should strike a nerve or send your entire body into shock. Shock your mind as well as engulf every human emotion in your entire body. Every vein and vessel that runs blood throughout your body, and your heart as to what is taking place on the Ivory Coast of Africa and Ghana on the Cocoa Plantations with these five year old boys and girls you think Black Genocide started in America no it never stopped in Africa. These children have no protection; they have no father or mother to protect them. As I stated earlier the Cocoa Plantations are documented as being the worst form of slavery ever. It is much worst then slavery as we have ever known it to exists even in America. The worst noted ever in American or Western European history. These are five year old children I am talking about. Where is the conscious mind of the people the humane part that says this is all wrong. The treatment of these children is so grotesque one should puke at the mentioning of five year old boys and girls being beaten, raped, sodomized and possibly murdered. Why is this being allowed to happen? Slavery in America hadn't been abolished only pacified. I shouldn't use the word abolished I should say quieted down so genocide would not appear to be so obvious. With the stench of slavery and what is taking place on the Cocoa Plantations the memory of slavery in America still remains to be an embarrassing part of American history. A part of American history so degrading and immoral that it is rarely taught properly in the history classes of school for others to learn from. Americans would much rather sweep all of the graphic details as to how Blacks in America were stripped of their dignity, their families and culture under the carpet and keep it there then to expose how they became who they are today. As captured prisoners they were first called: Slaves, Niggers, then Negroid, Negros, Blacks, then finally African American. I will not for various reasons throw in the mix of name calling: Coon, Jigaboo, Sambo, Spook, Spec, Spade, nappy head, Uncle Tom oh and please do not let me leave out the n...word nigger the list goes on. These are just a few of the hardships Black men and Black women in America had to deal with not just during slavery but the name calling still exists to this day, let me remind you this is 2015. Americans would much rather hide the truth then discuss equality and fairness across the board because there is a fear within the infrastructure. A fear of thinking if they know what we know then maybe they will not think we are as superior as we think we are when in all actuality you are not you have been exposed a long time ago. Hiding the truth only feeds the wounds and there still has not been a healing process even with the first official African America President Barak Obama. Pacifying the public with what the people wanted to see but never relinquishing a forum to make it a visual apology to all. It is no longer a secret as history slowly unveiled the hidden agenda of those who harbored so much hate by exposing the uncountable rapes and possible murders of slaves that took place in the United States of America. Black men and women being raped sodomized along with any other abuse they had to endure for the sake of their survival. Since there aren't any representatives on the Cocoa Plantations to bear witness as to how these children are being treated or would care to report. Since these children are not protected they haven't any rights or violations to report. Sexual consent with five year old boys and girls because of their age would never be granted in the United States and is also considered a crime in other countries. Their yells and screams will never be heard in the hidden jungles of the Cocoa Plantations. Charges will never be filed against their assailants; there will never be a hearing or a judge to rule on the violations they have suffered. There is one there to bear witness to the abusive violations these children on the Cocoa Plantations have suffered. There will be no charges concerning the violations of their rights because these children do not have any rights on the Cocoa Plantations.

NO FATHER NO MOTHER

When you think about the abuse taking place on the Ivory Coast of Africa and Ghana in the remote areas of the cocoa plantations, please keep in mind these are five year old boys and girls I am speaking of who are working 100 hours a week. It should be impossible for anyone to be able to close their eyes at night knowing these children working on the Cocoa Plantations are as young as five years old with the oldest being sixteen years of age before they are no longer considered to be useful to work the Cocoa Plantations. These five year old boys and girls are being sold into slavery for as little as $14.00 dollars or sometimes depending on the need of the parent the child will be sold for as little as a tire for a bike that has a flat. These children are scarred for life not just physically from head to toe but also mentally and emotionally. It is mind boggling how a child five years old would be taught to swing a machete? It is unheard of how five year old boys and girls are made to work 100 hours a week, and that is every week? There isn't any sick leave building up, or paid vacation time for the year because they have been such dedicated employees. There aren't any bonuses or employee of the week benefits for these children. I am quite sure you have not given their medical needs any thought? What are the high risk factors involving these five year old babies permanently wounding themselves. Accidentally cutting off limbs on their body by trying to chop down cocoa with a machete? They may receive some medical treatment but many of the children because of the seriousness of the wound will remain damaged for life. To the overseers on the Cocoa Plantations these children are just not worth the medical bill or hospital cost. What happens to the five year old boy or girl who falls out of a 40 feet tree onto a machete or breaks his or her neck from the fall? What happens to the child who twists a knee or breaks and arm, what is done with them since they are not worth the cost of a hospital visit? These children are not only being mentally and emotionally damaged but they are also being physically abused. They are being beaten constantly, sodomized, raped and possibly even murdered and buried in unmarked graves away from the Cocoa Plantations because the United States of America refuses to make the laws that are already set enforceable?

What logical or ethical reasoning do our American politicians have left to listen for in order to go to the Ivory Coast of Africa and do something? **Former Senator Tom Harkin of Iowa** and **Congressman Eliot Engel of New York** should have a lot of explaining to do to the American people for sitting back and allowing this kind of brutal abuse of five year old children to continue. There has been broken promise after broken promise, the politicians say, "We are going to fix it". My question is, "WHEN"? Just how much longer will these political figures and Senators and Congressman continue their amending processes before these babies are helped? These five year old boys and girls are being denied an education; they are denied the life of being a child which is something that cannot be repaid in any amount of money. These five year old boys and girls are working over 100 hundred hours a week. They are not being paid any wages and they are not fed nutritional meals, they are fed corn mush. These children have no father or mother to attend to their ailments or their aching bodies. Their hands and feet are blistered from their long hours of work. I have to ask this question," Who cares for them when they have fevers? Keep in mind these are babies working in the scorching heat from sun up to sun down. What happens to them if they have a toothache, a headache, a stomach ache? Who do they cry out to for help? The pain they feel on a daily bases, the pain and suffering they endure on a daily bases is continual every day. Regardless of how tired or exhausted they are when the door to their mud shed opens up they must be ready to work sun up to sun down. Abuse is the only thing their little eyes and minds are able to witness, their mind is being conditioned at such a young age, they are being raised to think the beating, rapes and sodomy is how life is all over the world. They are being raised to believe that children are being tortured everywhere and it is a natural way of life. This is not how the law is supposed to work concerning children's rights. As an American citizen I am not in agreement with what is taking place on the Ivory Coast of Africa, many things can be done differently. Our position as a free nation should be to step in and render these children some form of relief. As citizens of the united states we stand by and watch the abuse of these five year old boys and girls as if we have blinders on. There is legislation set forth, laws set in place for this cocoa plantation it is called **Cocoa Protocol** of which **Former Senator Tom Harkin** of Iowa and **Congressman Eliot Engel** of New York both democrats were put in charge of the Cocoa Plantations in 2001 to make modifications happen and nothing has been done to date. Why hasn't these politicians been on the battlefield for these children? What they have in print before them makes it clear and concise there are violations concerning child abuse as well as violations of child labor laws.

Who is there to speak for the children on the Cocoa Plantations? They do not have a father or mother. They do not know why they are being treated with such harshness nor do they know they are not supposed to be working. These children do not know they are being abused there isn't anyone there to protect them from the abuse. In their eyes it is a normal way of life because they have not been taught anything different. There isn't an ending to the overseers' behavior the children just hope the next day the overseers will find someone else to pick on? Who is there to enrich their life when all they have been introduced to is a back beaten with a bike chain and hard labor? Who is there other than the unwanted sounds of other children crying out for help? There isn't any father or mother there to bathe them at night and encourage them with their dreams or to give them hope to inspire to be something? No father or mother is there to play peekaboo, or tickle them and most of all love and care for them? No father or mother is there to make them laugh? Here is a big question I am quite certain you have not thought about, have these children on the Cocoa Plantations ever heard laughter? Who is there, they have no father and no mother to pacify their needs? Who is there when they are locked up in a mud hut twenty-four feet by twenty feet with eighteen other boys and given two cans one is for everyone to defecate and the other is for everyone to urinate in. There is an armed guard at the doors of these mud huts. Once the huts are locked up the children are not allowed to come outside until day break, time to go to work. There is no playground or swimming pool, no home cooked meals, no books, no education, no dreams of a future. All these children have is the scorching sun beaming down on their slave driven backs as they work in the scorching hot and humid Cocoa Plantations. Their freedom is only through an escape. These children are captive to the environment of which they are being raised. They are driven by their own survival knowing they haven't any other choice than to do whatever they are told or face other consequences. They are all suffering and their blood is upon the hands of those of you in high places. These are the principalities of darkness that my father in heaven says to be aware of but I am bearing witness to make you accountable for the injustices being done to innocent little children. Keep in mind that one saint of God is more powerful than ten thousand sinners and my intentions are to stay on the battlefield for these voiceless children until something is done.

How can we watch the emasculation of these children and do nothing to correct the abuse taking place? How do we stand by and allow money to become more valuable than life or happiness of innocent children? Children on the Cocoa Plantations will never hear the laughter of children having fun in a park or see children being pushed on swings in a playground. They will only feel the crack of a whip on their backside, and the yells and screams of other children pleading for their life trying to make it through another day. Children watching the daily routines of other children being taken by their oppressors to hidden areas on the plantation and sexually abused, where are their protectors they have no father or mother? Why do we stand and watch the horrific treatment of these children as though we do not have a voice. Yes the elected politicians are our voice. They are voted into office to protect the common welfare of people whose rights are being infringed upon. I pray that God Almighty has mercy on the soul of this nation because we all have to stand accountable for what we did not do as a nation of people to help these innocent children on the Ivory Coast of Africa. Ask yourself these questions are the children guilty because they are born in a poor country and live in the poorest parts of Africa? Is it because the United States of America who's leading all nations in producing and manufacturing chocolate feels the resources that are being imported to America to create thousands of jobs for families in America has a greater value than the lives of these children? Or is the United States along with other countries guilty for not furnishing the food and supplies needed because the investment of a better living for these children would not show a profitable gain. Yet the United States will go into other famished countries feed and clothe them and give them other added amenities because we want to help to emanate other nations due to our ties and affiliations?

Protocol What List

Former Senator Thomas Richard "Tom" Harkin of Iowa and **Congressman Eliot Engel** of New York once again both democrats are suppose to be the voice and protectors for these children. Nothing is being done on an expeditious level to stop further damage and abuse of these children. If you asked what is Cocoa Protocol I would have to say a protocol of order that has not taken place yet. When you think about protocol there is an order that needs to be followed and if the order is not followed there is a violation that has taken place. So what is the definition of the word Protocol- **"an original draft or record of a document, negotiation, etc. (2) a signed document containing a record of the points on which agreement has been reached by negotiating parties preliminary to a final treaty or compact. b) The ceremonial forms and courtesies that are**

established as proper and correct in official intercourse between heads of states and their ministers.

When I begin to dissect the word "Protocol" it is represented with a sense of order, a pattern of perfection, a format that has to be followed but only in conjunction with the itinerary of importance. I say again what does "Protocol" mean to you and what establishes an individual, a place or a thing to be accountable as such if any of importance. Let's take some example for instance to open your imagination. Protocol, there is the President and Vice President, rank has its privileges, there is the alphabet you know A-Z that is protocol. Only what place does the list of prioritizing come when such a word as Protocol becomes lucent in trying to make something that is not as important as all of the other stuff on one's itinerary to fit the needs of the people. What I am saying here is there are amendments to laws, meetings and consultations with other senators and congressmen taking place; there is an order to follow. There is personal busy that must be taken care of as well as one's personal life and needs that must be met. I can keep on shuffling things around but I am quite sure you've gotten the picture of what I am trying to draw for you. Let me make it a little plainer for you. Everyone knows that child abuse is a big No! No! In America child abuse is something that is just not tolerable and never overlooked when it comes to the protection of a child. So I am going to say the "Cocoa Protocol" appears to be what it is not, that is set up for the children on the Cocoa Plantations to protect them. Can this be the case with Senators, Congressmen and others who are involved with the chocolate industries here in America when we think about prioritizing and protocol?

Is it fair for me to ask the question just how low does the Cocoa Protocol fall on the protocol list? I know for a fact it is not first on the list because if it was so and these Senators and Congressmen along with the National Confectionery Association in the chocolate industry would have taken immediate action. To bring about immediate changes to the abrupt conditions under which these children are being forced to live while at the same time they are being abused and exploited. For whatever matter nothing has been done maybe, just maybe the senate and congress may have been on break and fourteen years later they just never got around to expressing their concerns of five year old children being trained to swing a machete or climbing forty foot trees. What is the protocol for child abuse would someone please explain it to me because maybe I just missed something. I did say child abuse, in America mothers are given court dates for child abandonment (leaving a child in the car while unloading groceries), leaving a child in a running car with the windows not crack in the summertime, while pumping gas, not having a child in the proper car seat. A newborn baby in America cannot leave the hospital without the parents having a car seat for the child to ride home in. These are laws that have been passed for the protection of children voted on by the same senate and congress the same elected government officials who have not done anything concerning the child abuse and forced child labor on the Cocoa Plantations. They prioritize the Cocoa Plantations as a project they will eventually get to. The only problem is on the protocol list of important things to do it just has not made it to that level of importance to be looked at. Has the Cocoa Protocol been voted on yes in September of 2001? Do key people in the senate and congress know what is taking place on the Ivory Coast of Africa, yes? I just don't want to stop with our government knowing what is taking place with these children but I also have to look at key people in the chocolate industry conspiring not to make the necessary changes needed hoping that somehow everything will just fix itself. That is not going to happen because of the conditioning process these people who are running these disgusting Cocoa Plantations have already been programed. Those who are in charge of the chocolate factories and those at the corporate level are only looking at the production of the product and not how the product itself is actually created from start to finish; I would like to believe that? I am certain the board members of the **Chocolate Manufacturers Association** along with **Susan Smith** who has been involved with Association management for the Confectioners Industry since 1984 or other members on the **National Confectioners Association** (NCA) would not allow their children to even set foot on a Cocoa Plantation. Just from the research I have gathered it would be too embarrassing of a situation to have not just their grandsons or granddaughters working on the Cocoa Plantations but any relative they cared about brought to an area of such degradation they would be humiliated to confess to being a part of. Can you honestly see the board member of the National Confectioners Association (NCA), board members of the Chocolate Manufacturers Association, Susan Smith who also serves as spokesperson for the United States Chocolate and Candy Industry, Former Senator Thomas Richard "Tom Harkin of Iowa and Congressman Eliot Engel of New York give their five year old grandsons or granddaughters two buckets and lock them up in a mud hut that is not efficient enough to house 18 or more boys and or girls and tell all of them to defecate and urinate in these two buckets for the rest of the night. I want you to see what I see so you can have a better understanding that all of these boys and girls defecating and urinating in two buckets is first of all not sanitary and second of all it is and should be considered inhumane treatment. I did not say using the same commode (toilet) where the feces or urine is able to be flushed but two buckets where these poor little children have to sit and smell this stench for the rest of the night. Oh please don't let this shock you but the ventilation inside these mud huts is not larger than the circumference of a baseball. I adamantly doubt it very seriously if any of these so-called humane and well educated individuals belonging to the board of the Chocolate Manufacturers Association, the National Confectioners Association, along with Susan Smith, Former Senator Thomas Richard "Tom Harkin or Eliot Engel would give their five year old grandson or granddaughter a machete to go out in their backyard to play with or have them climb a forty foot tree to cut down cocoa with the high possibility of cutting themselves or maybe even falling to their death. But you allow this to continue with five year old boys and girls on the Cocoa Plantations in Africa and Ghana.

This Cocoa Plantation, forced child labor, child abuse in its worse form, a situation beneath the normal functioning of a child's Adult Daily Living (ADL's), or should I say a child's normal living capabilities. The detrimental damage mental, physical and emotional being done to these children for life is not just what they have to live with, but we all have to live with. I have to question the employees of theses chocolate manufacturers, companies and distributors as well? Do they know the abuse taking place on the Ivory Coast of Africa and Ghana with these children and their hard work of 100 hours a week to get the cocoa pod to America for them to have a job within these chocolate producing industries, companies and corporations? If they know what is taking place would they continue working for **Doctor Chocolate Jekyll and Mr. Chocolate Hyde?** I wonder would I hear all the excuses employees make for not knowing their role of involvement with certain companies and their involvement in forced child labor (child abuse) how do they correct their current situation or will they give the typical excuse statements, I need my job, I have bills to pay, my family has to eat, I am putting my children through college or the infamous statement, I did not know they were doing this to children. Now that you know will you continue working for the chocolate industry? The Chocolate Industry is big business in America and abroad I did mention earlier America is first on the list in the world for producing and manufacturing chocolate. I will get to the list a little later in the book. In the meantime I want you to keep in mind what I just stated earlier about these chocolate industries being the Doctor Jekyll and Mr. Hyde of Chocolate by the way I will explain what I mean by this a little later in the book. Please keep reading. This is worse than child abuse maybe another name for child abuse should be created at this point Those in higher management only see green dollar signs and not the abuse and inhumane treatment these five year old boys and girls are going through. Money does talk but not in the case of the Cocoa Planation's.

"The International Labor Organization (ILO) defines child labor as work that "is mentally, physically, socially or morally dangerous and harmful to children; and interferes with their schooling by depriving them of the opportunity to attend school; by obliging them to leave school prematurely; or by requiring them to attempt to combine school attendance with excessively long and heavy work." Not all work that children do is child labor. Work done that is not detrimental to children's health, development or schooling is beneficial because it allows children to develop skills, gain experience and prepare them for future positions. (http://en.wikipedia.org/wiki/Children_in_cocoa_planations)

When I leave the house to go to a store or to get gas, go shopping at the mall, get groceries, or stop at a General Dollar store chocolate is being sold everywhere. This is how I began to understand just how easy it was for the Chocolate Industry to lose sight of what was taking place behind the scene. And only focus on the trillions of dollars they would make off the backs of five year old children, slave labor for free. Just think of all the little people working as distributors, clerks, vendors, managers, supervisors, district managers, regional managers and those at corporate level positions. All they can think of is how to market the chocolate products they are in charge of in order for their distribution and sales to look good at the end of the month. This would afford them the title of employee of the month, staff representative of the month and maybe a new position within the Corporation, an all-expense paid vacation and possibly a very large bonus check to purchase gifts during the Christmas festive season. Do they have an idea as to what is taking place on the Cocoa Plantations; they could probably care less as long as the people at the top of the chocolate industry are happy and their paychecks continue to get bigger? I understand the big picture they see is of course money, money, money. The importance of human life hasn't any value at all to them especially if it is not their own or their own kind.

This is just more exploitation without examination of one's investment regardless of who is suffering yet the abuse of these children continues to be nonstop through the years but kept quiet with only a little exposure through articles and maybe a news reporter on CNN will do a story every once in a while but for the most part the Cocoa Plantations are unknown to the consumers. The treatment of these children on the Cocoa Plantations is being kept very quiet. I am going to be a little optimistic here and say I guess all of the politicians have not forgotten to do something about the Cocoa Plantations. They are just on a rush called a Chocolate high and when they come down from all of those added bonuses like trips, and time share vacations and political campaign contributions being made out to their favorite foundations. I guess just maybe one day one of the politicians in Washington, DC will think about these five year old boys and girls and how they are suffering and do something about it. When the truth is finally uncovered I am certain it is going to be a **CHOCOLATE** mess. I say this because there isn't any logical reason as to why these five year old boys and five year old girls are living under such abusive conditions what's even more asinine is they are working with machetes. If you want to go for ludicrous, remember they are working 100 hours a week every week.

Hear My Prayers Father God

This is very painful for me to write about but I am compelled to do so because of my love for all humanity. There are consequences we all have to face but as I sit captivated over the degradation taking place not only on foreign soil but on American soil I cannot be silent concerning this matter. Many of you know what is taking place on the Ivory Coast of Africa and Ghana. You have turned your head not in shame or disgust but have turned your head to greed. I pray God Almighty has mercy on your soul. Fortunately for me and for the sake of these innocent little ones who haven't a voice to speak for themselves I say proudly "Use me Lord, use me." Let the flood gates be opened to unveil the abuse of these innocent children. Let your word move forward with a vengeance Father God, and let your hands my Lord bend the irons and break the shackles of hate weighing down the strongholds of sin. Please hear my prayers Father God. Please hear the cries of these children through the night for they are helpless and in need of your spirit Lord God to filter out the wickedness that has fallen upon them. Hear my prayers Father God. Reveal to the world this inhumane hate that has taken the lives of these innocent children. Jesus said in the book of Mark 9v42 **"And whosoever shall offend one of these little ones that believe in me, it is better for him that a millstone were hanged about his neck, and he were cast into the sea."** Let these words go forth Jesus and let the Christian nation stand in the gap for the intentional wrong being done to these innocent children. I stretch my hands to thee Father God for there is no other help I know. There is no one else I can go to who will come to the aide of these children on the Cocoa Plantations. I rest under the wings of God Almighty knowing the blood of these children being spilled will be avenged by my father in heaven. I pray their cries at night and the pain they do not understand be comforted by the Holy Ghost. What is permissible by mankind laws are not permissible by our Father in heaven. I pray for change and let it come quickly Lord God. These children have suffered immensely Lord God let them feel their relief through your glory. I ask in the name of Jesus that you come quickly and let not your raft be short of those who are guilty. You said to me Lord God to forgive 70 times 7 times a day I am your obedient servant Lord I forgive the Chocolate Industry for their greed. There is much that could have been done many years ago had the Chocolate Industry moved in a willing way to accommodate request made to help the children. I will pray and ask for their forgiveness in all of the wrong that is being doing to these children even with that being said Lord God. Everyone deserves a chance at salvation Father in Heaven and I do not want to sound unforgiving because I know you have the authority the power to fix all things including the grid that is in their heart.

Your Honor Father Your Respect

You have covered up the chariots and
Pharaoh's men in the Red Sea;
Pharaoh's heart was hardened and his army
drowned for the wrong he had done;
Let my people go was the cry heard throughout the land;
Egypt brought forth plagues through your anger Lord;
The children of Israel suffered it so in their
cries for deliverance, freedom,
Let your honor Father God be swift and without mercy;
The just will suffer with the unjust as
the earth trembles beneath,
They honor themselves in your glory Father
God without any respect to you;
The castrations are uncountable and the murders are countless,
In this land of milk and honey they spoil themselves with greed;
Yet these children ask for so little my Lord and Savior,
What does laughter cost, and when
does a smile embrace a whip;
Come quickly Father God to these children's rescue;
Their cries are being heard through the
land for your goodness and mercy,
Let those in position know you are to be
respected, you hold the reins;
Let the East winds come where there isn't any thirst,

Let the tides come with destruction just
by the wave of your hand;
Let my people go is the cry throughout the Cocoa Plantations,
Let lightning strike in places unheard of,
nothing can hide from you Lord;
Let the thunder roar with a vengeance and
be not far Lord, they need you,
Graves were opened and the dead got up and walked;
There is nothing too hard for my Father in heaven
or too large of a scale to complete,
Yet they still turn their heads in laughter and
greed, worshiping their filthy lucre;
Not trying to correct this wrong being
done on the Cocoa Plantations;
They have been warned: Let my people
go, but they do not believe,
You have warned them Father to touch not
the little ones, but they mock you;
You have warned them to not have any other God before you,
These are stiff-necked people, who only believe in their way,
They say there is no God and mock you
as they rise to their pinnacle;
You have warned them Father God just as
you warned Sodom and Gomorrah,
Be not far from these children in ending their pain and suffering;
They have your strong arm Lord for I cannot reach them,
Please hear the cries of your servants,
Almighty Father hear their cries, ease
their pain, sweat and blood;
These children do not know how to cry to you;
Let the voices of their ancestors be head
and their request delivered,
Our voice is now their voice for they know not how to pray;
They know not your name Lord, how
do they call upon you in need,

It is not their fault Father they have not been taught to pray,
They do not know how to worship and love you, can I intercede;
I cry out for their mercy, to cease the pain
that continues in their body;
I cry out for them for their screams that cannot be heard,
I cry out for the multitude of boys and
girls buried beneath the earth;
For they know not your name Lord nor do
they know the name of Jesus,
Let these children's tormentors feel the
vengeance of their injustices,
I know you can call the sea, the wind, the storms and lightning;
I know you can move the earth and stop the sun from shining;
Because of their greed and perverted desires
they feel they have the power,
They feel they have gotten away but they
word is sufficient with me Father,
"There is no good or bad deed that goes
unrewarded" reward them accordingly;
Uncover their hidden secrets, weaken their
armor, and bring light on their darkness,
Dismantle them quickly, they mock your word
my Lord and protest against you,
Some still say there is no God; this is what
the fool has said in his heart;
You said to suffer little children, and they
wait on a God they do not know;
While they are beaten, raped, sodomized and
murdered, they cry out for mercy;
Their oppressors gist with joy and have no fear
they continually say there is no God,
They frown on…Your Honor Father God and Your Respect

Written by: Author & Hall of Fame Poet
Raymond C. Christian

A Reflection by the Author (Do you recall)

As I sit in awe over many unresolved issues I feel important to write about. I first had to examine myself. I have to do some deep soul searching first to make a point and secondly to make sure everyone would have an understanding about the point I am attempting to make.

I pray those of you reading this book regardless of color does not get offended. I ask that God opens your mind, your heart and soul to give you a sound understanding to what has taken place very quietly behind the scenes concerning chocolate in America as well as chocolate throughout the world. There is an old cliché that says "What you don't know won't hurt you." Well I am going to have to disagree with the old cliché and make a new one that says, "What you don't know will not only hurt you but possibly kill you."

For those of you who are able to stand watch with me I am writing this book for many reasons not to cause wars or rumors of such but to enlighten your conscious mind. If I might pour a little ice water on you while you are in a deep sleep in order to shock your mind just a little. So you can move with an urgency and do something about this crisis of child abuse on the Cocoa Plantation I will do the very best I can to explain. To bring forth factual information in order to introduce you to a situation that must be changed. It is more than just a little something to make you think to open your mind outside of your comfort zone. It is a reminder of a dreaded past, a past that was once active and alive in the midst of America, slavery. Slavery was somewhat abolished in America because of the Emancipation Proclamation which only obscures the visual, but still being practiced in remote areas of the world? A past filled with misconceptions of a race of people portrayed as being ignorant and slothful. A race of people looked upon as being animals and without feelings or capabilities to function in society without a leash. I should not say it is something that was abolished because slavery never ceased read your Thirteenth Amendment. Slavery was never completely dismantled as we once knew it to be here in America. Of course, since we are aware of redirection, a change of course, rerouting the original plan and making the primary plan just a little obscured so everyone cannot see the bigger picture, "it still exist today." In today's society it looks even more catastrophic.

The primary plan now is the beginning of a new investment building prisons to legally house Blacks in America. Mass incarceration, controlling prison calls, incarceration of African Americans and other minorities, Latino's and Mexicans. With the intent of annihilation of the African American race as we know it. African American men make up 97% of the prison system. To my understanding Victoria Secrets has been named as a primary investor in building women prisons of which African American women make up more than half of the women prisoners population. Although we are looking at it from the perspective of a much broader spectrum which says, no more slavery in America at least as we once knew it. Slavery was being slowly filtered out of the American system. Slavery remained in practice and continued to be practiced in the International mother land, Africa. As we take a closer look at the Cocoa Plantations what we really see is nothing more than a reflection of what was once known as the cotton plantations. And just life the Cotton Gin was invented by Eli Whitney in 1793 to pick cotton and began to abolish slave labor as we once knew it on the cotton plantations. Modern technology today can get the job done on the Cocoa Plantations so they can stop using five year old boys and girls as an excuse to abuse and rape them. Now let's dig a little deeper. Let's go all the way back to the mother land, Africa where slavery has never ceased and refresh your memory to the abuse that has taken place on the Ivory Coast of Africa and Ghana on the Cocoa Plantations.

You can read this book with tears in your eyes or hate in your heart. Many of you will say, "Who does he think he is, to write a book such as this?" Well just look at me as a servant being used by God Almighty, doing the will and work of my Father in heaven. And to my understanding of scripture the Holy Bible says, do not fear the one who can mutilate the body but fear the one who can mutilate both body and the soul. My work is justified and sufficient with the Lord. Everything and anything in this world my Father in heaven has to first approve so I say let this book be a blessing and a learning tool to all those who fight against inhumane treatment of anyone. The sad thing about this whole picture I am drawing for the world to look at is that you cannot redo the past. There are reflection of hate involving and even bigger and deeper bitter hate towards African American (Blacks). There are some people who wish African American (Blacks) could just disappear. My question to you is what is God's plan? Yes the scab of slavery is once again oozing with puss. The Cocoa Plantations is something that needs to be uncovered, opened up and revealed to the world so everyone can see all of the worms wiggling beneath its crust. Unfortunately there are many things that cannot be repaired over night or forgiven but not forgotten. When I read the book "The Red Record" and all of the slaves that were murdered, hung, some entire families were hung together, some burned alive, some boiled in oil, some hung up for target practice and then shot full of holes. The list goes on and it is an ugly sore. America I must admit you now have an even greater opportunity to redeem yourself. You can do something to bring a positive change for once and for all by ending the abuse of these five year old children on the Cocoa Plantations. There is so much that could be done to help promote peace and tranquilly unfortunately the ugly monster of greed has warped everyone's thinking in the chocolate industry, politicians are overlooking laws that should be enforced and law enforcement is just looking the other way. The dates and time given to attempt to make some changes on the Ivory Coast of Africa and Ghana has exchanged hands so many times it makes you wonder will it ever stop being passed around. Will they ever get to the Harkin-Engel Cocoa Protocol of where the Cocoa Plantations can actually make it on the list of important things to do without moving the date of rectifying this situation further back. Once a promise is made it should be adhered to. I could talk about the 40 acres and a mule that was to be given to every African America (Black) serving in the civil war, that's another promise the infamous rubber stamp bounced on. Although the forty acres and a mule is a contractual agreement and documented, American politicians remain consistent with their false promises and very little hope. You might want to question what is written on the Statue of Liberty "Give me your tired, your poor, your huddled masses yearning to breathe free;, Words with meaning but never filled. Issues in the past that have shed light on the worst of situations once again promises made but not kept. What many people are privileged to is their own uncontrollable tongue, a muscle in the body that is considered to be untamable. There is an old saying that was taught to me as a child by my mother. She would always say be careful with what you allow to come out of your mouth and she taught me this saying: **"Words like eggs should be handled with care, because words once spoken and eggs once broken are not the easiest things to repair."**

Making promises and not making good to who that promise was made is just not going to cut the mustard; there are penalties for such lies. The old politician way of life appear to be saying, tell the people anything you think you can get away with and make as many false promises that you can and hopefully they will believe you and elect you to public office. In today's society people have become more aware of the politicians and their promises. The American people are just not falling for the same old routine any longer, you know the old let's see who can lie the best, believing the best liar is the right one to pick, who is more believable? American people are now searching for sound political figures. Politicians that say what they mean and carry out the promises made during their campaign for election. I cannot reiterate what I have said concerning the Cocoa Plantations to make it any clearer than I already have and this is the first portion of the book I am asking you to drink from. Let the cuisine of words I have just fed you sliver around in your mouth for a while before you swallow this distasteful mouthful of the **worst forms of child abuse** ever heard of in the history of the world. The pot will thicken as I stir in my concerns. I will continue to give you pertinent facts as you read this book to enlighten yourself with what is taking place on the Cocoa Plantations on the Ivory Coast of Africa and Ghana. There are changes that must be made if we, Americans are to continue to be able to call ourselves a civilized nation of people. Changes undoubtedly have to be made quickly to sustain the lives of these children on the Cocoa Plantations to instill hope for their future as well as the opportunity for a better life.

This pattern of abuse involving African Americans (Blacks) in American and abroad goes to the depths of what others would consider to be humane in the United States of America verses what is considered to be inhumane or should I say animalistic, the latter being inhumane. African Americans (Blacks) were once looked upon as being property and of course property cannot own property with either having the relevance to purchase. As this ugly sore of American secrets begins to become more and more irritated the history of slavery shall present itself again openly and without thought of the wrong being done but of violations of laws and ethics concerning human rights. Am I being superficial when I say American's will say, "We are so embarrassed about slavery?" That statement is questionable because of what has taken place through the years something's are better off just left alone. This is what many whites will say due to the embarrassment of what those who progressed during those years of slavery, those who used slaves as a means of profit (free labor), which is exactly what is taking place on the Cocoa Plantations, free slave labor and without pay. During those days a meal and a old shack to live in was good enough. Slavery is something America would like to put behind her, but the ugly faces of injustice keeps the sore covered and the wound which is never revealed is never allowed to heal? Slavery continues to be reintroduced due to the fascist behavior of others who still to this day feel African American (Blacks) are nothing more than animals. Which is how they were treated when they were first brought to

America by ship, slaves were chained together on what was once called slave ships that traveled down the Ivory Coast of Africa to Europe where those who were captured were taken from Africa and sold as slaves on the auction blocks in Europe. Slaves were not given freedom to roam around the ship during the months of long travel. Slaves were handcuffed and shackled together to prevent their chances of escape. In the process of slaves wanting to go to the bathroom in private there was no such thing. Slaves were made to defecate and urinate where they sat and slept. Female slaves that had their monthly cycles were not given any privacy. They were not released from their shackles they had their monthly menstrual cycles where they sat and slept. On the slave ships they were not given plates such and silverware to eat from. Their food was thrown to them the same as pigs in a pigs sty were feed. Slaves were feed like hogs on a farm. Well there is that animalistic behavior I was talking about. I wonder how it all got started the animal behavior that is or is that another book as well. You see the pot calling the kettle black is not a pretty thing. Slaves were fed all the scraps of food others did not want it was just like feeding slop to hogs, well there is that animalistic behavior again. Do you think whites will ever admit to treating humans like animals? I must admit times in America have changed just a little. Now there is bi-racial everything not only married couples, but children in mixed families, grandchildren in mixed families, and mixed families in mixed families did you laugh yet well guess what I am cracking up at this point. Because when it all comes out of the wash everyone will figure it out that God's plan is the plan that is going to work. He is our father. I better stop right here I hope everyone got the memo.

True Life Story What Would You Eat

I often find myself thinking about the time I had just gotten out of the Marine Corps and I was attending college working on my Associates Degree. I was in class and listening to the Professor (Terry) who just happened to be a female teaching Introduction to Sociology in Oklahoma. I just happened to be the only male in class with about twenty women. The question that was presented to the classroom was "If it came down to your life would anyone eat a dog?" I remember my professor making the statement that she did not care how hungry she had gotten she would never stoop so low as to eating a dog. She asked a few other girls they responded "No." She finally asked me and my response was, "did you say this person was hungry or starving because there are different levels of hunger? I responded there was a time I would have given the same answer "No" but during my training in the United States Marine Corps one of the training methods a Marine is taught is survival. Marines are trained that if you are in a situation where you are pinned down in crossfire or you are in an area that you are not able to get out of and there are dead bodies around the fatty part of the dead soldier's buttocks has the most nutrients for your survival. Be assured as a young man and marine I thought it sounded gross as well but until that situation occurs do you really know what you would do? I hadn't any idea that part of my training as an Infantry Officer would be to sleep in a cemetery with dead bodies all around me but that did happen; of course I was not the only one sleeping out there. So given this classroom scenario I thought it was important for the professor as well as the students to know my training in the Marine Corps was very stringent in many areas and if the situation was to present itself in reference to one's survival. I was taught to do what was needed and necessary. I continued to tell them "I am happy the situation did not present itself to me, but it is important for them to never say what they will and would not do until they were actually presented with a situation such as, eat dog or die."

Another situation that happened to me while training to become an Infantry Officer we were out on patrol and this was a situation where we had to stay up for three days without sleep. We were given our perimeters to protect and then we had to move to other locations throughout the day and night. This training required both night and day patrol, travelling and stopping to set up perimeters and no one could sleep. Each future officer watched the strengths and weaknesses of the other officer. I am not saying it to be funny but in case a war was to break out you really want to know what kind of a person you are in a war zone with. What we were watching for is to see who would go to sleep on their perimeter watch, who would be careless enough to fall asleep and possible get everyone killed. We had two very strong training sergeants I will never forget Staff Sergeant Sims, and Sgt Dagley two good men. Sgt Dagley was always trying my mental strengths. He just happened to be the Sergeant over this particular mission I remember him taunting me telling me I would not make it the three days without any sleep. That he would be breathing down my neck to make sure I did not get the opportunity to close my eyes for one second. Well the mission was long and of course we had our meals to eat while others stood watch. Well this was the last day and we were on our last march to close out our training cycle before graduation. We set up our perimeters and it was chow time. I was called to go eat but I noticed the other officer with me was famished and could not hold up another second so I told him to go ahead before me I would be okay. Sgt Dagley would later have a soldier come to relieve me. The only problem was when I got to the chow line all of the food was gone. The only thing that was left was a plate sitting by the garbage. I asked Sgt Dagley where was my plate he pointed right there, the one sitting by the garbage and laughed. I thought to myself was this a test of my manhood or was this really a plate left over with other soldiers scraps they did not eat. Please do not let the outcome shock you I had to face this demon and I did knowing at this point I was also in need of nourishment and this was the last meal until five the next morning. I knew there was no way I would have made it if I did not eat because we had more patrolling to do and I was already riding on empty. I never had any regrets about giving the other officer my spot to go before me, he was on his last leg and that's just what we do for each other. Would he have did the same for me that's a question you have to ask yourself? Remember I did graduate IOBC and I did become a United States Infantry Officer amongst many other things I will not mention. This is where the importance of knowing how to pray and what prayer is for comes into play. I grabbed that plate of food that was by the garbage and a fork and began to eat. I kept my mind on Jesus not knowing what this plate was really left for me or someone else's left overs. I did eat and I thank God that I did because our missions were not done and it would have been impossible for me to make it if I had not eaten. We traveled all night with very little rest. We finally got to our final attack and everyone was told to run full steam ahead to our mark. That was a happy time for all of us we had made it at the end of the three day mission we were all blessed with the opportunity to meet General Colin Powell he had just flown in by helicopter to congratulate us. He gave us a brief "that a boy" prep talk and said he would be meeting us back in the rear, "You have one hour to get cleaned up and be in the auditorium." I never had the opportunity to ask Sgt Dagley about the plate of food by the garbage. When it is all said and done it really doesn't matter, I did eat it. When your survival for life is challenged you will find out it is not a game. Remember it is written in scripture Matthew 15 v 11 "Not that which goeth into the mouth defileth a man: but that which cometh out of the mouth, this defileth a man." Some things in life you have to experience for yourself in order to understand. Now you should be able to see the bigger picture of what's taking place with captive slaves on a ship shackled together for months barely fed, eating and sleeping next to their own feces and hungry. I wonder if I should present the question to you and ask you would you eat? Do you think the slaves on the slave ships had time to wonder where their food came from? The answer is no they ate what they were thrown. Now let me present the question to you would you have eaten the meal I ate? But you really cannot answer that question because you are not me and you are not aware of all of the circumstances involved during my time of starvation.

So whatever was not considered to be edible by whites or whatever made whites sick was given to slaves to eat and to feed their children. A slave's question of being considered to be human remained in question as they reached Europe's slave trading post. The auction block is where African men, women and children were made to strip down to nothing exposing themselves in front of everyone in order for the slave to be sold for a profit. Oh please don't let me forget that many of the slaves did not make it to Europe. In reference to American history books there were over 100 million Africans who were captured and taken from the mother land (Africa) who either died, was murdered, jumped overboard, or was murdered by other slaves, in travel through the middle passages. They were either thrown overboard, jumped overboard, or just murdered in cold blood and thrown overboard for the sharks to eat. Because of the living and eating conditions of which these captive Africans had to live under at times they were forced to kill one another for the sake of their own survival. To whites they were nothing more than animals and that mentality remains conducive with many whites in their way of thinking today. Remember Mass Incarceration is the perfect example of racial hatred. Case given facts are wild animals locked up if you answered yes a point for you now relate that to caged up human being (African American Blacks to be discrete), case closed. This is why I am writing this book about the abuse and rape of these five year old children on the Ivory Coast of Africa and Ghana. You see it starts off as an international problem and ends up being a world problem because although the American politicians have jurisdiction to help no assistance has been rendered to help these five year old children on the Ivory Coast of Africa and Ghana working 100 hours a week on the Cocoa Plantations. The conditioning process starts early and perpetuates itself into a cause and purpose of why certain things have been allowed to happen. Many people here in America would never believe that slavery would raise its unwarranted face again but racism is still quietly practiced, (It still exists today). Please take note of the conditioning process and how it not only affects animals but humans as well making both very difficult to deal with.

Introduction of Theory a Conditioning Process

Let me give a few examples of which I will use one theory by Ivan Pavlov. Someone I studied in high school and college. Ivan Pavlov was a Russian physiologist known primarily for his work in classical conditioning. I chose to write about "classical conditioning" because it fits what I am about to explain perfectly concerning the conditioning process which Blacks in America have gone through and continue go through as the guinea pigs by force not by choice. By force it would be considered to intentionally hold back jobs, food, housing, medicine to get someone in need which is usually located near a ghetto to get Blacks to forcibly volunteer. A person does not have to be hog tied or hung to be made to do something they do not wish to do. The sacrifice of one will save many so the power to be intentionally introduces hardship, causation to a reaction which usually renders the response needed. These people only appear to be making these choices themselves but that is not the case African Americans (Blacks) are victims of "classical conditioning" almost similar to "Willie Lynch" but just a little more discrete, less practical and unobvious, at least that is what they would like for Blacks to think. Yes! The cat is out of the bag the three basic necessities of life, food, shelter and employment takes the three away and what you have is a broken man or woman unable to take care of their self. These needs must be met in order for life to exist as they know it and so does the individual or individuals who are driving the heard. No one is confused they are just made to appear confused because of the conditioning process. Do they really want to do it, no? Do they have to do it in order to survive, yes? Who will get the blame they will for doing it anyway and this is where Ivan Pavlov classical conditioning experiment comes into play. Please follow me carefully:

My Theory of "Classical Conditional" in Human Form

"During his research on the physiology of digestion in dogs, Pavlov developed a procedure that enabled him to study the digestive processes of animals over a long period of time. He redirected the animal's digestive fluids outside the body, where they could be measured. Pavlov noticed the dogs in the experiment began to salivate in the presence of the technician who normally fed them, rather than simply salivating in the presence of food. Pavlov called the dogs' anticipated salivation, psychic secretion. From his observation he predicted that a stimulus could become associated with food and cause salivation on this own. If a particular stimulus in the dogs' surroundings was present when the dog was given food in his initial experiments, Pavlov rang a bell and then gave the dog food; after a few repetitions, the dogs started to salivate in response to the bell. Pavlov called the bell the conditioned (or conditional) stimulus (CS) because its effects depend on its association with food. He called the food the unconditioned stimulus (US) was the unconditioned response (UR). The timing between the presentation of the CS and US affects both the learning and the performance of the conditioned response. Pavlov found that the shorter the interval between the ringing of the bell and the appearance of the food, the stronger and quicker the dog learned the conditioned response.

As noted earlier, it is often thought that the conditioned response is a replica of the unconditioned response, but Pavlov noted that saliva produced by the CS differs in composition from what is produced by the US. In fact the CR may be any new response to the previously neutral CS hat can be clearly linked to experience with the conditional relationship of CS and US. It was also thought that repeated pairings are necessary for conditioning to emerge, however many CRs can be leaned with a single trial as in fear conditioning and taste aversion learning." (_http://en.wikipedia.org/wiki/Classical conditioning_) Pavlov was a genius, there were other experiments that Pavlov used such as Forward conditioning, Delay conditioning, Trace conditioning, Simultaneous conditioning, Second-order and higher –order conditioning.

Herding, I must state is taking place with African American (Blacks) today. The same as what has taken place with the dogs in Pavlov's experiments is nothing more than a process to condition the dogs to salivate. This is where I began to take you to the unemployment ratio in America of which African Americans have the highest unemployment ration with Latino's and Mexicans combined, which also explains why the prison system is so over crowed with African American (Black) men the problem is so clear Pavlov may have been a genius before his time concerning "classical conditioning". You really don't have to look any further at what is taking its toll on the entire African American race which clearly defines the word genocide or annihilation in a different way, I must say in a quiet and subtle way.

My Analogy of "Classical Conditioning"

If you would like to look at the salivating dog experiment and relate it to what is taken place in modern day history. Everyone would have to be realistic and see where the confusion began. When we look at the economic social structure we are looking at status. Status in America is where a family or an individual falls on the list of protocol. I say there are four social classifications of people you have the elite status, rich, middle class and poor. Dependent upon an individual's income this is going to determine where this family of people will be structured in life. Of course there is always the exception to the rule just remember everyone who is not classified in a certain class level do not always remain outside the status quo. Less fortunate people do make it to higher levels of social status due to their hard working efforts but that is only a few. Many on the outside will never take the opportune time to even try to figure out their pinnacle in life because they have been environmentally conditioned that they are not good enough and never will be good enough no matter how much money they make. Their environment is the mark of being "classically conditioned" trained by the "leash theory" that plague many African Americans (Blacks) that the social ladder of freedom is too high for them to climb and they will never infiltrate. In laymen terms it is called getting over the hump. A conditioned to a response is in relations to a third party in the case of African American (Blacks) progress in America it has always been based on their place of employment. An environment of which many may or may not have been able to get out of to be given the opportunity to excel in life, many end of stuck in their situation and very bitter. Some African Americans (Blacks) advance because they were able to focus on bettering their educational level. They wanted to be successful in life they wanted to move forward while others remained victims of the "classical conditioning" you only eat when I feed you. While looking at Ivan Pavlov's experiment "classical conditioning", I am going to relate it to what African Americans and other historians called the "Leash Theory".

My Leash Theory

My Leash Theory in actuality is in comparison to human beings (African America Blacks) to a dog or animal chained to a tree or stake to restrict a certain amount of movement for a very long period of time. By this dog or human usually an African American slave being chained to restrict movement the dog after being chained is fully aware after a while just how far it is supposed to go before the leash jerks the dog back. After the dog is released from the leash the dogs mind and his ability to run freely has been contained so long that it has become conditioned to being restricted. When the leash is taken off the dog is no longer being physically restricted. The dog will not go any further than what it has been conditioned to go. This "leash theory" also applies to human beings. Especially African American (Blacks) those who suffered for long periods of time from being restricted from any progressive movement. The "classical conditioning" or might I add the "leash theory" due to the mistreatment and abuse they suffered conditioned their progressive movement. They have become mentally conditioned to any progressive advancement. They are now conditions to the response of the word no, failure, lazy, uneducated in the same like manner as the dogs used in Ivan Pavlov's experiment. The conditioning process or should I say the abuse they had taken for so long conditioned their minds to not to want this kind of abuse any longer. So the individual now accepts the restrictions that have been whipped and beaten into them they are mentally defused and they become emotionally unable to cope with the possibility of even having a better life. So when the time comes for them to take a chance on life and relinquish the leash to be free men and women on the plantations many of them did not want their freedom. They wanted to stay on the cotton plantations as slaves, it was safer for them. The conditioning of their mind through the abuse they had endured for such a long period of time conditioned them to what they had become servants (slaves). The "Leash Theory" would later become a reality in 1863 when the Emancipation Proclamation was put into effect supposedly ending slavery in America. Due to the "leash theory" an option of leaving the cotton plantations or staying there and continuing to work but not as slaves was given to them. Many of the freed slaves chose to stay and continue their same duties not as slave but as free men and women. And this is what the "Leash theory" is all about. The many who stayed and continued to work for "the good master that had beaten, raped and whipped them." They were free physically but mentally their mind and dreams had already been tortured out of them, dream for what? Free but not really free, stagnated in a dilemma of not knowing what to do once the shackles and chains had been broken. The invisible leash had now been broken but the mind of the slave was still shackled not being able to see past that cotton field. Still on the leash of not wanting to disappoint the "master" of the plantation they continued to work for. Whites only water faucets, restrooms, restaurants, schools, clubs, gulf courses, etc. remained segregated, and it was called "separate but equal. You should take the time out and read the case law on, "Plessy v/s Ferguson". It was many years later when African Americans were allowed to go into the segregated areas or even drink for whites only water faucets, attend the same schools or be served by a white waitress at a restaurant.

True story in 1979 at the passing of my grandfather in Canton, Mississippi I and my two uncles went to a restaurant in town to have breakfast and noticed a fat African American (Black) woman washing dishes in the back. All White (Caucasian) waitresses were out front waiting on other white customers. Getting our order in was not going to happen any time soon until finally we noticed the African American (Black) woman who was all dirty from washing dishes in the kitchen approached our table to take our order. She was still wiping sweat and grease from her hands. It was obvious then that my oldest uncle Andrew said "let's go I see they don't want white waitresses waiting on us. My uncle James had to calm my uncle Drew down and remind him we were in the south. My uncle James always had a little joke to tell to calm the worst of situations down. He said, "We are already down here for one funeral and I like my neck just where it is Drew on my body in place and not with a rope around it." He said man they are still hanging Blacks in Mississippi, maybe they get some kind of a thrill listening to your neck crack and then watching you urinate and defecate all over yourself. And I don't want to be found with feces and pee in my pants, let's go." They still had issues in 1979 with serving African Americans (Blacks)in Canton, Mississippi. I do believe to this day had it not been for the sake of my grandfather's funeral coming up my uncle Andrew would have sat there a little longer." Both of my uncles believed in fighting for their rights but being wise men they knew the odds being in the south were great and not in their favor. I also believe they did not want to jeopardize my safety.

The leash theory is not something that affected the majority of Blacks from the northern states but I must keep in mind that many African Americans migrated from the south when African American (Blacks) were supposedly emancipated from slavery and the cotton plantations. I say supposedly due to the ugly demon of hate raising its factious face once again. *"The time is 1960 he is now known as the greatest boxer of all time. He had just won the Olympic Gold Medal in the Light Heavyweight division. Yes! I am talking about The Greatest, Muhammad Ali. He walks in a restaurant in Louisville, Kentucky and Muhammad Ali at the time known as Cassius Clay is denied service inside the restaurant because he is an African American (Black). I do not know the name of the restaurant but Muhammad Ali stated in his autobiography published in 1975 that he took off his gold medal and threw it in the Ohio River."* Any man who had just won the gold medal in representation of the United States of America should be able to return home having won and earned his respect from everyone. For Muhammad Ali this was not the case he was proud to represent America but knew he had a few more hearts to change.

Now we are looking at the time 2008 when racial tension continues to build with the first African American President Barack Obama elected into office. The treatment of President Barack Obama and his family as President of the United States of American clearly explains the hypocrisy taking place in America. The first insult he received as president, someone sends a truck to the White House filled with watermelons and dumped it in front of the White House. This was supposed to be an inside joke that all African Americans (Blacks) like watermelon so they dumped the truck at the White House. Even with this truck filled with watermelons being dumped in front of the White House many people still want to deny there are racial problems in America. I will not mention how many times First Lady Michelle Obama has been called out of her name neither will I mention the names she has been called, they have not been respectful of the First Lady at all. And we ponder on issues of slavery to this day, north and south, blue states and red states. While looking at the "lease theory" it makes me wonder who has really been conditioned. This is the United States of America yet issues of racism still persist today. Even today the racial hatred is deeply rooted in the blood of those who choose to harbor it.

The mind of the slave remained captured by its once white captives and the invisible leash continues to pull at their neck it is a reminder of the whip that once thrashed the backs of slaves. America saw the inhumane treatment of African American (Black) families in slavery as well as the degrading way slaves were treated. Christian White Americans could not stomach the embarrassment any longer thus ending slavery in America as we know it; although there are many who still practice slavery. Which leads me to discuss the environment African American (Blacks) were herded like animals into, the word (herded) is not a misplaced word in context it explains how Blacks in America are treated like animals, feed them if you can pay them if you want to, but make sure you work them until they are broken and no good to themselves. Yes I use the word herded because animals are herded around which explains how Blacks in America are looked upon as being nothing more than animals.

There is an social environment called "the ghetto" an environment that contains a viscous cycle of what Blacks in America who are still caught on that invisible leash will never leave. It is vicious cycles where teens have babies and young men are locked up for the most part both male and female suffer from the lack of education. I do not want to get into "Willie Lynch" but I just thought I would mention it to reveal the effect and combination of a list of things that continue to haunt African American (Blacks) due to the environmental control Blacks in America have had to live under and many who are for the lack of a word in need are still being herded around like animals.

Environmental Control

The environment each person whether rich or poor grew up is normally how they are able to perceive life. This is why you hear so many people say when something goes wrong the person was a victim of his or her environment. The social status also enhances the reality of certain people not ever getting out of their environment which depends on whether or not the individual fought to bring about some form of change in their life and it is not based on just Black American. There is a ghetto in every race it just that those who control the wealth are a little more discrete with their less fortunate of which they are informed of better programs and housing to avoid impoverished areas. Many people become victims to their environment are not able to leave. Please do not stereotype the ghetto by thinking everyone there is a victim. Some leave after they receive their education and some stay to help those who are less fortunate and try to guide them to a better life. Many become numb to the situation they are familiar with and learn the rules of the game called survival whether it is in the hood or Hollywood. I am still talking about Ivan Pavlov's theory "classical conditioning" but I am applying it to today's form of thinking and reasoning. You see dogs are conditioned to salivate, to eat, even at the sound of a bell. But on the other hand African Americans (Blacks) were conditioned according to where they were herded like animals to, there is a much bigger picture behind the picture many of us are allowed to visualize and that what is on the other side of the wall. I see I used that word again, herded. I use the word herded very freely because this is how Blacks in America have been treated like a herd of animals. No job, no money, no food, can't eat and no place to sleep.

Now you have what is created to assist and hinder Blacks at the same time you created something called "welfare". Hey! Let's herd the African American's (Blacks) over here, this is where they are giving away free government cheese, food stamps to eat, section 8 housing for very little pay and a check for every African American (woman) who has children a very low income and unable to feed her family. Who's salivating now it's no longer the dog? This is nothing more than a humanistic version of "classical conditioning" without the dogs but now with humans. Mentally trained, conditioned to be channeled where they are intentionally led to go. The majority of the ones being herded today are none other than African American (Blacks). African Americans (Blacks) have been victims of their environment since slavery making them a part of the system from which the leash theory came from. Many still wear the invisible lease because the leash is only visible to the mind of the individual who choose to allow past experiences to hinder any forward motion. Slavery was once considered to be unbearable and inhumane in America concerning Blacks. Slavery on the Ivory Coast of Africa and Ghana in relations to the Cocoa Plantations is one hundred times worse today for the children in Africa then any known slavery that ever existed in the world.

"The Channeling Affect" African Americans (Blacks)

This form of channeling African American people has been going on for years. They have been working jobs others did not want to work and would not work due to other dangers involved concerning health issues. I can recall many Black men in the late 60's and early 70's dying from black lung disease and from working hazardous jobs in the steel mills. Working in areas of such intense heat that their lungs were damaged for life in a company once called Inland Steel. Many of these Black men never got a chance to enjoy their retirement due to illness and early death. Because Blacks were in need of jobs and they would work any job given to them and Whites companies knew it. African American (Blacks) had to work in the positions of which Whites who owned corporations and companies knew Blacks were going to have to apply for those jobs and knew they needed Blacks to work. Which were normally jobs Whites would not do because of the danger of future health problems such as cancer, black lung etc. would affect their health as was not safe?

"The Channeling Affect" lead to companies and corporations opening factories and mills, in the suburbs close to areas that housed low income or impoverished Blacks. These were steel mills, factories and other companies that would be polluting the water in the area and contaminating resources that Whites did not want near their families. So everything that was not considered to be resourceful and positive was placed near the areas where African Americans (Blacks) were being herded and raising their families. I guess what you are saying to Blacks in America is since you are going to contaminate the father you might as well pass it through his genes. African Americans (Blacks) who needed the jobs most of the time lived close enough to make it back and forth to work. These where jobs that Whites already knew would cause health issues within the Black race but the only thing the business owners where concerned about was making a profit. They were not concerned with the Blacks who worked for them because they rendered a service (a job with pay) for a product. Keeping in mind the White business owners kept their conscious clear by telling themselves "the Blacks came to me for work and I hired them." What Whites are not expressing is how they channeled the jobs in those particular communities intentionally. You will also find many school districts that have the local steel mills and foundry's do not focus on the academic level of preparing the students in the area for college. The education level is more so structured toward preparing the students who will probably get out of school with less than a fifth grade reading level to stay in the community and work in the steel mills just like their parents did. This was so typical and I could see it coming because this is the kind of area I grew up in I just happened to be one of the students to be blessed to want to go to college and make a difference. I don't want to make it personal but I can literally speak about the Channeling Affect that takes place in many communities just like the one I grew up in because I worked in Blaw Knox Mill & Foundry right before going off to college. I had never seen so much dirt and filth in a work area but this was a trade that paid good money to a kid out of high school. To me it was an experience because I knew I was going to college. To others it was their life and this is where they would live and work until the day they either retired or died. The targeting of poor areas has always been a rich man's ploy. People in general have to eat in order to function. When you look at the Channeling Affect you must come to some kind of understanding. Finding a job to take care of family for a Black man in America has always been difficult. Many times African American men and women take certain jobs regardless of dangers involved. Not having the proper education to sustain or apply for certain positions they had to rely on who they knew and this is what we call having an inside connection to get them in. Who had the connection inside the steel mill or factory would be based on the level of danger of the job he would have to work. If he was in a good position then he would be considered to have what people call today, "pull". If not then he usually ended up working very difficult jobs with a short life span. "The Channeling Affect" is still in operation today and it runs deep in the ice cold veins of white America. What many African Americans have forgotten is how in the early 60's they fought together for the right to work and called it "Affirmative Action" civil rights leaders stood together to fight for positions in companies and corporations. To make certain that African American's (Black) men and women would have jobs and be able to work to feed their families. The threat since 1960 concerning equal work for Blacks got better for only a few years. It has actually gotten worse since 1993 when the North American Free Trade Agreement went into effect causing jobs to go overseas and business to relocate. Affirmative Action was the bases for equal employment in America for African American (Blacks). Equality on the job site or was it, no it was never balanced equally and never will be. Only through preparation by the elite whites what was once looking like a prominent America where people of all color, race and ethnicity began to thrive has now become "a secret with an hidden agenda". The way it appears to be seen is this agenda does not include the African American (Blacks) at least not as part of the job market, but more so as laborers working jobs without any room for promotion. It is an agenda with a plan that pretends to have accidentally and incidental overlooked African American Blacks but it was all intentional from the start. I would have to go into the National Free Trade Agreement (NAFTA) or the Central American Free Trade Agreement (CAFTA) to get down into the loss of jobs in America and how it would affect the primary targeted race, African American (Blacks) and nobody would care. Let me briefly discuss Affirmative Action and how doing away with such a bill would cost African American (Blacks) their freedom in America as it is perceived with having the ability to work and take care of their families. I will also relate Affirmative Action to how the Cocoa Plantations will have a detrimental effect on African American (Blacks) in America.

Affirmative Action

Before I get started on Affirmative Action I want to give those of you who are not aware of its meaning the official definition: Affirmative Action is a federal agenda initiated in the 1960's that's designed to counteract historic discrimination faced by ethnic minorities, women and other underrepresented groups. To foster diversity and compensate for the ways such groups have historically been excluded, institutions with affirmative action programs prioritize the inclusion of minority groups in the employment, education and government sectors, among others.

Best Example: Affirmative Action programs have allowed women and minorities entry into professions formerly off limits to them.

Affirmative Action in hiring is when race, ethnicity, disabilities, military background, socioeconomic status, and/or gender are considered when making hiring decision as a means provide equal employment opportunity. Affirmative action (which include outreach, training programs, and other efforts) help to prevent discrimination in employment practices and to promote equal employment opportunity. Affirmative action, the set of public policies and initiatives designed to help eliminate past and present discrimination based on race, color, religion, sex or national origin, is under attack.

"Civil rights programs were originally enacted to help African Americans become full citizens of the United States. The Thirteenth Amendment to the Constitution made slavery illegal; the Fourteenth Amendment guarantees equal protection under the law; the Fifteenth Amendment forbids racial discrimination in access to voting. The 1866 Civil Rights Act guarantees every citizen "the same right to make and enforce contracts...as is enjoyed by white citizens. The actual phrase "affirmative action" was first used in President John F. Kennedy's 1961 Executive Order 10925 which inspires federal contractors to "take affirmative action to ensure that applicants are employed, and that employees are treated during employment, without regard to their race, creed, color, or national origin." The same language was later used in Lyndon Johnson's 1965 Executive Order 11246." by (Marquita Sykes...August 1995).

With the American system going through a change of history with the abolishment of slavery beginning to take full effect concerning the demands African American (Blacks) were now making issues began to develop. African American (Blacks) were receiving better education and better chances of employment although many were educated and not accepted on certain jobs they still applied and were turned down. Even though there is an old saying "An honest day's work for an honest day's pay." White's did not want African Americans (Blacks) working in their place of business regardless of how educated or qualified they were. To this day January 27, 2015 there are still major problems concerning job discrimination and African Americans rights to work. There is a deeply rooted hate in the United States of America that extends beyond the arc of the universe and runs deeper than the bottomless sea and reaches out from the dark boundaries of the gates of hell where I dare not enter. Pressed upon my worn temples where I lay my head in question and ask this question so many have before me, **"Why"**. I am not trying to give light neither will I avoid wearing my feelings on my sleeves but I do know something about the Holy Bible that says "love thy brother". Where is this love that will not feed a man who is hungry? Where is this love that will not allow a man to work when such is available? I am transcendent of thought when it comes to what would be considered to be morally logical in doing what is right and humanly kind verses playing the role of a wolf in sheep's clothing. This material universe is in an overabundance of resources and surplus for many thousands of years to come but many still fight over table crumbs. Do humans consider themselves to be animalistic in nature? Do we hunt one another for prey as animals to delight in others pain? If these aforementioned statements were not in question there would not be a need to have a law called Affirmative Action? What is quite comical about all of these racially related laws such as Civil Rights of 1964, Plessy v/s Ferguson, Equal Opportunity Employment Commission, Fair Housing, Due Process, Voting Rights Law of 1965 etc., is the reason for their creation which is usually based on someone being discriminated against but only in denial whites would rather say racism does not exist. As we look at society today and racial statements made against African Americans by prominent whites has finally taken its toll. What was once discussed amongst whites concerning their little Black people jokes has now come full circle while the torch is being passed and whites continue to lose their power status their prowess behavior is nullified by statements made by whites prominent whites. I will not go into name calling but for the past five years now many whites in position have been fired for talking about African Americans in such a negative way. There isn't any joy in seeing this happen I do understand that forgiveness is the righteous thing to do but how do you save a person when they have knowingly swam past the half way marker knowing it is impossible for them to make it back. People make statements without thinking and after they are caught then and only then are they so sorry for making the statement. So often on our way to the top many of us forget how we got there. Then once we get there we feel like we are untouchable and can say and do anything but that is just not the case in todays society.

Although things are supposedly changing for the better there is still a fight for equality in America. It is an evolving circle and the benefactors of it all are those who continue to believe not the truth about racism that it does exists in America. This is why African American (Blacks) have to hold on to the struggle as insensitive as it may seem and continue the fight for Affirmative Action, just as Maynard Jackson had done.

Maynard Jackson was the first African American Mayor of Atlanta Georgia. He died of a heart attack at the age of 65. Mr. Jackson was a major landmark in the southern U.S. city's history. His position of being the first African American (Black) mayor signposted a change of guard in the local political class from white to black; no white person has since been elected mayor of Atlanta, Georgia. Maynard Jackson's fight was to make sure African Americans (Blacks) had employment. In his first two terms, he rattled Atlanta's old cozy business relationships, alienating some, but wooing them back in his third term with deft deal making skills. In 1978, he signed a law requiring 25% of the city's projects to be set aside for minority firms. The policy, which still operates today, made Atlanta the most hospitable place in America for black entrepreneurs. He also pushed through an affirmative action program that made it mandatory for contractors to take on minority-owned businesses as partners, and forced the city's major law firms to hire African American (Black) lawyers. He threatened that "tumbleweeds would run across the runways of Atlanta airport" if blacks were not included in city contracts. Maynard Jackson massive heart attack happened in the airport of Washington, DC while he was in preparation of getting ready to go speak on the Green Carpet in Washington about the need to keep the law pertaining to Affirmative Action. As one might say "he fought with his last dying breathe". Maynard Jackson had some famous quotes of which one in particular stands out, **"If you don't like affirmative action, what is your plan to guarantee a level playing field of opportunity?"**

The biggest question I have to ask is where were the other African American (Black) leaders during such an important affair on the green carpet concerning such a viable law as Affirmative Action? Maynard Jackson knew exactly what would happen to African Americans without the Affirmative Action Law in place. White business owners would not comply with hiring African Americans unless they were forced to do so. On the other hand with affirmative action in place whites who wanted to hire African American (Blacks) would not be accused by their white counterparts as being called nigger lovers. What Affirmative Action did was to nullify the playing field and opened up doors for African Americans who were not able to work in certain positions, whether educated or not. Who would be there to speak up for African American (Blacks) and the unfair policies white business owners practiced concerning job applications, job qualifications and job interviews? African American (Blacks) saw major changes in America in the late 60's. Blacks and Whites were getting along and the job market was booming. Businesses and jobs were everywhere and in every city. African American leaders got complacent and began to ad hoc to the situation concerning African American (Blacks) and employment thinking that white business owners were going to be fair and the Affirmative Action Law would no longer be needed. Unfortunately since the law concerning Affirmative Action has been abolished the job market today for African Americans has plummeted continuously and the prisons remain filled with Black men and women. Is it by accident or mere coincidence that African American (Black) men and women in American cannot find employment? I must beg to differ and say no it is not a coincidence on a higher scale of probability I would say intentional. This is why Maynard Jackson fought so hard to keep the Affirmative Action Law in affect. He put forth the effort and asked congress what is the solution to Affirmative Action? Looking at unemployment as not being a problem that may occur but a problem that already developed into a macro problem concerning job opportunity with African American (Blacks) in America with unemployment in the 70's at an all-time high. What would be the common ground nullifier to assure himself and other civil rights activists that African American (Blacks) would have descent employment enough to take care of their families. With the fight for Affirmative Action being on the green carpet to be abolished what assurance did African Americans have for stability? What leverage did African American (Blacks) have to fight with once Affirmative Action was abolished? The problem had presented itself and Blacks could not find employment and a white person with a criminal history was still able to find employment and get hired before an African America Black without any criminal history. I do not see how the question of should we have Affirmative Action in place for African American (Blacks) should even be in question. When the extensive process of graduating high school and going to college to be able to attain a respectable position in society and still suffer by trying to do the right thing in America is just not enough and holds no water in the hearts of white employers. What is being depicted is not a level of common ground with consideration to the fact of a man having to work for a living in order to feed, cloth, provide shelter for his family and take care of his household. I must state that everything concerning Affirmative Action of which was never totally equal and still quite biased which does not leave me with any pretentious notion of fairness or equality. It's sad to say but it is quite the opposite when it comes to showing concern for the African American families. The struggle for fair housing and fair employment still exists todays and the victims at the top of the list are African American (Blacks). It is a hatred that runs so deep in America that it is African Americans who are continually under pressure trying to do what is right. To keep a clean record and stay out of trouble, go to college and graduate at the top of their class not realizing although they graduated with a 4.0 or 3.5 (G.P.A) they will still be overlooked. A white male with a criminal record will still be selected over them. Below you will find a report I discovered during my research please read it carefully.

White Convicts are likely to be Hired Before Blacks with No Criminal Record

by Ezekiel Edwards

"...disadvantage in the job market, but also that, again, black ex-prisoners are in a much worse position: positive responses from employers towards white applicants with a criminal record dipped 35 percent, while for black applicants similarly situated it plummeted 57 percent." Just to be fair about what is taking place with the research in this article and I insist you read the article in its entirety. It is stated that although whites would have criminal records they were esteemed to be hired before African America Blacks who had not been to prison and also had college degrees. This would also be a reflection of on why African America (Black) ex-cons recidivism ratio is so high because they are less likely to be hired anywhere if they have any kind of a record. Racism does run deep in the job market as it relates to Blacks obtaining employment, of course the background check is a killer, not only as it relates to jail or prison time. There are other checks on minority's records that will also keep him unemployed, a very poor credit score and of course the ultimate killer in the rears on child support. And please don't let me forget the final straw that broke the camel's back he just happens to be African American. This is one of the main criteria that is taught in African American households, staying out of trouble and out of the system. Trying not to become a statistic in society because of the strikes already against you if you are African American, first strike is you are black, second no experience and third not enough education, today there is a forth over qualified. Anything to keep you from being employed and not given the same opportunities as their white counterparts leaving most Blacks with very little hope of being able to have a chance to change their life around or work and take care of their family.

"Last hired and first fired" as the old but still in practice cliché goes. Making it very difficult for many to believe that African American (Blacks) really want to work. They are stigmatized with being slothful, unlearned, lazy and unclean, exactly who would want to work around or with someone like that. Well the truth of the matter is what was being said was just not the truth. They could not work because they were not being hired in any form of work that was paying well and as we research what has taken place in the past. We are now in the year 2015 there are more African American (Black) men and women in prison than there were slaves during slavery, and that is hard for many to people to understand. How can a country unified under one flag put over 841,000 African American Black men and women in prison and call it justice? Let me clear the 830,000 prison inmate this is the number given for Black men in prison. I have not calculated the Black women in prison well let me give you the total of Black women in prison 64,800. Which brings the total amount of African America Blacks in prison to 905,800 that is the 2009 consensus. Does the United States of America have a legitimate answer for investing over $185 billion dollars a year in prisons? Private companies and corporate businesses are having prisons built for future use. Prisons are what they are investing in which appears these investors will need prisoners to fill the prisons they are investing in. The rich have invested in prisons and of course when someone is investing in anything they want a profit in return no matter what the cost. Mass Incarceration is the going trend of which for every 100,000 Americans 137 will be placed in some form of formal confinement. The very same investment that has taken place on the Cocoa Plantations in Africa is the same investment taking place right here in America. Chocolate is a trillion dollar industry not only does it involve child abuse and forced child labor, it also involves sex-trafficking and prostitution etc. There is just not enough that can be said concerning the Cocoa Plantations or Affirmative Action they are both in need of balanced scales. There are similar in so many ways when comparing the two I hope you are getting the message. The Cocoa Plantations promote slavery and abuse of children, Affirmative Action promotes the same. If a man is not allowed to work and is denied the right to be hired the logic behind this is he will eventually commit a crime and more than likely be incarcerated. Incarceration is in fact a form of slavery in accordance with Amendment XIII. African Americans have to deal with the high unemployment ratio but Whites in America do not want to admit they would much rather hire a convict out of prison than a Black man that just graduate college. Are Blacks in America hired on a company's quota needs? **"In 1981 the service recommended that state employment agencies adopt a race-conscious way of re-computing test scores on the Employment Service aptitude test battery to avoid adverse impact when referring job applicants to employers."** www.nytimes.com/1990/08/01/opinion/1-hiring-quotas-exist-but-employers-won't-tell **(Please read this article in its entirety)**

With the Affirmative Action law in place there would not be a need to try and hide the truth about the secret "hiring quotas". African American (Blacks) would have a sound stance on what would be an official document of legal representation to research when it came down to employment rights. For this purpose of unfair labor practices that has been taking place since African American (Blacks) were allowed to work side by side with their white counterparts. Filters a need of omission concerning equal playing ground and of course an honest referee who would look African American (Blacks) right in the face and call a ball a strike. Since the playing ground is not level to this day 2015 and has never been, only with gratuity of those in power who had pets at home could relate that even their animals needed to hunt to survive. They showed some empathy to the conditions under which African American (Blacks) in American had to live under in relations to the control they needed to keep to maintain their position in power. Many Whites today do not view African American (Blacks) as human I guess they have failed to read their own theories and philosophies of life. This would explain "classical conditioning" and also "environmental control" of which should help my white brothers and sisters come to an understanding as to why their views of animalistic genealogy of African American (Blacks) is so adamant in thought. How does one person depict another as being human or not, I wrote this prose to help you with your funnel of dark thinking.

"How Do You See Me"

How do you see me?
Is it the color of my skin?
Or, is it the shade,
I come in.
Are my features too strong?
My teeth are showing,
Of course, can't you see!
Well, that's nothing new,
Only something you taught me.
I often smile with my eyes,
Sure! I know you can't see my heart,
It is so full of life.
The cruelty of this world will not make it tart.
As I climb and climb,
To find my way out,
My spirit is kindred and free,
My thought is, do you think I am human?
Really! How do you see me?

Written by: Raymond C. Christian
Author & Hall of Fame Poet

Why is there so much joy to thrive on others pain? What's in question here is once again why are we still talking about slavery in the year 2015, affirmative action laws, the 1964 Civil Rights Act, unfair labor practice? The Constitution, Emancipation Proclamation, the Thirteenth and Fifteenth Amendments, Brown v/s the Board of

Education, let's not fool ourselves with what I have brought to your attention. We are still talking about it because many of you still have not let go. You do not know where you stand and it has nothing to do with the right wing or left wing of politics it has everything to do with filtering out your own personal hate. A Hate which runs even deeper than many of us think, I am posting this article to support such evidence of this hidden hatred which has obviously divided The United States of America.

Jobs for White Felons,
Blacks continue to struggle

Although they do not have criminal records and have attained some form of education African American (Blacks) are still looked upon by White owned corporations, companies and businesses as not employable. This would be considered an EEOC violation which involves background checks and in some jobs criminal record checks and finger printing does the race card have a part in this? It would be hard to say no when job descriptions are clear and background checks are factual and true evidence of a person's life history. Why are African America Blacks frowned on when it comes to receiving fair treatment? After African American (Blacks) have suffered through the struggle of receiving the proper credentials of education needed to be hired. They have kept their record history clean Blacks find it even harder to attain jobs they most certainly meet all of the qualification for but are still not able to be hired in the positions they are qualified to do. The studies are listed below revealing the almost impossible feats African America (Blacks) have been struggling with for many years. With knowledge of this research which reveals the inequality and unfair treatment of Whites against Blacks very little has been done to correct the injustices done to African American (Blacks) today.

A study which involved the Federal Reserve data by the Economic Policy Institute reveals that in 2004 the media net worth of white households was 134,280 black's households once again would receive the least recognition in relations to jobs and income for the household. It is imperative to say Blacks do not want a better life, better living conditions or better things to enhance their life. It is obvious by now that Blacks in America were never to be given a fair chance of enjoying the amenities of life nor the privileges in America. Especially when corporations, companies and businesses would much rather hire Whites with felony records before hiring Blacks with no criminal record. That is just part of the equations being drawn up the rest of it involves the data reports by the Economic Policy Institute where the stats given for African American (Blacks) income were so low it would be impossible for a husband and wife team together to make it. In 2004 the Federal Reserve data by the Economic Policy Institute revealed the median net worth of African American (Blacks) was $13,450. Five year later the median net worth for white's households would drop 24% giving them an income of $97,860. Although it would seem like the average median for African American (Blacks) would increase due to their immediate struggle it did not. It plummeted 83% to a whopping $2,170.

When we talk about circulating the powerful dollar bill within the different race groups we find that a dollar bill will circulate within the Black community at a rate of zero to six hours before it leaves the Black community. Blacks are noted for not supporting black owned businesses. Whites support their own in very high standard meaning their dollar bill will circulate zero to one time in the black community with a life expectancy of its circulation to be zero to six hours. Blacks may not realize it but they have a spending power of $507 billion dollars, to spend within their own communities but it never occurs. There are many reasons why the popularity of shopping within the Black business areas, product of merchandise, cost, and of course security issues. These areas of concern are critical to any shopper. Because of their spending power if African American (Blacks) were to take into consideration their spending power and the control of the outcome of things they could really make very positive changes and earn the respect of all corporations, companies and small businesses divided against them. Just do not shop there; it's just that simple people. Your hard earned African American dollar has the spending power to keep a business in operation or close it down. Maybe while you are reading this segment of how Whites with felonies are preferred to be hired over and before Blacks with criminal records. You just might begin to say hum... I think I finally got it and figure out there is a greater need to shop within your own communities. And do things in a diplomatic way by talking to your senator, congressman, mayor and alder person about the types of changes you are looking for and expect those changes to occur.

The statistics of the Federal Reserve data by the Economic Policy Institute makes it more concise and clear in 2004 when it was researched. In 2009 for every dollar bill that went into white households the African American (Black) household received two cents. This is not only a reflection of the negativity surrounding African American (Blacks) to succeed in America but it exposes the reason why Mass Incarceration was created. My perspective of Mass Incarceration another Willie Lynch plan for African American (Blacks) in America to fail by Whites intentionally not hiring (Blacks) for job they qualify for. The plan is simple do not give the (Blacks) jobs to feed or enable them take care of their families. First the rule for Whites in corporate America, is to tell African American (Blacks) they did not meet the qualifications, when their cousin or best friend, son or daughter does not even have a college degree or did not finish high school, next they will tell African American (Blacks) they do not have the needed experience to run the operation, when they started training their relatives and children while they were in high school but still they haven't a college degree and may or may not have a high school diploma. The entire plan is to keep African American (Blacks) unemployed with the master plan being annihilation of the African American race through Mass Incarceration, put the African American (Blacks) in prison. At the current time there are 841,000 African American (Black) men in prison and 68,000 African American (Black) women in prison. Now you can answer the question for yourself and I am certain by now that you should be able to see the plan. Even with the lack of African American (Blacks) being denied employment the system went a little further and began to cut programs that once assisted Blacks in qualifying to work certain jobs. Now African America (Blacks) has to deal with the pre-existing conditions that are set up by the system for their failure. Along with other stereotypical conditions of African American (Blacks) being labeled as lazy, uneducated, non- family oriented, and worthless. It does not explain how they were able to excel into new heights of success in America no it was not the "Spook Who Sat Behind the Door" that gave Blacks a chance at success in America. It was said to the extent of not needing any help and doing things for their self when the Godfather of Soul James Brown came out with the song in the late 60's titled, "Open the Door and I Can Get It Myself".

What is really bothersome to me is why Whites would continue to create minimal jobs for Blacks to do and not want to give them any benefits and barely give them a salary to take care of and feed their families' if they are so insecure in their abilities to excel before Whites. Although it is not fair across the board Whites along with Blacks in America has help to bring the condition of humanity back to civilization somewhat in America. With Mass Incarceration of Blacks in America being the target for the massive number of Blacks. The Cocoa Plantations says just the opposite for children born in the worst of impoverished areas on the Ivory Coast of Africa, Ghana. Children being trained as slaves, five year old girls and boys raped, sodomized, whipped and beaten to please the eyes of those who are being paid to cultivate two products the cocoa bean being one and slavery being the other. The free labor of these so called lazy and slothful five year old children working the Cocoa Plantations to produce the cocoa bean for chocolate factories in America to be able to produce chocolate is being done illegally. These five year old children are not being labeled as being lazy because they are not receiving any pay for their labor neither are they making any demands because they are children, and no one is complaining about them working 100 hours a week and not receiving any kind of formal education whatsoever. But here in America Whites complain about African American (Blacks) with PhD's, Masters Degrees and Bachelor Degrees to not be educated enough or for the lack there of experienced to work high salaried positions they are qualified to work. While in Africa five year old children are not receiving any education to prepare them for a better future. African America (Blacks) who are unable to find employment will at some point end up in the prison system because it is a form of living. To a man who has no place to go and is not able to feed himself with bills piling up and children to feed, whether he has to beg, borrow or steal he has to be able to take care of his family. The hurt of not being able to take care of his family like his White counterparts the burdening some pressure so gets to his inabilities to function adequately which leads him to breaking some form of law. I am not saying it is just but it is how the African American (Black) man is caught in the devises setup for his failure and without recourse. He would much rather go to jail then starve to death at least there he is promised three meals a day and a bed to sleep in. Is this fair to Blacks in America? The answer is of course no but what Blacks do not see is the bigger picture in prison is where you want them because your threat is lessened with each Black man or Black woman that is incarcerated. I will not get started on the prescribed drugs given to African American (Black) children in elementary, junior high and high school that is an entirely different book.

When you think about education and the years one has to apply their self to achieve such a high degree and level of understanding. Whites basically feel they are already ahead of African American (Blacks) although I question that thought. Just because your father is white and may own the business does not mean you should not attain the degree to be employed as the senior ranking person. Changes in the American economy should reflect what the American dream is about? But many Whites feel they do not have to apply their self toward receiving a formal education. On the other hand Whites feel that African American Blacks should be pushed to the limit and made to produce the necessary documentation to attain a position in the company. On the flip side of the picture a friend of the family who happens to be White and has a felony attached to his record walks in the company with the proper credentials, his Caucasian skin, and welcomed aboard. He will more than likely be paid a fair salary for the lack of knowledge whereas the African American (Black) who just may get the position is hired to oversee the non-degreed individual and his salary will be less than less only because he is African American (Black).

"Employers Prefer White Felons Over Blacks With No Criminal Record; How Will Blacks Feed Their Families"

"You may remember the 2003 University of Chicago study by Devah Pager that sent young white and black "testers" with randomly assigned "felony convictions" to apply for low-wage jobs. The study found that whites with felonies were more likely to be called for interviews than black applicants without criminal records."

(by Kathleen Cross, Mon Jul 11, 2011) **(Please read this article in its entirety)**

How long must you travel in a circle not realizing the truth is in your reach and you can't see it? I have presented this question throughout this book "why are we still talking about slavery and affirmative action in the year 2015? Let me give it to you scripturally as to why the Holy Bible is such a potent book. Not only because it was written by inspired men of God but because it has the potency of revealing the ugliness of this world many of do not want to see. This is as humorous as I can get it, you know in order to kill a snake you have to cut the head off or that snake will continue to wiggle. Does anyone know where that head of the snake of racism is I hope you brought the axe just maybe we can get it over with quickly. I am going to try to take you through a discovery walk with me in this walk I will use scripture from the Holy Bible and quotes if possible to bring your mind to a visual picture as to what is taking place in America and throughout the world. I will show you how opposite ends really do have a strong probability of meeting.

My mentor Dr. Albert Lee Powell Sr. although deceased was a wise man with many years, he had written this in a bible he had given me. He read what he had written in it before giving the bible to me, Of course, I still have it today. He wrote, "The answers to all questions and the solution to all problems are in this book." The ultimate purpose of what was said to me is to pick it up the bible and study it. So I did as my mentor instructed me and this is what I was able to interpret from my studies biblically and historically concerning African American (Blacks) and unemployment, Affirmative Action, Mass Incarceration and the Cocoa Plantations. It is all based on time, adequate timing in order to make things work. And while making the corrections at the same time cover up one's flamboyant mess. A mess that says the statistics speak for themselves and the numbers as close to accurate as they may be concerning the article of why "Employers Prefer White Felons over Blacks with no Criminal Record" says a lot about our society today when everything is look upon as a whole as it relates to the treatment of African Americans (Blacks) in America. The statistics given are so high it will almost make you wonder how the African American (Black) race of people are able to exist and are not extinct. You really cannot expect African American (Blacks) to be on the same level of intellect when of course we did not create the Intelligence Quotient (IQ). African American Blacks may not be able to score as high in many areas because the designer(s) of the IQ did not take them into consideration when the IQ test was created. This puts the entire race of Blacks behind the eight ball, they are the last to receive any recognition. The eight ball being the last ball to be given any attention would be similar to the attention African America Blacks get in America when there are jobs involved. Still to this day the last hired and the first fired. There isn't any condition given to their needs of survival or how they are supposed to make it in society and be respectable people in their communities when there has been fowl play taking place since their birth.

The Children of Israel, Slaves in America
and the Cocoa Plantations

There is a watering down or maybe I should say a filtering down to weaken the soul and spirit of people who believed in truth, justice, and the American way. Dr. Martin Luther King Jr. spoke on nonviolence and stated in his speech that the Moral Arc of the Universe bends towards justice and that African Americans can win the battle by not becoming violent. Dr. King felt that African Americans would someday become a big part of the future for America and things would get better. He felt this in his heart and delivered himself as a personal sacrifice for people of all races who wanted to believe that equality would filter into the hearts and minds of those in control and cultivate a system in need of a complete overhaul. Without Blacks and Whites joining one another and working together side by side problems would become magnified and more lives would be lost? There is a filtering out process needing to take place in the old south and throughout the rest of the world. Those who have left the Red States and try to invoke their beliefs on others concerning racial hatred are fully aware of what they are doing. Unfortunately they may have physically left south but they carried the mentality of their deeply rooted southern racial hatred with them. They may live in Blue States now but there is an old saying that surface from bible scripture," Everyone that says Lord, Lord is not going to heaven." And everyone just because they say they are against racism may or may not have other motives. If you look closely at what took place in the Holy Bible concerning the Children of Israel what you will find is in their search for the promise land there was a waiting period. Everyone who was told about the land of milk and honey did not get a chance to see it. Before crossing the Jordan more lives would be lost. God did not want a particular age group of people to make it out of the wilderness. It is written in scripture that everyone twenty and younger would make it to the promise land and all others would die off in the wilderness. They would roam around in the wilderness for forty years. Forty years was the number given by the Lord for the old ways to be forgotten concerning the men and women of war that participated in the attacks? There is a filtering down process a change in ones heart to do the will of God and not mankind. The Filtering Out Process is not based on a weaker generation but a generation more virtuous in wanting to do the will and work of God. God decided it would take forty years tp filter out the old. Why would it take forty years when you look at the Affirmative Action Program, Mass Incarceration and the Cocoa Plantations notice there is a Filtering out Process. A process which stripes Blacks of their dignity and respect? Making them defenseless, helpless and hopeless in their attempt to do anything productive in life dismantling their thought process of ever having ownership of anything, not even themselves. Comparing their human existence to something that is less than a dog and bringing them to a place called America. Where their needs for survival is equivalent to that of any man but because the resources are not divided equally the attitude of whites in charge succumbs let the Blacks makes it the same as any animal on the street. We will render them very little resources to be able to survive. Blacks are to have nothing more than a mere existence. Their presence will remain unnoticeable and they will be recognized as nothing important but something that is beneath white, stripped of all superfluities of life.

Introduced to an authoritarian system controlled by Whites or should I make it more formal and say Caucasian (White) Americans based on one's ability to function which will suffice the intentions of what those who are in control want to do. You should ask yourself the question of why are there so many prisons being built? Why are there so many African American (Blacks) men and women in prison? God knew it would take forty years of roaming around before the last of the Children of Israel that he did not want to see the promise land die off. Land marks in the bible have always been used by those who had some form of influence in society. It all ties in with scripture concerning the approximate time it takes to not only contain what is not wanted but to kill the spirit of what others were trying to attain.

The Significance of Forty Years in the Wilderness

If you would carefully follow me to the King James Version of the Holy Bible please do not get confused. I am still talking about the Cocoa Plantations but I am trying to lead you to a point of deep thought. I will take you to a place where it all ties in so you can see the bigger picture of what is actually taking place in America in a combination with the Cocoa Plantations and slavery. If you have a King James Version Holy Bible turn to the book of Joshua and read **(Joshua 5v6)** which talks about the Children of Israel and what God wanted them to do.

"For the children of Israel walked forty years in the wilderness, till all the people that were men of war, which came out of Egypt, were consumed, because they obeyed not the voice of the Lord: unto whom the Lord sware that he would not shew them the land, which the Lord sware unto their fathers that he would give us, a land that floweth with milk and honey." The Lord speaks a little more in **(Numbers 32 v 13)**" And the Lord's anger was kindled against Israel, and he made them wander in the wilderness forty years, until all the generation, that had done evil in the sight of the Lord, was consumed."

As things slowly progress in society what is not being taken for granted and watched even closer is the progress of one race meaning (Whites) over that of (Blacks) not in a small way but very marginal jumps. Which makes it even more apparent as to what is being brought to the attention of others concerning the annihilation of the African American (Black) race, there is a slow process of slavery taking place as I speak. The forty years God gave the Children of Israel could closely reference the need in today's society. A preparation period for the stronger race of African American (Blacks) to go through a filtering out process where a lack of concern to keep African American (Blacks) employed and working is now reverted back to giving African American (Blacks) the minimal of everything which will only condition their minds to not (half of the glass being full but half of the glass being empty). All positive reinforcements are in the near future of which has already taken place, to be denied. Whites are taught that at an early age do not give Blacks anything, not even a fighting chance to make it. Not even African American (Blacks) of other persuasions will be adhered to in the future. One of the great philosophers of the U.S. Constitution John Locke states," According to Locke, political power is the natural power of each man collectively given up into the hands of a designated body. The setting up of government is much less important, Locke thinks, than this original social–political "compact." A community surrenders some degree of its natural rights in favor of government, which is better able to protect those rights than any man could alone. Because government exists solely for the well-being of the community, any government that breaks the pact can and should be replaced. The community has a moral obligation to revolt against or otherwise replace any government that forgets that it exists solely for the people's benefit." With the benefit being for freedom just and equality. John Locke also made it very plan when he wrote a similar quote, Once you have shackled a man and you have allowed him to have some form of freedom you have either of one of two choices. You can either shackle him down completely or free him. He will not be subject to one hand free or one leg free. In his search for complete exoneration he will find a means of freeing himself. Since we are in America and the United States Constitution has been sent forth by the Founding Fathers of this great nation. Please help me to understand your aggression and inconsideration of African Americans (Blacks) in America. One of the Founding Fathers John Locke talked about the shackling of an individual be it mentally or physically expressing his findings of thought openly. So I have to present this question to all Caucasians (White) Americans. Since freedom has already been presented to African Americans in this country and John Locke has stated that you cannot shackle a man once he has tasted freedom. In partially in shackling him what you will do if one arm is shackled he will free himself by any means necessary and if a leg is shackled he will also free himself from it. With this information known to humanity when it concerns human nature what road is America going down concerning the new Mass Incarceration System when it comes to African American (Blacks). We all know change is inevitable the purpose of change is for procreation but there isn't any procreation when the focus in America today is building prisons of which 98% of the prisoners are African American (Black men). African Americans (Blacks) having fought for their freedoms in America under the laws that govern this land are now facing a race of annihilation due to the racial hatred that stunts this countries growth. You the reader are being made aware that in order for America to move forward in a positive way Americans cannot continue to hide behind their racial hatred. What is being depicted here in America is envy concerning the progress made by African American (Blacks). Only instead of getting an all (White) militia and going through the cities of the United States of American and killing African American (Blacks) on sight. Which is what was done concerning the Tulsa riots with hundreds of African American (Blacks) slaughtered in their homes and on the streets of Tulsa, Oklahoma. So instead of shackling the African American (Blacks) down you are just taking away their jobs, their grants, and any other means of being able to function here in American to be able to enjoy life, which leads to nothing more than a slow and painful death. The sad thing about it is you think you are doing this in a legal since but in all actuality you are not, you double books of justice speaks for itself. You cannot have justice where there is none. You unbalanced scales and separate but equal books of law should disgust you every time you rule against a African American Black man who commits the same crime as a White man knowing your ruling is already biased.

Let me help to clarify what appears to be a bit conspicuous concerning your religious conscious beliefs.

When Pontius Pilate had the opportunity to free Jesus he did not because the people wanted him to have Jesus Christ crucified. Pontius Pilate negated the authority of being a positive ruler and role model for the people. He thought by turning Jesus back over to the Jewish people so Jesus could be tried by Herod that his hands would be clean. When in all actuality Pontius Pilate hands were as dirty as the Romans who murdered Jesus. Pontius Pilate could not wash away his authority; his power just by washing his hands of Jesus crucifixion it did not relieve him of any blame. Blood was still on Pontius Pilate hands just as it was on King David's hands for intentionally sending Uriah to his death. I must make it known to everyone that if you are in business and you are not hiring the less fortunate here in American then you cannot symbolically say you are doing justice to those in need while you intentionally starve and stab African American (Blacks) in the back thinking your hands are clean and it is okay because it is not okay. You will be accountable for your actions. The Holy Bible makes it clear that we are accountable for the less fortunate. (Romans 15 v 1) **"We then that are strong ought to bear the infirmities of the weak, and not to please ourselves."** There isn't any justice or due process for the weak when the United States of America is incarcerating 841,000 African American (Blacks) with a total capacity imprisoned being 2 million incarcerated in America. African American (Blacks) makes up 98% of the prison occupancy. There are more African American (Blacks) incarcerated today then there were slaves during slavery. If you want to look at it technically a prisoner according to the 13th Amendment is a slave, they haven't any legal rights. The United States is also guilty for not abolishing forced child labor and child abuse of 2,000,000 children in Africa who are in slavery. It is still in existence today in the year 2015 on the Cocoa Plantations on the Ivory Coast of Africa and Ghana and known as the worst form of child slavery in the history of the world.

Caucasian American (Whites) today are fully aware through time and study as to how long it would take before the lack of jobs in America for African American (Blacks) would turn into chaos within the African American race. Whites are looking to increase on their investments of $185 billion dollars a year in building prisons. They are looking for a profit this is why people invest to make a profit. The profit being made will be off of the incarceration of Black imprisonment. This might sound a bit hypothetical but I have always been under the impression that everyone know the importance of being able to work for wages in order to feed and take care of your family. In return what they would create would become an even bigger profit for monopolized investors due to their investment in building prisons to create what is now called Mass Incarceration. And rest assured with the highest unemployment rate being that of the African American (Black) race. Rest assured the targeting of African America (Blacks) had already been determined before the investors ever made their investment. Their silent cry out is to put as many African Americans (Blacks) in prison as possible creating a wave effect across the nation which has already been put into play to recreate slavery under a different precept of American laws.

Filter Out Process

Please pay close attention to the filtering out process. It is taking place right before your very eyes so please do not blink. The filtering out process of getting one to forget or express what is to take place once it was introduced and agreed upon based on what those who would normally be considered to be in power want to take place in America. It is quite similar to what took place with the Children of Israel and their crossing the Jordan. What people are not paying attention to is the process of how much time it would take to filter out what is not wanted and start over again? How long does it take to retrain, uneducated and capture the minds of those who are not of the so-called white persuasion. Whites have begun to take away the majority of the government funding that was once put in place for the advancement of the less fortunate. There is very little assistance given anymore to the less fortunate. Things that were once put into place to help those who needed aide are now being given to the rich.

After I began teaching school for awhile in the Mideast of the United States I found that children were not receiving the education they needed to sustain themselves in life. Children who attended public schools received metal sensors and security cameras. Poor training facilities to enhance their talents and poor classroom ventilation meaning not any air conditioning to relieve their minds of the sweltering heat so they could study. There wasn't any carpeting on the hallway floors and of course no MacDonald's, Wendy's or Pizza Hut in the school for these less fortunate children to have lunch. Their level of reading did not meet the qualifications pertaining to the grade they were in and their writing skills and science lacked the comprehension level needed to actually be passed to the next higher grade. On the other hand children in predominantly white areas are given all of the amenities other public school areas are not given. Don't say it is not true I have witnessed this for myself. It is really hilarious to think that African Americans are naïve enough to believe the funding that was supposed to go to the minority school system somehow went to the more prominent white schools. Do we actually believe that Plessy v Ferguson which implies separate but equal facilities is considered to be abolished or was school districting another way to keep less fortunate children from receiving a better education, SHAME ON YOU? This is what Caucasian Americans (Whites) are perceived to be saying (Well we cannot call it Separate but Equal because African American (Blacks) are going to be upset. So we will call it school districting this will be a more legal way of trying to keep the African American Black children away from our white children. Since Blacks cannot afford to stay in the same privileged school district because of their pay and inability to afford a house in the school area our white children will receive the better education. In order to filter out the youth today and separate them from the system of success this is what we will do first, change the school zoning codes and school district. First we will start by stripping them of their cultural American Inheritance by first giving them improper reading instructors and they will not learn how to read properly secondly we will not teach them good writing skills and arithmetic skills. We will deny them a legal right to have a proper education because we are the ones (Whites) to prepare the legal boundaries as to what is sufficient and what is not acceptable for children of today who are not of the (White) race persuasion to excel in anything. This method of the Filtering out Process once implemented will not give African American (Blacks) the opportunity for any hope of recovery. The next thing that is occurring right under your nose is the current introduction of minimum paying jobs designed to lessen the expectations of a better life. Of which the final outcome is to involuntarily, voluntarily force them back into a culture of life many have given their life to change for the betterment of this great nation and that is to re-introduce slavery across the nation. You should be thinking about what is the purpose of mass incarceration and the intentions of those investing in prisons? Can I now sing KUMBAYA my Lord?

Keep in mind that Willie Lynch was already past its filtering process of what it would take to turn African Americans (Blacks) against themselves. Willey Lynch was designed to make African American (Blacks) hate one another, not trust one another and if implemented properly they would end up possibly even killing one another. This analysis was developed by a man from India. Where they tortured and studied African American (Blacks) for years. To come up with this concept of (Willie Lynch) and how this plan would work also in America if they would pay him well to teach White Americans in power how to treat African American (Blacks) to be against one another in America. What is taking place here in America is still being taught throughout the world but because of the wisdom God has given African Americans and because of the changes that have to take place in order for things to change it is inevitable that change must occur. Dr. Martin Luther King Jr. made it very plain to all of America when he said, "He believes Blacks are a part of the American dream and he believes Blacks can win it." This speech was in reference to remaining none violent. I say, "What war can be won with sticks and bricks battles are no longer won with bows and arrows or even bullets it is now a war of power and position. African American (Blacks) haven't neither power or position, yet the most compassionate people on the face of this earth are close to suffering extinction.

With the help and practice of what is called (**The Willie Lynch Speech**) put into practice. If you will read the Willie Lynch speech carefully you will find such practices taking place today within the Black community. If you would be kind enough to read the Willie Lynch Speech to your children of all races for those of you who are trying to gather an understanding of what has taken place with African American (Blacks) in America. Just keep in mind a person cannot be classified as none intelligent, lazy, stupid or incompetent if they are never given equal resources or a chance to make things better for themselves. This is what Whites in power have done to African American (Blacks) in America. Please read the entire speech carefully I understand many of you are not even aware of this speech ever being in existence. My thinking is at some point in your life you will have to look at the African American (Blacks) race and say to yourself, why are these people so hated, why are they so disliked and what did they do to be treated so badly by people all over the world? Why are African American Blacks the most used people, abused, neglected and rejected people on the face of the earth? What threat could a race of people who have nothing be to a people who control everything? Why is the African American (Blacks) so feared? Me personally I have been wondering since the age of 10 when I first found out about the bibles in Rome why there are bibles in Rome locked up and under guard? Why would something so sacred and so historical not be public knowledge to everyone who wanted to read the bibles? Why hasn't these bibles been released for everyone to read is the missing bibles the key to who African American (Blacks) really are? I now present to you:

A Summarization of Willie Lynch

By Raymond C. Christian

I have given you the Leash Theory, Voluntary/Involuntary action of African American (Blacks) in America and how a conditioning process determines how many of them will react to certain situations. The Willie Lynch Letter will give you some concept of an idea as to why Blacks in America react the way they do. It is a letter created while studying Africans in captivity. This was created by people in the West Indies paid to come to America to teach White slave owners how to maintain their slaves. If the processing of their training was to be implemented properly it would cause discouragement amongst the slaves for approximately 350 years. The entire plan orchestrated was to depicted slaves against slaves and the process was to be followed to the letter in order for the 350 years to remain in effect by causing African American slaves to hate and distrust one another.

The Willie Lynch Letter was a plan devised a by those in the West Indies. A man from the West Indies was hired to come to America to teach Whites how to keep their slaves in line. Part of the plan was to win the trust of the slaves and the slaves were to listen to and trust only the Whites not slaves.

The Willie Lynch Letter was designed to cause discouragement only amongst slaves and cause them to be put at odds in compromising situations with one another. The plan concerning the Willie Lynch Letter was to put old age against young age, to use color against color in accordance to the shade of the slave. They also looked at the level of intelligence and used the smarter slaves against the somewhat slower slaves. The size of the plantation the slaves worked on was part of their mind manipulation. Willie Lynch used sex against sex, male against females and their status as slaves on the plantations. Even hair texture, of whether the slaves hair was fine or coarse it all played a part in keeping slaves hating one another. The height of the slave was used against other slaves depending on who was tall and who was short.

If you read the Willie Lynch Letter in its entirety what you will find out is that slaves where more than likely caged like wild animals and studied to find out their reaction to certain situations.

Some slaves were given more food than others.

Some slaves were allowed to do things other slaves were not allowed to do in order to make some certain slaves feel they were more important than others.

Some slaves were put in charge of other slaves with intent to cause division.

Some slaves were put into cages like animals while other slaves who were not in a cage paraded around in front of the caged slaves not to antagonize them but they followed instructions of what they were told to do to cause dissention. This is how the plantation owner got the slaves to distrust one another. After the other slaves were gone the plantation owner or someone white on the planation gave the caged slaves food and water, pretending to be their friend. This is no different than feeding or training caged animals that were hungry. Once pain is inflicted upon an individual not matter who the individual refuge is then sought after. Nobody is going to complain about receiving some form of assistance out of their struggle. Whether it be food, clothing or shelter. You will notice how quick a person will say thank you just for opening a door for them, yes even that is considered to be a relief.

The time limit of effect that was supposed to stay in tack was 350 years of struggling for the slaves. The Willie Lynch Speech or Letter however you wish to read it. Was implemented in the early 1700's, as sad as it is to say African American (Blacks) still remain divided. How can one be so holy and go to church knowing a divided house cannot stand?

With "Willie Lynch" being implemented in America the damages done remain unforeseeable by those who willfully and willingly enforced its practice. As we look at things that began to unfold daily concerning racism in America those who are in tune to what is taking place appear to be quite shameful. Knowing the behavior of many who are for racism has not been the behavior portrayed by those who are not in support of racism. It is a fact and I am certain there is no need for a survey that many hidden secrets or should I say true colors are coming out of the old skeletal closet which involves skin tone hatred. What is being White enough, Black enough, Porta Rican enough, Hispanic enough etc. the bottom line is we should all be in support of one another? The humorous side of skin color is why are there so many tanning salons? Why are so many Whites trying to tan to look like they are African American Blacks? Why are so many Whites braiding their hair like African American Blacks? Remember the gecko is not always its true color it is just there long enough to blend in to get what it wants before it moves on. The unfortunate truth is there are so many diversions taking place to get those in position to help to not focus on the areas that really need the attention and changes that time, energy, man power and dollars are wasted before anything gets done. Before a solution is rendered we find more damage is done and fixing the problem becomes almost irreprehensible. Just look at what has been allowed to take place on the Cocoa Plantations for so many years now. Here in America we know what is taking place on the Cocoa Plantations with these five year old children. Yet, nothing has been done to discourage the illegal use of forced child labor and child slavery. There isn't anyone who can justify five year old boy and girls working over 100 hours a week. These children are not receiving any pay, no education, no childhood memories and no one to vouch for them through there years of growing into young men and young ladies. My heart bleeds for some form of reparation to be given to these children whose life will never be the same no matter what is restored to them. What is being allowed to take place on the Cocoa Plantations is horrific and it horrifies me to think how everyone can keep the party going and not speak of some solution concerning these five year old children whose lives are endangered without question and nothing is being done?

Willie Lynch and the Cocoa Plantations

It is imperative that something is done quickly about the Child abuse taking place on the Cocoa Plantations, on the Ivory Coast of Africa and Ghana. There is a message being delivered there that stinks worse than the sewage of dead bodies rotting in a corn field. The message is progressive slavery is in motion and unless the attention at this time is given where it is needed we all stand to be looking at a cycle of history repeating itself with very careful preparation taking place where slavery began for the states as you once remembered the Cotton Plantation. You cannot continue to walk around and think the Cocoa Plantations and the $300 million dollars invested in Hershey's new foundation to make more chocolate at a faster pace was invested for Hershey's to take a loss. No one invest $300 million dollars to take a loss on anything. The larger the investment the larger the return, with Hershey's building a larger and more modern plant foundation in Pennsylvania more workers are needed in America. By the main ingredient in chocolate which is the cocoa bean comes from the Cocoa Plantations on the Ivory Coast of Africa and Ghana. There are going to be more children needed to work the Cocoa Plantations which is going to lead to more child abuse, more raping of children, more sodomizing, more child sex slaves, more child organ trafficking. This is why I am telling you to pay attention Willie Lynch is very much in affect and working against the odds since there are now those in Washington, DC who can do something about what is taking place with these children. We have senators, congressmen, National Confectioners Association, Chocolate Manufacturers Association, political leaders, politicians and government officials could have stopped this a very long time ago.

Please read The Willie Lynch Speech (in its entirety)

Taken from the book titled "Willie Lynch" "Why African Americans have so many issues written by Marc Sims

(The challenges we encounter in life are often paved with our ability to overcome obstacles. How are these children able to overcome anything when they know nothing about their own inheritance, culture or background most of all they do not know anything about God?) I present to you another prose I have written titled:

"The Abusers Who are They"

In the shadows of my mind hidden secrets lie there;
A cross that stands over an empty grave of fear;
I see how you look at me in your ugly way of disgust;
It was me, I know I am sorry for laughing too
loud, I know that is why you beat me.
When you passed by me did you smell
the soiled odor on my clothes?
You see, I haven't any water at home to
wash with, please forgive me;
Once you get to know me you will see I am really a good person;
I will make sure I stay my distance so you will like me, okay?
I must stand to stay awake; I had a long and sleepless night;
I was up listening to the little girl down
the hall, being beaten all night;
I thought for sure I would be next, so I
was afraid to close my eyes;
I wondered, if I would have closed them, when
I opened them who would be there?
No one knows the abusers, their faces and gender is hidden;
They are empty souls with a damaged past,
hidden in a reality we don't understand;
These abusers are normal people, quote, the always nice guy;
They are regular people, yes, people you and I know.
Can you see the inside scars, they are trying to heal;
The prayer that is needed for the victim is shared;
With the abuser who was once the victim and scared;

Not knowing how to let go of being the
victim of a victimized past.
Dreams and visions of a neglected life,
disbelief in a fore thought;
Still able to hold up my head and look in the mirror;
Telling the world I am a winner with God;
I dream to seek; I ask in order to be able to receive;
Not from you but God he is the only one who knows my fate;
I deal with my accusers every day, not just Satan but you as well;
The demons which are around me cannot
penetrate the positive forces;
Forces that are channeling my life, the
strongholds are pulled down;
My God, my God, what a blessing it is to know;
You are my final destination my suffering is not in vain;
My abuser will be brought to justice, yes, justice it must prevail;
Even though I have been abused;
I am still saved, sanctified and Jesus Christ is my redeemer.
My innocence was just taken away, although I pray;
I continue to get up to regain my strength, my composure;
The abuser will be dealt with; I know the word of God,
Will not come back void remember the double edged sword?
I know the Holy Bible speaks of Gods
little ones, "Abusers beware";
It is better for you to get into a boat and
go to the deepest part of the lake,
Tie a milestone about your neck and jump in
then to me with one of Gods little ones;
This is the word of God; this is where I stand;
Please do not worry about the tears forming in my eyes;
May I ask you this question, without insulting you?
Tell me why are the children suffering, what have they done?
I heard a voice out of nowhere saying
forgive the sinners who abused you;

I answered back and said father I forgive
them for they know not what they do;
You are the abuser, my father which art
in heaven said he still loves you;
Yes, I love you too, I forgive you of the sins
you have committed against me,
I ask that God's mercy be with you always;
Now, you, the sinner have to ask forgiveness for the
sins of abuse no one else knows about but you, you
know the sins you repeatedly had gotten away with.
Say a prayer of repentance on your knees, I
am sorry little boy, I am sorry little girl;
I am sorry wife, I am sorry for verbally, for
physically mistreating a child of God,
I am sorry, I am sorry, I am sorry, I am
sorry, I am sorry, God bless you.

Written by: Author/Hall of Fame Poet
Raymond C. Christian

Getting back to the reality of the Cocoa Plantations the research I have done and the evidence others have recovered speaks for itself. For the record those who I have personally encountered from South Africa have been very open with me concerning the Cocoa Plantations and how these children are treated and have stated: "The reviews of the Cocoa Plantations and the documentation that has been released is only scratching the surface of what is really taking place. The overall situation is must worse than I would think it to be." My response was that I can imagine. His response to me was "no you cannot imagine the unjust things taking place there. You really should go to the Ivory Coast and witness the things you are writing about." When I think about all of the stuff being swept under the rug we should all marvel at the numerous times corrections that should have taken place were rerouted and never changed? It never fails to amaze me when I see African American (Blacks) out in the public sector of stores and businesses. I ask them about the

Cocoa they never seem to know what it is. So who is allowing this victimization of these children? As the prose titled, "The Abusers Who are They" clearly states who are the abusers?

I would say that America and all the other countries involved directly or indirectly can start pointing fingers at one another to continue to make excuses as to why the abuse of these five year old children on the Ivory Coast of Africa and Ghana has been allowed to go on for so long. Is there an equitable amount of guilt that can be equated to the many sleepless and hunger felt nights these little boys and girls have had to endure must this vicious cycle continue?

I have already mentioned the Chocolate Industry is being a trillion dollar money maker for many. There are a lot of hands in this cookie jar and no one wants to admit who stole the last cookie. For those who are in the decision making positions setting your sights to achieve the American dream does not excuse the inacceptable behavior of child abuse or the abuse of others. The sky is the limit in America but what are the limitations when it comes to child abuse, any form of dignity and the value of human life? Oh! Yes I keep forgetting you do not consider these children to be human. If you go to Webster's New Collegiate Dictionary you will find the word:

Human

Defined as "of, relating to, or characteristics of man (2) consisting of men (3) having human form or attributes." Of course, I do not want to sound sarcastic but at past times and to other nationalities to this date in time of 2015 African American (Blacks) were not considered to be human. They were labeled as apes, monkeys, coons, jigaboos, bud, and boy and of course nigger. Very rarely will you have Black men in America referred to as sir, Mr. or man. Although times have changed somewhat many of the words aforementioned are still used by many whites and others today so the abuse and racial issues are not only being corrected in America. It is still in existence On the Ivory Coast of Africa and Ghana. Places of such that many of you go visit to be reminded of how it was back in your good old days when slaves were treated like animals. Are those the days whites in America are longing to have back? I will throw in a little sense of humor and say "I guess that good old boy system was so good that for many of you it was just too good to let go of."

Promises Made

The meeting that took place in 2001 with many of the power houses in the chocolate industry left no question of the abuse on the Cocoa Plantations concerning these children that it was emphatically time for change and renovation. The leading Companies in the Cocoa Market listed below agreed that enough was enough. The abuse of these Children on the Ivory Coast of Africa has to come to a halt. I personally feel that nothing has been done to rush the process of change because you first have to fill that some form of law has been broken. Secondly the law has to be in reflection to what is human and what is not because an animal cannot commit a crime. Therefore with possession being 9/10ths of the law an animal hasn't any rights because it is considered to be property so there wasn't a need for these six leading chocolate companies to react to what was exposed since the children on the Cocoa Plantation would have been considered to be animals (of which once again animals haven't any rights). These six leading companies signed the Protocol in 2001 agreeing to commit significant resources to voluntary standards. We are now 13 years behind quickly moving into 14 years by the time this book is published. Below I will list for you the six leading companies that signed in agreement with changes that needed to be made on the Ivory Coast of Africa. Keep in mind these six companies including the United States of America are fully aware of the Cocoa Plantations being the worst form of forced child slavery in the history of the world.

Six Leading Companies in the Cocoa Market:

1. Gary Guitland President of Guitland Chocolate Company
2. Emond Opler, Jr President World's Finest Chocolate, INC
3. Bradley Alford President Nestle Chocolate & Confections USA
4. Paul S. Michaels President M&M's/ Mars, INC
5. G. Allen Andreas Chairman & Chief Ex Archer Daniels Midland Co
6. Henry Blommer, Jr Chairman of the Board Blommer Chocolate Co

With trillions of dollars being made off of the backs, blood, sweat and tears of these children five year old children nothing seems to want to make these leading presidents, executives and chairman to want to tighten their belts just a little and make the corrections necessary to allow change to take place, once again change is inevitable the sooner it occurs the better. How many more meetings are needed to be held and at what point with those who have invested in the cocoa industry feel they have made enough money off of the backs of these children? There have been at least five delays that I can account for while doing my research on the Cocoa Plantations involving necessary changes needed for proper treatment and working rights of what is taking place on the Ivory Coast of Africa. We have to look to Senator Tom Harkin and Congressman Eliot Engel as to why better care and concern has not been given to such a sensitive matter. Wanting to do what is right is one thing but intentionally negating to do anything at all and just push things up due to amended changes and minor technicalities brings many issues to question?

Harkin Engel Protocol
www.cocoainitiative.org/en/reports/harkin-engel-protocol

"In September 2001, chocolate and cocoa industry representatives signed an agreement, developed in partnership with senator Tom Harkin and Representative Eliot Engel, to eliminate the worst forms of child labor in the growing and processing of cocoa beans and their derivative products wherever cocoa is grown.

The agreement, known as the "Harkin Engel Protocol" prescribes a comprehensive, six-point problem-solving approach along with a time bound process for credibly eliminating the use of abusive child labor in cocoa growing. It marked an important first an entire industry including companies from the United States, Europe and the United Kingdom, taking responsibility for addressing the worst forms of child labor in its supply chain. In 2010, a Framework of Action to Support Implementation of the Harkin-Engel Protocol was agreed." Once again nothing has been done to help these five year old boys and five year old girls on the Ivory Coast of Africa and Ghana. This reminds me so much of a similar conversation Dr. King had with President Kennedy when Dr. King brought President Kennedy to the projects in Chicago and President Kennedy told Dr. King to tell his people to chill. And Dr. King's response was, "If they chill any longer they will go into a deep freeze. All Dr. King was saying is that his people needed help now and the chill process had already been used up. This is what I am saying about the Cocoa Plantations the time limit needed for anyone to do anything to help these children are past the stages of trying to find aid or assistance. It's more of a question of why hasn't anything been done. And this question needed to be asked to Former Senator Thomas Richard "Tom Harkin and Congressman Eliot Engel, why is the help these children urgently need taking so long?

Foreseen Intentions the Real Agenda

Different continents of the same spiral constellation
struggling to be completed. Two opposite ends of the world
waiting to meet, waiting to complete
the cycle of what others hope
and wish for (the days of old)will slavery
ever return. There are so many who
stand in their law making courtrooms trained from birth on how
to slide papers in between cracks in the
wee hours of the morn, documents that were not there.
Beating the pavement of justice saying in God We Trust,
Yes, but in what God are they referencing, the god of Baal?
They plan for others demise saying, deplete the school programs,
legally take away their jobs, kill Affirmative
Action, and put them in jail
for any violation. Are the opposite ends of the
spectrum closing? Look at slavery
of the youth on the Cocoa Plantations of which
a physiological death is occurring.
In America mass incarceration has been
incorporated to take a different
breed of men. Physiologically destroying
them to bring them to an end.
Living In a captive environment satisfying the
impurities of hate others have for them,
this is why the gate keepers are in support of
investing billions in building prisons.

Mass incarceration lessens the challenge of
their extinction while reuniting power
and control back to its original source. While
the Cocoa Plantations continue to
justify the 1965 Voting Rights Act, have
you really been (Emancipated)?
Is the Justice System in America really
based on equal rights and if so,
Why is Marissa Alexander facing 20 years
in prison for firing a warning shot
Yes! "Stand Your Ground" in full affect. But
on the other hand Trayvon Martin,
A seventeen year old African American (Black)
child is cold in his grave murdered
by George Zimmerman a self-appointed
neighborhood watchman set free for murder..
This is why so many issues in America are
still at the forefront today. Tie all of
this in with the abuse, rape, sodomizing
and murder of five year old
boys and girls working the Cocoa Plantations
on the Ivory Coast of Africa and Ghana
and what you will find is that slavery is no longer a hidden agenda.

Written by: Author/Hall of Fame Poet
Raymond C. Christian

Slavery the Route Traveled

When I think of the Cocoa Plantations on the Ivory Coast of Africa and Ghana, it reminds me of what I read years ago in my high school history class. I noticed as I begin to study the issues concerning the Cocoa Plantations the same route traveled to capture five year old children on the Ivory Coast of Africa and sale them to the plantation owners was the same route traveled by the Europeans to capture and bring slaves to Europe sale them so they can later be transported to America.

Never forget there were one hundred million Africans who lost their life as the ships picked up slaves on the Cote d'Ivoire (The Ivory Coast of Africa) traveling through the Mid Passages to sale their slaves. We will never know the true number of lives that were taken whether thrown overboard or murdered? We will never know the number of women who were raped? We will never know the number of babies killed at birth? Just remember those of us who have survived the storm know it is not over yet. In the words of my friend Dr. Margaret T. Burroughs an brilliant woman before her time, Dr. Burroughs started the first African American Museum in the history of America. She would always say: **"There is still so much work to do".**

The Number Grows

Because no one cared their numbers grew quickly over the years. The most recent studies show there are over two million children working on the Cocoa Plantations. They say children I say babies because the Plantation employees start these little boys and girls off as young as five years old. Teaching these five year old babies how to climb forty foot tall trees and also how to swing a machete. Of course, medical attention is needed because five year old boys and girls should not be taught to use a machete or climb 40 feet high trees. In the process of these five year old babies being taught how to swing a machete keep in mind one wrong swing could cost the child serious medical injuries. They can cut off limbs, toes, slice their calves and legs or possibly fall to their death. These children do not receive the best of medical care due to the distance from the nearest hospital. Also because of the expense to treat the illness or the possibility that a snake bite or cut will save the plantation owner money by having it treated by old custom ways at the plantation. The mistreatment of these children appears to be continual with no one really caring enough to pay attention to the needs of the child. There isn't any consideration being given to the extreme heat they have to work in from sun up to sun down, the proper diet for food they are fed corn mush, there isn't any care for these children they are treated like field ox. Work all day and rest at night for the next day, these children are driven daily to the limit of their work abilities and each day to them is the same. The many violations of children rights being broken are insurmountable and the Cocoa Plantations should be restructured when it comes to legality as it refers to age restraints and the conditions under which these children are forced to work. The hours worked a week for a child in Africa and Ghana is not acceptable when compared to an adult in America 100 hours a week for a five year old child working the Cocoa Plantations is ridiculous. The age violations, working conditions, and how these children are being sold for hire should be enough illegal activity for the United States to step in to stop the abuse and admit these Cocoa Plantations are nothing more than modern day slavery plantations.

Just like any child in America cries out in the wee hours of the night for their parents. These children on the Cocoa Plantations do the same and their suffering is much greater than any child having a nightmare. Their blood is being spilled needlessly. How much longer can the politicians in America and other countries sit back and pretend like there is nothing wrong? When I think of the pain and suffering these children are going through it behooves me as to how our American politicians can ignore it, let alone how these politicians can sleep at night.

Who is underneath those Hoods

"Many Questions Left Unanswered"

For all of you God fearing church going Christians who are out hanging, murdering, and burying Blacks in unmarked graves. Know there is only one God and believe it or not we all serve the same God. Jesus said on his return he will come quickly and your reward is with him.

These hangings and murders of African Americans taking place in America are being uncovered. The hatred so many Whites feel goes unjustified in the murdering of innocent Black men and boys.

The sad part about all of these merciless murders is that Whites who are committing these crimes feel they are justified in doing so.

What many of you don't know is that as, far back as the 1783 it was legal for a white person to kill a Black man if he felt he wanted to kill him or his whole family on sight. This is where the word picnic was derived from Pic-a-nic to hang for the highlight of the day.

The Klu Klux Klan are no longer in their white hoods, they are in business suites, sitting in your conference rooms, sitting in political positions, siting in public school classrooms, sitting in church, for some of you even your next door neighbors. They have even infiltrated into our government systems some running as Democrats but are really Republicans.

The hangings taking place with the most recent being March 19, 2015 In Port Gibson, Mississippi Otis Byrd 54, Dec 15, 2014 in Bladenboro, North Carolina Lennon Lacy 17, Dec 16, 2014 in Killeen, Texas William Dowler 47. Oh let me mention again the 55 bodies found buried near a Florida reform school Feb 5, 2014 near Florida State University. The school closed in 2011. The question is how long had the bodies been there? Could this be the missing link to the Atlanta murders? Who is really behind all of these African Americans being murdered? One Black man did not do all of this. Okay, okay, okay.

I am Elder Christian in Jesus name.

I have one thing to say, God help us

A Trillion Dollar Industry

When you look at the Cocoa Plantations you are probably thinking a million dollar industry. Well let me inform you that cocoa is quite lucrative it is used in many products all over the world and there are many countries including the United States that have bought into the chocolate crave. Unfortunately many of you are not enlightened on the ways and means of getting the much needed cocoa throughout American and the rest of the world. When you think about chocolate I personally think all of the monies spent on advertising and promoting chocolate is not fare to the children working on the Cocoa Plantations because of the conditions of which they are treated, which is more in the sense of property than of human character. What needs to be looked at is the lack of progress being initiated in support of correcting the inhumane treatment of the five year old children working over 100 hours a week on the Cocoa Plantations. This is a blatant injustice that cannot go over looked any longer. We cannot say these children do not count when we know how they are sold for summer work and never returned to the parents. You cannot say they are not our concern when child abuse is a big part of this picture and these children are not accountable on the Cocoa Plantation. Did you ever ask yourself what is the real death toll per year from tree falls, rapes and suicides?

You cannot say this matter will be taken care of by Former Senator Thomas Richard "Tom Harkin or Congressman Eliot Engel when the years set for bringing this matter before congress has been changed so many times. It all boils down to who cares enough to speak up and do something for these children. It should be obvious to everyone by now this matter of cocoa and chocolate is not going to take care of itself by some magical whim that is just not going to happen? The attention needed concerning this matter to create change on the Ivory Coast of Africa and Ghana is going to be through media and networking. The networking needed is from all Americans who have a heart in matters such as this. We have to start with something so I say again flood the senate and congress with your letters of disapproval as to why there have been so many delays in helping these children and also question why Senator Tom Harkin and Eliot Engel have not been brought to the green carpet to be openly questioned as to why these delays have been allowed to take place when the agreement for change was signed in 2001. Americans have always taken pride in standing up for what is right and we have always stood together even in our own division. We can make a difference for these little five year old babies (boys and girls), change must occur. Institutionalized slavery or slavery of any sort is not acceptable in today's world. I say institutionalized because it is not reaching the entire world but used in a controlled area of poverty where the mind set is to control the people on the Ivory Coast of Africa by keeping them in a captive environment they will never get out of. These children are not held by force under armed guards. They are victims of environmental control, very poor cities within South Africa, few jobs and family that have to be fed.

I Sold My Child

The children on the Ivory Coast are sold by their parents. I know this sounds horrible but once again they are given an involuntary/voluntary choice with these choices not being in favor of the parent's decision. The children are sold by their parents to work the Cocoa Plantation in order for the rest of their children to be able to eat. This is very similar to bartering for a better way of life. Let me give you an example: A person who is hungry will find a way to eat. The Cocoa Plantation owner who is in control of the situation because there is a demand in relations to the children they need to work on the Cocoa Plantation will pay the parents of the child just enough to satisfy their immediate needs. What the parents who just sold their child so the rest of the family can be fed does not know is they will never get out of the condition they are in. Their need to sustain life and take care of the young children in their bartering for food is much greater than the child who is sold in order for them to no watch them or the other children starve to death. In order to feed the rest of the family the male child or female child is sold at the age of five years old some as young as three years old. Here is another good example involving involuntary/voluntary action, Example: Take a mother strung out on drugs for instance with her needs being greater than the request for drugs many times if she has a female child that is desirable to the drug dealer the mother right here in America will sale her daughter for that fix. I know this sounds a bit graphic so please save the "I don't believe they sold their child on the Cocoa Plantations for money, it happens every day on the market." Save the judging until you have lived under such circumstances, with your family starving what would you do? Let me go to a question presented in the earlier parts of the book, will you eat dog? Because South Africa in many small cities or provinces within its continent is so poor the environment is preyed on by these plantation owners. The plantation owners know where to find these families in need and how to barter for their children. Not only on the Ivory Coast and Ghana but Burkina Faso as well, these are three very poor countries in South Africa.

Let me not deviate from the Cocoa Plantations briefly to give you a little insight one of your favorite lingerie and panty stores to shop. I am certain this will shock you just a little. **Victoria Secrets Corporation has been tied in with forced child labor. Victoria Secrets have been reported for using girls ten years of age from Burkina Faso, Africa to plant seeds for its organic panty line. These young girls are planting seeds with their hands at the length of ten football fields. They are also reportedly being raped and sodomized. Forced child labor and child slavery of African girls, unheard of?**

The mother's in these poor countries continue to get pregnant as a means of supply and demand. Meaning the mother's supply of children is the plantation owner's demand. As long as the mother continues to produce children as a means of the plantation owners needs and the demands being met concerning young children needed to work the Cocoa Plantations the mother and the rest of family will have shelter and food. Deals are certain to be made ahead of time with promissory agreements paid in advance that once other children reach the age of five be it boy or girl it will go to work for the Cocoa Plantation owners. I say again an involuntary/voluntary action to an unwarranted situation. This is an institutionalized pattern of slavery, although the conditions are kept this way intentionally those who are in power will not admit to the dilapidated conditions under which the people are forced to live under in order that their supply & demand is met to continue on with their "Trillion Dollar Chocolate Industry".

Relief

The big question is where does their relief come from? Who will be the bigger nation to stand up and say enough is enough concerning the abuse of these children and what is noted to be "the worst form of child slavery and child abuse in the history of the world." I wonder just how many of these senators and congressmen will be willing to put a price tag on their child's head before its born into this world knowing in three to five years they will never see this child again. The help or should I say **Relief** comes from the Free World. We do not need another twenty years of this kind of horrific abuse of these children to continue. It is obvious these politicians and Cocoa Plantation owners are not going to do the right thing by making the necessary corrections and come to the aide of these children. The apprehension of those in Washington (senators and congressmen) who are able to help these children I would assume comes from pocket padding and favors being done behind the scene, in remote areas of the world. I will repeat it again that is only my assumption. I wonder what the real reason could be that nothing has been done to help five year old boys and girls who are being raped, beaten, sodomized and possibly murdered and working 100 hours a week from sun up to sun down. Maybe it is beyond my moral thinking and better judgment that just maybe these political figures, congressmen and congresswomen as well as the chocolate industry founders; presidents and vice presidents of these chocolate factories are making their children and grandbabies work 100 hours a week. Just how far in amenities would a president or chairperson or chief executive of a trillion dollar industry be willing to go to keep the chocolate industry untainted. So their trillion dollars chocolate industry can continue to function so people all over the world will continue to keep buying chocolate? By exposing this kind of unfair labor practice, forced child labor and forced child slavery, corruption such as this we can help make this a better world for all to live in. The key here is what we will and will not tolerate. Is supplying the world with chocolate greater than the need to give innocent children a chance at life? God forgive these politicians, government officials, and chocolate industry executives for taking so long to make the right decision, Father God have mercy. It is written in (Heb 6v12) "For we wrestle not against flesh and blood, but against principalities, against powers, against the rulers of the darkness of this world, against spiritual wickedness in high place." Let the darkness that rule over this land be uncovered and brought to light and let the four winds of the corners of this world continue to blow in all that is due to bring them to the judgment table.

What God Do They Know

These children do not have a voice Father God they do not know of you or how to cry out to you so please Dear God let me be a voice for their suffering. A voice for those who suffered and died those who suffered and had their life beaten out of them, let them be redeemed through the spirit you have given me and let me stand in the gap for their protection, Father God. Let the children on the Cocoa Plantations who are crying out for help be heard in every home, every office building, every church, and every room where their oppressors lay their head to rest. Let the citizens in darkness be given light and let them bear witness to the suffering of every child, every parent let them understand the torture of these children on the Ivory Coast of Africa and Ghana and come to their relief. How do they cry when they know not pain, and how can their emotional needs be heard when all they hear is the crack of a whip? Please hear my words Father God it is not only my responsibility but the responsibility of every breathing human being to question what is not taking place on the Cocoa Plantations. In the Holy Bible (Rom 15v1-3) "We then that are strong ought to bear the infirmities of the weak, and not to please ourselves. (2) Let everyone of us please his neighbor for his good to edification. (3) For even Christ pleased not himself; but, as it is written, the reproaches of them that reproached thee fell on me." If we do not protect our children then please tell me who are we to protect. When we speak of morals and ethics exactly what are Americans speaking about? Do they only apply to a certain groups of people, and are there any specifications as to who or whom we are speaking to or about. Especially when we are all taught the same standards of life where do these children go to pray when they have never been taught how to pray? Who will teach them morals and ethics and how to survive they have no father or mother. Remember **"In God We Trust"**. If it is not our responsibility than might I ask whose responsibility is it to help them. Do you ever wonder how many dead bodies have been found or uncounted dead bodies that will not be found on the Ivory Coast of Africa and Ghana? Due to the neglect Former Senator Thomas Richard "Tom Harkin and Congressman Eliot Engel have effortlessly pursued in not pushing the issue of (Harkin and Engel Protocol) hard enough to do anything for the children on the Ivory Coast of Africa and Ghana. Harkin and Engel Protocol is the name of the bill passed when referencing the Cocoa Plantations a well keep secret to be continuously amended to be kept off the floor of congress and the senate so any could do something to bring about change for these abuse and tortured children.

True story, in the year 2014 in the United States of America the remains of 55 bodies were found buried near a former Florida reform school. Could these children have been a part of the Atlanta hate crimes of which the (Atlanta Killings) were taking place? Is Wayne Williams the man who was convicted of the Atlanta Killings also responsible for burying all of these bodies in Florida as well? The majority of these bodies found in Florida were also young Black boys? Professionals have already stated Wayne Williams's sentence of being found guilty is questionable. Wayne Williams is doing life in prison without parole he was convicted. But not beyond a reasonable doubt, pertinent evidence pertaining to his conviction due to several professional witnesses' testimony was not substantiated and remains in question to date? Everyone is aware of Stone Mountain in Atlanta, Georgia and of course the Klu Klux Klan is very prominent in the area. The hatred concerning the murders of these young Black males still remains a mystery and unresolved. Many of the cases concerning the Atlanta murders remain open and ongoing to this date. There are many who testified believing that if would have been impossible for this one man to have killed so many boys in the various areas they were murdered considering where he was in place and time. I wonder will Wayne Williams be convicted of the Florida murders as well.

Remains of 55 bodies found near former Florida reform school

By Bill Cotterell Jan 28, 2014
http://news.yahoo.com/
remains-55bodies-found-near-former-florida-reform-232708887

"Excavation at a makeshift graveyard near a now-closed reform school in the Florida Panhandle have yielded remains of 55 bodies, almost twice the number official records say are there, the University of South Florida announced on Tuesday." (please read entire article)

In the article written by Bill Cotterell he stated that eleven families had been contacted concerning the boys who had been lost over the years at Dozier. They are hoping to find the other families in order that the DNA can be matched with the missing boys bodies through the family members being tested and possibly giving the families who had given up hope of ever seeing their son some relief.

This news breaking story published in Jan 28, 2014 made it very clear the majority of the bodies found buried were of young black boys. Keep in mind these murderers and display of hatred towards young African American (Black) boys is taking place at Dozier School for Boys in Florida, right in the good old United States of America in the year 2014. What I am trying to get you to see is if the murder of these young African American (Black) boys is taking place here in America at a boy's school. Then I am not one to speculate but with all of the supervision at a boys school and these bodies were said to be missing and were not found until 2014. What exactly do you think is taking place on the Cocoa Plantations on the Ivory Coast of Africa and Ghana, I do not want to leave out the abuse and possible rapes taking place in Burkina Faso with these ten year old girls. And as far as missing children are concerned who's on the Cocoa Plantations to report a child missing. First of all how will they get the opportunity to report anything when they are lead around by guards? Secondly who is going to listen to them or even believe what they are saying to be true? 55 bodies found buried near former Florida reform school in 2014. Just think how many boys and girls have been either buried or thrown to the alligators on the Cocoa Plantations. This is an area where no one is requesting the whereabouts of their child. A bill of sale for a child's life there are many things here that just don't add up to a happy ending for these helpless children. They have no mother or father to go back to. I have not heard of any records being kept so if these children are ever released they haven't any home of record to return to.

Love and Hate Becomes a Conflict
The Chocolate Industry a Bitter, Sweet Taste

When you want to cry wolf this is one perfect example of deception at its highest. The Chocolate Industries in America is the largest producers and manufactures of chocolate in the world. Of which the cocoa bean being the main factor for all chocolate being made. It is pertinent to first grasp an understanding that on the Ivory Coast of Africa and Ghana there are 5 year old boys and 5 year old girls who will work on the Cocoa Plantations all of their life. These children are sold into slavery at the age of five and have to work the Cocoa Plantations for the rest of their life. When they are too old to work the Cocoa Plantations they are then used in other ways, sex trafficking, sex slaves etc. Just keep in mind as these young five year old boys and girls get older they are developing into young men and young women. The rapes, sodomy, beatings and abuse occur throughout their length of stay on the Cocoa Plantations with a strong possibility of some of these children trying to escape and being shot (murdered). The actions of the slave Cocoa Plantation owners would not be any different than if they were chasing down a slave in American that tried to escape. The slaves were usually hung and left hanging for public display if they were caught. So in a remote area with no one watching what is taking place, the situation with these children on the Cocoa Plantations, anything goes?

I am talking about the Cocoa Plantations a well- kept secret until now. The only problem is that whether it is a well-kept secret or not the United States Senators know and the United States Congress knows what is taking place on the Ivory Coast of Africa and Ghana.

So does every manufacturer and distributor of chocolate which also includes the Chocolate Industries of America.

It is really a bitter sweet deal and no one is going to be able to explain this away. It is obvious no one really cares because there hasn't been a real live scare as to the horrific child abuse taking place on the Ivory Coast of Africa and Ghana. Who is really the blame? What part can the American people play in helping to change the conditions these children are having to live under? There have been a few children who have escaped from the Cocoa Plantations but not many who have lived to tell about it. What happens to them when they are caught? Where are the dead bodies? How does one read when they do not know how too? How does one explain things when they do not know logic or have not been taught logical reasoning? How does one pray when they do not know God? The Cocoa Plantations is a well-kept secret with hidden agendas and the Chocolate Industry is right at the head of it all.

"The Whip" (Prose)

I am tied between two trees. My skin is soaked profusely with sweat from the heat. My skin is already tender and sensitive to touch as I await my fate from the slave masters whip.

Man it is really hot out here. The sun is scorching my skin. My people have been ordered to come outside to observe my executioner and watch my merciless beating. As my mind flashes through the two possibilities that will happen to me within the next few seconds, first my body will be ripped to pieces by the master's whip. Then my beating will continue until I am either dead or as close to death as possible.

I am handcuffed, and my feet are shackled I have a rope around my neck and waist to hold me in place. I can barely move. As the whip slashes and snaps repeatedly ripping my skin. I began to lose count while fading in and out of consciousness. As I watch my blood pour out of my body, I can see the slave master raise his whip once again.

I can still hear and feel the crackle of the whip whisking across my back, slowly slicing my skin to pieces. My skin is swollen now from its continual beating, splitting in half. I can only feel with is left of its tingling sensation with my mind.

I began asking myself this question, how does my skin look? Is it still there? My skin is hanging by its torn veins, while my blood continues to pour out of my body staining the butcher's floor. I can feel my heartbeat getting slower and slower. I know there is not much life left in me, it won't be long.

My mind is drifting off to all the lynching(s) and beatings of all the other men, women and children whipped to death for things that do not make sense. Things like spitting on the ground, walking on the same sidewalk as whites, drinking out of white's only water faucets, whistling while walking, going in the front door, and for smiling too much.

Snap, once again, I am being beaten senseless for a reason that is not worthy of this kind of punishment. Just for holding up my head and looking the plantation owner eye to eye. My back is so hot from the whips burning slashes my life is slipping away.

My conscious mind is saying, hurry up and get it over, come on with your whip. As I close my eyes and silently beg God Almighty for mercy. Please take me Lord I cannot take it anymore.

Well, nothing can save me now, as my worthless life listlessly drifts away. I cannot cry because I can no longer feel the pain. My body has become numb from its continued abuse. My eyes are blood shot revealing the unbearable pain of my body crying for help. Can someone please stop this?

But there is no more snap, that had once ripped my skin apart. Things have gotten quiet, although I have lost consciousness, I am still conscious. I can hear pleads for my life, the yells and screams of mercy of pity. Men and women yelling to the slave master to stop. Please stop master, he cannot take anymore, please stop master you are killing him, master please.

Finally, a familiar voice orders my release. I am numb from the crown of my head down to the soles of my feet. I could no longer feel my body; my executioner has been ordered to stop.

I am being released from my shackles and dragged away. I am being taken to a place for my wounds to heal. The scars, they will always be there, the memory of the pain I suffered will always be in my mind. After all that beating and blood loss I will only be able to stay in bed for a few days until my wounds close and I can work again on the plantation.

Well, I am still alive and from what I know history does repeat itself. Knowing myself as a Man, a Man I said I am, a Man. I will look that slave owner in the eyes once again. I already know the consequences; I will be shackled and whipped once again. I do not know about you but his is not the life of a man, being bound and shackled all of his life.

Disrespected and called boy, bud, coon...etc. in front of his family, and his wife called gal never lady or woman. I wonder, why do they always want me to look down at the ground when I speak? They may not realize it but I am a child of God and I was born with the same inalienable rights.

They probably think by holding my head up I might see what they have been trying to hide all these years, the truth. What the truth actually boils down to is, in all reality they are no better than I am. So since you have cut my foot off so I cannot run, you have castrated me, cut off my limbs and continuously spit in my face. I will continue to hold my head up and I will always be prepared for... The Whip!

Written by the author: Raymond C. Christian

The Chocolate Industry/the Cocoa Plantations

I would say this is one chocolate mess and it is not at this point going to get any better.

"The school currently serves 1,818 students, and plans to grow to 2100 students by 2013), it is the largest residential education program in the US. The Milton Hershey School was established on November 15, 1909 it is located in Hershey, Pennsylvania." (http://www.ResidentialEducation.org/ (Please read the article)

I believe it was not the intentions of Milton Snavely Hershey or his wife Catherine Sweeney Hershey to support the abuse taking place with these children on the Ivory Coast of Africa. Their dream was not to abuse children in order to get the cocoa bean to America. Neither was it his intentions to deny the children who worked the Cocoa Plantations their right to a childhood, an education or freedoms they are entitled to. I will say that over time like so many things when founders pass and others take over their corporation the real intent of the (mission statement) gets lost. The original conception of the organization gets buried with the founder. When rulers are replaced so are their dreams and goals replaced with new ideas and a new mission statement is created. There is a lot of pain in this bitter sweet story as it relates to Chocolate and the cocoa bean and how Chocolate as it developed in America became a trillion dollar industry. It is a known fact that absolute power corrupts and the love of money ruins the good intent which leads to its roots of evil. I do not believe the way the Cocoa Plantations are today is the way Milton S. Hershey expected it to be. No one starts an orphanage school to help children in need then turn their dreams of helping poor children in to a nightmare of disbelief. Will the truth ever be known on how one man's love for children and mankind has turned into slave trafficking, sexual abuse of children, rape, sodomy, beatings and possible murder? Taking children off into hidden remote areas on the Ivory Coast of Africa and Ghana and having their way with them is this part of the dream of the Chocolate Industry Empire? How many years has the abuse been going on and just how long did the Cocoa Plantation owners think it would continue to go undetected? Five year old girls and boys working 100 hours a week is tragic. How is it that the American Chocolate Industries are associated with the worst forms of child slavery, child abuse, and child trafficking in the history of the world? Do you think Milton Snavely Hershey would be pleased with what is taking place on the Cocoa Plantations today? From what I have read about him, I would have to say no. From what I have researched about the schools he has created, the jobs he has created. The monies as a philanthropist he has donated I would have to say if he could scream out from his grave he would ask those in charge, "What are you doing"? This is not the legacy of the foundation Milton Snavely Hershey wanted to leave behind, child abuse, child slavery. The kind of abuse these children on the Cocoa Plantations are going through was not a part of his plan. There was so much thought, time and consideration put into taking care of children and getting them a positive start in life. I will once again ask those in charge of the Chocolate Industries today to give a lot of thought as to what the real mission statement Milton Snavely Hershey and his wife Catherine Sweeney Hershey wanted. Milton Hershey believed he had a product that was so delicious the world should know about it. And he wanted to make sure everyone who did not know of chocolate had the opportunity to taste it. Having the brilliant mind he had as a founder and the foresight of seeing where the Chocolate Industry could be he had a vision. Yes, Milton S. Hershey as brilliant a was Milton Hershey had to have known that in time modifications would have to be in the Chocolate Industry as changes would be needed in the Chocolate Industries relations to the Cocoa Plantations. I would like to believe he was preparing for those modifications with an understanding that because of his love for chocolate and wanting the rest of the world to know how good it was, that modifications to the Chocolate Industry would be needed in the future? Milton S. Hershey was a founder and like most founders and leaders they are usually prepared for change because they are great visionaries. Visionaries are usually months and many times years ahead of themselves before the change that is going to occur ever presents itself. Changes were occurring and with new laws coming into play. Milton Hershey new he would have come up with a better plan a better way for the Chocolate Industry to keep their demands for chocolate in sync with the Cocoa Plantations and what was taking place involving their much needed product the cocoa bean. He knew without the cocoa bean getting to the Chocolate Industries in America there would not be any chocolate. Milton Hershey new this would be a life time relationship in relations to how the cocoa bean was being harvested and how it was going to be shipped from the Ivory Coast of Africa and Ghana to America. He sounded like the type of man who wanted to look out for those who were not able to look out for themselves, the least fortunate. Milton Hershey was compassionate enough to appreciate those who were working hard to make him wealthy and do whatever possible to make life easier for those who were loyal to him. The team work and effort was there as well as the connections and Milton Hersey new that chocolate would become world renown someday and sold in every store not just across the United States but worldwide.

Enclosures of a Vision Statement

What mission is there to continue when you look at Hershey's Vision Statement? Of course you can find Hersey' Vision Statement online: It clearly states Hershey's as having (**a commitment to children**). I am referencing Hershey's Vision Statement because there are many children on the Ivory Coast of Africa and Ghana who are not receiving such a royal commitment as it relates to the vision statement. The words Hershey's corporation is supposed to embrace in their vision statement (**a commitment to children**) leaves questionable doubt as to whether the commitment is being fore filled in a way Hershey's may or may not want it to be. Due to the factual evidence of five year old children being raped, sodomized, abused and are working 100 hours a week. I am not able to envision Hershey's vision statement of having a commitment to children and if I were given the opportunity I would personally ask Hershey's to take another look and investigate their focus on supposedly having (**a commitment to children**). This is a vision statement lost within

After careful review of Milton Hershey's Vision Statement it is only appropriate to say those who are in charge today have taken his dream of sharing chocolate with the world to heights beyond his imagination. Milton Hershey's hard work in relations to chocolate and sharing his dream of making chocolate known to everyone all over the world would come true not just for himself but for many who continuously create and build on new dreams and goals for the Chocolate Industry. The new presidents and Chief executive Officers need to take a look at the original legacy of what Milton S. Hershey's left behind. Is it possible to lose the founders dream and turning it into a chocolate mess? You can clearly see from reviewing Milton

Hershey's Vision Statement that he does list "having a commitment to children." This makes my research even more concise and evident that child slavery, child trafficking and forced child labor and abuse was not something Milton Snavely Hershey or his wife Catherine Sweeny Hershey would be please with today concerning the Chocolate Industries connections with the Cocoa Plantations. Maybe I should say involved in as it relates to the horrible things taking place on the Cocoa Plantations. The Chocolate Industries love and concern for the youth would be quite contradictory to what is taking place today on the Cocoa Plantations. If I may speculate here and say from what I have researched about Milton Hershey he would not have had any involvement with what is taking place concerning the Chocolate Industry and how it is tied in with the Cocoa Plantations today in such a negative way. Milton Hershey was a man who wanted his dream like all men to turn into an empire and he was able to do it. Although the empire was established due to Milton Hershey's hard work and dedication there is a down side to this great and really remarkable success story. You can call Milton Hershey a visionary if you so choose, because of the love he had for children, his work, and his hunger to help those in need gave him the fortitude he needed to make Hershey's what it is today. When I look at the twist in Milton Hershey's legacy, when I look at his vision I would say it has turned into and ugly nightmare. You have to ask yourself has the dream of sharing chocolate with the world been lost. And if so is the dream pass that brink of being able to reach back and grasp what is being lost and the way it being lost to make it redeemable. If Milton Hershey were alive today what would he say to the Chocolate Industry to make everyone involved know the importance of finding out a better way to fix issues (preventive maintenance) of embarrassment as they relate to the Cocoa Plantations and reflect negatively on the Chocolate Industry.

At some point someone has to take the blame for the abuse taking place on the Cocoa Plantations and I am not saying the Chocolate Industries have any involvement at all as it relates to the Ivory Coast of Africa and Ghana. Although many significant factors that has been in print and on CNN News over and over again about, abuse on the Cocoa Plantations that spells illegal child labor, child trafficking, child abuse, rape, sodomy, beatings of five year old boys and girls and the selling of these children as slaves who will never see their father or mother again. **Who gets the blame? Who are all five fingers pointing at? Is it the Chocolate Industries of America, legislators who are not enforcing the International Labor Organization Laws? Or could it be the Cocoa Plantation owners and the illegal policies they are operating under? Take your pick, who is the blame?**

A Trillion Dollar Chocolate Mess

The Trillion Dollar Chocolate Industry under new management has become so wrapped up in making a profit that it is really no longer about chocolate but "show me the money". At all cost the vision that Milton Hershey once had (to give everyone a tasty chocolate treat) is gone. Now the involvement of the Chocolate Industry new leaders may knowingly promotes a different kind of chocolate, human chocolate or is it the Cocoa Plantation owners who are involved in auctioning off the lives of little African boys and African girls. Forced child labor, child trafficking, child slavery is illegal nationally and internationally and the pot only thickens with all involved. Is the Chocolate Industry noted as being a part of the worst forms of child slavery ever? I want to say to all men who are fathers to their children. Take a look at the bigger picture and keep in mind your own daughter developing in front of your eyes at home. As a father and like most fathers we do not want a man looking at our daughter (in that way). On the Cocoa Plantations there are thirteen year old girls beginning to develop into their womanhood there isn't any sanctity in this because rape has already been notated on the Ivory Coast of Africa? Former Senator Thomas Richard "Tom Harkin and Congressman Eliot Engel are the developers of the Harkin-Engel Protocol. A law passed to bring positive changes to the Cocoa Plantations but nothing is done, no movement is made to help these innocent children whose lives are being taken from them daily. Milton Hershey was a promoter of education, helping the needy, donating to charity and being a servant to the nation. Because of what he was able to do with the cocoa bean (chocolate) he made life easy for so many people not just his family but people all over the world. What is the relationship here with the Cocoa Plantations on the Ivory Coast of Africa and Ghana wanting to invoke child and adult trafficking onto a menu that does not include chocolate? They have taken all the good that Milton Hershey has created and turned it into a revised version of slavery with the support of the United States of America leading the way. Milton Hershey's legacy and love for children once spoke through the one thing he attributed more than anything else and that was his love for children and his wanting to help. He contributed so much of his time and money in creating positive things as a result of his investments made from chocolate.

Milton Hershey has the wealthiest and largest boarding school in the nation. **With $7.5 billion in assets for 1,850 students, Hershey spends about $110,000 a year per student, according to its nonprofit IRS tax filing, more than the nation's most expensive prep schools."** What the Chocolate Industry has done to Milton S. Hershey's dream to share chocolate with the world is to my opinion allowing the Cocoa Plantations to have the Chocolate Industry tied in with such horrific stories being printed and talked about here in America about the Cocoa Plantations. Negative ties usually lead to negative results and of course you do not have to have a billion dollar business to not want to be tied in with so many irreproachable occurrences that are taking place on the Cocoa Plantations. There is an urgency to correct the abuse of these five year old boys and girls on the Cocoa Plantations. And the abuse of these men and women who have grown up on the Cocoa Plantations and forced to be a part of the child and adult trafficking. There are changes that need to be made I guess we should ask Former Senator Thomas Richard "Tom Harkin and Congressman Engel the big question is what's the delay for now? More delays, more investigations more monies to invest in your campaign, these are children on the Ivory Coast of Africa and Ghana and they do not have a clue as to what is taking place in their life. But you politicians in Washington, Dc on the other hand have firsthand knowledge and reports to show you are aware of what is taking place. I am certain by now you should have a clear and concise understanding and the citizens of America are holding you accountable. We are all watching and waiting to find out the next move for a positive change concerning the Harkin-Engel Protocol as it relates to the Cocoa Plantations.

You say you do not have the funding to make the correction on the Cocoa Plantations but I see you have a medical school:

Hershey's Medical School

"In 1963, The M.S. Hershey Foundation offered $50 million to The Pennsylvania State University to establish a medical school in Hershey. With this grant and $21.3 million..."(please refer to Hershey's medical school)

The Chocolate Industries
Plans for the Future

With all of the investments being made in schools, colleges and factories, one would think that millions of dollars had already been put aside for the renovation of the Cocoa Plantations. The aforementioned information shows monies have already been set aside to renovate but what will these monies be used for. It would be impossible for a man with such a brilliant mind and salesmanship would not have a primary, secondary and alternate plan to keep his dream alive. There would not have been any other avenues to pursue other than to look ahead at the bigger picture and prepare for changes to the Cocoa Plantations in order for the Chocolate Industry to continue to grow. Changes that would have occurred would have been changes needed to build a better future and preparing for a more modernized and sophisticated Cocoa Plantations. One of many problems today which stems from issues on the Cocoa Plantations is the lack of schooling and education for these 2 million children. What solutions could have been reached prior to media exposure? There was so much more the Chocolate Industry could have done to better prepare the children to have a future and childhood. These children do not receive any education which means after they are no longer useful to work on the Cocoa Plantations and reach the age of fourteen to sixteen they would not have any education or skill to offer for employment. There is no trust fund set up for them to have a little account or anything set aside for them to be able to make a withdrawal from the bank. Neither is there any agreement or understanding of what they will do for survival if they are allowed to leave the Cocoa Plantations. It is a plan as far as their life is concerned already considered to be a failure, remember failing to plan is planning to fail. I am certain you will not believe what my next question will be so I will not delay you any longer.

I was just wondering what happens to all of those young girls and boys who cannot read or write? They haven't any survival skills or formal education. What use are they to the Cocoa Plantation owners if they can no longer climb the forty foot trees for the cocoa bean? Let's not procrastinate any longer sex trafficking children, men and women if given just a little thought would be the next solution for profit. Once a person has been denied the privileges of learning they began to perfect other things within themselves.

This really reminds me of American history which involves the Emancipation Proclamation I spoke on this a little earlier in the book. On many plantations in the south once slaves where considered to be free in 1963. Many of the plantation owners gave their free slaves an option to both stay on the plantation and continue working for them or they could leave and try to make it on their own. Many slaves in America decided to stay on the plantations and continue working for the slave masters, and many left. This is a very good reason why education is stressed so much today especially in African American homes. Of which the understanding of having an education goes all the way back to African Americans not being able to receive an education. Yes, reading is fundamental but you first have to be taught how to read. Since American slaves were not allowed to go to school just as the children on the Cocoa Plantations are not allowed to go to school, keep them uneducated. American slaves were not allowed to learn as did their white counterparts then of course slavery would become more prevalent; education once again was the key to unlocking shackles.

The same strategic strategy that was once used in America to keep slavery going and slaves oppressed is being used on the children in the Ivory Coast of Africa and Ghana on the Cocoa Plantations today. Those who are in charge of the Cocoa Plantations will not allow these children to receive an education. Please note that keeping these children from receiving an education affects those captive on the Cocoa Plantations it will also affect future generations learning capabilities as well. This is a stench that is deeply rooted involving oppression but it all starts with taking away things of value and making these children on the Cocoa Plantations have to rely of their plantation owners for everything. These children sleep in mud huts and the ventilation they have to breathe out of is the size of a baseball. They are given a pot to urinate in and a pot to defecate all eighteen boys use the same pots. They are locked up at night in the hut where an armed guard outside of the mud hit watches to make sure no one tries to escape at night. My question is raised again if these children are not being shot in the back or murder in any other way then what is the purpose for the armed guard at the door? You do not expect me or anyone else to believe that out of the over 100 years the Chocolate Industry has been in existence and the Cocoa Plantations has been supplying the cocoa bean in order for Americans to be able to make chocolate that not one of the children have ever tried to escape. Even on the slave plantations in America when a slave was caught trying to escape he or she was made an example of and was either whipped to death in front of the other slaves or they were shot or hung. So please let me revert your mind back to the Cocoa Plantations and make this very clear that these children are living under uncivilized conditions. We are not even sure of the actual number of head counts out there. We just know it is well over 2 million according to reports I have read. So please tell me once again if I am completely wrong for suggesting that if a slave in America would try to escape the cotton plantations. I am just as certain a child slave would also get tired of being beaten at some point and find a way to escape? If caught the results would be the same as for the cotton plantation slave in America who was killed and more than likely the same thing happens to the child on the Cocoa Plantations if not worse?

Is all fair in love and war? The answer to this question is yes all is fair but to whose scope of understanding. War is not suppose to have any rules and regulation but the Geneva Convention was established for the protection of those waving white flags and situation concerning medical evacuations when a soldier is considered to be wounded and harmless. Unfortunately this is not a way out for those who manage and operate the Cocoa Plantations. Children are given the title of child or children v because of the status they fall under.

Child, defined in the Webster's New Collegiate Dictionary:

(a person not yet of age). Meaning this young person should not be subject to trying times or mistreatment for any reasons more especially a five year old child. As a nation of people we have to come to a more precise way of thinking when it involves injustice. And note that an injustice is such but is not treated as such across the board it sways and swaggers and the pendulum is not lowered according to is rotation but according to who is in control of its movement. Must I bring up the past and state as Dr. Martin Luther King stated, "An injustice to one is an injustice to all". We as a nation of people will not grow and we cannot balance the scales of justice with two different books or different sets of laws that are on the contrary "Separate but equal" yet considered to be fair…did you laugh yet. That's right I know you did not laugh because it is not funny it is hypocrisy within itself. African American (Blacks) get more time for the same crimes as Whites. This is what the American Judicial system has allowed. Sadly enough African Americans have not formed an alliance to rectify such a hypocrisy of injustice. But we stand in wait for better times even with our White allies close by, but the pressure on the ceiling has now began to crash in on everyone. Not in America or on the Ivory Coast of Africa and Ghana will such a behavior as child abuse which is what's being noted throughout the pages of this book be accepted as fair? There is a facultative way of thinking especially when it involves a child in one area being abused and the abuser being punished. In the same scenario child abuse such as what is taking place on the Cocoa Plantations and nothing is being done about it by the two American politicians jointly responsible and the six leading corporations that signed on to make correction and have not. The American Senator over the "Cocoa Protocol" is Former

Senator Thomas Richard "Tom Harkin or the American Congressman over the "Cocoa Protocol" is Congressman Eliot Engel both have the ability to make a difference for these five year old abused children but nothing seems to be important enough to inconvenience their regular day concerning their personal agenda or protocol. May I allude to a double edged sword and the bitter sweet taste of what appears to be a blessing to so many because of what is provided to one group of people verses what is taking place in other remote areas of Africa will help to understand this facultative way of being involved with one set of people and two different kinds of standards. Let me introduce you to the Chocolate Industry and how things are working toward the betterment of some while in the same process killing others. This double-minded way of thinking should and will justify that something must be done in order to save these children from the worst form of slavery in the history of this world. Meaning what is taking place with these children concerning slavery is a mockery to every law ever created concerning the annihilation of slavery. It is a mockery to every American citizen who has children. It is a mockery to everyone who sits on the board for Preventive Child Abuse that would allow such an injustice to continue. In its very existence knowing children five years of age are being beaten, raped, sodomized and possibly murdered. What would the founders of the Chocolate Industry have to say involving their facultative gestures of one side in the United States taking care of so many children at the Milton Hershey School yet on the Ivory Coast of Africa and Ghana on the Cocoa Plantations the owners of these plantations are purchasing children or should I say in support of forced child labor on the Cocoa Plantations. As I began to further my studies and do my research concerning matters of the Cocoa Plantations I could only think of all of the Chocolate Industries making a profit on the backs of these five year old children in Africa and Ghana. What is public record is that there are certain company's within the Chocolate Industries that makes 60 billion dollars a year and another company that makes 30 billion dollars a year. In relations to the Chocolate Industries operations of getting the cocoa bean from the Ivory Coast of Africa and Ghana to America in order for United

States citizens who work for the Chocolate Industry to produce chocolate. Chocolate is then made in the factories here in the United States of America where jobs are created. People work in these chocolate factories hoping to someday retire with a pension. They work in these chocolate factories to feed and clothe their children, pay their bills, and for hourly wages to receive a check. They work in these chocolate factories to hopefully someday send their children off to college in order to provide them a formal education. These are the benefits afforded to those fortunate to be employed by the Chocolate Industry worldwide. Oh! Please do not let me forget the Chocolate Industry employees who are hired world- wide, they have medical coverage, hospitalization and affordable dental care it is included in their hiring package. These are benefits these five year old children are not given as they work from sun up to sun down 100 hours a week.

In the United States adults work in the chocolate factories but they only work a forty hour work week with weekends off. On the flip side of it all the workers on the Ivory Coast of Africa and Ghana are not adults they are five year old babies sold into slavery and working for no pay with a work week that totals 100 hours a week every week whether they are sick or not. They haven't any benefits and they are not able to prepare themselves for a better future because they haven't any future to look forward too. It is true slaves haven't any rights no matter how young or old. A slave is considered to be property. There are just too many inconsistencies of trying to correct a problem that should have been taken care of and resolved a very long time ago, when the discussion was about righting the wrongs on the Cocoa Plantations. It is my understanding to some of the information I have researched that chocolate has been around since the early to mid 1800's. I know you are saying show me the facts well here is my researched documentation. Since it is not a given as to who actually invented chocolate. Go to http://www.facts-about-chocolate.com/chocolate-history

"Chocolate history starts out in Latin America, where cacao trees grow wild. The first people to use chocolate were probably the Olmec of what is today southeast Mexico. They lived in the area around 1000 BC, and their word, "Kakawa," gave us our word "cacao." Unfortunately, that's all we know. We don't know how (or even if) the Olmec actually used chocolate.

"We do know, however, that the Maya, who inhabited the same general area a thousand years later (from about 250-900 AD), did use chocolate, a lot and not just internally. It is with the Maya that chocolate history really begins."

"The cacao bean was used as currency. 10 beans would buy you a rabbit or a prostitute. 100 beans would buy you a slave. Some clever person even came up with a way to counterfeit beans- by carving them out of clay. The beans were still used as currency in parts of Latin America until the 19th century!"

"The Maya also used chocolate in religious rituals; it sometimes took the place of blood. Chocolate was used in marriage ceremonies, where it was exchanged by the bride and groom. (I think I will have to revive this tradition), and in baptisms. They even had a cacao god."

"But the Maya prepared chocolate strictly for drinking. Chocolate history doesn't include solid chocolate until the 1850's." Although chocolate was being used for various things including being, "prescribed by doctors for curing fevers, cooling the body, aiding in digestion, and alleviating pain, it was considered a health food and a medicine. In fact the church also approved it as a nutritional supplement to take while fasting. (That might have been a bad choice, as one bishop was poisoned for refusing to allow his parishioners to bring chocolate to mass.)"

Chocolate soon made its way to the rest of Europe. Well, the rest of the rich people in Europe, that is. It was a big hit in Louis XIV's court. In 1657, the first chocolate house opened in London."

As far as chocolate being in its first solid form it is documented in its first solid form in 1850.

The Cocoa Plantation owners have been evading any corrections needed on the Cocoa Plantations for so long they have become complacent in their thinking to even want to take on the challenge of trying to make such a horrific wrong, right. Once again let me refresh your memory and restate, the Cocoa Plantations are considered to be the worst form of slavery (child slavery) ever in the history of the world. Yet the politicians and government officials still allow the cocoa bean to enter into the United States through slave labor of which is supposed to be prohibited in America. America is the number one producer of chocolate in the world. Is the United States of America a big contributor to child abuse, child slavery, and forced child labor? I have listed just a few of the laws being broken concerning these under aged children on the Cocoa Plantations

Guilty by Association

I stated earlier in the introduction pages of this book that I would show how "Guilt by Association" is tied in with all of these countries. Mainly because of their refusal to stop the abuse of what is taking place on the Ivory Coast of Africa and Ghana and give aid to these slave driven children. It has been documented over and over again with journalist doing articles and news reporters exposing the abuse of children on the Ivory Coast of Africa and Ghana yet nothing is done. With laws in place to help these five year old babies no one has established what it appears to me to be is enough gumption within their own moral ethics to step in and say abuse of a child is not right in America or anywhere else in the world. Since America is the largest producer and manufacturer of chocolate in the world that would make every Senator, Congressman, Congresswoman, politician and government official guilty by association. "Guilty by Association" is what is not being adhered to concerning these children on the Ivory Coast of Africa and Ghana. It's obvious that Former Senator Thomas Richard "Tom Harkin and Congressman Eliot Engel have not pushed hard enough to express their concerns which involve the wrongful treatment of these children. Nor have they exposed what is needed to be given to the media concerning the harsh treatment, extremely poor living conditions, and nutritional diet of five year old babies who work 100 hours a week. Of which it is not acceptable for American politicians to sit back and allow this to continue. There is no need for further delay through investigative teams being sent to report back as to what is taking place Ivory Coast of Africa. The political figures in America have all of the information we need in order to pursue legal avenues of forced corrective measures. American officials are fully aware of the tragedies taking place on the Ivory Coast of Africa and Ghana; I will not forget Burkina Faso. Three very poor countries where African men, women and children little girls and boys are being taken advantage of. American officials are fully aware and it saddens me to say but the very people we have voted into office and trust them to uphold laws both in and out of country, domestic and foreign do not feel obligated to enforce what they were sworn into law to enforce, the law. Of which international laws do apply to the Cocoa Plantations. I have the researched documents right in front of me showing the lists of countries involved in forced child labor and it continues as if these children do not have a life or anything worth salvaging. American politicians are aware of: these children on the Cocoa Plantations being only five years old. American politicians are aware of these children working 100 hours a week. American politicians are aware of these children very poor dietary meals (these children eat corn mush). American politicians are aware of the beatings these children are taking daily. American politicians are aware of these five year old children being trained to swing a machete. American politicians are aware of these five year old children climbing 40 feet high cocoa trees. American politicians are aware of these children being denied a right to an education, they are aware of these children being sold, some kidnapped. American politicians are aware of the rapes and possible murders. What say ye as the judge hit the gavel to give the accused American politicians the verdict? You American politicians and other countries involved have all been found "Guilty by Association". I am almost certain as to what you are going to plea away and say that you were not there. You are going to say you haven't any records of such crimes because none have been committed. You are going to say where is the evidence of these young five year old children being beaten, raped and sodomized where are the hospital records of such or the police records of such crimes? What I am saying to each of you who has their hand in the others pocket. To all of you who have gotten in bed together knowing these innocent children's blood is being spilled and refused to do anything about it. I tell you there is no court higher or gavel more powerful in the closing of cases then the one of God Almighty. How can you allow such inhumane treatment to continue and do nothing about it? I will present the legalities in this book to show that America does have jurisdiction and the ability to enforce the laws that are being broken by the Cocoa Planation owners. With all of these violations of these children's lives taking place on the Cocoa Plantations everything is being kept quiet know that my father in heaven hears everything. And he hears the cries of these children. How do you close your eyes politicians with a sense of peace thinking you have served your obligation to this country each night knowing children are being put under lock and chain by and armed guard on the Cocoa Plantations? Knowing some of these children on the Cocoa Plantations are taken off in remote areas and abused. Yes! I say you stand accused and you all will stand trial for the abuse you have allowed to happen to these innocent children. You are hereby found guilty for the rape of every child on the Cocoa Plantations, you are found guilty for every child molested on the Cocoa Plantations, you are found guilty for every child sodomized on the Cocoa Plantations, you are hereby found guilty for every child beaten on the Cocoa Plantations. You are hereby found guilty for every child who has cut of a limb with a machete and for every child who has not received wages for their honest day's work. You are found guilty for every child purchased or kidnapped and forced to work on the Cocoa Plantations, you are found guilty of locking up innocent children against their will, and you are also guilty of possibly murdering innocent children. It is perfectly understood that you did not have to be there to participate in the rapes, beatings and abuse of these children. By law it is stated children (meaning not of age) are not eligible to work, yet you force them to work 100 hours a week and nothing is being done to correct the problem. You watch them lose their childhood, their education; literally lose their life working for no wages, and no benefits. You are hereby found "Guilty by Association".

Guilty by Association, legal definition:

"refers to the attribution of guilt without any proof on individuals solely for the reason that those whom they associate with are guilty."

American politicians and every country involved in either trading or receiving the cocoa pod for use of producing or manufacturing chocolate or any other product involving cocoa is guilty of every wrongdoing concerning forced child labor on the Cocoa Plantation. By law the founders, business associates corporate executives, chief executive officer and vice presidents of such, both foreign and domestic of which are associated with state, government officials, political figures, corporations and companies are guilty by association. These people are smart enough to distance themselves by not being directly involved with evident cases of rape, abuse, sodomy and possibly murder. What is even worse concerning the murder cases is how you can account for a child of which there is no record of ever being there. These are the disheartening facts where a lack of evidence will provide the guilty to go free without a conviction. For those of us who believe in God in accordance to scripture Proverbs 11 v 21 "Though hand join in hand, the wicked shall not be unpunished; but the seed of the righteous shall be delivered." Proverbs 11 v 23 "The desire of the righteous is only good: but the expectation of the wicked is wrath." What good can come of those who seek their vengeance upon the poor, the helpless, those in need? Of course the retribution that should be awarded to these children that are found alive if the plantations are ever renovated and they are not too severely damaged emotionally, physically or mentally for life. The debt owed will be considered to be unredeemable. I am quite certain the intent throughout the years has been intentional of which recovery of this trillion dollar industry was to be kept a hidden secret forever. Fortunately Proverb 15 v 3 says, "The eyes of the Lord are in every place, beholding the evil and the good." For over 100 years these children have not received any wages for their hard labor. What amount of retribution would be acceptable at this time? I personally do not feel there is a price of payment that could be reached. There is not any amount of payment that would be considered acceptable for the abuse suffered by the children on the Ivory Coast of Africa and Ghana working the Cocoa Plantations. Neither is there an explanation that could be given that would substantiate why such opened forced child labor and abuse of these children is still being allowed to this day. I like to say it would stop before this book is published or maybe Former Senator Richard "Tom" Harkin and Congressman Eliot Engel would put more pressure on the six chocolate manufactures that were at the meeting in 2001. Stating this was a matter of urgency and needed to be stopped and modifications needed to be made concerning the abuse and cruelty under which these children where having to work and live. Once again it was noted "The Cocoa Plantations are the worst form of not just slavery but child slavery in the history of the world yet nothing has been done to rectify this horrific problem it is now February 1, 2015. Who might I ask is going to accept the guilt for all that has taken place with these children? Slavery in any form is not acceptable. What really gets to me are the so-called God fearing Christians who say child abuse is wrong, sexual abuse of children is wrong, sodomy and acts against the laws of the land are wrong and of course murder is wrong. We could even take a look at the American laws of which is stated child endangerment just for leaving a child in a running car, or inside a car alone, or even home alone, a parent or guardian would be given time in jail. So what American politicians are saying here is that abuse of a child is okay as long as it is not an American child? What I am trying to show you is that abuse is abuse in any country and of any child under age and not of sound mind to give consent to any such act of being violated. I will close out Guilt by Association because I know it is impossible at this time to clear your conscientious mind that is if you have one? You are hereby and forevermore found to be "Guilty by Association" until such a time of change has occurred for these innocent children on the Ivory Coast of Africa, Ghana and for not trying to make things better for children all over the world.

Hide and Seek...They Turned Their Head the Other Way

God does not support the abuse of children and everyone who could help appear to be turning their heads the other way because they are being appeased in another fashion and it is not by receiving an extra bar of chocolate. We are talking about Christmas bonuses; we are talking about bonuses at corporate level, bonuses at regional levels, and bonuses at district levels. Remember the Chocolate Industry is a trillion dollar industry at all costs what is the bonus for a general manager who business vendors the most chocolate for the year. Yes, you finally got it; it's all about how much money they can receive for being number one. Unaware of morals and ethics the Chocolate Industry managers have not matured to that level of compassion since it doesn't go any further then the rims of their pockets, money. It most certainly does not touch the trips and vacations promised to the top three sellers of the year. Oh yes! Don't let me leave out the opportunity to meet and have dinner with the head of the Chocolate Industry family at the end of the year. Or maybe an invite to sit with the VIP's at the banquet table at the end of the year with all that is being said there isn't a prize or a reward monetarily large enough or a trip far and exotic enough that would be sufficient in continuing the pain and suffering of innocent children. For all of you who say you did not know or were not aware, you are hereby found **Guilty by Association.**

The Chocolate Industry Employs all over the World

One of the leading companies within the Chocolate Industry employs 13,000 people all over the world. From research of (Spotonlists) http://spotonlists.com/bizarre/top-10-highest-chocolate-producing-countries-in-the-world they list the **"Top 10 Highest Chocolate Producing Countries in the World"** This information will be taken from http://spotonlist.com and I will list from 1-10 on the list from the most producing chocolate countries to the least. I must inform you the United States of American is the number one leading country not only in production but also in manufacturing chocolate. Out of all the meetings these leading chocolate producers along with Senators and Congressmen and women involved the bitter sweet story of the Chocolate Industry and so many other company's selling chocolate in America and abroad continues. The abuse of these children continues to be overlooked nationally and internationally with investigations being extended and laws to make changes for better working conditions and better protection of these children prolonged. Due to what I have observed concerning the dates and changes taking place to only entangle things more renovation may perhaps never be agreed upon concerning the modifications needed to protect these under aged five year old boy and girls from any further abuse.

Documented to date below is listed the:

Top 10 Highest Chocolate Producing Countries in the World"

1. America:

(Authors View Point)

In honor of the United States of America, how does America become the biggest producer and manufacturer of chocolate? After being informed and well in the know as to the abuse taking place with these 5 year old boys and 5 year old girls on the Cocoa Plantations on the Ivory Coast of Africa and Ghana? The United States of America supposedly frowns on child abuse and is so quick to go into other countries for peace keeping missions yet nothing is done to protect innocent children that cannot defend themselves in Africa and Ghana. Why are we not knocking down doors on the Ivory Coast of Africa and Ghana to free these children from their oppressors, is this the same America, give me a break? I clearly understand Former Senator Thomas Richard "Tom Harkin and Congressman Eliot Engel who are jointly in charge of the (Cocoa Protocol) have done some good. But for the purpose of my research they have not done enough to protect the lives of innocent children from abuse, sodomy, rape, and have not provided a program for these children to be adequately taken care of as children and provide them in life with the fundamental skills to be able to survive. These children are not receiving any education, or training skills viable to enhance their future, no wages or benefits to sustain their life once they are no longer useful for the Cocoa Plantations. If there was a ball to drop the United States of America being the number one producer and manufacturer of Chocolate definitely dropped the ball when it comes to doing something to correct the wrongs concerning the lives of these innocent children on the Cocoa Plantations on the Ivory Coast of Africa and Ghana where the Cocoa Plantations are noted as being the worst form of forced child slavery in the history of the world.

2. **Belgian**
3. **Switzerland**
4. **Mexico**
5. **Spain**
6. **Germany:**
7. **France:**
8. **Italy:**
9. **United Kingdom:**
10. **Denmark:**

My next question is how does a five year old child form a union for better rights, treatment and benefits? I thought I would be just a little facetious. In so many words I am asking just what exactly are you expecting five year old children to do? This is quite hilarious when you really look at the only part of the picture I have drawn for you. Keep reading please just maybe you might grow a conscious and at least try to help. Try to imagine these children on the Cocoa Plantations are your children then ask yourself this question (How hard would I fight if this was my child)? Hey! Have you called CNN, ABC, CBS, BET, Oprah, Wendy Williams or The Talk, did you write a book and get it published with Author House Publishing because you were so concerned? Someone has to do something and if you want to play hide and seek? You have just been tagged you are it. Yes this is a topic everyone will be discussing soon. Have you made your phone call yet? I guess you are still contemplating getting involved. Let me say at this point I would be calling everyone I can. Just a little FYI the Cocoa Plantations are now beginning to develop plantations inside of the United States the two states Florida and Hawaii are already in operations. Can I ask the question again have you picked up the phone to call the President, Senator or Congressman, Black Caucus is anyone listening? These are five year old boys and girls working 100 hours a week under laws that are not being enforce, which makes it all illegal.

You might be asked this question in the very near future right here in the good old U.S.A. if your child comes up missing, "Do You Know Where Your Child Is?" Amber Alert is not going to be able to help you. Haven't you noticed throughout this book it's people in high places involved? I did give you the name of the Cocoa Plantation bill passed. For the umpteen time it is called the Harkin-Engel Protocol that means Former Senator Thomas Richard "Tom Harking and Congressman Eliot Engel and Susan Brown she is the Senior Vice President of Strategic Communication for the National Confectioners Association (NCA) and Bradley Alford President of Nestles Chocolate and the Confectioners Association these are powerful people in high places. If you do not read the Holy Bible and you are not aware of (**Ephesians 6 v 12**) I have quoted it for you once again and you will probably see it again before this book is completed, **"For we wrestle not against flesh and blood but against principalities, against powers, against the rulers of the darkness of this world, against spiritual wickedness in high places."** This is the darkness of what is taking place on the Cocoa Plantations on the Ivory Coast of Africa and Ghana. Some of these children are asked to work for a while during the harvest season and the parents never see their child again. In America we have teens running away from home and never seen again. Once they are tricked into going with a stranger because they are hungry or need a place to sleep or food to eat etc., where do you think they are ending up? These children haven't a voice to speak up for them and many are found years late just like the American children bodies that were found buried under an old Florida reform school in January 28, 2014, the last report I read was 55 bodies and they were still digging. Things will get worse the longer we allow such abuse to take place and continue to do nothing about it. Right here in America bodies were found near a Florida reform school buried in unmarked graves. The majority of the bodies found where the bodies of African American young (Black boys) who had been missing for many years this was uncovered Jan 28, 2014. I am trying very hard not to be redundant but giving notice to the point I am making I must state if we are just finding bodies of dead black boys buried and cases unresolved and probably never will be? How long have these young African American (Black boys) been missing? How do we not begin to suspect the worst of what is taking place on the Cocoa Plantations on the Ivory Coast of Africa and Ghana. Just think the Chocolate Industry has been in business for over 100 years. Will there be bodies discovered when the renovation starts or will those doing the renovation decree that the digging be done on a new site for a new start for all involved? I am certain the cover up concerning all of these bodies will astound you but there will be no one there to speak up for these children. Yet America remains the largest producer and manufacturer of chocolate in the world. Is American politicians totally at fault by themselves the answer is no but America politicians have always taken the lead to correct major problems such as this chocolate mess on the Cocoa Plantations in Africa and Ghana. When America leads others usually follows. Turning away is not the solution and there is not going to be anything resolved at this point in time due to dates continually pushed further up to prevent positive changes on the Cocoa Plantations concerning renovations, of which I am certain is going to cost the chocolate industry millions. When you look at this in a logical sense of the understanding it remains evident that since these children are not receiving any pay for their hard labor. Neither are they receiving any form of education which is required by law for minors. The monies that should be paid out by the Chocolate Industry in America and around the world would not be enough to correct the damage that has already been done.

There is also denial from other countries that the Cocoa Plantations on the Ivory Coast of Africa and Ghana are not in violation of the accusations made as it pertains to the rape, beatings, abuse and highly probable murders of these 5 year old boys and girls. The hierarchy of the chocolate industry feels because these are Africa children their lives are not worth the time or effort to bring to the American public and rest of the world a need for to make changes involving the emotional, mental, verbal and physical abuse taking place with these under aged children on the Cocoa Plantations. The **Harkin-Engel Protocol** was designed to stop **the worst forms of child labor, child slavery, child rapes, child sodomy, child abuse, child beatings, child mistreatment, child abduction and possibly child murder of these children five year old boys and five year old girls working 100 hours a week on the Ivory Coast of Africa and Ghana.** Due to a lack of concern by American politicians, government officials in Washington, DC that are able to bring immediate change on the Cocoa Plantations. It is contingent that although American politicians and government officials and many other countries are aware the abuse of these children exists. Their interest in correcting this matter is secondary to them due to the nature of the children being violated on the Cocoa Plantations are of African origin or for a better word not in accordance to them these children haven't any self-worth. They lack any value of human importance or life and should be looked upon as being non-human a product of purchase equal to what would be considered nothing more than animals.

There is a very high probability that many politician and government officials would like to think that nothing will ever be done this is why they continue to vote on amending dates and investigations for later. By changing the dates for renovations to start and pushing them up the calendar nothing will ever get done and everyone will continue to get their chocolate. Keep in mind just as Abraham the father of many nations was told to go to the top of the mountain and there he was to take Isaac's life this was a test to see if Abraham was obedient and if he would follow through with the Lord's request. Is there any righteous amongst you who is going to do the righteous thing and set everyone straight as to helping these children. Who is going to complete the task God has already sent forward? I want you all to keep in mind God is the same today, yesterday and forevermore. Just as there was a ram in the bush for Isaac there is also one in the bush for these children who are suffering. Just as Abraham said in

Genesis 22:8 "God will provide…" **"The protocol was negotiated by Former Senator Thomas Richard "Tom Harkin and Representative Eliot Engel in response to a documentary and multiple articles in 2000 and 2001 reporting widespread child slavery and child trafficking in the production of cocoa."** (http://en.wikipedia.org/wiki/Harkin%E2%80%93Engel_Protocol) **(Please read the article in its entirety)**

There is clearly any need for further delay in rectifying this problem. There isn't any reason to not believe the rapes, sodomy, beatings with bike chains, abuse and possible murder of these children are not taking place. But we are dealing with spiritual wickedness in high places (the gate keepers) who would much rather remain in denial as to what is taking place with these children, look these politician and government official in America and other nations in the face and say it is not so these issues are really taking place and change must occur. **"Other media followed by reporting widespread child slavery and child trafficking in the production of cocoa. The cocoa industry was accused of profiting from child slavery and trafficking."** (http://en.wikipedia.org/wiki/Harkin%E2%80%93Engel Protocol) **(Please read the article in its entirety it will astound you)**

They are not Animals they have Human Life and Value

The European Cocoa Association called the reporting of the rapes, beatings, sodomy and children working 100 hours a week "false and excessive" of which was later found to not be true. The "false and excessive" statement made was later retracted the statement of this type of treatment concerning these 5 year old boys and girls sold into slavery, raped, beaten, abused and sodomized to not be taking place on every Cocoa Plantation unfortunately working conditions were found to be unsatisfactory and children rights were being violated and possibly murdered. May I please present this question to you and say what five year old child knows about their rights on the Cocoa Plantations and if the child's rights were violated exactly who would this 5 year old child complain too. This is what makes so much of what is being done on the Cocoa Plantations so bizarre and unfashionable in relations to the illegal activities taking place with these children. As well as the plantation owner keeping these children under an armed guard, lock and key once these little boys and girls have worked from "SUN UP to SUN DOWN". What is being put down on paper is not being incorporated in a plan of action to eliminate the worst forms of child slavery, child labor, and child abuse and child exploitation in the history of the world. Many positive changes on the Cocoa Plantations could have occurred if the abuse of these children would have been rectified over fifty years ago but unfortunately politicians, government official and executives got comfortable and the abuse has since than escalated in to child sex trafficking. Unfortunately there are people all over the world that defy the laws of the land for their own selfish reasons, usually for the love of money. Laws that are in place to protect children and keep them safe must be adhered to in order to bring such violators to justice. Right now in the year 2015 we are looking at 2,000,000 children on Cote d'Ivoire (Ivory Coast of Africa) and Ghana in slavery working the Cocoa Plantations. I do not want to leave out the 5 year old and 10 year old girls being used in forced child labor in Burkina Faso another impoverished small town in Africa to plant seeds by hand in order for Victoria Secret to have an organic cotton panty line. Once again these young girls are planting these seeds by hand in field's equivalent to ten football fields. This is Victoria Secret well-kept secret. What the politicians, government officials and other nations need to be looking at are more modern technology, equipment, housing, dietary plans, educational schooling formal and non-formal, medical and hospital plans and wages. There is so much that should be given to these children as retribution for the life that was taken from them, a childhood they will never have and a father and mother, siblings they will never know.

CNN News Covers the Story on the Cocoa Plantations

According to CNN report "The Human Cost of Chocolate: Ending Modern Day Slavery" (Please read this article) **(thecnnfreedomproject. blogs.cnn.com /2011/09/19).** CNN reporter stated Senator Tom Harkin and Congressman Eliot Engel negotiations where pushed back from when it was first agreed upon to be corrected in 2001, and then pushed it back to 2005 then 2008 then 2010. My question is when is the Protocol agreement going to be enforced? Because my recent research shows the new agreement to correct the Cocoa Plantation is now 2020 and I am almost certain that will be pushed back even further to maybe 2030 in the very near future. This is due to the anticipated retirement of Former Senator Thomas Richard "Tom Harkin rumors having it that he will be retiring in 2015 and moving onto new adventures in his life. I am certain the new senator coming in may or may not inherit the Cocoa Protocol which means more delays in renovation. Of Course! With the new senator on board there will be a need to further investigate new documentation and reports to support the new incoming senator's reviews. Should something have been done a lot sooner? Why of course! Former Senator Thomas Richard "Tom Harkin and Congressman Eliot Engel have had since 2001 to start the ball on the Cocoa Plantations going. It is now 13 years later of which there is still abuse, rape, abductions, sodomy, and beatings and possibly murder that has taken place. Due to the conditions these 5 year old boys and 5 year old girls have to live under. What would take 13 years or more to make positive changes available for so many small children who are living under conditions not fit for animals to live in? With abuse being the key factor here in so many articles and reports I have read of which have stated the Cocoa Plantations are the worst forms of child slavery in the world. Nothing should take 13 years especially with the millions of dollars that have already been invested to start the process. Changes could have been made many years ago but nothing has changed due to amendments introduced by congress and the Cocoa Plantations renovations are still on hold until Congress can come to some form of agreement. Is abuse of a child illegal or not? Have the rapes been reported? Have the abuse been agreed to be taking place in so many reports? Are young girls and boys being raped? Are five year old boys and girls working 100 hours a week? Are these children being held by armed guards? Are they locked up at night so they won't escape? Are these children possibly murdered? To every question asked the answer I have documented is, yes! The next question I have is quite simple are these American politicians, government officials and other nations planning on stepping in to help?

Renovation Plans a Myth

The Chocolate Industry a trillion dollar industry, are the entities in America which manufacture and produce the chocolate aware of the abuse of children taking place? By investing in **the worst form of child labor,** child abuse and child slavery in the history of the world the chocolate business seems to be well kept and quite silent on these issues. A proposal does exists of which there is a renovation plan to make changes but to this date February 2, 2015 nothing has been done, the proposal is called **"Framework of Action to Support Implementation of the Harkin-Engel Protocol".**

Explanation of the Framework of Action

Congress continues to extend the renovation due to unnecessary ongoing investigations and probing in order to prolong delay. Congress fails to come to an agreement of action as to when a given date of renovation should or if it would ever began. "**Framework of Action...**" was drawn up to appease the eyes of those who needed something in print. To report in the investigative documents that progress concerning the Cocoa Plantations has been made. Yet in actuality there is no intention to start renovating the Cocoa Plantations neither is there any intention of bringing any relief to the lives of these 5 year old boys and girls. It does not take from 2001 to 2020, nineteen years later to correct problems of child abuse especially when it is taking place out in the open where many new teams, journalist and others have reported the abuse of these children. "**Framework of Action**" signifies nothing more than a document on paper which walks us through changes that are supposed to take place of which in reality there isn't a plan for any renovation to take place now or in the future.

Below is the printed and agreed upon proposal in its entirety for renovating the Cocoa Plantations. "Framework of Action" concerning the Cocoa Plantations as stated: This document really lets everyone know political figures and government officials are aware as well as those in power in other nations who help to operate the wheel of the trillion dollar chocolate industry. Corporate owners of chocolate, executives, chairman and chairwomen, founders, chief executive officers, presidents of chocolate corporations, manufactures and producers and distributors. Political figures in the United States of America and other countries all over the world all know what is taking place on the Ivory Coast of Africa and Ghana. Not just with the working conditions but also with the beating, rapes, the sodomy and possible murder of these children. Nothing is being done to change the inhumane and unsafe conditions these children are in. Life on the Cocoa Plantations as we would see it in America would be unheard of. Five year old children boys and girls are working 100 hours a week. What are you waiting on have you called anyone yet?

I must continue to reiterate that these young girls who are taken at the age of 5 grow up on the Cocoa Plantation of which they become young women at some point. Their bodies are developing; changing into womanhood each year. The rapes that are occurring because the men on the Cocoa Plantations guarding these girls are take them off to remote areas and raped repeatedly. What happens to the girl if she gets pregnant is there some butcher shop set up for the abortion? I will also cover the International Labor Organization, **ILO Convention 182** and International Labor Organization, **ILO Convention 29** after the "Framework of Action".

"The purpose of the Harkin and Engel Protocol for the growing and processing of cocoa beans and their derivative products was to bring practices in West Africa into line with ILO Convention 182 of the International Labor Organization concerning the prohibition and immediate action for the elimination of *the worst forms of child labor.*"

"According the other research Former Senator Thomas Richard "Tom Harkin has also been active in combating **the worst forms of child labor.** The trade Development Act of 2000 contains important child labor protections authored by Senator Harkin but only after reports of child trafficking and child slavery associated with the Cocoa Plantations in West Africa surfaced in the media." Once again it is not by either Senator Harkin or Congressman Engel own fruition that they were at one time trying to do something about the problems involving the Cocoa Plantations it is only because of the media. And what the media was getting ready to exposure concerning the cruelty of what was taking place on the Cocoa Plantations with these children that Senator Harkin was pressured to cover himself and create a document to show he was doing something to help implement into action the Harking-Engel Protocol.

The smoke front has not cleared up yet as to any renovation taking place on the Cocoa Plantations which makes it obvious that Former Senator Thomas Richard "Tom Harkin was only putting up a smoke front window to come up with a plan that only looked and sounded good on paper. There were never any intentions of any renovations on the Cocoa Plantations to take place. Everything Senator Harkin came up with in year 2000 was to protect him from any scrutiny. The document looked good on paper but it was nothing more than a store front window it looked good only no one was buying. There was never any intention for anything to change on the Cocoa Plantations. Chocolate was a well-kept secret to a trillion dollar business. Who cared about the treatment of these children as long as chocolate continued to be sold and the money continued to flow into the pockets of those on and off the payroll?

Protocol and 2001 Joint Statement

The Harking –Engel Protocol is a voluntary public-private agreement to eliminate the worst forms of child labor (defined according to the International Labor Organization (ILO)'s Convention 182) in the growth and processing of cocoa in Cote d'Ivoire and Ghana. The Protocol was a voluntary agreement that partnered governments, the global cocoa industry, cocoa producers, cocoa laborers, non-governmental organizations. The agreement laid out a series of date-specific actions, including the development of voluntary standards of public certification. The Protocol did not commit the industry to ending all child labor in cocoa production, only the worst forms of it. The parties agreed to a six article plan:

The Six Article Plan

1. **Public statement of the need for and term of an action plan**- The cocoa industry acknowledged the problem of forced child labor and will commit "significant resources" to address the problem.
2. **Formation of multi-secretarial advisory groups**-By 1 October 2001; an advisory group will be formed to research labor practices. By 1 December 2001, industry will form an advisory group and formulate appropriate remedies to address the worst forms of child labor.
3. **Signed joint statement on child labor to be witnessed at the ILO**-By 1 December 2001, a statement must be made recognizing the need to end the worst forms of child labor

and identify developmental alternatives for the children removed from labor.

4. **Memorandum of cooperation**-By 1 May 2002, Establish a joint action program of research, information exchange, and action to enforce standards to eliminate the worst forms of child labor. Establish a monitor and compliance with the standards.

5. **Establish a joint foundation**-By 1 July, 2002, industry will form a foundation to oversee efforts to eliminate the worst forms of child labor. It will perform field projects and be a clearinghouse on best practices.

6. **Building toward credible standards**-By 1 July 2005, the industry will develop and implement industry-wide standards of public certification that cocoa has been grown without any of the worst forms of child labor.

A 2001 Joint Statement extended the protocol to also identify and eliminate forced labor (defined according to ILO Convention 29) in the production of cocoa.

The protocol laid out a non-bind agreement for the cocoa industry to regulate itself without any legal implications, but Engel threatened to reintroduce legislation if the deadlines were not met. This agreement was one of the first times an American industry was subjected to self-regulation was used to address an international human rights issue.

Although Congressman Eliot Engel did threaten to bring this matter to legislation, after seeing that nothing has been done for almost 14 years when did Congressman Eliot Engel or Former Senator Thomas Richard "Tom Harkin expect to reintroduce the worst forms of child slave labor in the world to legislation. Or was it intended as I had stated to just go unforgotten. As far as legislation is concerned this matter has never been brought to the carpet to be addressed openly to the American public. The other part of the 2001 Joint Statement that does not make sense to me is when the 2001 Joint Statement agreement was prepared for the chocolate industry to make changes. They came to an agreement that the industry was not going to stop all child labor only the worst forms of it. This would only leave other avenues open for them to continue the abuse of children in other ways this is in reference to the Six Articles. There is no subtle way to deal with child abuse, once it is observed to be happening all forms of it should be stopped immediately. As for the parties which are in agreement to the six article plan. It is stated that five of the articles has already been completed. They are only waiting on the Sixth Article to be completed unfortunately Article Six is going to be very difficult to fore fill because of what is stated in the caption of its purpose. Of which I will reiterate for you:

Article Six

Article Six: By **1 July 2005, the industry will develop and implement industry-wide standards of public certification that cocoa has been grown without any of the worst forms of child labor.** Because of the continual delays through amended policies and ongoing frivolous investigations there is no medium of balance to come to any form of completed reports. Due to the facts stated by the **Chocolate Manufactures Association** earlier which said they did not see any wrong being done to these children on the cocoa Plantations. They said the abuse and the forced child labor was not taking place on every Cocoa Plantation. For this reason I have to say due to the fact of which was stated by the **Chocolate Manufactures Association** that every Cocoa Plantation cannot be covered to come to such a conclusion of forced child labor is not being used in any areas of the Cocoa Plantation. And for this purpose Article Six will never be considered to be totally satisfied therefore this investigation of Article Six will never be completed. Now I am certain we are right back to what is called an ongoing investigation. Of which means in American terminology that nothing will be resolved if possibly ever.

Shocking Evidence a $300 Million Dollar Investment

The not so shocking information on the next page will astound you in reflection to all of the proposed renovations and monies already sent to invest in the Cocoa Plantations. To make changes to help with the dilapidated conditions these 5 year old boys and 5 year old girls are living under on the Cocoa Plantations of the Ivory Coast of Africa and Ghana. Renovation is being made but not to the tune of what is needed to prevent more forced child slave labor and child trafficking. The tune that is being played is to the Chocolate Industry's investment of $300 million dollar in plant upgrade. This investment of $300 million dollars is not designed to help the children on the Ivory Coast of Africa and Ghana but it does deliver a very large increase towards the revenue of the Chocolate Industry. The Chocolate Industry ensures a strong local workforce while they promote growth globally. The Chocolate Industry is growing; where there is growth renovation is needed unfortunately the growth and change needed on the Cocoa Plantations is not happening. A well know company within the Chocolate Industry has expanded a plant in Pennsylvania at an expense of $300 million dollars. It is one of Pennsylvania's largest manufacturing investments in 20 years. The plant contains 10 miles of pipes and enough concrete to pour a sidewalk stretching 65 miles. Computers control the manufacturing process.

I did not attempt to get permission to have the picture of the new 300 million dollar Foundation displayed in this book. If you would like to view the new addition to the Chocolate Industry just google what is highlighted below:

(The New $300 Million Dollar Chocolate Factory)

A New factory WOW!

Space-age robotic arms hoist cases of finished candy. What better way could one of the world's leading company in the Chocolate Industry invest its money then to afford the most modern technology to make things more suitable for their workers. It would be a productive move in the very near future to begin so form of renovation on the Cocoa Plantations to also make things a little better there. Happy workers bring better production and the demand for chocolate will continue to go up. It has been known throughout history that strong workers bring about better products and smart workers develop new and better means of technology. This goes as far back as the days of Moses when he opened the dead pharaohs mill for the children of Israel to eat. Therefore he was able to prove to his king that it took strong and able bodied men to build his new kingdom and they would do it in less time. I am relating this to to Cocoa Plantations because these children are not being fed properly, they are not being educated, and they haven't any means of supporting themselves. If nothing changes for them very soon what we are doing as a nation is watching the disaster of children happen right before our very eyes. You cannot say you have not been informed because you have. There is also a need to renovate the conditions under which these 5 year old boys and girls have to work. Due to the renovations that have taken place the $300 million dollar upgrade to one of the Chocolate Companies in Pennsylvania they will be capable of churning out 70 million Hershey's kisses a day. Because of the millions of dollars invested in the best of modern technology and man power putting forth the effort into making this company more productive officials say substantial manufacturing in this particular company is assured for 50 or more years.

A Chocolate Industry Employees Wages

One particular company in the Chocolate Industry has about 13,000 employees nationally and internationally. **"They also employ about 100 temporary employees who work as needed. The pay scale for union workers begins at $18.59 an hour and raises to $28.14 an hour with some maintenance workers earning slightly more."**

The Need for Milk
(What makes Chocolate)

John P. Bilbrey, the CEO of Hershey's. "He pointed to the company's local heritage, and its ties to the Milton Hershey School and smooth-running processes that enable it to obtain 350,000 gallons of fresh milk daily from farmers within a 90 mile-radius." (http://www.pennlive.com/midstate/index.ssf/2012/09hersheys_300_million_plant_upg.html)

Of course you cannot have chocolate without milk. This is a well thought out plan to maintain employment in the state of Pennsylvania. And to keep a good rapport with the surrounding cities of Pennsylvania with the adjourning farmers to keep Hershey's factories going. These are all tell signs where I see a lot more could be done to help the worst forms of child slavery and adult slavery in the world on the Cocoa Plantations. $300 million dollars is nothing to laugh at. I must ask the question, could some of these monies used to build a 300 million dollar foundation been used to help renovate the Cocoa Plantations on the Ivory Coast of Africa and Ghana. In accordance with the six point plan of action to abolish the use of forced child labor, how if ever will any renovations start to make it better for the workers and conditions on the Cocoa Plantations if they are investing in new factories which are bigger and able to produce more chocolate? A larger factory of course means a greater need to produce more cocoa beans and a need for more workers on the Cocoa Plantations. A definite fact that the Chocolate Industries supply and demand will be on the prowl for more cocoa beans since the foundation is being enlarged. Meaning since the demand for chocolate in America is greater the Chocolate Industry is going to need more cocoa beans to produce and sell more chocolate. Because of this the Cocoa Plantation owners will need more children to work the Cocoa Plantations. They will also need more Cocoa Plantations to grow more cocoa beans.

Chocolate Investors Waiting to Invest

Where does the greed stop? It doesn't. Now that one of the leading chocolate factories has invested the $300 million dollars people who are looking to make money are looking for a faster turnover for their investment. With the proposal for the Harking-Engel Protocol it would seem that the $300 million dollars would have been invested in renovations for the Cocoa Plantations, if not all but some of the monies unfortunately more investors are waiting to get on board. It appears to be a heartless effort on everyone's part to bring some relief to these children. It is nothing more than a smoke screen hanging over the plans to correct any problems concerning the 2 million children in slavery, working 100 hours a week on the Cocoa Plantations. Investors continue to pay close attention to the Chocolate Industries expansion now that other powerful players are established. It is also noted that the Chocolate Industry is focusing much of its international effort in fast-growing regions, including Mexico, China, Brazil and India. My question is if millions have already been invested to renovate the Cocoa Plantation where did the renovations take place? And once again I have to ask, why hasn't this situation concerning the Cocoa Plantations been expedited until an alternative plan can be implemented to help remedy and cease the rapes, beatings, and sodomizing of these children. I must continue to mention the possible murderers as well? How are the bodies of the dead children being disposed of, where are the grave sites and how did the children die? These children are taken at such a young age to work the Cocoa Plantations are they even taught a language, do they have any social skills? How can politicians and government officials in the United States of America stand by and knowingly watch what's taking place and pretend as though nothing is wrong?

The Chocolate Industry a Trillion Dollar Empire

Let's take a look at the protection of children as it stands not only in America but in the world today. It is not by default that we are willing to give up or let things continue to go as stated, we are trying very hard to get away from "business as usual." Meaning as civilized American citizens we can no longer say we are not aware of what is taking place on the Cocoa Plantations. There has been article after article printed, journalists have covered the stories and CNN News has also done some coverage of the Cocoa Plantations. American news is already talking about the problems with the raping, sodomizing of five year old children. It gets worse than that and I would like to put it in a softer context but I cannot. The abuse of these children has been going on for many years now. The Chocolate Industry has been around for over 100 years of which means the Cocoa Plantations have been in use just as long. I would have to say I do not feel all of the articles and journalist as well as news media who have been covering the stories on about the rapes and abuse these children are suffering from can all be wrong. I do not see the delay for immediate action to come into play for the protection of these young children on the Ivory Coast of Africa and Ghana. Concerning the abuse of children even if it was found out one year ago I would say these children have been suffering too long. I was only trying to be a little coy with stating one year of suffering for these children let's try one day or how about one second of the day would be too long for these children to have suffered.

From my research and understanding the auction block for these children on the Ivory Coast of Africa and Ghana is worse than the auction block today than it was for actual slaves in America, when slavery was permitted. I am not saying that slavery in America is over with but the actual conceptualization of it would be considered to be emancipated at this time. I will not get into the "Voting Rights Act of 1965 that is an entirely different matter. We have just gone from slavery in America to Mass Incarceration which is even more trivial. When I look at my research and see the bargaining table for these children working the Cocoa Plantations the selling price can be a little as a bike tire. The question that continues to arise is do the Chocolate Industries in America have a clue as to what is taking place on the Cocoa Plantation a "No" response would be very hard for me to believe. The Chocolate Industries have been in the business of making chocolate for over 100 years now. I would like to think the Chocolate Industry is not aware of the raping, sodomizing, abuse and selling of these children is not something they are privileged to but it has been all over the news media for a while now. If you are a trillion dollar industry that is very hard to miss what is taking place with your personal distributors of your main product. With the Cocoa Plantations being noted as the worst forms of child labor ever the citizens of America would like to know what is this involvement of five year old children working on the Cocoa Plantations this is not something that is has just popped up. I would have to ask the Chocolate Industry to please don't insult my intelligence and say they did not know. It continues to be covered by the news concerning these under aged children and rapes taking place on the Cocoa Plantations. These violations of children on the Cocoa Plantations are also stated in the laws of the International Labor Organization this why the laws were created. The abuse was found in the reports to be true concerning these children being made into sex slaves, sex trafficking on the Cocoa Plantations and nothing was being done to protect them. The laws speak for themselves because they have been ratified which means the laws set in place are now enforceable. To find the laws I have listed them in this book please go to the "Table of Contents" which will direct you to the section in this book which covers the laws of the (ILO) the (CRC) and the Convention Laws. There isn't one law that I have read stating it is okay for these children on the Ivory Coast of Africa and Ghana to be working at the age of five 100 hours a week. The Cocoa Plantations are considered to be the worst form of child slavery and child labor in the world.

Out of the 100 percent of which is considered to be the entire crop of cocoa beans the Ivory Coast of Africa and Ghana produce 60 percent of the cocoa beans. The other five countries producing the cocoa bean that also use children to work the Cocoa Plantations are Indonesia, Nigeria, Cameroon, Brazil, Ecuador and there are still children working the cocoa fields of Romano. But the other five countries percentages of demand for the cocoa bean are not as demanding as the Ivory Coast of Africa and Ghana. Once again laws are being violated and nothing is being enforced to deter the Cocoa Plantations for abusing or using these five year old children in their work force. The Chocolate Industry is a trillion dollar empire. What I am saying here is that it is impossible for any corporation of that magnitude to not know what is taking place within the realms of its business when the main product that is needed to produce chocolate is coming from a source that is being scrutinized, the Cocoa Plantations. The Chocolate Industry should not only know what its operating procedures are under the law but also know the intricate part that operates the ramifications of its Cocoa Corporation as a whole. It is important to know if someone is operating illegally and of course and how it is going to affect your Industry if something was to go wrong. It is critical to make all of parts of the operation known to those in charge. This is why I find it very hard to believe as much as it is been on the news in America that the Chocolate Industry does not have a clue about the child abuse, the illegal use of children and the forced child labor taking place on the Cocoa Plantations when the Department of Labor distributes reports concerning child labor and forced child labor. Some people would say these are mere allegations being made? I beg to differ with this as an allegation, why would small children need an armed guard to prevent them from escaping if they are not being held against their will? And if the child does attempt to escape is the child going to be shot in the back? These are all legitimate questions and if those who operate the Cocoa Plantations have nothing to hide then what is the purpose of these children being locked up at night with an armed guard at the door

It is imperative that the quality control person as well as the operation manager know the quantity of cocoa beans coming in as well as the amount expected from each country per shipment. There has to be a list of cocoa beans showing their amount of purchasing on each shipment so I guess I can add the purchasing agent as well on this list. This list should break down how many tons of cocoa beans are needed to keep each factory or foundation of the Chocolate Industry running. The operation manager for the Chocolate Industry would have to know how many tons of the cocoa beans are needed each day to keep each factory or foundation operating fully. They would also have to know how fast the cocoa beans grow pursuant to the number of children needed to work the thousands of cocoa plantations on the Ivory Coast of Africa and Ghana. Since the demand for chocolate is do high each month there should be an expected shipment weekly or monthly of how many tons of cocoa beans are coming in from the Ivory Coast of Africa and Ghana. Chocolate is a big deal in America and all over the world the operations managers have to keep in mind all the holidays, birthdays, fund raisers, different events and activities that will be taking place throughout the year in their regional area because once again everyone loves chocolate. The operations manager has to stay abreast of the needs of the Chocolate Industry and that its corporation's needs are being met. Due to the thousands of Cocoa Plantations which are located in remote areas of Africa and Ghana the number of children needed to work will vary but the hours of work does not. These children are transported from plantation to plantation seven days a week. The growth of the need for chocolate puts pressure on the children who work the Cocoa Plantations to work long hours. Due to the laws and Convention 182, 183 and Convention 29 these five year old children should not be working at all.

Would you say the Chocolate Industries are not aware of the laws being broken and the broadcasting of these children being violated all over the news in America has not graced the door steps of their corporations? That I must say is a very good question because if the operations managers are doing their jobs corporate knows what is taking place before the news media gets the story, you could say different, what do I know I am just a writer, huh. In the operation of a trillion dollar industry it would be vital for any industry to know its contacts and how they operate from the ground up. It is vital to have this information in case something was to go wrong and a change of plan is needed to be implemented immediately. Starting a business for anyone is being able to first understand how it operates from the ground up. Which would again mean to have the knowledge of knowing how many workers are needed on each Cocoa Plantation but that would not have anything to do with the Chocolate Industries now would it? Especially if the cocoa bean is coming from a major entity of their operation concerning what they need to keep everyone employed and working at the factories and foundations in America. They would have to know shipping procedures as well as how many tons of the cocoa bean is set for arrival and at what time will the shipment arrive. Is customs involved? Statements made about five year old children working 100 hours a week is very discouraging especially to those cannot just overlook what is being said and not try to find the truth out about it unfortunately the stats speak for themselves.. With the Chocolate Industry barring the burden of trying to disprove they are not aware of the Cocoa Plantations on the Ivory Coast of Africa and Ghana working five year old boys and girls 100 hours a week to get the cocoa bean to its much needed areas of production to the factories and foundations in America. Article after article has been covered over the years for those who are concerned for the safety and welfare of these children have made adamant statements about the abuse taking place. Not just with five year old children being used as workers on the Cocoa Plantations but also of the physical violations that continue to take place concerning the abuse these children are suffering from. Along with the legal issues of the Chocolate Industry may possibly not be aware of such legal recourse due tied in with all the other violations that have been aired in America.

The Chocolate Industry in no doubt should be ashamed of the trillions of dollars made off of the backs of these young children working on the Ivory Coast of Africa and Ghana, if they are aware of such legal issues? I will continue to say the founders of the Chocolate Industries must be totally disappointed with how this situation is turning out. How many articles need to be written, how many reports have to be reviewed and how many more children need to be raped, abused, beaten and sodomized before something is done to correct these obvious problems on the Cocoa Plantations. Remember I said I do not think the American Chocolate Industries knows what is taking place, and if you believe that then you can also believe the story of "Jack In the Bean Stock" is real?

Now that I have discussed what is being done on the Ivory Coast of Africa and Ghana with the children. I also want you to make note of the other countries and their involvement with the Cocoa Plantations in relations to the Chocolate Industries. What about the other five countries? With the Ivory Coast of Africa and Ghana being noted as the worst form of forced child labor in the world it should make you wonder what is taking place in the other countries. Indonesia is the first to be in question as being the second or third country on the list of the top 10 countries to produce the cocoa bean. The fourth on the list is the country, Nigeria which produces 0.383 million metric tones a year to be distributed to factories around the world. I am not aware of the abuse of children or maybe it just has not been covered by the media of what is taking place in Nigeria. What I am aware of is the 39.8 percent of the children on the Ivory Coast of Africa are working under aged children at the age of five years old to fourteen years old. Some of these children are held forcibly on the Cocoa Plantation to work 100 hours a week. Because these children are guarded so they will not try to escape if they make an attempt to escape they are beaten.

The one thing that bothers me the most concerning the children's attempt to escape is the choice of word being used here. The word escape refers to someone who is captured, a person who is a criminal, a person who does not have a right to leave an area without permission, someone whose rights have been taken away, or someone who is a slave to someone else a form of property. A child runs away from home. The use of the word escape is much more difficult and leaves a lot of room for explanation since it encompasses something that is not considered to be free?

I am certain you are grasping onto what I am saying here. The Chocolate Industry is a trillion dollar business, are there any limitations the Cocoa Plantations are not willing to go to hide the chocolate mess they have gotten not only themselves but the Chocolate Industry will also be involved because the cocoa bean is the main ingredient to the product they need to make chocolate. If you look at it logically I would say it is impossible for anyone in the chocolate Industry to not be aware of what is taking place concerning their entire operation of chocolate, they must know their operation from the ground floor up?

I am really hoping that all of these intelligent people working for the Chocolate Industry would not expect me to believe that there isn't one single person not only in the corporate office. But I am talking about one single person out of the 13,000 employed throughout the world that the Chocolate Industry could say they did not have a clue as to what is happening on the Cocoa Plantations? How will the Chocolate Industry attempt to convince, domestic child abuse agencies, Child Protective Agencies, Child Abuse Agencies, the National Labor Association, they did not know what is going on with the under aged children working 100 hours a week? How will the Chocolate Industries convince the International Labor Organization, the Convention of the Rights of the Child, the Convention Laws as they relate to child abuse that they did not have a clue as to how they were able to receive tons of cocoa bean for their chocolate and not know any parts of their operation? Would you say they are "Guilty by Association" or just victims of circumstance. The liability would be too high in relation to whatever quantity would be needed to come in each week in order for the Chocolate Industry to maintain their level of production and keep up with the supply and demand for chocolate in America when the Cocoa Plantation owners know that using five year old children is against the law. It is not only illegal in Africa and Ghana but with American ties to Africa and Ghana in relations to the International Labor Laws.

Would it be practical to say the Chocolate Industries not only in America would have to know what is taking place on the Cocoa Plantations? Or should I say it is practical to say not only is America in this mess knee deep but every Chocolate Industry and Chocolate foundation in the world is trying to keep quite their involvement in the worst forms of forced child labor in the world. Not just because of the abuse these children have to endure physically by working 100 hours a week but also because of the emotional abuse and mental abuse they are suffering from. There is so much involved concerning what is already notated with the children being used as sex slaves, they are used in child trafficking. I would like to say the Chocolate Industries do not know what is taking place on the Ivory Coast of Africa and Ghana but that is just not the case. It would be highly improbable that the Chocolate Industry would not know what is taking place with these little children. What has to be considered is the need of the main ingredient the cocoa bean which comes from the Cocoa Plantation on the Ivory Coast of Africa and Ghana who uses forced child labor to pick the cocoa beans. To have a trillion dollar industry such as the Chocolate Industry where the cocoa bean is being shipped from several countries the Chocolate Industry would have to know the operation of the industry and how each section operates from the ground floor up. With the tons of cocoa beans coming into America how could the Chocolate Industry not now what is taking place concerning the child slave labor on the Ivory Coast of Africa and Ghana? The operations manager, the inventory supervisor, and the distribution manager would all have to know what is coming in on each shipment in order to keep the

Chocolate Industries in America running at full operation. It would be improbable for anyone to believe the Chocolate Industry is not aware of not only the production of how the cocoa bean is being harvested but also how so much of the cocoa bean is being able to be produced. Which does not negate the fact that someone would have to have knowledge of the illegal use of the children on the Ivory Coast of Africa and Ghana? Do not let me forget Indonesia, Nigeria, Cameroon, Brazil, and Ecuador. Keep in mind that Indonesia is running close to second in some places concerning the statistics but for now I will continue to say the Ivory Coast of Africa and Ghana produces 60 percent of the world's cocoa bean which is the main ingredient to produce chocolate. That means millions of tons of the cocoa bean is brought into America each year. If you want to take a look at the top ten countries involved in making the Chocolate Industries filthy rich Below I will list them for you and then I will list the conversion from the metric tonnes to the United States tons. As we all know number #1 is the Ivory Coast of Africa is leading the way in the percentages of the cocoa bean. Number #2 being Ghana both Africa and Ghana combined is responsible for 60% percent of the cocoa bean. Number #3 is Indonesia, number #4 is Nigeria, number #5 is Cameroon, number #6 is Brazil, number #7 is Ecuador, number #8 is Mexico, number #9 is Dominican Republic and number #10 is Peru. Although Nigeria is listed as fourth on the list of the top 10 countries to produce the cocoa bean the activity within Nigeria involves fourteen of its thirty-six states. This list contains the names of the fourteen states in Nigeria that grow the cocoa bean: Abia, Adamawa, Akwa Ibom, Cross River, Delta, Edo, Ekiti, Kogi, Kwara, Ogun, Ondo, Osun, Oyo and Taraba. The Cocoa Industry was liberalized in Nigeria in 1986, when the government abolished the Nigerian Cocoa Board, a government bureau that controlled the marketing of cocoa, and deregulated the industry. This should really make you wonder how many states inside of each of the countries listed and not listed are actually involved in forced child labor in relations to the cocoa bean.

Below is the list of the top 10 countries and the amount of cocoa beans each country produces a year they were listed in metric tonnes. I have used a conversion chart to let you see just how many tons of the cocoa bean is produced each year this is only the top 10 countries. I have converted their chart to United States (tons).

Top 10 Countries Producing the Cocoa Bean in Metric tonnes to US tons

	Metric Tonnes	Tons
1. Ivory Coast of Africa	1,485, 822	1,637,838
2. Ghana	879,348	969,315
3. Indonesia	740,500	816,262
4. Nigeria	412,300	464,403
5. Cameroon	256,000	282,191
6. Brazil	253,211	279,117
7. Ecuador	133,322	146,962
8. Mexico	80,000	88,185
9. Dominican Republic	72,225	79,614
10. Peru	62,492	68, 886
		Total = 4,829,773

Looking at the numbers as you can see they do not lie. You can also see that almost five million tons of cocoa beans are produced by the top 10 countries a year.

Do not forget there are other countries that did not make the top 10 list.

Unfortunately it is the Overseas Development Institute (ODI) that claims it is much easier for the cocoa bean plantations to be operated by the small farm holders than to be turned over to the large corporate farms. (WorldAtlas.com)

In order to remedy a situation that has clearly gotten out of hand to gain more control of not only the massive harvesting of the cocoa bean into a more centralized and controlled area that corporate would bring. The Chocolate Industry would much rather give control to the small older farms. Which also alleviates them from knowingly being tied in with any illegal activity taking place on the Cocoa Plantation that involves any illegal activity with the under aged children on the Ivory Coast of Africa and Ghana. Why would an industry as large as the Chocolate Industry not want to take full control over the Cocoa Plantations after they have been made aware of the problems not only of forced child labor but also sex trafficking and child abuse as well? Why would the Chocolate Industry not want to take control of this situation in order not to show the Chocolate Industry was not aware of the violations of law taking place with these under aged children and the forced child labor taking place to get the cocoa beans to America? With their refusal to step in and make the necessary changes what sometimes is better not said in a situation such as this that involve little children five years of age. No response usually incites guilt.

Will We Pay the Cost

As we begin to look at other issues concerning the Chocolate Industry we have to make ourselves aware of other issues that involve this trillion dollar industry and how it will affect the rest of the world. I have already explained the expansion that has taken place of which a very large invest was made within a certain foundation in the Chocolate Industry of which will only enhance the need for more workers, longer hours and more small independent farms on the Cocoa Plantations to come up with the supply for the much needed cocoa bean. Business as usual is at its peak on the Cocoa Plantations with the use of small under aged children whose ages range from as young as 5 years old to 14 years old. In some of the areas of the Cocoa Plantations the age range has been reported to be as young as three years old. With the demand for chocolate on an increase and the Chocolate Industry continuously growing will the industry at some point began to see the necessity for a better trading market within its operations.

I have given you the numbers on the cocoa bean of which there is almost 5 million tons being produced a year. Please keep in mind the 5 million tons comes from only the top 10 countries a year. There are other countries that did not make the list merely because they do not produce as much cocoa beans involved with cocoa farming on the Cocoa Plantations.

The Chocolate Idustry and the Cocoa Plantations have to at some point admit to their union and come to an agreement that there is a need for renovations to be made on the Cocoa Plantations. Renovations needed in respect to the hazardous conditions under which the under aged employed children are working, the poor dilapidated mud huts these under aged employed children are forced to live in, the unreasonable hours the under aged employed children are having to work under. As noted from what I have just recently mentioned the children are under aged that would be another change the Cocoa Plantations would have to make an adjustment for better change. I do not want to go into wages not being paid to the workers, why? The main ingredient which comes for the production of chocolate comes from the cocoa bean but the country of which the cocoa bean is needed does not pay its workers. And from what I have reviewed concerning the workers being paid that if they ask for their payment they are beaten and made a mockery of. Let me go a little further concerning the adjustments needed for a brighter and better future as it relates to the Chocolate Industry. Education is the key to a brighter and better future and of course it is something that is not happening on the Cocoa Plantations and I am certain you have figured it out. If a five year old child is working 100 hours a week on the Cocoa Plantations the child is more than likely not going to school and receiving a proper education. With many violations already noted it is impossible to overlook the legalities being revealed. With millions of dollars being spent on expansions taking place in America in the Chocolate Industry and with trillions of dollars already made, there should not be renovation focusing on making the Chocolate Industry bigger. The renovations that need to be made is money that should be put toward making the Cocoa Plantations more livable which would mean better housing, and safer surroundings for the children meaning snakes and other issues that hazardous to their safety should be disposed of. The children do not deserve to live under such dilapidated conditions. A lot of involvement in correcting the worsening conditions is funded by the United States Department of Agriculture. Which also helps to improve the infrastructure such as paying for paved roads so farmers can have a place to dry their cocoa beans properly which will help to increase their sales. The United States Department of Agriculture also helps to provide within their programs training for the farmers. Training that will help them to learn how to rehabilitate old abandoned cacao trees. Due to their bartering abilities and small farmers wanting to get a better price from the sales of the cocoa beans many have joined together to combine their harvest. Other programs the Agricultural Department support gives the cocoa growers a better way of understanding how to produce a better product of cocoa beans to make their cocoa beans more marketable.

The way things are looking for the Chocolate Industry in America is that chocolate still remains to be a trillion dollar Industry. But no one is able to account for the legal problems that continue to persist involving the use of under aged children. When I look at the Department of Agriculture and compare what is legal when it comes to children working on the Cocoa Plantations I find myself in awe because plantation owners lack concern for their safety and lack of compassion for their age. When the laws were put into play concerning the make and the reality of this field I find them to be quite cunning when I look at the articulate way the laws were written. It was always the law maker's advantage concerning what was needed to take care of the agricultural products and how the children would be needed to work on the Cocoa Plantations. The age of the child as you can see from reading the agricultural regulations limitations the age of the child was probably thought about. But the way the laws were drawn in relations to agriculture and non-agriculture it appears as though the law makers were saying, I guess a child working to pick up fruits and vegetables was not considered manual labor.

Children were intended to be a part of the workforce all the time. Although the Fair Labor Standard Act made the provisions for children to be allowed to work on agricultural jobs they made specific restrictions to those who violated the non-agricultural jobs but the laws are still not being enforced. Those who had the foresight and vision to understand how the two would interact made certain the children at some point would be used as workers on the plantation but only in the agricultural areas of work. When we look at supply and demand on the Cocoa Plantations a child's life does not rate very high especially if it is a five year old child. It really does not make a difference because they are still being used no matter what the law says. The child's best interest is not taken to heart as it relates to the agricultural laws of labor for children. Although the Fair Labor Standards Act makes specifications as to how long a child can work and the age a child is able to work stipulations are still ignored. In America (FLSA) which is also known as the "Wage-Hour-Law" applies to minors employed in nonagricultural occupations and the FLSA reflects the wage, overtime and recordkeeping. The United States Department of Labor Wage and Hour Division have put in place laws to help with children who in the past have been used illegally in the United States. Laws that cover once again the rights of the child but in all reality of what is being said here, do you really expect a child 14 years old to actually know how their rights to not have to work certain jobs nor the extensive hours they are forced to work regardless of the laws put in place to protect them. The famers are not getting such great deals on their crop and the use of children does not appear to be going anywhere anytime soon because the company's and corporations want to get away with not paying these children what they are worth. If you someone is not educated and have not been trained to count the odds of them having a say so over there rights is null in void simply because they do not know they have right. This is why the need for those who are in government and have concerns of Fairtrade for the children have to make sure the laws are enforced. I continue to stress this throughout this book that laws are in place and ratified but they are not being enforced. If the laws are not being enforced in America you can really imagined how bad it is in the rest of the world. What is even more so even uglier is out of the entire globe of the earth the Ivory Coast of Africa and Ghana are the worst for child abuse. The Cocoa Plantations are in the spot light today because people are tired of the abuse that is allowed to take place with the little children. Farmers continue to be under paid for their cocoa beans which are many times sold on the black market for a better price. The Farmers are seeking to have the United States Department of Agriculture pay for created programs to help better the infrastructure for their marketing capabilities.

They want paved roads so they can have a clean place to dry their cacao beans properly. The problem I have with having the roads paved for the farmers to create a better product through United States funding is there is no mentioning of a school for learning being built for the children on the Ivory Coast of Africa and Ghana who work the Cocoa Plantations. It's not only noticeable by watching the recent investment of 300 million dollars being invested to create an even more stable foundation for the Chocolate Industry and made to increase the Chocolate Industries productions in America and secure jobs for another fifty years but nothing for the children on the Ivory Coast of Africa and Ghana. I know it might sound a little coy to some of you reading this book. But if you take the whole situation and not look at it as a one win and one lose matter of concern you will realize that no one has to lose. The Chocolate Industry can maintain their elite trillion dollar Industry and children will not have to be bartered off by their parents to work the Cocoa Plantations for the rest of their life.

There is so much going on with the Chocolate Industry and its ability to service mankind with one of the tastiest treats in the world today chocolate. That they have forgotten about the law makers and laws create to combat such abuse with children that the Chocolate Industry will try to act as though they haven't any idea as to what is taking place when in all actuality they do. Along with keeping things quiet within the Chocolate Industry those who are in the decision making positions concerning the child abuse and child slavery are fully aware of what is taking place on the Cocoa Plantations. It has already been documented first of all from the voting that took place by congress in favor of doing something to correct child slavery. Other problems the Chocolate Industry was dealing with involved congress who voted in 2001 with a vote of 291 to 115 to do something about the problems on the Cocoa Plantations and once again changes were to occur by 2005 for renovations to take place. Labeling of child slavery was to appear on products coming in to America revealing that children were forced into slavery on the Cocoa Plantations to produce such products. Remember the lobbying became a big factor because of the greed of the Chocolate Industry senators George Mitchell and Bob Dole were hired to lobby against the bill congress had created and "it did not go to vote". Why the bill never went to vote is not of my knowledge. We are all fully aware as to what takes place behind closed doors but first you would have to be one of two or more people behind such doors in order to understand what took place. I have to differ with the meeting of congress and their proposed plan simply because there are children involved. And when there are children involved under such circumstances as these, in military terminology we are going to do the white glove test meaning everyone are supposed to put their best foot forward for the betterment of the children only that is not what took place. The Chocolate Industry had to fear what the American people would do. Although African American (Blacks) were not in slavery as it was before 1862 in effect of the Emancipation Proclamation. And looking face to face with the year 2011 what could be said about the progress that could have been made through the years. If the lobbying by senator George Mitchell and Bob Dole had failed and products were allowed to be ship or flown to America with the labels showing slave labor. Exactly what kind of message would African American (Blacks) in America be receiving from white own businesses and corporations when it came to unloading such products to be sold in their stores and purchasing products with labels revealing child slave labor. You should not have to wonder if this was a so-called judgment call due to the problems white owned business and corporations already perceived as happening. America had already been through the change and in fact is still working tremendously hard to combat the racial issues of the past and not create new racial problems in 2001. Whites and Blacks were now working together in a unified effort to help change things in the past. Was the lobbying meant to buy time and give the Chocolate Industry some space in trying to come up with a solution that would work? A solution that would give the Chocolate Industry something they could be proud of without sending African America (Blacks) into culture shock. With the Chocolate Industry having no respect of person and fair trade was not on the table the Chocolate Industry wanted chocolate to continue to be able to be produced without bringing negative attention to its buyers. Freedom in America is a big pot being filled with many people from many and this is why it is called "the great melting pot". America has every ethnicity, religion and race mixed in the bowel together. Due to its own embarrassment of enforcing slavery at one time and still not able to live down the ugly reminders of the treatment of African America (Blacks) in America before the abolishment of slavery. The need to show labels of slavery on clothing and ask African American (Blacks) in America to purchase the clothing would have been a very big mistake. Why would the Chocolate Industry want to bring attention to them and uncover the truth about force child labor? It did not want to have a shadow over its head so the Chocolate Industry fought against having its product that was partially produced by forced child labor labeled as a warning for Americans to make a choice to purchase. I would say more than likely because of the use of children the Chocolate Industry in America and possibly the rest of the world would have been boycotted.

The Chocolate Industry
is not Invisible any longer

Although the Chocolate Industry would like to appear to be sweet and innocent that is just not the case. The Chocolate Industry moves in the shadows of the Cocoa Plantations but soars within the rings of the elite trying to not be noticed in the process of pretending to not know about the exploitation of these children. Children who work form sun up to sundown to give the Chocolate Industry the main ingredient it needs to produce chocolate, the cocoa bean. The Chocolate Industry continues to want more and more blood from slave labor to quench the cravings of Americans who want chocolate at the same time making more money off of the backs of laboring under aged innocent children. Children who once lined the streets of the Ivory Coast of Africa, Ghana, Mali and Burkina Fasa, they were poor and homeless but what gives the Cocoa Plantation owners the right to make them workers on the Cocoa Plantations for the rest of their life. Although they may not have been wanted they still had the right to do whatever they wanted with their life. All of their freedoms changed once they were taken to the Cocoa Plantations. Anyone who pours 300,000,000 million dollars into building a new foundation are looking for great returns concerning their investment which guarantee's people that want to work for the chocolate Industry another fifty years of employment. But will there be another fifty years of under aged five year old children to work the Cocoa Plantations without any benefits to sustain their health or any wages to help to prepare them for a different future. Although the Chocolate Industry remains behind the scene of the Cocoa Plantation it has already been notated that the Chocolate Industry is not the invisible ghost it was at one time. It became even more apparent the Chocolate Industry wanted their cocoa beans delivered no matter what the cost. The unadulterated truth was now transparent when it came to the Chocolate Industry doing what was right for the sake of children on the Ivory Coast of Africa and Ghana. With the truth of the matter being the Chocolate Industry did not care then and still does not care to this date of 2015 considering the facts that nothing has been done to rectify the treatment, living conditions, age, hours of work, lack of wages and better treatment of the children who work the Cocoa Plantations. The Chocolate Industry's "true crust of earth" is slowly being revealed and once the last thread of covering has been pulled back the embarrassment of what the Chocolate Industry will have to suffer with will be devastating. I feel this tragedy of deception being unclothed could possibly be avoided by showing a better hand of not what the Chocolate Industry intends to do but to bring about change by making a move to begin to starting the children on the Cocoa Plantations on a newer and brighter path. A path they are more than deserving of one that says to the world the, "Chocolate Industry cares about the children." It seems to me that greed has over powered the President, Chief Executive officer, Regional Directors, District Managers, and Supervisors throughout. No one wants to be at fault concerning the abuse of these children but now it is all out in the open. Congressman Eliot Engel stated he was disappointed in the industry because he would have thought the Chocolate Industry would have gathered some kind of social conscience. It is just not right for the Chocolate Industry to continue to pour money to better the Chocolate Industry and not do anything for the children. Along with myself and a few others I know I wonder just how many people are continuing to eat chocolate. There are those in the Chocolate Industry who have big names those who would much rather break the backs of small children than to better the children's chances at life. The Chocolate Manufactures Association is a trade group that represents U. S. chocolate producers, who also brought in allies such as the Grocery Manufacturers of America that also represent Kraft and General Mills. There is so much to consider in doing the right thing but not when it comes to children. When the senate and congress look back at the lobbying that took place to keep the "slave free" labels from being confirmed and passed on the floor of the House of Representatives it is going to leave a very bitter tastes in their mouth. I am not just talking about just any man or woman I am talking about men and women in Washington, DC those in the decision making positions who have the authority to make positive changes in the United States of America which also carries a lot of respect abroad. Susan Smith a spokeswoman for the Chocolate Manufacturers Association said the "slave free" would hurt the people it is intended to help. She had already envisioned this "slave free" label leading to boycotts of Ivorian cocoa. This was not a missed calculation on her part but in doing the right thing she thought would help. The Chocolate Industry as a whole would have been able to stay under the radar and move forward with even greater numbers had they not tried to hide the truth and attempt to continue with busy as usual. While trying to stay in the shadows of pretending to not know what was going on was not a wise decision on the Chocolate Industry's part. Now at some point in time change is going to occur because the Chocolate Industry (balloon) that was once new and secretly growing has begun to seep over the years and the V.I.P.'s that once kept this trillion dollar industry afloat has begun to slowly dwindle. The power that they once had in covering up things quietly now has the world's attention. People are not so quick any longer to cover their ears and turn their head. Modern technology has allowed common everyday people to become great film makers just by the touch of a phone. And now common everyday people are looking for lawful answers that make sense and not that old, that just the way it is. When I think about Congressman Eliot Engel telling the Chocolate Manufacturers they should be ashamed let's be realistic that's just not enough. This is not some kind of a tag team (your it) when it comes to children in slavery. What was the Chocolate Manufacturers Association supposed to say, (Ring around the roses). Give me a break was that the best defense for children who are being raped, a lot more could have been said. But once again since these children are of African descent its almost as though everyone is walking around saying oh well. There was definitely a fear of the Chocolate Industry being boycotted not only concerning the Ivorian cocoa. Once word got out about the abuse these children were taking and the long hours they were working along with all of the other stuff going on there would have been a boycott on cocoa I am most certain all over the United States. Protestors in America would have been walking around with big picket signs saying, "DON'T BUY CHOCOLATE", "CHILDREN WORKING AS SLAVES SO AMERICANS CAN HAVE CHOCOLATE" or how about "ARE YOU COOKOO NO COCOA". Because of the unity in America and the love and protection we feel for children I could see Americans going to battle with the Chocolate Industries until this situation of child slavery was corrected. It should have been corrected many years ago. Congress appeared to be on top of this situation for labeling chocolate products at one time but after a while lost its teeth in the bite and nothing once again was done. Although there were children involved and not only was the government on the Ivory Coast of Africa and Ghana aware but what is even sadder is the United States of America politicians, government officials and political leaders knew exactly what was taking place. As well as the Chocolate Industries in America founders and corporate heads are still aware of the abuse taking place with these children on the Cocoa Plantations. In fact the Chocolate Industry cannot dispute the fact they did know because the Chocolate Manufacturers Association were the ones who hired Senator George Mitchell and Congressman Bob Dole to lobbying to not let the "slavery labeling" bill go through. I must agree somewhat with Congressman Eliot Engel and say, shame on you "government officials" for not stepping in to make changes for these children a (go). I really don't know how such a bill to be passed in favor of "slavery labeling" which is the labeling of products to be singled out and receive a vote in congress of 291 to 115 in favor of labeling the products as they came into the United States and have the bill dwindle to nothing and not be passed. And shame on the Chocolate Industry for not caring enough about the children to want to step in to show some concerns that these little children's life matter. The Chocolate Manufactures Association could have made changes years ago but for whatever reason refuse to want these children to not have any freedoms at all. It is impossible for anyone to look at the Chocolate Industry at this point in time and say they have nothing to do with the abuse, rape, sodomy, beatings, and possible murdering of these children because Americans are now getting the full picture and we know what is taking place with the children. This will be an embarrassing situation for the world to look at as a whole. And we as Americans citizens need to pay more attention to the products we are allowed to import into the United States of America. Is America reverting back to the old ways of slavery? Is slavery the kind of bondage we as a nation who believe in the freedoms of all races, religions, ethnicities, and gender will be supported in our country? One of the greatest presidents of our time President Abraham Lincoln signed the Emancipation Proclamation to abolish slavery in the United States of America so why should we support slave marketed products. It is not right and the Chocolate Industry does not have a leg to stand on because it knows about the child sex slaves, the Chocolate Industry knows about the child sex trafficking, the Chocolate Industry knows about the child organ trafficking, the Chocolate Industry knows about the organ trafficking of these children on the Ivory Coast of Africa and Ghana but does not want it exposed that they are aware not only of the abuse taking place but the hazardous and dilapidated conditions under which these children are forced to work. Why would the Chocolate Industry (Empire) so full of wealth and riches not want the best for everyone all the way around. The price these children are paying is like a living death where everything has been taken from them and all they have is a hard road ahead of them. A road that has no ending until they are either dead of escape from the Cocoa Plantations where there is approximately two million children captive and working throughout the continent of Africa.

When I talk about the abuse, beating, rapes and sodomy taking place with these five year old children on the Ivory Coast of Africa and Ghana it should make you think what would an adult male want with a child in that way? For now I want you to keep in mind although all of it is disgusting there are other extracurricular activities taking place with these children: They are being used as **Child Sex Slaves** on the Cocoa Plantations, to be more explicit when you think about a slave doing what they are told to do in order to please their master the same relationship goes with the child who is now a sex slave and it takes a sick mind of an individual to think this child is enjoying themselves. This would be considered role playing but this is not a man role playing with his wife but with a child who does not know right from wrong. There is also **Child Exploitation** on the Cocoa Plantations of which is referred to as any person who employs, uses, persuades, induces, entices, or coerces any minor to engage in or who has a minor assist any other person to engage in, or who transports any minor in or affecting interstate or foreign commerce, or in any territory or Possession of the Unite States, with the intent that such minor engage in any sexually explicit conduct. With this explanation alone concerning the Cocoa Plantations as it relates to child exploitations and the under aged five year old children who work their this description alone should be enough to close the Cocoa Plantations down immediately until matters concerning these children who are being exploited have been corrected. On the Cocoa Plantations there is **Child Trafficking** of which is referred to as the sale of children. On the Cocoa Plantations to make it even more impersonal, child trafficking is the sale of children illegally and without any form of documentation or legal papers drawn up to track their whereabouts of the child who is sold. There aren't any adoption papers drawn up, there is not birth certificate to disclose the child's parents. This child is trafficked which means it is sold on the black market without a trace and will more than likely be never seen again. I would go a little further and say the child trafficking is closely tied in with child organ trafficking. **Child Organ Trafficking** on the Cocoa Plantations involves children on the Ivory Coast of Africa and Ghana which are more than likely are being exploited for their body parts that may be needed by a recipient. The transfer of the child's organs is without consent from the child and it depends on which organ is needed that could reflect the child's ability to function in life or could lead to the child's death. The human organ transplants can range from the liver, the kidney, pancreas or even the heart of which we are all certain that you cannot live without a heart. This is where the child trafficking comes into play since there aren't any papers drawn up for adoption, since there isn't a way the child on the Cocoa Plantations can be traced as being alive or dead. Their organs are very easily removed and since there isn't any trace of the child if by chance a heart is needed for the transplant. That child will never be missed or even spoken of again. This is why these people go to the poorest parts of the world because many of these children are living in the streets. Homeless, poor and hungry when they are taken the parent more than likely will report it to the police department and sometimes get the child's name on the missing child's list. Once these children are kidnapped they are taken out of the country and are never seen again.

Fair Trade

There is a lot to consider when we talk about Fair Trade and improvements concerning the Cocoa Plantations. The immediate improvements needed are the ones I just mentioned the child sex slaves, child trafficking and child organ trafficking on the Cocoa Plantations. This most certainly does not need to be delayed any longer and just because these children come from the poorest of countries in Africa no one seem to carry about their welfare. With all of this being said do you think the children are a part of the fair trade act or do they just simply slip between the cracks and are never missed. There is not enough public awareness being exposed to Americans and the rest of the world. The Chocolate Industry's cliental is the public. We are the voice of reason when it comes to what this monumental chocolate empire has now become. We the public can make trade fair and in the same sense of humanity make the Chocolate Industries all over the world aware that (We the People) will no longer support their force child labor. We will not support the illegal use of under aged children to get the cocoa bean to America. Fair Trade is not what it is considered to be this book will be the first of many to come so let the unraveling of the Chocolate Industry begin. The Chocolate Industry is wrapped up in so much of taking care of its own production that it does not care about preparing for the children on the Cocoa Plantations and their future they only care about getting more land and stretching their Cocoa Plantations out as far as they can get them. More land means of course more Cocoa Plantation and more Cocoa Plantations without a doubt means more money coming in. The Chocolate Industry is not innocent at all when it comes to knowing about what is taking place not only with the children but also with guilty of destroying rainforests for Cocoa Plantation production as you can see there is no end to their madness. The Chocolate Industry knows that as long as there is child slavery on the Cocoa Plantations the cost of chocolate will remain low but exposure is bringing about change and of course time is catching up with the Chocolate Industry. The Harkin-Engel Protocol may not be in effect as of now but it is still in existence. I personally believe that a change is going to come mainly because there are good people still in the world today who care about what is taking place with the five year old boys and girls on the Cocoa Plantations who are working 100 hours a week. Child slavery keeps the cost of chocolate down which allows major corporations to keep their chocolate cheap. It would cost the Chocolate Industry more if they had to pay the children for their labor on the Cocoa Plantations which would reflect as a lost or should I say reflect less of a profit to their already trillion dollar industry. What is not considered to be fair trade is how these children and parents are fooled into believing they are going to be paid for their labor? This is how parents are fooled into giving up their child for a summer which usually last a life time or until the child escapes of dies. Once they are taken to the Cocoa Plantations they are paid for a short period of time after a few months of work they are not paid anything. Many of the young children who are able to ask for their pay thinking they are going to be able to send the money home to their parents are severely beaten. It is a no win situation for the children there as well as the small farmers who run the Cocoa Plantations so they can trade their cocoa beans for a profit. But not only are the children being cheated but the small cocoa farmers are cheated as well. Many times they are quoted prices far below the market value and the farmers have to sell their cocoa beans on the black market to get a better price. The labels for slave free chocolate should have been allowed and I can see the lost and how this would have affected the purchases of certain chocolates that came into America in a very big way. I must say the Chocolate Industry may seem to be immovable but there is nothing too hard for God. Change as it relates to children in slavery, children being raped and sodomized, children being used as sex slaves, for exploitation purposes and for organ trafficking this is the kind of change that is inevitable and will occur regardless of who is at the helm of the Chocolate Industry.

Fair Trade at this point in time is really what is needed and with fair trade being implemented it will make those who are trying to do the right thing feel a lot better about what they are trading. Saying "shame on you" is just not enough to make the necessary changes needed on the Cocoa Plantations. Do we need more meeting to come to a solution of change I would say no? The Chocolate Industry needs to call a national conference meeting and say "we can no longer do business as usual." Unless this meeting is held the Chocolate Industry is setting itself up for a hardship. It would be better to invest the money needed for change than to wait until the bottom drops out and then start to do something. Fair Trade is needed and is crucial for the survival as we know it concerning the Cocoa Plantations and the Chocolate Industry all over the world. The Chocolate Industry cannot wait to begin to clear up the scandal around its name. There are so many usages of chocolate the Chocolate Industry must not wait until the last minute to start correcting the problems that are currently haunting the Cocoa Plantations it must start now. The after effect will not be as bad if you start to clear up these slavery problems now. You do not want until the last minute because just like process of getting things to change for the better concerning the abuse you have allowed to continue for so long was a slow grinding change so shall the recovery of the Chocolate Industry be even slower.

The Framework of Action speaks clearly on the changes that need to occur. It breaks down the importance for change and makes it known that the Ivory Coast of Africa and Ghana are being recognized as the worst forms of child labor in the world

There is Light at the end, He's there

"Going to the Cross"

When you think about Jesus Christ going to the cross. What really captures your mind? What entertains your thoughts of the Son of God being allowed to be put out on display before those who mocked him, spit on him, stoned and bricked him, did all manners of things to him and then were allowed to humiliated by watching him die on the cross.

Are you asking yourself at this point what is God's plan? What plan does the Father have to rescue his children from a world that hated his son Jesus without cause? Do we stand a chance? Jesus had the authority the power the will to call on legions of angels and never did. How do you see his power now, he did not abuse his authority. Jesus did not leave the love of his Father for temporary gratification. If you look at the crucifixion carefully, please allow me to speculate for one second. [Jesus must have been smiling on the inside saying do they really believe they are going to kill me. I am Jesus Christ the Son of God.]

Remember he carried the cross, he laid down on the cross, he allowed them to drive the pins in his hands and feet. They lifted him up and scripture was fore filled, "If I be lifted up I will draw all men unto me." We all have a cross to bear. The servant is never greater than his master. Jesus stayed on the cross, leading the way for the edification glorify God Almighty. Letting his children know it's okay and we don't have to fight with the world. We don't have to run and hide ourselves. But to be able to stand up for justice and for righteousness sake and not be afraid to go to the cross for his purpose for his glory, "It is better to have suffered for righteousness sake."

I am Elder Christian in Jesus name.

There isn't any place to run when you are serving Gods purpose. Pick up your cross and follow Jesus. Come on everybody he is waiting

Framework of Action to Support Implementation of the Harkin-Engel-Protocol

The following is a Framework of Action for efforts aimed at a significant reduction in **the worst forms of child labor** in cocoa producing areas of Cote d'Ivoire and Ghana. The Framework is intended to support the further implementation and realization of the goals of the Harkin-Engel-Protocol.

1. **Propose:** The overarching goal of the Framework is:

By 2020, the worst forms of child labor as defined by ILO Convention 182 in the cocoa sectors of Cote d'Ivoire and Ghana will be reduced by 70 percent in aggregate through joint efforts by key stakeholders to provide and support remediation services for children removed from **the worst forms of child labor,** including education and vocational training, protective measures to address issues of occupational safety and health related to cocoa production, and livelihood services for the households of children in cocoa growing communities; the establishment and implementation of a credible and transparent sector-wide monitoring system across cocoa growing regions in the two countries; and the promotion of respect for core labor standards.

To reach this overarching goal, the Framework will support the development of thriving cocoa communities fostering safe, healthy, and productive environments for children and families through coordinated support for new or expanded initiatives in Cote d'Ivoire and Ghana in the following areas:

a. Removal of children from the worst forms of child labor, including hazardous labor, in cocoa growing areas and provision of appropriate remediation services, including education or vocational training; or in the case of children/ youth or legal working age, removal of workplace hazards and other steps necessary to bring conditions into conformity with national laws and international labor standards;

b. Prevention of children's involvement I **the worst forms of child labor,** including through increased access to schooling and vocational training and improvement in the quality and relevance of education:

c. Promotion of sustainable livelihoods for the households of children in cocoa growing areas;

d. Establishment and implementation of community-based child labor monitoring systems (CLMS) in cocoa growing areas, linked to the provision of remediation for children identified as engaged in **the worst forms of child labor;** and

e. Continuation of nationally representative child labor surveys, recurring at least every 5 years. Nationally representative baseline data is established as the most recent data coming out of the 2008-2009 Tulane field surveys. The next nationally representative surveys in both countries will be in the field during the 2013-2014 harvest seasons, with a report made in 2014, and again in the field in 2018-2019, with a report in 2019. These surveys will provide comparable data for the ongoing assessment of child labor prevalence in cocoa growing areas and a commitment to make publicly available the related survey methodologies, all raw data, and reports based on the finding of such surveys. In addition to such nationally representative surveys, efforts should also be made to incorporate a child labor component into existing national household surveys to support efforts to combat the **worst forms of child labor nationally** in each country.

2. **Key Stakeholders:** Stakeholders under this framework are defined as follows:

a. **Cocoa growing communities:** This group includes children in cocoa growing areas and the households of these children where efforts to promote sustainable livelihoods will address root causes of child labor.

b. **Producer Governments:** This group includes the national, district, and local government agencies of Cote d'Ivoire and Ghana.

c. **International Chocolate and Cocoa Industry:** This group includes companies participating in this Framework which are engaged in the growing of cocoa, processing of cocoa, and/or production and sale of its derivative products.

d. **Foreign Donors:** This group includes the U.S. Government (the U.S. Department of Labor, the U.S. Department of State, the U.S. Agency for International development, and key Congressional Offices- Senator Tom Harkin and Representative Eliot Engel). Other donor entities, such as the European Union and other international donors, are encouraged to fund projects that will support the goals of this Framework.

e. **Social Partners and Civil Society:** This group includes employer and worker organizations, non-government organizations (NGO), and community-based organizations in both, Cote d'Ivoire and Ghana, as well as the international counterparts of these groups.

f. **Implementing Organizations (including International Organizations and other Non-governmental Organizations):** This group includes among others, the international Labor Organization's International Program on the Elimination of Child Labor (ILO-IPEC), the International Cocoa Initiative, the World Cocoa Foundation, and other organizations possessing expertise related to the initiatives under this Framework and whose projects or other inputs are integrated and supportive of achievement of the Framework's goals.

3. **Financial Partners:** The key stakeholders defined above include a subset of partners, including the U.S. Government

and the International Chocolate and Cocoa Industry, that have committed to provide new financial support for new or expanded interventions to achieve a significant and sustainable reduction in **the worst forms of child labor** in the cocoa sector of Cote d'Ivoire and Ghana and whose actions are supportive of achievement of this Framework's goals. This subset also includes the Governments of Cote d'Ivoire and Ghana, who will transparently communicate their financial and human resource commitments under this Framework to the Child Labor Cocoa Coordinating Group (CLCCG) and its Principals, (See Section 6.)

It is further noted that the group of financial partners may be expanded over the life of the Framework to include other partners, such as other private sector entities, NGO's or international organizations. In order to ensure that new initiatives are supportive of the Frameworks goals, proposals for new partners and their programs will be subject to review by the CLCCG and its Principals.

4. **Roles, Responsibilities and Commitments under this Framework:** This Framework considers the roles, responsibilities and contributions of financial partners as noted below:

a. **Producer Governments:** The Producer Governments play critical roles in planning, implementing and monitoring progress toward achievement of their respective national plans that are the foundation for reducing **the worst forms of child labor.** The Producer Governments must ensure coherence between project efforts under this Framework and the national plans for the purposes of national and local ownership and sustainability. Producer Governments also will ensure adequate human, financial, and organizational (e.g., decision making and internal advocacy) resource capacity in appropriate government agencies, as well as working in partnership with financial partners and other key stakeholders, to provide the following services:

o Data collection and monitoring at the community and national level through supporting a nation-wide, community-based CLMS and by developing, funding and conducting nationally representative surveys as described in this Framework:

- Remediation for the children removed from **the worst forms of child labor** through the provision of education, vocational training, and by increased support for programs to improve livelihoods for the households of children in cocoa growing communities;

- Prevention of other children from involvement in the **worst forms of child labor** in cocoa growing communities through the provision of education, vocational training, and increased support for programs to improve livelihoods for the households of children in cocoa growing communities;

- Development of physical and social infrastructure, including roads, wells and schools in cocoa-growing areas; and

- Enforcement of laws intended to protect children from **the worst forms of child labor.**

b. **International Chocolate and Cocoa Industry:** The Harkin-Engel Protocol and accompanying Joint Statements of 2005 and 2008 serve as a commitment by the representatives of the International Chocolate and Cocoa Industry to carry out the industry's responsibilities to ensure that cocoa beans and their derivative products are grown and processed in a manner complaint with internationally-recognized standards on child labor. Specifically, in the Joint Statement of 2008, the International Chocolate and Cocoa Industry committed itself to "continue to support efforts to eliminate **the worst forms of child labor and forced adult labor** on cocoa farms and to help cocoa farmers, their families and communities by continuing to work with the national government to ensure that the certification process, including remediation and verification are fully implemented." It is further noted in the Joint Statement of 2008 that the International Chocolate and Cocoa Industry will work with the governments of Cote d'Ivoire and Ghana to have a sector-wide certification process "fully in place across each country's cocoa-growing sector." **With this Framework of Action, the International Chocolate and Cocoa Industry, in partnership with financial partners and other key stakeholders, will:**

- Continue to support data collection and monitoring at the community and national level through a credible community=based CLMS.
- Through relevant local institutions and stakeholders, support the provision
- Of appropriate remediation services for children based on the CLMS data, national survey data, and other credible sources of information, with the goal of protecting children from *the worst forms of child labor* in the cocoa growing areas of Ghana and Cote d'Ivoire.
- Provide sustainable livelihoods for the households of children in cocoa growing communities in order to protect children from *the worst forms of child labor* and ensure thriving cocoa communities.
- Provide technical advice to assist in the refinement and implementation of the ILO-IPEC project referenced as: "Towards Child Labor Free Cocoa Growing Communities through an Integrated Area Based Approach."
- Strive to ensure their cocoa supply chains use safe and responsible labor practices, including combating *the worst forms of child labor.* Individual companies will inform their employees who buy and sell cocoa and its derivative products of the relevant ILO Conventions, the International Cocoa Agreement, relevant labor legislation in the two countries, the Harkin-Engel Protocol and the Framework of Action.

Reflecting their commitment to the production of cocoa and its derivative products without the involvement of *the worst forms of child labor,* and as an immediate pledge, the International Chocolate and Cocoa Industry is committing $7million to further the goals of the Harkin-Engel Protocol and the Framework of Action, of which $2 million will support an ILO-IPEC Public-Private Partnership and $5 million that includes the expansion of significant current industry work on cocoa which has demonstrated the value of partnerships of this nature. This funding will be spread out over a five year period, and the amount and timing of outlays will be discussed during CLCCG consultations. The Industry is making a further pledge to explore the possibility of committing an additional $3million for remediation activities that further these goals.

c. **U.S. Department of Labor:** The U.S. Department of Labor will play an active role as a donor supporting projects that reduce *the worst forms of child labor* in the cocoa sector in West Africa, committing $10million in 2010 for a new, multi-year program to be implemented by ILO-IPEC that supports the efforts described in this Framework. The U.S. Department of Labor will continue to report on progress being made to address the goals of the Harkin-Engel Protocol and the goals and objectives of this Framework, with a specific emphasis on the progress made by the ILO in the program noted here. As a donor, the U.S. Department of Labor will have substantial involvement in the design and development of the project and will work in partnership with financial partners and other key stakeholders.

5. **Benefits:** By promoting improved coordination and more integrated planning, implementation, and assessment of interventions, this Framework offers a number of important benefits:

a. For cocoa growing communities, this approach can lead to driving cocoa communities fostering safe, healthy, and productive environments for children and families.

b. For Producer Governments, the approach helps to focus and coordinate assistance on meeting national goals related to the elimination *of the worst forms of child labor,* provision of universal basic education, poverty reduction, and employment creation. National capacity will be built in data collection, including nationally representative surveys; monitoring, including CLMS; impact assessment and remediation.

c. For Financial Partners, the Framework offers a coordinated approach that will help maximize impact in target areas. Moreover, by demonstrating an effective model of cooperation, the Framework can serve as a platform for attracting increased funding from other donors, including other chocolate and cocoa companies, other manufacturers who purchase or use cocoa, chocolate and their derivative ingredients, and other international agencies with an interest in tackling *the worst forms of child labor.*

d. For the International Chocolate and Cocoa Industry, the Framework provides an integrated approach to enable the sustainable supply of cocoa in a manner consistent with the commitments made under the Harkin-Engel Protocol.

e. For social partners and civil society, the Framework provides opportunities for the involvement of social partners and civil society in dialogue on how best to support sustainable change.

f. For all stakeholders, the Framework provides mechanisms for promoting greater transparency and accountability for all parties.

6. **Governance:** In order to meet the objectives of this Framework, the participants will operate within a well-designed and articulated structure of governance.

a. Within the context of governance, it is noted that there is a significant difference between "Key stakeholders" (those with an interest in the issue) and "financial partners" (those assuming a direct responsibility for the management and ultimate success of the Framework of Action). The development of governance structures will include mechanisms for stakeholders to be informed of and to comment on the governance structures, while reserving direct and strategic decision making to the financial partners.

b. The CLCCG will serve as the initial coordination and steering group for the implementation of this Framework. The CLCCG is currently composed of (1) Principals representing the U. S. Department of Labor, the Harkin and Engel offices, the Governments of Ghana and Cote d'Ivoire, and the International Chocolate and Cocoa industry and (2) a larger working group of representative from these organizations. It is envisaged that the CLCCG could be expanded to a broader group of participants. The CLCCG will consult with technical experts on matters as necessary (e.g., the development of indicators and common monitoring and evaluation frameworks).

c. The CLCCG will work in the coming months to define the governance structure under the Framework and the roles and responsibilities of the CLCCG itself.

7. **Coordination:** The Framework will offer a means for improved coordination of interventions under a more holistic approach for significantly reducing *the worst forms of child labor* in the cocoa growing area of Cote d'Ivoire and Ghana in support of the National Plans of Action in each country. This will be achieved by the following actions:

a. Each of the CLCCG members will designate a resource entity and person(s) who will serve as the point of contact for efforts under this Framework, be available to coordinate on matters related to the Framework, and have the capacity to update partners on relevant initiatives;

b. The CLCCG will meet on a regular schedule to be determined. The U. S. Department of Labor will help facilitate the convening of the CLCCG.

c. The CLCCG will assess progress toward the goals of the Framework on an ongoing basis and engage in consultations on what is needed to achieve these goals.

d. Programs funded by the Financial Partners and implemented by the Governments of Ghana and Cote d'Ivoire and implementing organizations will be designed to operate in support of national plans and goals, including those related to the elimination of **the worst forms of child labor,** provision of universal basic education, poverty reduction, and employment creation;

e. Efforts will be made to effectively target communities with a high incidence of **the worst forms of child labor** in order to maximize the impact of the actions taken;

f. All stakeholders will be encouraged to share learning and experience, collaborate to pilot new models, and actively explore ways to ensure sustainability and scalability of effective strategies;

g. Key stakeholders will engage in joint monitoring and evaluation of programs where feasible and beneficial; and

h. Regular public reports will be issued on progress and lessons learned under the Framework.

8. **Monitoring of Progress:** Progress under the Framework will be monitored as follows:

a. The nationally-representative surveys on child labor in cocoa will provide standardized information about the situation of **the worst forms of child labor** in cocoa in each country and be used to measure progress on reducing the number of children in **the worst forms of child labor** in the cocoa sectors of Cote d'Ivoire and Ghana.

b. The CLCCG, in consultation with technical experts, will discuss and come to agreement on a monitoring and evaluation design for use by all participants in this Framework.

c. The CLCCK, in consultation with technical experts, will discuss and come to agreement on a set of common indicators that clearly track interim progress towards the goal of a 70 percent reduction in **the worst forms of child labor** in Ghana and Cote d'Ivoire, and other key parameters that will be reported on a regular basis.

d. In the periods between the national surveys, information from the CLMS will provide ongoing information on the child labor situation in specific communities.

e. Individual projects launched under the Framework will measure progress towards the specific goals of the project, report on an appropriate subset of common indicators, and include transparent impact evaluations. Where feasible, the integration of randomized control trials or other rigorous evaluation methods will be used to identify interventions that are both effective and cost efficient so that they may be promoted for future replication and scaling-up.

f. A series of milestones, or performance goals, will be developed to assess the progress being made to significantly reduce **the worst forms of child labor** in the cocoa sector of Cote d'Ivoire and Ghana. The benchmarks will be unique for each country and will be based on the commitments of specific action on an annual basis.

g. A progress evaluation of the Framework itself will be conducted two years after implementation of the Framework begins, and an annual review will be carried out every twelve months subsequently.

9. **Timeline to Launch the Framework:**

a. A meeting of Principals will be held on September 13 to issue a Declaration of Joint Action, including this Framework, and a joint and media announcement will be made.

b. The Principals will deposit copies of key national plans (in the case of the Governments of Cote d'Ivoire and Ghana), identify Framework points of contact, and agree on a schedule of meetings (the next to be held by December 31, 2010) to begin implementing this Framework.

c.   Meetings of the CLCCG will be held in Washington, DC and in Cote d'Ivoire and Ghana on a rotating basis. These meetings will be organized around concrete agendas to address program design, financing, governance, and other matters necessary to fully implement this Framework.

I For the purpose of this document, **remediation services** are defined as removing children from hazardous or exploitative labor through the provision of direct services. This includes education and livelihood services, protective measure to address issues of occupational safety and health related to cocoa production, and social protection services for trafficking victims. Education services may take the form of formal or non-formal education and vocational training. Livelihood services improve the ability of the family to care for the child and protect the child from the worst forms of child labor. By providing protective measures to address issues of occupational safety and health related to cocoa production, youth of legal working age who are engaged in hazardous labor could be withdrawn by transitioning them into safe, acceptable work that is in conformity with both national laws and international labor standards. Children who are victims of trafficking may need to receive social protection services including rehabilitation and repatriation services.

II For the purpose of this document, **livelihood** is defined as a means of living and the capabilities, assets, and activities required for it. A livelihood encompasses income, as well as social institutions, gender relations, and property rights required to support and sustain a certain standard of living. It also includes access to and benefits derived from social and public services provided by the state, such as education, health services, and other infrastructure. In turn, sustainable livelihood programs seek to create long-lasting solutions to poverty by empowering their target population and addressing their overall well-being.

(http://pdf.usaid.gov/pdf_doc/PNADR399.pdf)

Set Backs by Congress No Renovations
(Cocoa Plantations)

Are the Boycotts Needed to impose upon others to do the right thing and bring the Cocoa Plantations up to par as far as working conditions, living conditions are concerned. Other inclusions in the renovation process would entail a proper education for children of a legal age that could actually be allowed to work on the Cocoa Plantations. Not 5 year old boys and girls that are taken from their families and never get the opportunity to see their father or mother again. The children need vocational training and if possible college outside of the country, and social services to step in and assist them with formal and non-formal educational challenges as payment for all the years and lives that were lost prior to the Cocoa Plantations being exposed.

Background

"In 2001, US Representative Eliot Engel introduced a legislative amendment to an agriculture bill. This amendment was given the U.S. Food and Drug Administration (FDA) $250,000 to develop a label to indicate no child slave labor was used in growing or harvesting cocoa. This label would be similar to the "dolphin safe" labels used for tuna. The amendment was approved in the House of Representative vote of 291-115. The bill appeared to have similar support in the Senate. The international cocoa industry strongly opposed it and the Chocolate Manufactures Association hired former senator George Mitchell and Bob Dole to lobby against it. The cocoa industry faced potential consumer boycotts and harmful legislation if the bill were to pass. Mitchell and Dole encouraged the industry to make a deal. And before the bill went to a vote in the Senate, the cocoa industry agreed to address the problem without legislation.

Former Senator Thomas Richard "Tom Harkin and Congressman Eliot Engel negotiated a deal with the cocoa industry to create the Harkin-Engel Protocol. The protocol was signed in September 2001 with the objective to eliminate the **"Worst forms of child labor"** and adult forced labor on cocoa farms in West Africa. It was signed and witnessed by the heads of eight major chocolate companies, Harkin, Engel, Senator Herb Khol, the ambassador of Cote d'Ivoire, the director of the International Programme on the Elimination of Child Labor and others."

((http://en.wikipedia.org/wiki/Harkin%E2%80%93Engel_Protocol)

My Angels Stand Guard Over Me

I close my eyes to sleep at night comfortable in your arms,
Cradled under the wings of the one I trust, my Father in Heaven;
There aren't any hidden thoughts of the
peace that has befallen me,
The twilight hours await my soul, my
body is at peace within itself;
Losing sight of consciousness and this physical
world as I know it, I sigh in relief,
I reflect briefly on the joy that once filled
my day in my prostrate position;
I yawn in relaxation as my tense body
reaches its final stage of surrender,
I can feel the air moving about my presence, it is so surreal;
There is no guarantee of my eyes ever
opening again, nothing can revive me,
I am subjected to the will of my Father in Heaven, to God alone,
In my walk today I can only say I gave my
best before I closed my eyes;
I can feel deep spiritual warmth a calmness one with nature,
A wanton to not fight any longer, I have
reached my stage of exhaustion;
All that will let it come, I cannot defend
myself any longer, it is God's will,
Yes, it is my Father in Heaven who will determine my destination;
In all actuality it was always up to the Father, he has all power,
I haven't any authority without his confirmation, he is king,

He has the power to lay down life and take it up again;
The power God gives is of his will, nothing
overshadows the Father,
Nothing could give me more pleasure then
my sleeping visit with death;
Not knowing if God will ever wake me up
again, is my mission complete,
I recall the words to an old church song "all
day all night angels watching over me;"
Because of my labor to do what is sufficient
in his will, to please only him;
My earthly walk is not quite finished yet
so I thank you Father God,
I thank you for my peaceful rest as:
"My Angels Stands Guard over Me"

**Written by: Author &Hall of Fame Poet
Raymond C. Christian**

These children have no mother or father. What more can I say other than that I will continue speaking on this issue. Of course, I am asking everyone to get involved and call your senators, congressman and government officials and ask questions. Why do these children have to wait until the year 2020 for the abuse to stop? Trillions of dollars as stated has already been made off of the backs of these children what more is there to wait for concerning the exploitation of these children. They haven't a father of mother to speak up for them or to care for them. They do have appointed officials senators, congressmen and government officials in place to legislate in their behalf as to what is considered by many to be immoral and unjust. These government officials are put in position to control the international laws of which we as Americans see as adverse child abuse. The two named politicians are Former Senator Thomas Richard "Tom Harkin and Congressman Eliot Engel.

Former Senator Thomas Richard "Tom" Harkin

Democrat

PICTURE DELETED

Brief Dialogue on Former Senator
Thomas Richard "Tom" Harkin

Former Senator Thomas Richard "Tom" Harkin (born November 19, 1939) is the current junior United States Senator from Iowa serving since 1985, and a member of the Democratic Party. He previously served in the United States House of Representatives (1975-1985). He is a graduate of Iowa State University and The Catholic University of America's Columbus School of Law. He served in the United States Navy as an active-duty jet pilot from 1962 to 1967. Thomas Richard "Tom" Harkin won a race for U.S. Senate in 1984 by a wide margin. He was an early frontrunner for his party's presidential nomination in 1992, but dripped out in support of eventual winner Bill Clinton. On January 26, 2013, he announced his intentions to retire from the Senate after completing his fifth term in 2015. Harkin attended Iowa State University on a Navy R.O.T.C. scholarship. "In 1969, Harkin moved to Washington, D. C. and began work as an aide to Democratic U.S. Congressman Neal Smith. During his work for Smith, he accompanied a congressional delegation that went to South Vietnam in 1970. Harkin published photographs he took during the trip and a detailed account of the "tiger cages" at Con Son Island prison in Life Magazine on July 17, 1970. The account exposed shocking, inhumane conditions treatment to which prisoners were subjected." (http://en.wikipedia.org/wiki/Tom_Harkin)

My question here with all due respect earned is why is the ball being dropped concerning the fight for these five year old boys and girls working over 100 hours a week on the Cocoa Plantations? The meaning of the word,

Abuse

Accordance to the Webster's New World Dictionary it means, "to use wrongly; misuse; to hurt by treating badly; mistreat.

When looking at child abuse all over the world the mistreatment of a child is considered to be child abuse no matter what color, creed or gender of the child. It appears that Senator Harkin is truly the man for the job because of his experience and knowledge in the political field. He has served in the Senate longer than any Democrat in Iowa's history, and only Neal Smith has served in Congress longer among Iowa Democrats. This is why it is so hard for me to take this cup so lightly, not forgetting to mention child abuse is involved along with what is also recognized by the United States Department of Labor as forced child labor. I would like to know how much more time and delay is needed. When it is not just the United States but all of these companies, countries and corporations have made trillions of dollars off of the backs of these abused children in slavery and it appears as though everyone is going home to their families at the end of the day enjoying life. What is important to me here is that Senator Thomas Richard "Tom Harking signed on to get what needed to be done on the Cocoa Plantations corrected. He is well informed of what is taking place with these children and the need for new corrective measures to be employed. It would be impossible to not be a United States Senator with your name on a law and not know what the purpose of the law is or the changes that need to be made within the realms of the law created. Senator Harkin knows what is taking place on the Cocoa Plantations because of the legal ramifications involving the worst forms of child abuse taking place on the Ivory Coast of Africa and Ghana. Along with these five year old boys and girls being trafficked into exploitation on these farms, to put it more bluntly these children are being taken off into other areas and used sexually when it comes to just working on the Cocoa Plantations. Since 2001 changes to the Cocoa Plantations were supposed to be made it's now 2015. It appears as though every Senator, Congressman, Congresswoman; every government official and every executive of the Chocolate Industries all had a case of amnesia about the same time concerning the help these children need on the Cocoa Plantations. The evidence is quite explicit my lack of understanding is that nothing has been done. I would have to wonder if the Cocoa Plantation policies concerning the Harkin-Engel Protocol have been voted on again. Or was it just accidentally dropped in the trash, or swept under the stack of other things to do, or is it that no one wants to speak about it. I must say this is so unbelievable because the United States government has not stepped in to monitor the sexual abuse taking place with these five year old children, and of course the verbal abuse is just as worse. Don't let me forget about the mental abuse it ties in with the emotional abuse. Many of the articles I have read talks about the physical abuse. Since there isn't any counseling set up for these five year old boys and girls we would have to look at the physiological abuse of these children and what they have to live with each day of their life, they have no father or mother to protect them. I would like to assume they are not being helped because the American politicians and government officials who should be involved could not take the graphic treatment of these children so in order for them to keep from getting their hands dirty they just chose not to do anything at all…are you kidding me? The worst form of child slavery in the world as graphic as it may sound does not have a need to be put off any longer than what it already has. These are children no matter how far away from our eyesight they may be, no matter how poor, unlearned, and under privileged they may be these are still our children.

Below you will find another article written this article came out from early researchers:

h t t p : / / w w w . c h a n g e . o r g / p e t i t i o n s / stop-the-traffik-end-the-trafficking

When this article came out it was written to the National Government, European Parliament, Stop The Traffik: (please read the article in its entirety)

"Please take parliamentary action to stop child trafficking in the cocoa industry.

West Africa produces 70% of the world's cocoa. 1.8 million Children are working on 2 million cocoa farms there. Many of these children are trafficked into exploitation on these farms..."

More than ten years ago several of the top companies had gotten together and decided to get rid of the child abuse. These companies I would say began to grow a conscience and want to do the righteous things? As time as rolled along and greed continues to set in I would say it has become even harder for those who wanted to do the righteous thing and get rid of the child trafficking that is taking place and stop miss treating the children on the Ivory Coast of Africa and Ghana. They just can't seem to get their hands out of their pockets without thinking about the money that will be falling out. They have come up with ideas to use to show the imported products coming into the United States that came from slave labor is tagged with the symbol of forced child labor. And are asking the American citizens not to purchase them these products that are marked? The Chocolate Industry is not hurting for money and due to the demand on chocolate probably never will be hurting for money because so many people love chocolate. The Chocolate Industry has earned trillions of dollars on the backs of these children on the Ivory Coast of Africa and Ghana. Although the Chocolate Industry has thrived and grown into an Empire it has not benefited the children working the Cocoa Plantations any. They are still without an education, a childhood, and the inability to come and go off of the Cocoa Plantations as they please. They do not receive any wages for their work. These children on the Cocoa Plantations on the Ivory Coast of Africa and Ghana are, five year old children are working 100 hundred hours a week. These five year old Children are being used as sex slaves, in sex trafficking and organ donations. With all of the promises being made by the Chocolate Industry to not use children illegally on the Cocoa Plantations nearly 40 % percent of the workforce are children between the ages of 5 -14. Some of the children are sold as young as three years old. With trillions of dollars being made only 0.0075% percent goes toward some form of improvement for the children nothing significant. I would guess the 0.0075 % percent is just a little something to show on paper but where does the money actually go. These children are still living in mud huts and breathe out of a ventilation hole in each mud hut about the size of a baseball.

Laws are already in place but are not being implemented to help bring about the positive changes needed to help not only the children on the Ivory Coast of Africa and Ghana but children working the Cocoa Plantations all over the world.

As far as putting together some form of Legislature it would be suggested that Former Senator Thomas Richard Harkin who was once a senator in Washington, DC and just recently retired in 2015. And Congressman Eliot Engel who is still seated in Washington, Dc of which both men were named individuals in relations to the Cocoa Plantations. Had the bill that was passed into law in 2001 called the;

Harkin-Engel Protocol they the Cocoa Plantations primary source of action for change. I wonder what happened to all of the reports, which involved the delays for these children. I wonder what happened to all of the meetings, notes taken and the investigation if any occurred. Where are they when CNN News, ABC News, CBS News, 20/20 reports, written article, news media coverage and journalist reports clearly state what is taking place on the Cocoa Plantations with these children and the Chocolate Industry merely stands by and pretends the information never got to them. There is a change that needs to occur not only from American citizen but citizens all over the world who have compassion for the innocent lives of these children. Children who are looking for the adults to do what is right and not just stand by and watch.

Special teams need to be created to help stop the abuse of these children so that reports can be filled and followed up on not over looked. There should also be progress reports as well as pictures taken to show the changes that have been made as well as the new workers. Workers who are not five years old and working 100 hours a week to get the cocoa bean to America. Criminal suites need to be brought up against those who are involved in criminal activity such as rape, sodomy, child abuse, the purchase of children as slaves. Children who are being used as sex slaves, in sex trafficking, and organ trafficking. People who are involved in such crimes legal actions should be held against them. The Cocoa Plantations and their affiliates of the Chocolate Industry need to have sanctions brought against them for continuing to use under aged children this is a violation of the International Labor Organization Laws, the Convention of the Rights of the Child, and the Convention Laws 183, Convention 182 and Convention 29. Please do not let me forget those who have assisted in supplying the children to these wealth tycoons who fly to Africa or who have these children flown to the states for personal pleasure. Each one should be prosecuted to the full extent of the law.

The suffering of these Children is a Reflection on You

How much more time is needed before the Chocolate industry gets the message that the treatment of these children is not considered as being civilized or humane enough to say they are even trying to be fair. The abuse of five year old children is despicable, distasteful and mortifying to Company or Corporation in their sense of profiting from the blood, sweat and tears these children share within them daily. The Cocoa industries are aware of the corruption but refuse to eradicate the problem after over 14 years now with this year being 2015. Not only are the Cocoa Plantations big money but child trafficking is also part of it. It makes me wonder just how many of the wealthy fly out to Africa just to go out to the Cocoa Plantations and purchase these young girls and boys for a few hours or for a night. I have been drawing mental pictures for you throughout this book I cannot express my heart felt pain to imagine what is being done to these children. There are so many sick minds in this world today. There are so many people with hidden agendas and ill intentions to want to stoop so low as to have forced sex with children. It appears to be alright on the Cocoa Plantations in Africa and Ghana as long as the five year old African boy is being raped or as long as the five year old African girl is being raped. Child trafficking is big business. The exploitation of these helpless children is what several articles speak of and the savage way they are treated. I am aware of the principle of people in high places of which they are the same ones who have control over the situations concerning the chocolate. The very same people we are pleading to in Washington, and the Chocolate Industries and the Cocoa Plantations. The same people in government who pretend to not know what is taking place on the Ivory Coast of Africa and Ghana but sit and smile with your Black American friends and their children. It takes a feeble and sinister minded individual to suppress such hate and continue on with their day as though everything is alright in your world.

The doubled edge sword is a powerful sword it may miss you when the first stroke is coming forward only you forgot one thing. There is a second blade coming and it will not miss your children, or maybe your children's children. With all of the money you have made and have secured within your family for generations to come it is ill gotten and will diminish as it is this very day right before your eyes. With every little boy and girl who cries out with pain because some sick minded pervert with money is able to afford to purchase a child for his or her desire know there is a price to pay and even in your being pleasured. Mark my words God will bring it back to your memory. **There is no way in God given earth this kind of child abuse or child trafficking should even be heard of in the year 2015. Know that you are responsible for what you do and also for what you do not do in helping to bring this nightmare of the Cocoa Plantations to an end.**

Congressman Eliot Engel

Democrat

PICTURE DELETED

Brief Dialogue on Congressman Eliot Lance Engel

Eliot Lance Engel (born February 18, 1947) is the U.S. Representative for New York's 16th congressional district. He is a member of the Democratic Party. In 2013 he became the ranking minority member of the House Foreign Affairs Committee, replacing Howard Berman, who lost his re-election bid in the 2012 elections. Engel was born in the Bronx, the son of Sylvia (nee Bleend) and Philip Engel, an ironworker. His grandparents emigrated from Russia. Eliot grew up in a city housing project Eastchester Gardens and attended New York City public schools. In 1969 he graduated from Hunter-Lehman College with a Bachelor of Arts in history and received a master's degree in Guidance and Counseling in 1973 from Herbert H. Lehman College of the City University of New York. In 1987, he received a law degree from New York Law School. He began his political career in local Democratic clubs. (http://en.wikipedia.org/wiki/Eloit_Engel)

Congressman Eliot Engel, once again a perfect candidate who should have understood even more so the abuse taking place on the Cocoa Plantations with these children and requested immediate action be taken to stop what was going on. Somehow, somewhere the buck was passed, heads were made to turn and nothing was done. When I say the buck was passed I am relating this to a money not a male slave. Yes money was distributed whether you want to accept the truth or not. There are some things you can just look and see in people to want to do right considering where they came from and the struggles they had in getting there. This is like a living nightmare to have to write about and fortunately for me I am not on the other end of the spectrum. With Congressman Engel having the experience in Foreign Affairs and with himself and Senator Harkin being lawyers with their experience and knowledge in politics immediate action should have been taken an investigation should have been pursuant to the allegations of child abuse and sodomy on the Cocoa Plantations. And immediate action concerning the urgency of children being raped and beaten along with the children being under aged the Cocoa Plantations should have been shut down until further investigation could be conducted. But remember I already told you the Chocolate Manufacturers Association had already found these findings of rape, abuse, sodomy and beatings to be true.

The National Confectioners Association

The National Confectioners Association was founded in 1884 in Chicago by representatives of 69 confectionery manufacturing firms. The National Confectioners Association is one of the oldest trade associations in the world. It is currently based in Washington, DC. In 2008 it merged with the Chocolate Manufacturers Association of the USA which is now called the Chocolate Council. The association has 700 members which include domestic and international confectioners. The total number of confectioners in the United States was not given and neither was a number given for those on the internationally level. Once again this is just a clear and concise statement confirming that the United States political leaders are fully aware and in the know of what is taking place with these children on the Cocoa Plantations on the Ivory Coast of Africa and Ghana. The confectioners are the manufacturers and suppliers to the industry. It aims to meet challenges and problems in the confection industry.

The National Confectioners Association (NCA) offers education and leadership in manufacturing, technical research, public relations, retailing practices, government relations, and statistical analysis. The National Confectioners Association (NCA) has an Annual Exposition. It sponsors a yearly exposition of candies, gums and other snack foods at the McCormick Place Convention Center in Chicago, Illinois. Up until the year 2009 the event was called the All Candy Expo. The trade show has hundreds of booths staffed by representatives of dozens of companies debuting their latest creations.

The United States government along with the National Confectioners Association (NCA) should have stepped in years ago to correct this atrocity. It is not beyond the level of simple common sense. In other words if you have not figured it out by now it does not take a rocket scientist to figure this one out, there are a lot of hands in the cookie jar and a lot of mouths being feed. By people looking away from the truth people who are in position to make changes such as Former Senator Thomas Harkin and Congressman Eliot Engel. Since chocolate industries are all over the world this is one horrific situation that will not go over looked any longer. May I reiterate the NCA was founded in 1884? The NCA has an exclusive membership of 700 members designed to meet challenges and problems in the confectioner industry. The United States political leaders should have set in place the second those contracts were signed by Former Senator Thomas Richard "Tom Harkin and Congressman Eliot Engel in September of 2001 to close the doors on the Cocoa Plantations since charges of child abuse had already been validated. We are now in the year 2015 and these children on the Ivory Coast of Africa and Ghana who are working 100 hours a week on the Cocoa Plantations has yet to receive any help. The big question here is where did these politicians lose the knack for their initial reason for wanting to be representatives for the people? Where is the ground pounding taking place now? When you have closed your eyes just because the wrong is being done in another country and there isn't anyone there to witness the wrong and foreign citizens cannot affect your being re-elected to office, where is the humane effort moving forward concerning this matter? Well I have to go back to morals, loyalty, integrity, honesty and a sound conscious mind. From what is taking place on the Cocoa Plantations with an estimated 2 million children so far being counted in slavery on the Ivory Coast of Africa and Ghana in the year 2015? I do believe the United States of America political leaders must be on a euphoric cocoa high and by the way remember the National Confectioners Association in 2008 did move to Washington. There is nothing right about the child abuse taking place with these five year old boys and girls in Africa and Ghana. Something must be done and it must be done expeditiously. American politicians and leaders in other nations have gotten too comfortable with allowing the rapes and abuse of these children, what kind of message is being given to the rest of the world. Is the message being sent **"Eat chocolate while you watch us rape, sodomize, beat, abuse and possibly murder a child, no need to get upset they are only African children, slaves?"**

I am going to assume this is the kind of respect politicians, government officials, and the Chocolate Industry workers give their children when they get home from a hard day at the office. Because if you are not treating your own child like this than why would you allow someone else child to be treated with such humility.

My Statement before CNN Report

Before I get into the report let me state that I do understand that forced child labor is a problem all over the world. There are many countries who are suffering and there are many children being used in forced child labor and I will list them for you. But just keep in mind with all of the abuse taking place with these children the Ivory Coast of Africa and Ghana are still considered to be the worst form of child slavery and forced child labor in the world. The abuse these children have to endure is unimaginable and something needs to be done about it, expediently.

CNN Reports: The Dark Side of Chocolate

By Richard Quest (please read the report in its entirety)

"Before you bite into a chocolate bar or take a sip of hot cocoa, where did it come from? It may be that the treat is the product of someone else's hard labor. The person who may have sold it or who may have made it may not even be an adult."

The ten largest cocoa producing countries are: **the Ivory Coast of Africa and Ghana, Indonesia, Nigeria, Cameroon, Brazil, Ecuador, Mexico, Dominican Republic and Peru.**

The Ivory Coast of Africa and Ghana are the largest of the producers of the cocoa bean which is the main ingredient needed for the production of chocolate. The Ivory Coast of Africa and Ghana are producing nearly 60% of the global cocoa production. Are we failing our children? This is the question needing to be asked, is their life value worth the same as an American child's. Let me balance the scales for you very quickly in case you are in deep thought. An apple is an apple in any part of the world regardless as to what orchard it is grown from. And a child is a child, they are all birthed the same from whatever part of the world they come from. Child abuse is child abuse there isn't any standard level of acceptance that I know of in any part of the world that says it is okay for a man of any age to have intercourse with a little girl or boy five years old. There isn't any law that says if a child is not an America child and is said to be from another country that the child has to endure, rape, sodomy, beatings with bike chains, abuse, child exploitation and child trafficking because the laws to protect them are not being enforced. There are national and international laws in place for these children's protection that are not being adhered to what exactly are these laws in place for if they are not going to protect the citizens they were made to protect. Because there are innocent children involved with 38.9% percent almost 40% percent of these children are being used illegally on the Cocoa Plantations.

I must say the bottom-line to what makes this Cocoa Plantation issue so news worthy is the need for the Chocolate Industry and investors to find another way to sharecrop the cocoa bean another way in order to bring some form of relief to the children who are working and end the abuse taking place. Not only with the way the cocoa seeds are gathered but once a new system is figured out and children are not being abused it will give a new and different meaning to chocolate all over the world. The use of modern equipment such as using the same mobile equipment used to change our street lights here in America, equipment used to trim and cut trees is the same type of equipment needed on the ivory Coast of Africa and Ghana to get the cocoa seeds out of the forty foot high trees these five year old children are climbing. What I am telling you here is there is an easier way to get the cocoa pods out of the trees. This will also minimize 5 year old children from falling out of forty-foot trees to their death. It will also keep them from severely cutting and maiming themselves permanently with the machete they are trained to use to cut the cocoa pods down. It is paramount that other means of support need to be given to assist the Cocoa Plantations in the future. So the responsibility of the work does not fall on helpless five year old little boys and girls.

The Harkin-Engel Protocol is also referred to as the Cocoa Protocol. It is an international agreement aimed at ending the worst forms of child slave labor. According to the International Labor Organization Convention 182 and forced labor (according to the ILO and Convention 29). The purpose of Former Senator Thomas Richard "Tom Harkin and Congressman Eliot Engel combined efforts was to find a workable solution to end such an horrific act of child abuse in coercion with child slavery ever known in both national and international waters. The Protocol was signed in September of 2001. It is a mockery, the United States of America a nation that is so against child exploitation has become a part of the abuse taking place on the Cocoa Plantations. Due to America being the largest producer and manufacturer of chocolate in the world. With American politicians, government officials and the National Confectioners Association have knowledge of these five year old boys and girls being sold into slavery to work on the Cocoa Plantations for the rest of their natural life? The United States cannot deny they do not know what is taking place on the Ivory Coast of Africa and Ghana because the U.S. has a United States Former Senator Thomas Richard "Tom Harkin from Iowa and a United States Congressman Eliot Engel from New York which is who the Cocoa Protocol was named after. The United States is a part of the crimes involving the Cocoa Plantations because of the child abuse taking place, the child slavery and forced child labor of which are all violations of the International Labor Organization Laws. When we look at the legal terminology of it all the United States must comply with the legal term "Guilt by Association" whether the United States wants to admit to knowing what is taking place on the Ivory Coast of Africa and Ghana hasn't any relevance to what has already been admitted by Senator Harkin and Congressman Engel. The United States is considered to be a contributor of all that is taking place due to its involvement with the chocolate industries and Susan Smith is the Senior Vice President of Strategic Communications for the National Confectioners Association (NCA), she is the Executive Director of Chocolate Confectioners and Policy Issues in relations to the chocolate industry. Of which the National Confectioners Association moved their headquarters to Washington, DC in 2008. It's quite fascinating how everything just circulates around Washington, DC with all of the politicians and government officials and the Headquarters of the National Confectioners Association (NCA) all sitting right in Washington and no one has mentioned a word on how stop the illegal use of these children on the Ivory Coast of Africa and Ghana. Neither has anyone stepped in to say the abuse of these 5 year old children must be stopped. Not one soul has spoken up neither has anything traumatic occurred to correct the exploitation of these 2 million children working the Cocoa Plantations. What is even funnier in a facetious way is how the National Confectioners Association moved their headquarters to Washington, DC in 2008 the same year our nation elects its first African American President.

Of Course! Everyone knows that when a wrong is done or being done and the laws are broken and no one steps in to enforce the laws being broken, there is a cover up somewhere and it's usually close by. Anyone who knows someone is breaking the law and does not do anything to correct the wrong being done is just as guilty as the person or persons committing the crime. Although the Harkin-Engel Protocol was signed in 2001 with an agreement to end the suffering of these babies or should I say 5 year old boys and girls. The legal process to initiate the corrections appears to be on a continual delay. I guess you readers should be saying who's at fault for the delay of something being done to give these children some relief? Is the United States at fault? Or is it a combination of all the countries involved in the producing, manufacturing and distribution of chocolate let's just say the Chocolate Industry as a whole? Someone has to take responsibility at some point in time and say enough is enough. Just keep in mind we are talking about trillions of dollars, and a lot of people's pockets getting fat off of the blood, sweat and tears of these children. The bill was signed in 2001 and we are now in 2015 what seems to be the problem in making changes to the Cocoa Plantations to come to the rescue of these helpless children.

It started with the first delay and has only escalated since, more delays by congress and still waiting on a start date to renovate. The delays in pushing the dates up or should I say by not bringing the bill to the floor so the amendment can be heard and given a new start date since it is not heard it causes more delays. I guess congress is saying, let's see how the years of correcting the problems on the Cocoa Plantations can be extended because the longer we extend the more money continues to come in and it just keeps getting better and better.. Renovations were to begin taking place on the Cocoa Plantations in 2001 which was then delayed until 2005. From 2005 to 2008 in 2008 a Joint Declaration, in 2010 extended the commitment to address the forced child labor problem. We are now in 2015 and all these children who are in slavery have are nothing more than broken promises. It remains unclear as to what is going to be done to help these children. If any relief will ever be given to these children at all. I question those who are able to help and I hold my head in disgust, in wonder of all you politicians and government officials, and the National Confectioners Association, senators and congressmen for knowing what is taking place and not doing anything about it. This is a state of emergency concerning these children but you sit twiddling your thumbs because these are not your children and you don't have enough compassion in your heart to do the right thing. When will you consider at some point in your life that these innocent children should have a decent chance at life?

When you think of servitude what surfaces to the brim of your mind? I have to ask, do you know the chances of these children on the Cocoa Plantations ever having the opportunity to have the kind of life style American children have. That is one question that should not take long to answer and neither the senate nor congress should have to take too long in deliberating. They know the odd of those children experiencing what an American child has is too far from their reach. But being a man of God I also have to ask this question is there anything too hard for God? And if so what would be the percentage ratio more than likely less than 1% simply because they will never get the opportunity to be educated in America even though they deserve to be sent to the best of schools to receive the best education for all they have been through. This nation and others have to take the responsibility of what is being done to the lives of these children. I do not wish any harm on anyone but I know that scripture says, (Proverb 15v3) **"The eyes of the Lord are in every place, beholding the evil and the good."** These children have been left out in the cold and forgotten about. They are not given a second thought because they have no voice, no one to speak up for them. I am a believer and I know that God sees all. This is a joint effort for those of you who have a conscious mind to come together to see that these children are given some form of a decent life. A joint effort, a mission for everyone who cares about the safety of children, it's a joint effort because we are dealing with some very wealthy and high powered people. Scripture even tells us to beware of people in high places. Chocolate a trillion dollar industry, produce, manufactures and sells chocolate throughout the world. I would have to be inquisitive and say do you think nothing is being done for these children because of the monies being distributed or because no one really cares; either situation is a little distasteful. Do I need to take a survey on this question or are we in compliance with "Money is King". In all that is taking place on the Cocoa Plantations I have to revert to my biblical understanding my haven of peace which is the Holy Bible and say there is a God. He is the Father of Abraham, Isaac and Jacob and he said in his word, **"And the king shall answer and say unto them, Verily I say unto you, in as much as ye have done it unto one of the least of these my brethren you have done it unto me."**

No one really understands the conditions these children on the Cocoa Plantations are living under. Because of the love and affection we give our children here in America daily. What is happening on the Ivory Coast of Africa is difficult for an American who has a family to phantom, a child having to live under such conditions. It is very difficult to understand the abuse these children are experiencing on a daily basis, every day is a challenge for them. There have been several articles I have reviewed stating these children are being beaten with bike chains, they are being raped and sodomized. These five year old boys and girls are up at the first break of dawn and work until sun down. Let me remind you these are five year old boy and girls I am talking about made to work one hundred hours a week or more. These children are fed corn mush as a meal. Considering the circumstances of which they live they are denied any form of life's enjoyment. I may be a bit biased here but my understanding of what I have researched concerning child slavery on the Cocoa Plantations. These children are denied happiness in any form and are subject to do the work for which they have been purchased to do. They are slaves on the Cocoa Plantations and treated less than the animals that patrol the fields. There isn't any recreation for them. Of course, if they have never heard laughter before how do they laugh? What is the meaning behind their outburst is it an expression of joy or an expression of pain? What are they receptive to when the only things their little ears hear is the snap of a whip or another child crying out in pain. What comfort can their bodies feel when they are marched back to their mud huts which house as many as 18 other boys at the end of the day. The ventilation is so poor that the only form of air that comes into the mud hut is a hole cut in the side of the mud hut about the size of a baseball so they can breathe. As far as birthdays are concerned many of them who were kidnapped or purchased by the plantation owners will never know their birth date and will never have a celebration of such. How do you celebrate your birthday when you haven't any clue as to when you were born? I doubt it if they even know the cycle of days changing through the week, they work without thought and only seek what peace they can have in the midnight hours.

American Children take their Rights for Granted

As I reflect back through the years of my teaching in high school, junior high and elementary schools I can remember talking about the problems on the Ivory Coast of Africa and Ghana as far back as1995. I was talking to the American children about how blessed they are to not have to get up before the crack of dawn and be ready to go to work on the Cocoa Planation. I explained to them how these children are sold as slaves and would have to work on the Cocoa Plantations for the rest of their life. When I think about the situation on the Ivory Coast of Africa it saddens me. The wheels of justice appears to be turning even slower there than the due process of law for Blacks in America. Since time has passed it's almost twenty years later and the wheels of justice are turning even slower and the scales of justice are unequally balanced. American children will never know how the thrash of the slave owners whip feels? They will never know the agony of having to work long hours in the intense heat of the jungle. They will never know at five years old how to swing a machete. A machete that may cause them to inflict personal wounds on themselves or even cut off a hand or a foot with a machete in a five year olds hand anything is possible. There is an even greater possibility of these five year old children falling out of these forty-foot trees to their death. I don't want to forget about their poor hygiene from having to wear the same clothing each day. Not being able to wash and clean themselves properly just keep in mind they have had no one there to teach them how to take care of themselves since they were taken from their parents. They are more than likely wearing the same clothing day after day. These children haven't anything to look forward too, since they do not attend school to receive an education or books to read because they have not been taught there is most certainly not going to be any form of a graduation day for them to look forward too. Who wants to educate a slave are they really worth the time, money and effort? This is how these children are seen by the Cocoa Plantation owners, as nothing more than slaves. They feel it would be a waste of time and money to build schools to educate them or even allow them some form of enjoyment in life. Once again to them every day is a day they have no Monday, Tuesday, Wednesday, Thursday, Friday, Saturday or Sunday every day is just a day how sad. Unfortunately these children will till the land until they are no longer useful to the Cocoa Plantation owner. These children are kidnapped, trafficked and some are purchased for a price. Because the environment they are in is so poor these children are purchased for as much as 250 EU and for as little $14.00. They haven't any self-worth because the area in which they grew up is stricken with poverty. Being sold to the Cocoa Plantation appears to be a way out for many with no apparent future to look forward to. Let me ask you a question, what child do you know who is five years old in America is working one hundred hours a week or more? No need to brain storm there isn't any five year old child in America who you can think of that is working one hundred hours a week. And if an American citizen were to find out such child abuse was taking place child protective services would be called immediately. So why haven't the politicians, government officials and the National Confectioners Association of which all three are designed to correct the wrongs of those they are sworn to protect? How can they allow such malicious intent to take place on the Ivory Coast of Africa and Ghana with 2 million children? 2 million

African children are pretty hard to overlook or say you did not see the abuse occurring when you go out to visit that is impossible to believe. But from what I have read and the research I have reviewed I would say that just maybe these politicians, government officials and National Confectioners Association of 700 members are all walking around with blinders on.

American children are blessed to have a better life. A life many children in other countries only dream of. American children have options in what they want to do; places they want to go and countries they would like to visit. What they want to eat or drink from the refrigerator and how about an allowance for just being good. They are able to get together and go out with their friends meet at McDonald's and enjoy a "Big Mac". Oh! There are more choices how about Burger King (have it your way). Wendy's is a blast (where is the beef). If that doesn't work there is always DQ Dairy Queen, White Castles (watch those sliders). There are so many options for American children to grow up normal and enjoy life with the protection of their parents and laws set up to make sure they have as less stress as possible in their life. But what about the five year old boys and girls who work sun up to sun down on the Cocoa Plantation what friends do they have to visit other than the ones they are locked up with. What variety of meals do they have to look forward to other than corn mush? Do they brush their teeth, change their clothing, are these children given any relief other than being beaten, raped and sodomized by the plantation owners and workers.

Once a child's mind becomes captive their freedom of growth becomes limited. They can only see what they are shown and they can only relate to what they have envisioned before them. Their freedom of thought and expression is not free because it has become imprisoned by the whip, chains and cries of other children, yelling please don't beat me. This is the growth they have embraced concerning their normalcy of life. Their freedom of thought cannot be gratified without environmental change. This would not be any different than a slave taken from his home land as a baby without any memory to recall and asked to describe what their homeland looks like. It will be impossible to do so because the child doesn't have any memory to recall consciously or subconsciously. This is applicable to the children on the Cocoa Plantations because their enjoyment in eating the corn mush is all they know. This is considered to be their variety in life in accordance to what the owner of the plantations have fed them. These children whether sold in to slavery, captured or kidnapped come from very poor areas in South Africa. How does one seek a better life when they are not educated about the arts of life and the rest of the world, they only know one kind of life style, working on the Cocoa Plantations from sun up to sun down? The young girls end up doing domestic work and are taught prostitution at a very young age. It really make me wonder what is the age group for these girls who are being turned into prostitutes, how young are they? Are these children seeking a way out, yes, it is true that some do escape by running away? This is how I am able to write this book from true stories of children who escaped the Cocoa Plantations and were later questioned by journalist who saw the importance of publishing their stories. These children who do not see a better life for themselves nor do they see a way out of the jungles of Africa and the hidden Cocoa Plantations that has consumed their life. I am certain their crying out only cost them more pain. How does a child in pain hide their emotions inwardly without divulging a tear outwardly from the emotional pain he or she is enduring? Yes they hold it in, they do not know what they feel, and they can only express their feelings of what is allowed by the Cocoa Plantation owner for them to express. Their feelings are captured from fear of what will happen to them for not pleasing the Cocoa Plantations owners. Watching other children being beaten with whips and bike chains is mentally challenging to the mind of anyone witnessing such brutality. Many times the beating will leave deep permanent scars on these children sometimes down to the bone. Some are beaten within seconds of losing their life. The abuse is not unheard of concerning what takes place on the Cocoa Plantations. I wonder what happens to the children who are taken out of the area so the rest of the children cannot see and are beaten for running away. Do they ever make it back to the site or are they just beaten to death? What happens to them? Are they ever seen again or are they buried somewhere around the Cocoa Plantation beaten to death for not doing what they were told to do? I will make a wild assumption here and say if kidnapping, forced child labor and little boys and girls prostituting themselves is all legal on the Ivory Coast of Africa then I guess I should also make the assumption that killing a African boy or an African girl is quite the norm on the Cocoa Plantation. There are numbers that go uncalculated concerning what happens to the little boys and girls who try to escape as well as the ones beat to death for not complying. Countless numbers of children's blood is crying out from the ground of the Cocoa Plantation. Only no one has tilled the land in search of these children's bodies because there isn't any record of their ever being there and no search party to alert to consider them missing.

What kind of sick minds are we dealing with? We have the most ingenious minds in the world watching what is taking place with the Cocoa Plantations, nationally and internationally. Once again the bottom-line being is how much more money can be made off of the backs of these children? How much longer before this kind of child abuse will no longer be tolerable? The deaths of these children are unannounced because there isn't any connection to the parents after the child is taken, sold, or kidnapped. What papers are kept to show this child was ever on the Cocoa Plantations and if so are the names correct? The children who volunteer to go to work for a while on the Cocoa Plantations never end up being able to leave. At least not of their own free will, they either escape or they are killed. These five year old children work sun up to sun down under guard and at gun point. They are marched back to their mud huts at the end of their work day and the door is latched with a lock. They are not allowed to leave the mud hut for the rest of the night and a guard is left to make sure no one tries to escape in the midst of the night. The big question here is would a guard with a gun be needed unless someone has intentions of shooting a child trying to escape.

I could possibly be incorrect but I am not doubtful at all concerning children that could have been murdered and questionably buried in the forest area of the Cocoa Plantations. From the research I have done and articles I have read it is said to be at least two million children working on the Cocoa Plantations on the Ivory Coast of Africa and Ghana.

These children are being sold by their parents to work on the Cocoa Plantations but the parents are being tricked into believing that their child will only be gone for a short while. Many of the parents on the Ivory Coast of Africa and Ghana end up never seeing their child again. These Cocoa Plantations owners go to these poor villages making these parents believe they are their demagogues, cleaning up the mess others created. These demagogues were supposedly Christian people who wanted to do right but they did travel with the same guys who captured the slaves, raided and destroyed villages. During the times when the Europeans were going to Africa to capture the weaker tribes and bring them to Europe for slave trading? After all the raiding, raping and pillaging was done in the villages the demagogues were the ones who came in to correct some of the wrong. I have never seen or heard of anything more hypocritical in my life. The Cocoa Plantation owners make the parents believe they are going to give their child a better life, a better education, a better job and money not knowing their child is going to work as a slave for the rest of his or her life and be sexually exploited by being trafficked once they are no longer useful on the Cocoa Plantations. And all this is done for the sake of "chocolate". Let me give you the statistics once again and then you tell me where this is considered to be over reaching or am I being justified through the research I have read and used throughout this book. "West Africa produces 70% of the world's cocoa and 1.8 million children are working there on 2 million cocoa farms. Ten years of broken promises have earned the Cocoa Industry one trillion dollars with only 0.0075% of the profit being used toward the benefit of improving the working conditions on Cocoa Plantations. As of today nothing has changed to an extreme where this book is not needed. What I am saying here is the changes have been so minimal they are not even noticeable. The rapes, abuse, beatings, sodomy and possible murdering of these children are still taking place on the Cocoa Plantations; what renovation are you aware of if any? The children are not receiving any formal education to assist them in changing their life or advancing in some form of intellectual way. They must be given some form of a trade because they are only useful to the Cocoa Plantations up to the age of sixteen. Not knowing how to read or write, add or subtract they are not being taught any formal education where as they might have the opportunity to function as normal citizens outside of the Cocoa Plantations.

It is with great concern and compassion for these children that I must add that after working on the Cocoa Plantation for eleven years of their life and being taught nothing more than how to climb forty-foot trees and swing a machete. What other talent can be noted concerning these young boys and young girls' life? So how are these men who are released able to take care of their primary needs and be able to attain a healthy life and function in a society that requires monies to live? Yet they haven't any skills of being able to function to acquire employment. They are not prepared for the outside world because they are without any education whatsoever; they have neither job nor any other means possible for them to legally obtain food and shelter. They have not been given the basic ADL's to be allowed to function in life; their functioning levels may be closer to those of an eight year old child. What happens to these boys and girls who are now sixteen years old and haven't any life skills to present to anyone in order for them to be able to function as young adults as well as survive. Looking at this in a more holistic way while keeping in mind these boys and girls on the Cocoa Plantations were taken, sold or kidnapped at the age of five years old. They have been on these plantations all of their youthful life and they do not have any form of education. I must conclude with this analysis by interjecting that their functioning capabilities are lesser than or possibly equal to that of a child entering the third grade in elementary school. These children on the Cocoa Plantations are only concerned with surviving the next day. As Charles Darwin's theory would play a part here and that is "Survival of the fittest". This is not Vegas as the old cliché states, "What happens in Vegas stays in Vegas."

When you look at the nature of an animal and how they are driven to perform daily look at it this way: a horse pulls a buggy. A mule pulls a plow, animals being driven to the point of exhaustion. What better way is there to describe what is happening to the children on the Ivory Coast of Africa and Ghana then to put them in the same category as nothing more than housed animals? Please don't misinterpret what I am saying. I am not calling them animals but the treatment they are receiving is in conjunction with how an animal is taken care of by its owner. Just take a minute to look at the way they co-relate. First the animal is thoroughly looked over before it is purchased. Its teeth are checked, his paws are checked, the sex is checked then the animal is purchased. After it is brought home it is kept in a certain area of the house and fed, then it is made to sleep in certain areas of the house or outside of the house. Oh! Let me go back to the feeding part. The animal is not fed the same food as the owner. The animal is usually fed slop, stuff that no one else wants or would even care to sample. In the eyes of those who are guilty of treating these children life animals. They feel whatever they give that animal to eat that because it is an animal it should be happy to eat whatever it gets regardless of whether it tastes good or not. This is no different than the Cocoa Plantation owners purchasing and having to feed these five year old boys and girls corn mush and working them like animals from the crack of dawn to the end of day. I am still trying to figure out what exactly is corn mush?

It sounds more to me like hog slop, or pig's guts (chitterlings), all of the waste from animals the white slave masters would not eat. That is what was given to slaves to eat during slavery on the cotton plantations in America. Once again I must ask the question what is corn mush and what nutritional value does it have in sustaining these children working on the Cocoa Plantations for almost half of their life

I can't begin to imagine the humiliation they are subjected to daily, five year old boys and girls being beaten, raped, sodomized and possibly murdered.

Girls on the Ivory Coast of Africa and Ghana

Well, what about the young girls what is happening to them. Must I continue to elaborate and say the children working the Cocoa Plantations haven't any protection, no father and not mother? These armed guards, men on the Cocoa Plantations are having their way with these young boys and girls. This form of master, slave relationship takes me back to a recently released "Oscar" winning movie "Twelve Years a Slave". It was so real and based on a true story. I could hear the silence at the theatre as I focused on the scenes in the movie. I could see the disgust on some of the faces in the theatre. I must say I was a bit moved to see there were several ethnic backgrounds watching the movie. They finally start trying to figure out why Blacks in America are treated the way are. People mouths dropped open in shocked to see some of the conniving tricks pulled on Blacks during those times. They looked as though they were saying, "I don't believe this. The movie was so compelling that it took me back to other movies. I began to remember movies in the past that were made featuring black actors. Movies we do not see any more such as Roots, Mandingo, and The Color Purple. It made me think about the difficult times when Blacks in America had to fight for every inch of respect they could get. I began to think about books such as Jim Crow, I know Why the Caged Bird Sings, Black like Me, The West and the Rest of Us. I needed to make it even more personal so I thought about my first book, It Still Exists Today; A True Story of Racism in the United States Postal Service/The Story Oklahoma did not Want Told.

A true story about my struggles as a young Black American male in the mid 80's and early 90's due to the racial problem I was suffering from while working for the United States Postal Service. I resigned because of the continued racial harassment and discrimination problems the Oklahoma City Main Post Office was having. I began fighting to get my case against the United States Postal Service filed in the United States Supreme Court (pro se) and succeeded. The case is on file but has never been reopened to this date.

"Twelve Years a Slave" was a reminder to me of how much progress has been made for Blacks in America. It was a reminder as to how far we as a nation of people have not progressed. As I observed the role played by the young lady Lupeta Nyong'O playing the part of (Patsey) and how she was repeatedly raped by the plantation owner and not be able to cry out for help. The audience sighed with disgust. It was painful to watch but it was so evident and so true. Many of the slave girls were taken off of the plantations and repeatedly raped. There is only so much truth you can get into a movie in two hours' time. Should there have been a few sequels to "Twelve Years a Slave"?

In today's society when looking at the United States and the due process of which many African American Blacks are still waiting to occur. Many nationalities do not have a clue and cannot phantom the number of African American young black girls taken off the cotton fields away from their parents and repeatedly raped. Threatened and told if they tell anyone what had happened they will be whipped as close to death as possible. This is what happened in the movie "Twelve Years a Slave" what I am trying to get you to focus on is not in a movie but the reality of what is taking place on the Cocoa Plantations on the Ivory Coast of Africa and Ghana. What about the five year old boys and girls, who are being raped, beaten, sodomized and possibly murdered, what about them? This is not a movie it is reality and it is noted in the many journals and articles I have reviewed to write this book that to this date the Cocoa Plantations are the worst form of child abuse and child slavery in the history of slavery. Journalists that are aware of the abuse of these children on the Ivory Coast of Africa and Ghana are pleading for the mistreatment of these children to stop. It is all quite indescribable, just from my reviews it is enough to make you puke.

I am asking everyone to please open their mind and heart to have compassion on these boys and girls, five year old children working one hundred hours a week to get the cocoa bean to America so Americans can produce and manufacture chocolate. You have seen the movie "Twelve Years a Slave." At this point you should not have to wonder as to what is taking place with these young girls on these Cocoa Plantations on the Ivory Coast of Africa and Ghana and Burkina Fasa etc. Child slavery hasn't any innocence attached to it. Humility is too small of a word to use at this point yet there are those who are still waiting on the due process of law to settle into the conscious minds of what is quite evident of so many wrongs being done to these children on the Cocoa Plantation. There is so much shame attached to this situation on the Cocoa Plantation. Those who are turning the machine of chocolate to make a profit are so lost in the since of their productions and manufacturing techniques they have totally forgotten about their own human dignity. On the opposite side of the spectrum those who have taken over since the original founders have died. Has lost sight of the Chocolate Industry original ideas to share chocolate with the world and they did not intend for the success of the Chocolate Industry to become successful under the pretense of abusing children or have them suffer in any kind of way this was not the dream.

"Belle" Based on a true story

There is also another movie that ties closely in with the problems of African American (Blacks) in America. This movie is also based on a true story titled "Belle". It is truly a must have for everyone's movie library. It exemplifies the struggle of African American Blacks all over the world, not just in America. It depicted the hatred which exudes out of the hearts of those who hated slaves just because of the color of their skin. And did not acknowledge the fact of slaves being men, women and children but classified them as cargo. As defined in the Webster Dictionary (**CARGO**) "goods carried on a ship, aircraft, or motor vehicle." This is what the slaves were considered to be cargo, goods carried on a ship in the movie "Belle". "Belle" brought out the truth of how slaves were murdered in during the Middle Passage. What many people are not aware of is there were one hundred million slaves that were murdered and some died from sickness and were thrown overboard during the Middle Passage. For the purpose of broadening the readers understanding of just how far the hatred flowed I could not leave out the true story called the Zong Massacre remember the movie is titled "Belle". Not only can African American (Blacks) learn of their royal heritage but Whites as well can learn just how deep the blood of African slaves has mingled with the royal blue bloodline of England.

The Zong Massacre was a case built on insurance fraud. The cargo because it was not considered to be human was thrown overboard. The cargo was 132-142 slaves handcuffed together and thrown into the sea. The case was based on insurance money the ship's captain wanted for the so-called cargo of slaves he threw overboard. The case was built on the cargo being thrown overboard not humans but cargo handcuffed together. The insurance company was not forced to pay for the diseased cargo. The Zong Massacre was a landmark case of which it would soon change part of the course of history of how slaves would be considered. Although the cargo (slaves) did get sick it was determined that the ship's captain and crew were negligent because the Zong did not stop at any ports to restore the ships needed water supply. The cargos death was noted as being intentional because they passed by eight ports without replenishing the water supply thereby causing the cargo (slaves) to get sick. And since they became diseased the cargo (slaves) were handcuffed together and thrown overboard. The captain and crew were given the blame of contributory negligence for the lack of not giving their cargo proper nourishment. The cargo's health began to diminish from being malnourished. Since the 132 or 142 slaves were being seen as cargo and the case concerning the insurers wanting to be paid for diseased cargo was ruled in favor of the insurance company. Due to the decision rendered in favor of the insurance company slaves could no longer be called cargo therefore changing history and for the first time slaves were considered to be human, not animals or cargo.

In the case of (Gregson v Gilbert 1783) 3Doug KB 232) held that in some circumstances, the deliberate killing of slaves was legal and that insurers could be required to pay for the slaves deaths. The judge, Lord Chief Justice the Earl of Mansfield, ruled against the syndicate owners in this case, due to new evidence being introduced suggesting the captain and crew were at fault. A freed slave named Olaudah Equiano brought news of the massacre to the attention of the antislavery campaigner Granville Sharp. Mr. Sharp was unsuccessful in getting the ship's crew that had handcuffed the 132 or 142 slaves together and threw them overboard. This was literally nothing more than cold blooded murder. The way the ruling came out was that the insurers did not have to pay the insured. The murder concerning the 132 or 142 slaves did not matter they were just concerned of the matter of getting the insurance company to pay. The lives that were taken and thrown overboard never did spark an issue serious enough to fight for. This became obvious to me when I noticed the number that was thrown overboard varied from 132 to 142. It was really not important as to how many slaves were murdered but was important in the Zong Massacre was if the insurance company or the insured were wrong. The cargo at this point did not count because cargo is considered to be a perishable or nonperishable status. Therefore by the slaves being considered to be cargo they were not considered to have had any value of what would be valued life.

This case is so reflective of today's situation of what is taking place on the Cocoa Plantations on the Ivory Coast of Africa and Ghana with the raping, sodomizing, beating, sex trafficking and organ trafficking of five year old boys and girls organs including murder and nothing is being done to enforce the laws being broken. Could it be because these children are not seen as human but as property? I have been saying this throughout the book. Between cargo, and property when human life is taken it is considered under the law to be murder. The case of the Zong Massacre explains the value of life with slaves being classified as cargo, and when explained under the law cargo hasn't any life. Which isn't any different than a child five years old working 100 hours a week on the Cocoa Plantations because they are not considered to be human but animals? These five year old children's lives haven't any value other than the work they are able to produce. The legalities of having the freedom to kill slaves without a reasonable cause were abolished in 1783. Prior to (Gregson v Gilbert 1783) before the case was made into law. If a white person wanted to murder a slave for no apparent reason they could murder a slave and nothing would be done. What is taking place on the Cocoa Plantations today is similar to what was taking place prior to 1783, killing innocent children at will. The purchasing and slave trading of children in accordance with the International Labor Organization, Convention on the Rights of the Child and Convention 138, 182 and 29 entitles these children it have the rights of States Parties and International laws to reprimand those in violation. It is even sadder that not only in Africa but I the United States of America that many whites in the "Free World" feel it is okay to murder African American (Blacks) in America. The law "Stand Your Ground" is nothing more than the case of (Gregson v Gilbert 1873) over turned and reversed so it would be okay once again for a white to walk up to a black person or should I say his piece of property cargo I might add and murder him or her at will. This attitude of murdering blacks in America today is running ramped throughout the United States. So many unresolved murders committed by Caucasian people and Caucasian police officer have gone unresolved. And they have been let go on a basic technicality that it was merely a Caucasian person killing an African American. The bottom line of what it all appears to be is, whose life had the most value? With all that has been said to try to keep the peace between this ongoing feud of the White race against the Black race and vice versa. Once again caught on tape more racial problems, this time at a major university in Oklahoma young Caucasians males using the n... word as though it was just another form of expression for them? What value is there really on an African Americans life in America? Their bitterness is so deeply rooted and harbored in the emptiness of their souls that I am certain it will take an act of God to change the value of their thinking and read their own words in the inscription of "Lady Liberty" it reads "Freedom and Justice for all.

Sigma Alpha Epsilon Fraternity of Oklahoma University

The final straw that broke the camel's back concerning these murders taking place across the United States against African America (Blacks). And the violent out breaks throughout the United States of America I feel took place in the state of Oklahoma. This is a clear massage of how young Caucasian males have a lack of respect for African American (Blacks) in America. Are Oklahoma parents the blame? When we look at racism in the world we all know it is a learned behavior passed down from generation to generation taught to these Caucasian children by their parents through the years. White males attending Oklahoma University, students belonging to the Sigma Alpha Epsilon fraternity would feel so free and without fear of being so open to use the word "nigger" several times on a public bus ride without any fear of repercussion. At Oklahoma University Sigma Alpha Epsilon students were singing a chant song on a bus ride back it wasn't a normal fraternity chant it was a chant that repeatedly mentions the word "nigger." Part of the song "There will never be another N....ger President or SAE, You can hang him from a tree etc." No one is certain as to what the words being spoken but freedom of speech in America is just what it is freedom to say what you feel to be correct at least that is what most people presume. Fortunately freedom of speech does have some limitations if you are causing someone a form of pain Since the Washington Post stated "Though the words are not all intelligible" meaning they cannot figure out what is being said could it be geared toward the President of the United States at least that is what it sounded like to me. Remember President Obama was pictured in many detestable positions and one of those positions was him hanging from a tree.

The controversy concerning Oklahoma University seems to be the wording involved in what was being said and who it was being said to or about. The one word that is not controversial is the word "nigger" which was verbally expressed more than a few times by the **SIGMA ALPHA EPSILON** FRATERNITY. Since some papers like the Washington Post could not determine what to make of the words being song. I do recall several incidents where President Obama was used as an effigy and being hung from a tree of which much of this did come from the Southern States. There are several outbursts who openly expressed themselves on how they wanted to hang President Obama from a tree. The song the Sigma Alpha Epsilon's were singing has a very strong probability in relations to past expressions: In case you may have forgotten you can go on line and find these listings with the photos for support.

October 31, 2008, Two Arrested for hanging an effigy of Barrack Obama from a tree.

September 20, 2012 called the, Empty Chair "Lynched" by Anti Obama Texas republican Bud Johnson.

November 3, 2012 North Carolina shows effigy of President Obama hanging from a tree at shell Gasoline Station.

November 6, 2012 Houston Texas another effigy of President Obama hanging from Shell Gasoline Station

There is only so much of a mistake that can be made and this is the kind of incident of which college students being involved. For those of us who believe in freedom equality and justice for all. It is important that this kind of behavior is brought to its knees of pity because this kind of behavior cannot be tolerate in the workforce of America or with those who will one day possibly lead this nation in the position of President of the United States.

The openness and lack of guilt feelings exhibited on the bus ride by the Sigma Alpha Epsilon fraternity attending Oklahoma University for what took place March 9, 2015. Is a perfect example of why hatred is vastly growing in the United States of America? Here is a quick lesson for the Bible belt state of Oklahoma the Holy Bible says, "To train up a child." If this is the kind of hatred is what you are teaching your children a lot is already explained as to why racial violence continues to keep reoccurring. It also shows the lack of concern of the young white males who hadn't exhibited any remorse whatsoever in expressing their hatred and outlandish behavior. The unveiling of hatred before the world in one of the premier universities in the State of Oklahoma should make everyone wonder if it is something being taught in their fraternity house on campus at Oklahoma University. Or was it something they practiced during family night at home with their parents? Young male adults learning the ways of old, they are already practicing how to hate African American (Blacks) in America. There is not a whole lot left to be said after the video tape was released. **"Sigma Alpha Epsilon national headquarters has closed its Oklahoma Kappa chapter at the University of Oklahoma following the discovery of an inappropriate video."** www.washingtonpost. com/news/morning-mix/wp/2015/03/09/university-of-oklahoma

Daily Prayers for Good Old Oklahoma

Below you will find my original work, several captions of the Daily Word of which I send out to give comfort through scripture to those who are hungry for the word of God and seek to hear the truth daily. I also like to keep those who like to be informed up to date as to what is taking place concerning world issues. God said to watch and pray. The sermons below relate to the incident which took place on Oklahoma University involving the **Sigma Alpha Epsilon fraternity (SAE)** caught using the n.... word. The boys were asked to leave Oklahoma University.

Will They Ever Learn

Part 1 "A Reflection of the Past" Oklahoma Scandal (SAE)4

Unfortunately we live in a nation where some Whites still fight to overcome their hatred toward Blacks. A hatred that runs so deep Whites want to see African American (Blacks) killed, massively incarcerated, without employment and unable to take care of their family. How can White parents in Oklahoma pray in church but practice hatred in their homes by teaching their children to hate Blacks, You hypocrite?

The hatred I mentioned earlier is the same hatred passed down from generation. A hatred taught by older Whites in Southern States in order to attempt to control the upward progress of African American (Blacks).

What's even more trivial is these old Southern tactics of hatred are still being psychologically imposed in their children's mind today. The situation of Oklahoma University fraternal chapter (SAE) on campus blurted out their hatred not just toward (African-American (Blacks) but toward the President of the United States. The Oklahoma University (SAE Fraternity) where caught on tape singing "There will never be another nigger President (SAE)".

The State of Oklahoma is part of the Bible belt. Which god are they serving?

I wonder what kind of training is going on inside of these white parents' home in Oklahoma. This was not just something these young adults came up with. It was something they were inspired at home with their Father and Mother leading the way.

Hatred, not the Holy Bible is being taught in the homes of these children. Caught on tape proudly singing about the President being a nigger was a small portion of what really takes place. I now wonder if there is a hidden Klu Klux Klan fraternity on Oklahoma University campus. Oklahoma has never lived down the murdering of African American (Blacks) during the Tulsa Oklahoma Riot.

I am Elder Christian in Jesus name.

We wondered in the wilderness for 40 years to get rid of sick minds such as this. Shame on your parents

Copyrights Elder R. Christian all rights reserved ©

"Big Oklahoma Scandal"

Looking at the state of Oklahoma that appears to be religious and sound as I did my research to listen to the words used by the Sigma Alpha Epsilon fraternity at Oklahoma University. The question that has risen is what was said of which the Washington Post stated the words could not be made out to be clear concerning what nigger they would hang. Their choices of words are detestable and scrupulous.

It is obvious the state of Oklahoma did not care for President Obama since he has been in office. It is a fact when President Obama went to visit Oklahoma the Governor and Mayor just happened to be out on other business...really?

It is a noted fact Oklahoma is an advocate RED STATE (Republican) to the core. I am not shocked with the racial connotations used by the Sigma Alpha Epsilon fraternity in relations to the word hanging a nigger nothing would make them happier.

Keep in mind America these are young adults involved with this SAE Fraternity. Some of these young men will probably run for public office someday, be in charge of a business or corporation. Of which they may have to employ African Americans. This terminology nigger which is a racial slur should not be coming out of anyone's mouth. Let alone racial connotations from a group of young men in the state of Oklahoma which is a part of the Bible belt at a major University, Oklahoma University.

What is being taught in their fraternal meetings? What are the requirements to join? What did their parents teach them before they left home to move on campus? It's all being uncovered. I wonder what they call their football players and their basketball players.

I am Elder Christian in Jesus name.

It's obvious their hatred toward African Americans is deeply rooted. Are their parents teaching this at home? I ask this question because their boys look so relaxed on the video using the word nigger. I will end with you all need prayer

Copyrights Elder R. Christian all rights reserved ©

Sigma Alpha Epsilon Fraternity (SAE)
Just When you Thought it was, Over

Without a doubt Oklahoma University (SAE) students were being videotaped exposing to the world their liberal freedom of not having a problem at all using the word nigger. I was not surprised because these young future leaders of America are being taught to carry the torch of racism in America by their parents. A bloodline of racial hatred that runs deep in the veins of these young men's nourished hate.

I did say young future leaders of America because that's why people go to college. To some day be given an opportunity to lead, to bring about positive change, to progressively move America forward and to learn to become professionals and to do away with antics such as: name calling, bigotry, hatred, and defaming the character of the African American race.

The State of Oklahoma and Oklahoma University must be right proud of their boys. Their parents are right proud.

This may occur in their hooded meetings the older white men whisper to the young white boys and say, "don't worry about it your in Oklahoma nothing is going to happen to you here. We feel the same way. Just let it quiet down for a while and next time add a few more niggers to your song but just don't get caught. Next time keep your hoods on so they don't recognize you. We sit in high positions throughout the world, politicians, government, corporation owners, businessmen and business women. We are proud of you boys and we are going to stick with you.,

The one issue that has not been brought up is the Sorority the sisters to the Sigma Alpha Epsilon fraternity. What kind of songs are they singing and where are they getting their training tactics from. There are so many African American men set up on false rape charges and have done 10 to 15 years in prison for being falsely accused of rape. Is this what Oklahoma promotes.

I am Elder Christian in Jesus name.

SAE women speak up pull those hoods off

Who are the SAE at Oklahoma University referring to as another nigger (SAE) president

Copyrights Elder R. Christian all rights reserved ©

"It's Easy to Harbor Hatred"

It has been proven throughout history as well as through theorists of scientific research that people can be trained. Or should I say be lead in a direction without knowing where they are headed or why they are being lead there innocent children.

When I look at the United States of America the outline of its foundation has become the layout of a blueprint. Which only gets uglier as its foundation is being laid. The Sigma Alpha Epsilon fraternity (SAE) is a fraternity for young adults. Young adults who openly blurted out nigger without compassion and did not have any concern of being reprimanded for their behavior? Since we know hatred is a taught behavior that starts from home we also have to look at the source of its beginning, the (SAE) parents.

The hate is so deeply rooted that what these children are being taught by their parents remains to be the cause, of why America is so divided. Remember Pavlov's "Conditioning Theory" in his experiment he uses dogs "to prove a "response to a stimulus".

In these parents homes that teach their children hate niggers. They use rewards of toys, money, cars, video games etc. To teach their children to hate, a nation divided with racial hatred being taught in homes by parents who have a deeply rooted hatred against Blacks. Red States such as Oklahoma says niggers know their place it sad to say but the proof has been exposed now your children are saying the same things. Practicing what their parents taught them.

I am Elder Christian in Jesus name.

Did the Southern Red States really lose the Civil War on slavery? Or was the United States of America simply divided?

I wonder what kind of God fearing Christian's parents sit in church on Sunday and teach their children this kind of hate. Be careful who you sit next to while attending service in Oklahoma. They had a few cross burnings when I was there

A Heavy Price for an Unwarranted Behavior

"Penalties for Disobedience"

After watching all of the controversial happenings taking place in the state of Oklahoma for the past few days there's a hidden hatred beginning to be unveiled of which is reflective of the entire state. It is a strong hatred of which white parents have taught their white children how to hate and practice hatred against African American (Blacks) in America.

I say this openly because I once lived there. I experienced their racial hatred for seven years of my life. When you have time please read my true story "It Still Exist Today a True Story of Racism in the United States Postal Service". In the book I stated those who practiced racial tactics against me are forgiven. Twenty one cases of EEOC's were filed in a period of 6 years. I resigned after turning in a five page letter of resignation in 1992. This case now sits on file in the United States Supreme Court. The woman I loved and would soon marry later died from a brain aneurysm. What's so amazing about people in Oklahoma is how they pretend to love God.

The incident that occurred at Oklahoma University is being kept quiet. There is a hatred harbored in the hearts Oklahoman's a Red State filled with a disguised hatred. My God look at what's coming out of their children's mouths.

A rooted hate that runs deep, There have been African Americans walked off their jobs with 20 years of service to company's before they can get their pensions. There have been African Americans told with college degrees in Oklahoma told by company's "we will hire you but you won't get paid anything hire than this amount." While white owned companies in Oklahoma bring in their non-degreed Caucasian workers and place them in positions and higher paying salaries over the degreed Africa America workers.

God is fed up with the cover-up in Oklahoma. What the parents in Oklahoma are teaching their children is being unveiled for the world to see. Are the college students at Oklahoma University at fault?

I am Elder Christian in Jesus name.

It does not take a rocket scientist to figure this one out Oklahoma. Prayer is the key

Unclothed Before the World

"God Has Suffered It So"

What exactly do you see when you walk through the Malls shopping going in the same stores together? What do you see when you go to hospitals and see African American Doctors treating your White fathers and mothers? Or when your son receives his big break and a African American gave it to him?

How did you feel Oklahoma when President Obama the first African American (Black) United States President came to the state of Oklahoma? After losing every city and county of your Red State in the election after the natural disaster hit Oklahoma?

The first time President Obama went to Oklahoma the Governor conveniently left the state and did not want to meet with President Obama. When the disaster hit President Obama returned to Oklahoma and assured them funding and assistance. Oklahoma turned down over 50 million dollars from President Obama's Health Care Program. This is a state that is slowly being revealed to the world racism uncovered in the raw.

The world can see the depth of your valleys of racial hatred? The powers of darkness circumference your state, Oklahoma, and the stench of your hatred can be smelled for hundreds of miles. Unfortunately Christian Whites who live there and want change. Covering up the truth makes matters worse and not enforcing the law only delays positive change.

There is an old saying, "apples don't fall from the tree." The Holy Bible says, "You will know the tree by the fruit it bears." Parents in Oklahoma teaching their children racial hatred is uncovered. A racial hatred that has hung, boiled, tarred and feathered and skinned blacks alive will be open in the books on Judgment Day. Parents of

(SAE) students at Oklahoma University are responsible for the racial filth that came out of your children's mouths March 9, 2015.

I am Elder Christian in Jesus name.

Why do this to your children, Oklahoma why. The cycle will repeat itself until you get it righteous

Copyrights Elder R. Christian all rights reserved ©

"They Sneak and Hide Themselves"

Because our Father in heaven is a God of Love, Hope, Faith and Charity, Christians do not hide or try to trick people into serving God.

Those of you in the Red States, who are mostly on the southern boarders of the United States, serve your god of hate. Passing the torch of racial hatred off to your children to practice in hopes that one day the old south will rise again.

The Sigma Alpha Epsilon fraternity at Oklahoma University was a small layer of racial skin peeled back for the world to see. It was a portion served to the world that needed to be uncovered. Racial insensitivity in the South has become an open market.

Parents are teaching their children racial hatred. Parents who sit in some of the most prominent positions in Oklahoma are still having their private meetings.

True story: The passing of my grandmother in 1987 I headed south out of Oklahoma to the funeral. About an hour into my drive I was passing through a small town in Oklahoma. I looked to my right and there they were the Klu Klux Klan with torches burning in their white hoods and covering, going into the forest. That memory will stay with me forever.

We don't know the pledges being made to recruit. We see parents of the (SAE) boys but what about the girls they are being recruited as well. Policemen are killing unarmed young African American boys without a cause.

How deep does the KKK go just keep in mind they all do not wear hoods. Look inside the prison walls and see their hate, go to the corporations and companies and see the hate their lack of employment of Blacks, go to the Juvenile Detention Centers and see their hate. Yes they put our children in the system early.

I am Elder Christian in Jesus name.

When you think you have it all figured out God will peel back another layer

Copyrights Elder R. Christian all rights reserved ©

Once again when you begin to talk about freedoms concerning the right to be considered a human being you have to refer to (Gregson v Gilbert 1783) prior to this case in some instances it was legal to kill a slave at will. At the ruling of this case a slave was once considered to be cargo was now considered to be a human being, and now classified as a slave.

Which leads me back to the Cocoa Plantations since these children aren't considered to be human they would be labeled as property. And those of you on the Cocoa Plantations who are in charge and having your way with these children have forgotten that even your laws states they are not considered property but are to be protected and given a proper childhood in order that they may become more productive individuals in the future.

Without Excuse

Because I am an Elder I enjoy employing scripture to my books because it leaves the reader or the guilty party with no place to go. Remember for those of you who believe in God he said in his word he is the same today yesterday and forevermore. For those of you who are just reading for your own review to find out what is being said in this book. You're a politician, government official, an executive in the chocolate industry or a member of the National Confectioners Association in Washington, DC. I am saying not only are you all guilty by association but since you all have made a profit off of the backs and blood of these children the word of God says you are without excuse. **Romans 1v18-20: For the wrath of God is revealed from heaven against all ungodliness and unrighteousness of men, who hold the truth in unrighteousness; (19) Because that which may be known of God is manifest in them; for God hath shewed it unto them. (20) for the invisible things of him from the creation of the world are clearly seen, being understood by the things that are made, even his eternal power and Godhead; so that they are without excuse."**

The Cocoa Plantations has become the world's hidden nightmare. Intentionally kept in the dark because of the embarrassment it would bring to all of the executives, government officials and politicians involved I am certain they all have African America friends, girlfriends; some of them even have African America children and wives. I am certain you will hear all of the excuses such as: Oh by the way (I was not aware of this) that excuse is not going to work, or (I am sorry but we did not know) that excuse will not be acceptable. Especially when there have been meetings with Former Senator Thomas Richard "Tom Harkin and Congressman Eliot Engel, powerful men and women in Washington, DC who have made the nation aware by creating a bill called the Harkin-Engel Protocol. It is not just the United States of America but many nations are involved and responsible for the wrong they have done to these children. For taking these five year old children life from them by making them slaves, for allowing these children to be abused, trafficked and worked like animals. These children are being victimized and their innocence is being violated in the face of the world and nothing is being done about it. When we as Americans began to take others and their freedoms for granted than we have lost our value and respect of all mankind and have fallen submissive to what other countries would like to invoke on the freedoms of all Americans. This is why we fight so hard for our freedoms in the "Free World". So why does America remain so distant and stagnated in limbo and unwilling to help these helpless children who do not know how to cry out for help. Our laws here in America have a zero tolerance level when it comes to the abuse of children. We even have cruelty to animal's laws. It has been stated in almost every article I have read about the Cocoa Plantations that it is the worst form of child slavery and child abuse in the world. A baby, a child, a dog cannot be left alone in a car for one minute in America unless the owner or parent driving the car will be arrested for child abandonment or cruelty to animals. But a five year old child working on the Cocoa Plantations can be beat, raped, sodomized and murdered and nothing is done about it. Oh I must not be facetious, I must apologize something is being done about the abuse of these children? Since the bill was signed in 2001 the United States is supposed to step in to get these changes started in the year 2020. Did you get the joke yet? The politicians, government officials, National Confectioners Association just want to give the rapist, sodomizers, child abusers and murderers another nineteen years to cover up their mess before something is done. They haven't anywhere to run or hide they are all uncovered and... Without Excuse

The true story "Twelve Years a Slave" reopened many doors that people today would have liked to remain closed. It was a mind refresher to those who thought they had gotten away. A reminder of some of the humiliation Blacks in America had suffered. Blacks in America had to deal with the brutality of being treated less than human and at the same time deal with a double standard justice system. One that actually says equality and justice for all, it just forgot to add depending on your color. What's even worse are the hidden secrets that will never be told on the Cocoa Plantations of how these children are tricked and kidnapped taken from their parents' home to serve a life of slavery on the Cocoa Plantations never to be seen by their parents again. Now that you have seen the true story at the movies "Twelve Years a Slave" and watched the part Chwetel, Ejiofer played, a free man being tricked by whites kidnapped and sold into slavery. The same issues are taking place on the Ivory Coast of Africa and Ghana. A Black man walking around in America today reaps with such likenesses of the very same country of which our ancestors were taken from. The fear of being kidnapped and taken to a remote place no one knows of and put in bondage just because of the color of his skin. A Black child not only in Africa but in America is taught at a young age to run as fast as he can at night when whites are after him. It is not a myth to be ashamed of but the truth is that so many Blacks live in fear of being beaten up in alleys, framed for robberies, rapes and murders they did not commit, is this really taking place in America. Well don't hold your breath, I will put the answer to this question in all capital letters, YES, it is happening in America. So I say "Run, Run Little Black Boy Run. The movie "Twelve Years a Slave" prompted me to write this prose in respect to all Blacks in America and throughout the world. To every child, boy and girl on the Ivory Coast of Africa and Ghana know that you have not done anything wrong. You are innocent souls searching for some relief but understanding that if you get caught whether you did the crime or not the consequence you are going to suffer will be almost impossible to bear. To this day February 5, 2015 crimes committed against African American Blacks are unheard of or at least supposed to be. In America we have a young seventeen year old African American male by the name of Trayvon Martin murdered in cold blood by George Zimmerman a self-appointed neighborhood watchman, freed on a technicality. In America we have another teenager murdered, African American male, Michael Brown shot to death by police officer (Darren Wilson) with his hands in the air surrendering on video, freed on a technicality. In America an African American male, Tamir Rice twelve years old shot to death by Tim Loehmann a police officer for waiving a toy gun on the sidewalk, the officer was a rookie cop and was said to have not been trained properly. In America Jordan Davis teenage African American male shot to death by Michael Dunn a white male for playing his music to loud in the back seat of a car. There are so many more murders and false arrest taking place with African American Black men in America that I could write another ten pages just on the list itself. I will stop with the murder of Eric Garner. In America, Eric Garner was put in an illegal choke hold by police officer Daniel Pantaleo. After yelling out eleven times "I Can't Breath" Eric Garner was choked to death.

Don't feel bad when you read the prose I have written titled "Run, Run Little Black Boy Run" it should put you into a reality of what is real in America. I don't need to say it but to make sure everyone is on the same page, racism. Where the crimes against the African America Black men I listed above racially motivate. The truth of this matter is may I question, what is an accidental death? Although we live in the same America the rules of life and law has a tendency to change if you are not of the white persuasion. African American citizen's civil rights are being violated without thought. You would think it was 1853 and slaves had not been emancipated just yet. Many times back in those does of owning slaves White folks gave picnics and their grand finale was to pick any African America they wanted to hang and hang him or her for as little as spitting on the streets. Unfortunately for Blacks in America, Whites have a tendency to keep forgetting African Americans were emancipated in 1862. Africa American males are able to go to war and defend the same Constitution of the United States only to return home to a country prepared to give them the death sentence.

So in order to protect what little freedoms African American Blacks have in America I say, Run little Black boy run, is there somebody after you?

The prose below "Run, Run Little Black Boy Run" is to be read in the old Negro slang when words were enunciated the way people heard them. With great respect to Langston Hughes and William E.B. Dubois, Nikki Giovanni, Dr. Maya Angelou, Dr. Margaret T. Burroughs founder of the first African American History Museum in the history of the world. My hat is off to all of you who have put forth the effort and have run the race. It is because of your writings and the legacy you have left behind that others are able to understand the struggle of the African America Black man in America and the African American Black woman in America. Although both the Black man and the Black woman are intentionally divided there is a larger variable of understanding concerning the feelings of one another, the hurt, the cries, the pain, the laughter, the dancing spirit of life and entertainment? There is an unmentioned look of understanding, an alertness of interest and a vast volume of love when it comes to the soul of both the African American Black man and woman; there is an expression of piety, a connection of oneness with God Almighty that cannot be torn down. Although both souls long to be united the division is carefully maintained through the use of manipulation and environmental control. Even with a dividing spear even though our souls cannot touch we see the difference in our walk, our cloths, our hair styles our reason for being who we are so without further delay I present to you my prose:

Run, Run, Little Black Boy Run

No One Ever Saw Him...Alive Again

His eyes were bucked open and you
could see the fear on his face;
His mother yelled out what did ya do boy! What did you do?
He said mama I've got to leave home I've got to run;
They'll be acomin to get me before the day
is done, so I have to go, I got to run.
Run, Run Little Black Boy Run, we gonna chase ya for a while;
We got the noose out of the barn and the hound dog's acomin;
We can hear the twigs abreakin so ya better keepa runin;
Run, Run Little Black Boy, Run you won't
make it home by the crack of dawn;
My dog is gonna track ya until the mornin sun.
We dun went through rivers and swamp land too;
We won't give up we paid a fine price for you so you better run;
And don't ya get tired you little gigaboo?
I have the noose in my hand so I know ya better run;
Run, Run Little Black Boy Run;
You know when we catch ya we gonna have some fun;
Run, Run Little Black Boy Run;
When we catch ya we're gonna beat ya,
whip ya and listen to ya scream;
What were you doing with Sally Sue by the stream?
I saw your pants down and she was naked too;

I told you before our white women are off limits to you;
When we catchya, you better fight you're very best;
Remember you are out here alone no one
can hearya in the wilderness;
And no one will ever find where we will put your body to rest?
When they ask did we find you we will never confess;
So Run, Run Little Black Boy Run;
Before we string ya up to that old oak tree;
We gonna gouge out your eyes so you will never see;
So, Run, Run Little Black Boy Run, run away from me;
We gonna cut off your testicles and your penis you see;
Because of that white girl we gonna hang ya from a tree;
We gonna listen for ya neck to snap and
watch you shake for a while;
When I catch up to ya this is what I'm gonna do;
Shall I hang ya first or boil ya in oil.or just
skin ya alive for trying to flee;
I'll tell ya what, we'll just do all three, and
then I'll take ya out of ya misery;
The hound dog's acomin, don't ya get
tired I've pulled out my blade;
By the way my runaway slaves, they're
all buried in unmarked graves;
Can't ya hear the hound dogs and old Blue acomin;
Don't you give up you better keep on arunin;
Run, Run, Little Black Boy Run.

Written by Author/Hall of Fame Poet
Raymond C. Christian

The prose below "God Can Hear My Voice" is dedicated to every mother and father who never got the opportunity to see their son or daughter again. To every mother whose daughter was taken off and repeatedly raped it is a testimony of what we as Blacks in America have been able to overcome because the wheels of justice are not balanced. Ungodly spirits filled with bitter hate is a reflection of the murdering of our children without cause knowing that justice will not be fair but still the scales of justice are supposed to balance equally. To every unmarked grave, to every oak tree that held an innocent body on a noose. To every runaway slave that was captured and had his foot shopped off. To every slave who was castrated and never bore children? To ever slave that fathered white babies and the babies were murdered at birth. To every free man who was put back into slavery. For those who escaped and those who lived their life fighting to be freed. For those who never made it back to freedom and left families and friends wonder what happened many, many, years ago and still talk about them today. This prose I pray helps those who have lost loved ones and still suffer with an indefinite emptiness of not knowing what has happened to them. Although some changes for the better has taken place in America. The fight for a better America still remains constant in our hearts and you have not been forgotten. In memory of all those who were never seen again.

This prose I have written "God Can Hear My Voice" goes out to every little boy and girl, who was taken, sold or kidnapped on the Ivory Coast of Africa and Ghana. To every little one who was raped, beaten, sodomized, or murdered. To every child that seemingly vanished off of the Cocoa Plantations. To every little boy or girl who were unaware of the suffering they were going to have to endure and to every child, young man and young woman who are currently being used in sex trafficking, I say to the world hear my voice, hear my voice. My prayers are that the words in this book do not fall on death ears. My prayers are in knowing that "the eyes of the Lord are in every place". Hear my voice, Father God, hear my voice.

They Never Knew You Lord

Hear the voice of your children father God crying out from the wilderness. These children were taken before their time to know that they have a father in heaven powerful enough to change any situation that needs to be changed. I know the kings shall bow at thy feet father God along with all icons and idols. Where can they go to hide from you Father God when there is no such place? Why would the politicians, government officials and National Confectioners Association feel they are being justified by the wrong being done on the Cocoa Plantations with these children? What have these five year old boys and girls done to deserve such a judgment of slavery at birth? Their slayers show no morality, no compassion, no empathy or sympathy for the wrong being done to these children. They are hiding behind their deep cluttered thoughts of personal gain; personal wealth and they have an unwillingness to show compassion. They say with their tongue they believe in you Father God. But they praise themselves and glorify the beasts they serve and they do not ask forgiveness. Who is mightier than you Father God? Who is able to stand up to thy raft and overcome thy anger when you have not ordained it to be so? Children are suffering Father God and their destruction lies in the fate of those who rule over them. Touch their heart dear God in order that they may receive a better way of life for these helpless children on the Ivory Coast of Africa and Ghana. These particular areas in Africa are known to have the worst forms of slavery and child abuse in the history of the world. Let the founders of the Chocolate Industries; let the politicians, government officials, and the National Confectioners Association know this kind of behavior of exploitation with these five year old boys and girls is wrong. Let these people who sit at the conference tables with other officials who make decisions to continue such abuse of these children that you are watching Father God and you see all things. When I think about these high officials hiding behind their life styles and lavish yachts, clothing and fine linen on their beds. I think of those who are in service to this world. Knowing the father they serve is the father of this world Lucifer and not even he can hide from you Father God.

Please go to the book of Psalms 139 v 7-15) and read:

"Whiter shall I go from thy spirit? Or whither shall I flee from thy presence? (8) If I ascend up into heaven thou are there; if I make my bed in hell, behold, thou are there. (9) If I take the wings of the morning, and dwell in the uttermost parts of the sea: (10) Even there shall thy hand lead me, and thy right hand shall hold me. (11) If I say, Surely the darkness shall cover me; even the night shall be light about me. (12) Yes, the darkness hideth not from thee; but the night shineth as the day; the darkness and the light are both alike to thee. (13) For thou hast possessed my reins; thou has covered me in my mother's womb. (14) I will praise thee; for I am fearfully and wonderfully made: marvelous are thy works; and that my soul knoweth right well. (15) My substance was not hid from thee, when I was made in secret, and curiously wrought in the lowest parts of the earth."

Even the Rich and Wealthy Will Pay a Heavy Price

Let them see Father God they cannot hide no matter how rich or wealthy they are.

There is so much hidden from the least fortunate because of their lack of. Many feel the poor are not worthy of a place to enjoy life. To have the best of care because they are not wealthy and do not have the finances to say to those gone and they go. Or to say to those come and they come. But no man should be a slave to another because we are all servants of the Lord and only he is the master to all. No one should look down on another in a joyful way. A person who has fallen is not there for ridicule but for a change in life. There are millions of children on the Cocoa Plantations who will never have a chance to grow a chance to come into their purpose of life. To feel a need to be where they are at the right time and show the talent or talents that God has blessed them with. All of this is stripped away because of their lack of and no one is there to replenish or restore what is being taken from these five year old girls and boys. Children who work the fields of the Cocoa Plantations of the Ivory Coast of Africa and Ghana because there isn't anyone who cares about how they are suffering? Will riches and wealth cure your pain? You know the pain you hide behind in your loud outburst of laughter. Will your riches or wealth bring forth a baby out of the womb of your wife who cannot carry a child? Will riches or wealth bring back your dead son or daughter who was killed in a car accident or from a drug over dose that truly your wealth caused? How much further will you go into your shell and hide. Many things remain to be seen because you are able to hide behind your riches and wealth. Will you riches and wealth bring back the sight of your child who was born blind, paraplegic, limbs shorter than the other? A child you will never be able to run with teach how to ride a bike, visit in elementary school or see them graduate from college. The answer to all of those questions is no your money cannot change an act of God caused by your own selfishness, your own greed and uncompassionate ways. But even with all of your riches and wealth you sometimes wonder why all of this is happening to you? Not even the most expensive glass of wine will help your blotted way of thinking. Because your service to this world has already proven with whom your loyalty lies. In your suffering you try to hide your guilt because you know it is your fault. You know you could have made the right phone calls to make the necessary changes on the Cocoa Plantations. Only you continue to let the things that disgust you the most take place with these children. So why do you wonder with all of the riches and wealth you have attained that God has allowed all of these problems within your home and outside your home to happen to you. You can go into your deep thoughts all you like and you can try to play like you do not know about the selling of these children's organs, the sex trafficking of these little children, the abuse, the sodomy, the rapes and the murdering taking place with these children and you pretend like you do not know. Let me refresh your memory because I know you go to church every Sunday and I bet you pay your tithes and all of your children have been christened. I bet you even think you are doing the work of the Lord, I think you honestly believe that but you have forgotten one thing. And that is God loves all of his children and he left a special scripture for the rich and wealthy to take heed to: (Matthew 25v40) **"And the King shall answer and say unto them, Verily, I say unto you, inasmuch as ye have done it unto one of the least of these my brethren, ye have done it unto me."**

God Can Hear My Voice

Whose voice can be heard in a hollow and distant wilderness?
In a desolate and empty place where tumble weeds roll;
Where the wind blows freely without obstruction
and the wild chase their game;
Preying on those who are weak, alone and without protection;
The stars are hung to give light to the pitch black night;
I envisioned them before I closed my eyes
to the glory I sought from within;
I am in an empty land my house is now
vacant, and unpossessed;
I see them from a distance lowering that shale
into the ground, hiding their guilt;
My relief has come I am now abridged
from my tormentors grasp.
That body will decay in the grave they
have dug; there will be no trace;
No questions will be asked of my whereabouts;
I will not be remembered;
They took me into the forest so no one
would hear me scream for mercy.
I was so young, my blood was everywhere, my
tormentors won't remember my face.
As time goes on the leaves on this tree
will cover my rotting body;
The possums and crows will come to feast on their meal;

Underneath the soil of the earth alone
in a valley by a beautiful tree;
Death came quickly as I opened my eyes
and I looked to heaven and said:

"God Can Hear My Voice"

Written by: Author/Hall of Fame Poet
Raymond C. Christian

(An Inquisitive question from the Author to the reader)

I wonder if the two proses you just read **"Run, Run Little Black Boy Run"** and **"God Can Hear My Voice"** put you in a mindset of asking yourself the question of how many young boys and girls have been raped and possibly murdered for trying to escape the none ending nightmare they are living, daily on the Cocoa Plantations.

The Convention on the Rights of the Child (CRC) has been ratified for the protection of the children. The question is why haven't the agencies in charge enforce the laws passed to protect these children?

Convention on the Rights of the Child (CRC)

Article 32:

1. **States Parties recognize the right of the child to be protected from economic exploitation and from performing any work that is likely to be hazardous or to interfere with the child's education, or to be harmful to the child's health or physical, mental, spiritual, moral or social development.**
2. **States Parties shall take legislative, administrative, social and educational measures to ensure the implementation of the present article. To this end and having regard to the relevant provisions of other international instruments. States parties shall particular**

a. **Provide for a minimum age or minimum age for admissions to employment.**
b. **Provide for appropriate regulation of the hours and conditions of employment.**
c. **Provide for appropriate penalties or other sanctions to ensure the effective enforcement of the present article**

The well kept secrets of the Cocoa Plantations concerning these young boys and girls at some point have to make you wonder what is actually taking place there? Why do these children have to suffer when there are regulations in place? The Chocolate Industry is doing quite well. Some of them have universities and streets named after them. Even schools where children are allowed to go to school for free and the bills are taken care of by the sponsoring Chocolate Industries. The situation of what is taking place with the children on the Cocoa Plantations is in question and unacceptable. Children in America are being taking care of by the Chocolate Industry; children are being taken care of very well and graduating with the help of sponsorships by the Chocolate Industry in the United States.

On the Cocoa Plantations on the Ivory Coast of Africa and Ghana children are not being given an opportunity to receive an education. I am in no way blaming the Chocolate Industry for this. With other entities involved in getting the cocoa bean to America and other parts of the world someone operating a trillion dollar industry I would assume would have to know the basis of their operation. The Cocoa Plantation owners involved in the hiring and kidnapping of these children at some point have given someone in the chain of the operation a walk through on how the Chocolate Industry is able to operate and how the cocoa beans are gathered. African boys and girls are being beaten, whipped, raped, sodomized and possibly murdered. It should make you wonder what kind of deeply rooted hate anyone can have in their heart to live such a lie. Do you suppose the Cocoa Plantation owners are hiding the truth from the Chocolate Industry that would be hard to believe, when so many articles and journalist reports have stated how these under aged children on the

Cocoa Plantations are being treated? You can only close your eyes and play peek-a-boo for a little while and after a while everyone gets bored and wants to see what you are hiding?

The scenario appears to work this way, life and education if a child is in America it will be fully supported by certain entities of the Chocolate Industry to receive an education. A child working the Cocoa Plantations in headed for hard labor, abuse and working a 100 hour work week at the age of five years old. This is what the child on the Cocoa Plantations has to look forward to on the Ivory Coast of Africa or Ghana, a life of nothing more than abuse. In pretense Chocolate Industry is taking the earnings of the chocolate corporations and giving American families shelter and putting their children through school and college. In America the Chocolate Industry helps children. In Africa and Ghana and other parts of the world children are being misused and abuse for the labor of cocoa beans. Whether the Chocolate Industry has a part in what is taking place is questionable? And whether the Cocoa Plantation owners overall are directly or indirectly involved in helping to enslave children by allowing them to be beaten, raped, sodomized, whipped and possibly murdered leaves this matter with very little questionable doubt? Once again who is to blame is it the Chocolate Industry whose receiving their main ingredient the cocoa bean from the Cocoa Plantations? Or is it the Cocoa Plantation owners at fault forcing these young children to work. Take an even closer look at the people who are actually hired to operate the Cocoa Plantations where did they come from? What kind of person would want a job involving child slave labor of children? Do these supervisors, managers or whatever they call themselves who work on the Cocoa Plantations, those who are guarding these children have any kind of human decency whatsoever? What joy or work ethics of accomplishment could they possibly have at the end of the day or any day with being an armed guard watching children suffer each day and making sure they do not try to escape? What person in their right mind can stand back and watch the inhumane treatment of children and not do anything about it? I guess I am speaking of the

United States politicians, government officials and the National Confectioners Association of which are all in Washington, DC? I have tried to draw a mental picture for my readers to show the cruelty of what is taking place on the Cocoa Plantations with these five year old boys and girls working one hundred hours a week. Just the sound of it all turns my stomach. There is another side I have not addressed of which concerns the issue of five year old girls? How many rapes and violations are really going unreported it appears to be much worst of which I have been told then what is being reported by the media. What happens to the young girls after a long days' work and they are marched back to their mud huts? Who watches over the little girls while they are showering? Who teaches these little girls how to take care of themselves when they become of age and begin their menstrual cycle? What happens to these young girls when they begin to grow and are now ten or thirteen years old. What happens when they begin having menstrual cramps and cannot work, who is there to comfort them? They have no one to comfort them the girls are being beaten just like the boys and made to get up and go to work regardless of any association with pain. This is all being done in order for America and other countries to get the cocoa beans so America can continue to produce its chocolate. Yes the evolutionary cycle of supply and demand continues without remorse, one need and the other does not care how the need is met as long as the need is satisfied. Even with the supply and demand being needed in a very high quantity all most five million tons of the cocoa bean is produced by the top ten countries a year. The government, politicians, the National Confectioners and the Chocolate Industries can all work together in order for children to not be abused; I have already stated there are laws in place. People who are currently serving in the position of President or CEO of the Chocolate Industries are going about it the wrong way. It is quite evident that producing chocolate and manufacturing chocolate creates jobs for Americans and others throughout the world I understand that part of it. But there is a better way to gain profit other than through the abuse and illegal use of children who are forced to work under the oppression of child slavery and forced child labor. The rapes that are taking place on these Cocoa Plantations are a daily practice with the men there and nothing is being done about it. Is producing chocolate that important where laws are overlooked and raping a five year old boy or five year old girl is as easy as turning on a light switch? Let me give you an S.O.S. signal did you notice I used all capital letters, S.O.S. means HELP. I am intentionally being a bit facetious please forgive me but just how old are these young boys and girls who are being raped? Oh! Here comes the big question, what happens when one of these young girls are impregnated? How do they treat these young girls that are now carrying their babies? I do not want to overwhelm you with such tedious questions but do you think these young girls who come up pregnant are allowed to carry these babies full term? Or are they forced to have an abortion at the nearby Cocoa Plantation butcher's clinic? If these babies are allowed to be born what happens to them? How are they raised and where are they kept, children are in demand on the Cocoa Plantations? In all actuality slavery on the other hand is not that old. Have we forgotten how one Black male slave was actually put in the room and made to have sex with every woman in the room in order to impregnate them all? This is where the term "buck" comes from. Is this what is taking place on the Cocoa Plantations? Just maybe the babies are killed at birth like the babies born on the cotton plantations during slavery in the United States of America, just a little food for thought? Slavery has not been emancipated in America that long ago. Blacks in America are still having difficulties with voting rights. There are still issues of innocent Black young men being murdered by white law enforcement officers today and nothing is being done. Now the new fad for African American (Blacks) is look up for any reason or kill them for any reason and you will get away with it. America has now come up with (Mass Incarceration) with 841,000 Black males and 68,000 Black female in prison which makes up close to half of the total amount of 2 million people in the prison population. I do not want to get side tracked and start talking about (Mass Incarceration) excuse me but that is another book by itself let me stick to the current book about the Cocoa Plantation. I do want to refresh your memory in case you have forgotten about what happened when a black baby was birthed by a white woman, or a white baby was birthed by a black slave. When a female slave was raped by the master of the plantation and she became pregnant. The female slave usually stayed on the plantation and carried the baby full term. The white mistress of the plantation was kept in the dark and was never told the female slave was actually carrying her husband's baby. She was under the assumption that the female slave was carrying one of the male slaves baby. The midwives played a very important role in delivering these babies during these times. The midwives were smart enough to know the hair texture and skin color of whether the baby was going to have black or white characteristics, features. In some cases if the child was born with strong white characteristics the child was sold to another plantation owner, not to be raised by his biological black mother. If a child of strong black traits was born it stayed on the plantation and worked as a field hand with the mother. On the flip side many of the babies never lived pass a few hours. Once the new born baby was conceived and recognized of being of white decent that baby was immediately taken away from the mother and beaten until it was dead. The same scenario took place with white women on the cotton plantations who were sleeping with the filed hands when her husband was away. If she became pregnant and the baby was born with black characteristics she was told the baby did not make it. In actuality the baby was taken out back and bludgeoned to death or it was beaten against a tree until it was dead. My question to you is because the Cocoa Plantations are known as the worst form of forced child labor and slavery in modern day history of the world. How are these young girls and their half white babies disposed of on the Cocoa Plantations? It would be highly improbable that this is not occurring because the cases of rape are factual and eventually the young girls are going to become pregnant. Exploitation and trafficking of these children is big on the Cocoa Plantations. There are over two million children working the Cocoa Plantations what other use do they have to the plantation owner after they are no longer able to work on the plantation fields? Not only do we have to seriously consider what is taking place with these young girls but our concerns should also be the safety and treatment of every child. It should make you wonder if the plantation supervisors have an accurate accountability of names, numbers and gender concerning the children they have purchased and kidnapped. Are child labor laws in question concerning the accountability of how many African boys and African girls are actually working on the plantations? Child labor laws are being broken daily and there isn't any consideration being given to the International Labor Organization that clearly states five year old boys and girls haven't any business working and definitely not one hundred hours a week, it is illegal.

I question those who have made trillions of dollars off of the backs of these children on the Cocoa Plantations. I find you have no sympathy or compassion so I do not have a reason to bring up moral ethics because you have none. You have made it known that you haven't any compassion concerning the treatment of these children. Not even a mere speculation of (if my child was in such a situation would I want this to happen to my child)? Money is your king and it remains obvious that money is all you are concerned about. I am certain I can speak for everyone and say the answer to the aforementioned question would be that I am correct in saying, "You do not have any compassion or concern." No one wants their child raped or brutalized. Everyone wants their child to have a wonderful childhood; parents are the children's first line of protection their first line of defense which only makes the Cocoa Plantations even more horrific. The American government, politicians, the National Confectioners Association and the Chocolate Industries know what is taking place with these children. But they choose to allow what is taking place on the Cocoa Plantations to persist because Americans want chocolate in America regardless of what the cost maybe. Unfortunately for the five year old boys and five year old girls on the Ivory Coast of Africa and Ghana they are not considered to be human, by law I must state animals do not have any rights? Five year old children working 100 hours a week is just not heard of men having sex with five year old boys and girls are a very sick situation? If you would allow me just one more question are you the reader fed up with what is taking place on the Cocoa Plantations with these young children. To my understanding and please correct me if I am wrong but when laws are being broken and children are being abused investigations take place, schools and institutions are closed down, children are taken away, people are fired, people go to prison for the abuse of a minor. There are so many laws being broken concerning these children on the Ivory Coast of Africa and Ghana. I really don't know where to start with exposing these crimes being committed against these children. What baffles me even more is that Congress has agreed to give the Cocoa Plantation Operation until 2020 to start correcting the problems. Oh by the way what happened to the original agreement back in 2001 we are now in the year 2015.

As I stated the Chocolate Industry has made trillions of dollars off of these children but the children do not receive any wages, no health care benefits, no dental care, no education and any burial rights or benefits. Political officials, government officials and neither is the National Confectioners Association or the Chocolate Industries standing up for these children by saying the International Labor Organization (ILO) will no longer stand for such outrageous violations of laws being broken. These children haven't any father or mother to account for their treatment they haven't any one to monitor reports of illegal activities such as rape, sodomy, abuse, sex trafficking, child sex slaves, organ trafficking which is why things have gotten out of hand. Laws are in place to take care of such violations but nothing is being done.

Too Young to Know the Lord

These children were taken so young they do not even know how to call on the Lord for help. What religion are they being taught if any? Are these children being told about God and if so are they being told the truth about Christianity? I do recall in the movie "Twelve Years a Slave" the so called preacher who was giving bible lessons from the bible. At the same time he was changing words in the bible to fit what they wanted the slaves to believe. People put on many disguises with intent to mislead people down an ungodly path, Jim Jones, David Koresh, Charles Taze Russell, and so many others have given religion their own personal twist in order to get people to follow them. What religion are these children being taught on the Cocoa Plantations, they cannot read or write? Which means they are not able to openly question what they are being taught because they haven't any basis as to how religion got started, if they are being taught religion? It's sad how the politicians, government officials, the National Confectioners Association and the Chocolate Industries can overlook these children on the Cocoa Plantations. Five year old children are picking cocoa beans on the Cocoa Plantation from sun up to sun down and working one hundred hours a week. America is gaining because jobs are being created but because of the conditions they have to work under they are the ones being tortured. I am prayerful that you all have enough information to question this horrific situation even more on why the abuse of these children have been allowed to go on for so long and nothing is being done about it. As you can tell from my writings it is very hard for me to get past the actual facts of five year old boys and five year old girls being raped as well as having to work one hundred hours a week. I pray that I have irritated you enough for you to want to do something about it. Let me take you even further and say five year old boys and five year old girls are being raped, sodomized, beaten, mistreated, whipped, and possibly murdered.

Laws in Place for Children Rights

These are (ILO) laws Convention 182, Convention 138, Convention 29 and the Convention on the Rights of the Child (CRC) laws being broken and please do not let me leave out the fact that these children are not receiving any wages for their labor. Which makes Chocolate Industry more subject to what I am about to say. Because the Chocolate Industry sponsors putting American children through school for free and housing American children in orphanages the Chocolate Industry is spending more on their American students than the top Ivy League schools in America. The Chocolate Industry as a whole need to make things better for workers nationally and internationally. The Chocolate Industry must know the needs of the children on the Ivory Coast of Africa and Ghana they have been the ones who have slaved on the Cocoa Plantations in the scorching heat of day until the black of night to make the Chocolate Industry a trillion dollar business and not receiving any wages for their hard work. Once again from the trillions of dollars made on the backs of these children in Africa five year old boys and girls they have nothing to show for their labor. The Founder Milton Hershey is deceased now and I do not think he would be pleased with the way the Chocolate Industry is exploiting his dream of sharing chocolate with the world. There are new people in Chocolate Industry leading the way on producing and manufacturing chocolate. It appears as though they do not have the common decency to implement some form of change to better the working conditions concerning these children in Africa and Ghana. With America being the number one producer and manufacturer of chocolate in the world I must start with the good old United States of America and say when and where does fair and equal treatment come into play when it involves children being abused. American politicians and government officials are fully aware of the laws in place to combat such violations of children rights, forced child labor, laws of the CRC and National and International Laws like Convention 182, Convention 29 and Convention 183. The violations of the ILO concerning these children rights are being broke daily.

There aren't any rocks to hide under or trees to hide behind. America and the other nine leading countries in the production and manufacturing of chocolate should be called to the green carpet of the White House. There is a need to address these issues of child abuse. When these politician, government officials and members of the National Confectioners Association are brought to the green carpet for questioning let's start off with a very simple question such as: "What is child abuse"? Have any of you heard about the disgusting things taking place on the Cocoa Plantation with these five year old children? Since these children are five years old do you know the legal age limit these children are supposed to be allowed to work.

Because of the harshness concerning the way these children are being treated is there anything being done to bring about positive changes for these children? Do you know of the conditions under which these children are living? The year 2020 is when renovation is to begin on the Cocoa Plantations and this has been going on since 2001. I do have other documents that reportedly show exposure of what government officials already knew about what was taking place on the Cocoa Plantations since 1973. Of course the year 2020 date will be pushed up again. More delayed time to correct what has been exposed concerning abused children is ridiculous. Those in the law making positions, senators, congressman, political leaders, government officials, National Confectioners Association and chocolate industry officials are moving too slow to implement any positive changes for these children. Making them wait until the year 2020 before any changes will occur is far beyond my thinking when it comes to abused children. This is contradictory to the laws which have already been established in the International Labor Organization (ILO) which involves Convention 182 and Convention 29 concerning: Child abuse, forced child labor, children endangerment, and child slavery. Of which all are considered to be illegal nationally and internationally.

It is written (Luke 17 v 2) in the Holy Bible (King James Version) "It were better for him that a millstone were hung about his neck and he cast into the sea, than that he should offend one of these little ones."

My Daily Word concerning the Children on the Cocoa Plantations

What you are about to read below are mini sermons I send out to my followers daily of which depicts some of my writings to bring awareness to certain topics and issues I as an Elder feel my followers should be made aware of. It is important to know not only what is taking place in church as well as understanding scripture. It is also important to do just as the Lord has said, watch and pray. I began talking about the Cocoa Plantations years ago; I had no idea that God would put it on my heart to literally write a book about the ordeals taking place there. My awareness mini sermons are written to keep people informed. When you think about all of the holidays, and special days and birthday's that people go out and purchase chocolate. Not having any knowledge as to what they are really purchasing as it relates to the product or something they like. It is important as a consumer to be aware of what you are purchasing and supporting with your hard earned dollar.

Because of all of the abuse I have read about concerning the Cocoa Plantations. I began to wonder just how many people were not knowledgeable about these five year old boys and girls working 100 hours a week. Climbing forty-foot trees, getting raped, sodomized, beaten and abused daily, what person would not want to know about what is being purchased with their dollar? What is the truth behind the product?

Pt. 1 Bitter Sweet Chocolate

With research being inconclusive what has been told to you is dark chocolate lowers high cholesterol levels. What has not been told in studies is what the long term effects eating dark chocolate may cause?

Why is research on dark chocolate inconclusive? Chocolate is a trillion dollar business and brings in billions to the United States. The research is inconclusive because the United States of America is the largest producer and manufacturer of chocolate in the world. Why give you the long term effects keep the disadvantages hidden, right?

Another well-kept secret is an even bigger problem. 5 year old boys and girls on the Ivory Coast of Africa and Ghana climb 40ft trees with machetes for your cocoa beans so Americans can make chocolate.

What you are not being told America is there are 5 year old children little boys and girls working over 100 hours a week on the Cocoa Plantations. To this day these children are sold into slavery; they are being sodomized, beaten and raped. Some possibly murdered? These issues are being kept quiet because of the well-kept trillion dollar business and high political figures involved are you aware of the NCA that is the National Confectioners Association an important part of the Chocolate Industry.

Nothing is being and laws in place are not being enforced to help these 5 year old children. The political down side of what congress is doing is to just bury the truth with more investigations to make it appear the 2,000,000 children in slavery today will get some help. The dates to implement change are only pushed back stipulating more data needs to be collected. Former Senator Thomas Richard "Tom Harkin and Congressman Eliot Engel are over the Cocoa Protocol in Washington. PLEASE ASK THEM (WHAT DO YOU DO WHEN CHILDREN ARE BEING ABUSED, RAPED AND POSSIBLY MURDERED). Yes they are supposed to stop it. Senator Harkin is supposed to be retiring in 2015. I am certain more delays will occur.

I am Elder Christian in Jesus name.

Support what's right. My household will not buy chocolate for Halloween, no change no chocolate stand up America, PLEASE

Pt. 2 No Chocolate Treats

Former Senator Thomas Richard "Tom Harkin and Congressman Eliot Engel both sat with 6 of the top producers and manufacturers in the chocolate industry in 2001. They all came to an agreement that something must be done to protect the 5 year old children on the Cocoa Plantations. All six Corporate Executives including Former Senator Thomas Richard "Tom Harkin and Congressman Eliot Engel all agreed the Cocoa Plantations on the (Cote d' Ivorie) Ivory Coast of Africa and Ghana are the worst forms of child abuse and the worst forms of slavery ever.

These are 5 year old boys and girls being raped, and beaten with whips and chains, they are being sodomized and possibly murdered.

Where are the dead bodies of the children if there isn't any accountability? Who is there to account for the 5 year old boys or girls when they come up missing? How does a 5 year old explain they saw a 5 year old girl repeatedly raped or a 5 year old boy sodomized or beaten to death? They have "no father or mother" to protect them. Please speak up America.

For this reason I will not purchase any chocolate. When I listen to all of the problems of "Ebola" which originates from Africa and is now spreading throughout the nations it helps me understand God is the voice for these children.

For all of you who have a hand in the Cocoa Plantations on the Ivory Coast of Africa and Ghana. For the politicians, government officials the National Confectioners Association and the Chocolate Industry who have turned your heads to the rapes and abuse these 5 year old children are suffering daily and being worked 100 hours a week. Know that I serve a God, the father of Abraham, Isaac and Jacob and he reins over the just and the unjust.

I pray my father in heaven suffers it so as you all enjoy your chocolate remember these children on the Cocoa Plantations and why God said he will send his plagues throughout the world. And he has no respect of person.

I am Elder Christian in Jesus name.

Ebola is just a start of what is to come. Speak up America

Copyrights Elder R. Christian all rights reserved ©

Pt. 3 America's **Hidden Chocolate** Secret **(Your Trick No Treat)**

"The Cocoa Plantations"

What's not being told to the American public concerning the trillion dollar industry of Chocolate? The top company makes 60 billion a year from chocolate sales and a second company makes 30 billion a year from chocolate sales. What's not being told is the 5 year old boys and girls on the Cocoa Plantations on the Ivory Coast of Africa and Ghana are sold to the plantation owners and never see their parents again.

These children are watched by armed guards and locked up at night in mud shacks. 18 children to a mud shack where the ventilation is only the size of a baseball to breathe out of.

The renovation of which Former Senator Thomas Richard "Tom Harkin and Congressman Eliot Engel in agreement with 6 other top chocolate producers was to take place in 2001 due to the Cocoa Plantations being exposed as the (WORST FORM OF CHILD ABUSE AND CHILD SLAVERY) in the history of the world. The changes that were to take place moved from 2001 to 2005 then to 2008 then 2010 now the current agreement is 2020. It should be inexcusable for children who are notably being raped and abuse for help to take this long to come to their aide.

Do they really need more time to renovate the Cocoa Plantations? No! The Chocolate Industry has just invested 300 million dollars in renovating the chocolate factories for their 13,000 employees in America and abroad. But I have not heard Former Senator Thomas Richard "Tom Harkin or Congressman Eliot Engel going to the media about what's not being done for these 5 year old boys and girls who are being raped, beaten and possibly murdered. Children on the Cocoa Plantations are not receiving any education, no wages, and no future learning skills. You allow the Chocolate Industry to invest 300 million dollars as of January 28, 2014. While the Cocoa Plantation owners continue to be allowed to have more rapes and abuse of these 5 year old children. America supports The WORST form of Child Slavery in the WORLD.

I am Elder Christian in Jesus name.

Pt. 4 "A Trillion Dollar Industry"

There is an old saying in politics **"Be careful who you get into bed with"**

or is the old saying "Their all in bed together" or is it "All for none and none for all" it just keeps changing. Kind of like the dates to get those children some relief on the Cocoa Plantations, you just don't know what to believe.

After careful research and review the problems which are persistent on the Cocoa Plantations Former Senator Thomas Richard "Tom Harkin and Congressman Eliot Engel are both fully aware of the immediate action needed to take place concerning the rapes, beatings, sodomizing and possible murder and abuse of these 5 year old boys and girls who work 100 hundred hours a week on the Cocoa Plantations.

It is stated 23 times in the proposal I have read concerning renovation of the Cocoa Plantations 23 times "THE COCOA PLANTATIONS IS THE WORST FORM OF CHILD LABOR EVER".

It is also stated that America and other countries that are in bed with one another. Are fully aware of what is taking place with these 5 year old girls and boys. My question is how many times not just once America but 23 times would you have to list forced child labor or abuse of children (being the worst form of abuse of children) before something is done?

It saddens me that Congress could not see the urgency needed in this matter to make changes concerning the abuse of these children and voted to amend the proposal of September 19, 2001 causing intentional delay to not expose the (WORST FORM OF CHILD SLAVE LABOR EVER).

CONGRESS VOTED 291 TO 115 in favor to amend changes on the Cocoa Plantations knowing an amendment would cause further delay.

Chocolate is a trillion dollar industry it's been in business over 100 years. Yes Chocolate is in every store and every business. Every place you go you will find chocolate. Unfortunately it is a bitter sweet story. The Chocolate Industry has its own university in America helping to put American children through college. At the same time the Cocoa Plantations on the Ivory Coast of Africa are allowing 5 year old boys and girls to be raped, beaten and sodomized in Africa

I am Elder Christian in Jesus name.

Now that you have the Memo, are you still buying chocolate America

Pt. 5 Ministers God Is Waiting (A Chocolate Mess)

Men of God are put in position for a reason. That reason is to serve God not man. (Rom1v25) "Who changed the truth of God into a lie, and worshipped and served the creature more than the Creator, who is blessed forever. Amen."

God is watching (Pro 15 v3) "The eyes of the Lord are everywhere beholding the good and evil."

Ministers because of your calling you have an obligation to God to walk out on the water. Just as Jesus bid Peter to come out on the water. (Mat14v27-29) "...Be of good cheer: it is I: be not afraid. (28) And Peter answered him and said, Lord, if it be thou, bib me come unto thee on the water. (29) And he said, Come. And when Peter was come down out of the ship, he walked on the water, to go to Jesus."

Men of God you also took a personal internal oath to serve only God. The checks you are receiving from political figures of city, state and federal does not free you of your oath to God. The church is fully aware of the Cocoa Plantations. The church is fully aware of the rapes, sodomizing, beatings and possible murders. FIVE year old boys and girls being sold into slavery on the Cocoa Plantations and you still cash these checks. Checks that bind you from telling the truth about the Ivory Coast of Africa and the 5 year old boys and girls working 100 hours a week their blood is upon you.

Ministers don't insult me by telling me you did not know. I have been preaching on this matter for a while now. What say ye men and women of the, cloth?

Checks are sent to your private account; your home, direct deposit God sees it all.

Did you all of a sudden grow a conscious and like Pontius Pilate you want some water to wash your hands. Just as Jesus body could not stay in the grave. And Abel's blood cried out from the ground. So shall every child's spilled blood be justified by God? "Touch them not."

I am Elder Christian in Jesus name.

Pt 6 "God or the World"

Is there an acceptable excuse? This is the question I would like to bring to your conscious mind in your service to God?

In accordance to the word of God (Romans1v19-20) "Because that which may be known of God is manifest in them; for God hath shewed it unto them. (20) For the invisible things of him from the creator of the world are clearly seen being understood by the things that are made even his eternal power and Godhead; so that they are without excuse:"

Saying you love the lord is only lip service. You cannot have one foot in the world and the other out. There isn't any acceptance for those who straddle the fence.

Church Pastors, Men and Women of God, political figures there's an urgency when it comes to the lives of innocent children 5 years old working on the Cocoa Plantations. Choose ye this day whom you shall serve.

The Cocoa Plantations will not just go away. I have friends all over the world who see these children on the Cocoa Plantations being trafficked to different countries. And they have discussed with me how these children are beaten in public airports.

Pastors, men and women of God, who have lined your pockets with the filthy lucre haven't a conscious mind for what is just. (James1v6-8) "But let him ask in faith nothing wavering. For he that wavereth is like a wave of the sea driven with the wind and tossed. (7) For let not that man think that he shall receive anything of the Lord. (8) A double minded man is unstable in all his ways."

You cannot pretend you are helping when you know you really are not. God is still seated on the thrown and his words are not wavery or unstable. How do you all sleep at night knowing 5 year old boys and 5 year old girls are being raped, beaten and sodomized?

Pontius Pilate washed his hands from freeing Jesus he later committed suicide.

I am Elder Christian in Jesus name.

The storm will come I pray you catch the righteous wave

Pt. 7 Jesus Came So You Would Have No Excuse

"The Cocoa Plantations"

Preachers you stand behind the pulpit and preach about how Jesus was beaten and how he suffered. You preach on how the Children of Israel suffered and was delivered by Moses. Gideon and the Midianites and you say yes God delivered them.

What I am trying to point out to you concerning the 2million children in slavery on the Cocoa Plantations on the Ivory Coast of Africa and Ghana. This is going to take more than just one man of God speaking on it. I am asking all of my Brothers and Sisters in Christ to make the Cocoa Plantations personal. This is not just a one minute subject in church the Cocoa Plantations is an all-day sermon.

It all starts with proper leadership with wisdom playing the greater part. Men and Women of God have an obligation to speak on the wrongs doings of this world.

How do you sit back and watch 5 year old boys and girls being exploited beyond your imagination? The sexual abuse and beatings slaves endured in America is not comparable to what is being done to these 5 year old children working 100 hours a week on the cocoa plantations. In case you did not get the MEMO: THE COCOA PLANTATIONS ARE NOTATED BY THE SENATE AND CONGRESS AS BEING "THE WORST FORM OF CHILD SLAVE LABOR EVER" In the history of the world.

The power of the African American dollar is remarkable in America. If we do not purchase there is a shift in supply and demand a shift in power. You will find this out quickly once you decide to stop butting into slavery. It all starts by preaching on the wrong taking place on the Cocoa Plantations.

Harkin-Engel Protocol is the name of the law passed. A store front law put on paper but voted down by Congress to be amended 291-115 knowing the amendments would cause intentional delays to do nothing.

I am Elder Christian in Jesus name.

Be a voice for these children PREACHERS...HELP

"Statistics Do Not Lie"

One of my favorite scriptures (Pro 15v3) "The eyes, of the Lord are everywhere beholding the good and evil." God patients are not short with any of his children. He gives us a chance to repent. And he still has to make the decision as to whether he is going to punish us or blot out the sins committed.

I am trying to help you understand that we all fall short of the glory of God because of our imperfections and our need to be granted forgiveness at the throne of grace.

Take a closer look at these numbers I pray you understand my position as, an Elder. Affirmative Action Law has been voted down by Congress, which means there is no longer an EEOC policy to assure that Blacks in America have employment or the ability to take care of their families. Please pay ATTENTION

Out of 2,000,000 people in prison 841,000. 90% are Blacks who makes the prison total today. There are more Blacks today in prison then there were slaves during the times of slavery in America.

For every 1000 white young men between the ages of 24-29 that go to prison10, 000 black young men between the ages of 24-29 will go to prison. Is it Mass Incarceration or is it a legal Black genocide? Now when you look at the Cocoa Plantations you will see the bigger picture. There are 2 million children in slavery today on the Cocoa Plantations on the Ivory Coast of Africa and Ghana. Former Senator Thomas Richard "Tom Harkin and Congressman Eliot Engel go home to their families each day. Only appeasing the American public on paper saying progress is being made and it is not.

5 year old boys and 5 year old girls are being raped, sodomized, beaten, working 100 hours a week. Slave labor no wages, child trafficking. Yet Former Senator Harkin and Congressman Engel allow 300,000 million dollars to go toward the renovation of The Chocolate Industry remodeling its labor force in Pennsylvania. No renovation in Africa and Ghana, what about the children? When did American politicians start condoning child abuse.

I am Elder Christian in Jesus name.

So Sad

"King David Could Not Resist Her Beauty"

The Holy Bible talks about the irresistible beauty of a woman. I like relating things to scripture. Do you recall the story of King David and Bethsheba?

Bethsheba was a beautiful woman she was a Hittite. Meaning she was of the dark skinned people with yellow/brown mongoloid features. I also want to note that King Ramsey III was given the daughter of a Hittite King to marry to maintain peace agreement over the Mesopotamia.

Kind David could not resist the beauty of Uriah's, Bethsheba. (II Sam 11v2-4) "And it came to pass in an evening tide that David arose from off his bed and walked upon the roof of the king's house; and from the roof he saw a woman washing herself; and the woman was very beautiful to look upon. (3) And David sent and enquired after the woman. And one said, is not this Bethsheba, the daughter of Eliam, the wife of Uriah the Hittite? (4) And David sent messages and took her; and she came in unto him, and he lay with her,..."

This is a perfect example of how these men on the Cocoa Plantations are watching these young boys and girls for their own desires to be filled in a sexual manner.

Just as a King could not resist his own friend's wife these common men in remote areas are watching these young girls and boys develop. Child labor on the Cocoa Plantations is against the law and so is statutory rape, what agreement of consent can be given from a child?

Where are these young girls and boys bathing and who is guarding them while they are bathing. What happens when it is time for a young girl to start her minstrel cycle who teaches her how to take care of herself?

FYI: Senator Tom Harkin and Congressman Engel $300 million dollars was just put toward building a new Chocolate factory in Pennsylvania. Help these CHILDREN!!!

I am Elder Christian in Jesus name.

(Pro 27v20) Hell and destruction are never full; so the eyes of man are never satisfied

"God Is Not Pleased"

The Holy Bible clearly states, "vengeance is mine thus saith the Lord I will repay." I will start with Gods, vengeance because what I want everyone one to know is we are living in a world where "you will reap what you sow."

God has it all covered if you study scripture and get an understanding as to how life evolves. You will begin to see what is being unveiled for you. God is not short of anything so reaping and sowing is part of your self-worth of everything in life coming full circle.

The circle concerning people who have mistreated you or others, your circle encompasses things you have done behind closed doors that you will have to revisit someday. Whether good or bad you shall be rewarded for what you have done.

Longsuffering for many is hard to accept. Senators, Congressman, Businessman and others want your payoff NOW.

At the cost of the rapes, beatings, sodomy, the abuse and murder of these 5 year old children on the Cocoa Plantations You line your pockets with their blood and do nothing to stop their agony. Thinking you will never be caught?

While you are setting up a peaceful retirement for yourself remember (Luke 12v19-21) "And I will say to my soul, Soul thou hast much goods laid up for many years; take thine ease, eat, drink, and be merry. (20) But God said unto him, thou fool, this night thy soul shall be required of thee; then whose shall those things be, which thou hast provided? (21) So is he that layeth up treasure for himself and is not rich toward God."

I am Elder Christian in Jesus name.

Rest assured your circle has to be complete and God will give you a just reward. I pray you made it inside the circle coming to an understanding of your righteous walk in life. America those are 5 year old children on the Cocoa Plantations crying out for help...You still buying chocolate, Gods Vengeance. The Cocoa Plantations is the worst form of child slave labor in the world

"Gods Amazing Grace"

God Almighty protects us from all dangers seen and unseen

The question was asked hundreds of years ago, "Is there anything too hard for God." "NO" there is nothing to hard for God. He reins over the just as well as the unjust. The ultimate power of the Lord keeps those who serve him in perfect peace. We watch and wait for Our Father to move. Knowing there is nothing we can do without him.

He showed us his power when Jesus yielded up the ghost in (Mat 27v51-53) "And behold, the veil of the temple was rent in twain from the top to the bottom; and the earth did quake, and the rocks rent; (52) and the graves were opened; and many bodies of the saints which slept arose. (53) And came out of the graves after his resurrection, and, went into the holy city, and appeared unto many."

(Rev 20v13) And the sea gave up the dead which were in it; and death and hell delivered up the dead which were in them: and they were judged every man according to their works."

Senator Thomas Richard "Tom" Harkin and Congressman Eliot Engel you have a Protocol that has not been met concerning the Cocoa Plantations. There are children in the midst of this, situation and God is not pleased 5 year old boys and girls. Raped, sodomized, beaten, and sold into slavery.

These children's blood cries out from the ground help us America we haven't a voice, we haven't a father or mother to protect us. We were not taught about God. Teach us how to pray. The brutality taking place on the Ivory Coast of Africa is the worst forms of Child Slavery, Child Trafficking and Child Abuse in the history of the world.

I beseech you all to rethink what you are planning and doing. God is watching, have your way Father God grab hold your reins.

I am Elder Christian in Jesus name.

(Act 18v9-10)"...Be not afraid, but speak, and hold not thy peace:(10) For I am with thee, and no man shall set on thee to hurt thee; for I have much people in this city

"The Deliverer Is Sent"

Gods reins over the just and unjust, tidal waves, earthquakes, famine, and plagues these things shall come. Is there anything too hard for God?

The sea will give up its dead (Rev20v13) "And the sea gave up the dead which were in it; and death and hell delivered up the dead which were in them: and they were judged every man according to their works." Is anything too hard for God?

(Rev 21v1) "And I saw a new heaven and a new earth: for the first heaven and the first earth was passed away; and there was no more sea." Is there anything too hard for God?

(Rev20v12) "And I saw the dead, small and great, stand before God; and the books were opened: and another book was opened, which is the book of life: and the dead were judged out of those things which were written in the books, according to their works." Is there anything too hard for God?

Gods eyes are not short of anything therefore: he sees everything even in his taking of the just he suffers it so, with the Cocoa Plantations being called "the worst form of child slavery and adult slavery ever in the world."

I have to question the legacy of Milton Snavely Hershey in my research I have found him to be, a man of character and concern for the needy. It is his protégé who have bought shame to the Chocolate Industry by being a part of Child slavery, child rape, child beatings, child sodomy and possibly child murder. This was not a part of the Chocolate Industry legacy.

You cannot hide from the eyes of God Senator Harkin and Congressman Engel, corporate heads, politicians. Your sins will find you out and you will have no excuse (Rev 20v10) "And the devil that deceived them was cast into the lake of fire and brimstone, where the beast and the false prophets are, and shall be tormented day and night forever and ever.

I am Elder Christian in Jesus name.

When God sends his whirlwind there will not be one stone that will remain uncovered

"Storing up Treasures"

There are consequences for those who go against the word of God wanting to only please themselves to be looked upon as being more than the Creator. We were designed to bare the burdens of those who are weak (Rom 15v1) "We then that are strong ought to bare the infirmities of the weak and not to please ourselves." God tells us humble is the way. The mockery of what was considered to be abolished in America (slavery) is truly a MASS INCARCERATION.

The rewards you seek are phantom by your own delusion of thought and grandeur personality. Former Senator Thomas Richard "Tom Harkin and Congressman Eliot Engel, corporate heads, politician's, who have figured out their master plan knowing the Cocoa Plantations will never be renovated gives them foolish thoughts of superiority. It is an inside joke that they could go to Africa and still witness their inner personal desires to feed upon the souls of child slaves, and adult slaves. They think they are untouchable and have forgotten these children have a father who sits high in judgment. Not realizing that God controls the reins and when it does rain it rains on the just as well as the unjust.

Those who are serving in the body of Christ Jesus understands the sacrifice knowing it is for a much greater cause that a righteous child was put to death for the sake of righteousness. What say you the unrighteous? For if the righteous would rather suffer to be with the Lord. Exactly where do you think the unrighteous are going?

Do you truly feel that raping, beating, sodomizing and murdering children on the Ivory Coast of Africa and Ghana is Godly? Do you think that changing the renovation dates to correct the worst forms of child slavery in the world is okay? There are penalties for you and your children's children for embellishing in such hate.

I am Elder Christian in Jesus name.

The children of God are not foot stools, there is a penalty

"My Christian Duty"

Please Former Senator Thomas Richard "Tom Harkin and Congressman Eliot Engel hear me. Because you are over the Cocoa Protocol designed to help the children in Africa and Ghana. Understanding the Cocoa Plantations are the worst forms of Child Slave Labor and Adult Slave Labor and trafficking in the history of the world.

As Christian believers we have an obligation to God one that extends beyond the realms of the universe. Believing wherever we go we are taught to spread the gospel. We are taught to tell people about Jesus thee only begotten son of God.

I am not just speaking to Senator Harkin and Congressman Engel but to every Senator and Congressman who voted against renovations on the Cocoa Plantations in 2001 with a vote of 291-115 for delaying the help these children and adult men and women need. We have an obligation to God and to the United States of America being a peace keeping nation to correct a problem that is very fixable by making changes concerning the abuse of these children and adults.

Our duty as a free nation is to express the joy of our love for God which we were taught as children. Unfortunately the children, men and women working on the Cocoa Plantations since the age of 5 years old have never been taught about Christianity. They have not been taught about Jesus Christ. So who will come to their need and relief from their daily suffering? They don't know how to pray they were sold at 5 years old. All these children know is the thrash of a whip and the endless work of 100 hours a week. Milton Hershey did not start the Chocolate Industry off abusing children. Who will lead and teach these children about God.

I am Elder Christian in Jesus name.

I believe through faith and fasting God will unveil this monstrosity of human treatment to the world. You will be judged for their intentional inhumane treatment. By your own greed you shall be justified and condemned, have your way Lord

"Chocolate Hidden Secret"

What is not being shared with the American public is the abuse taking place with 5 year old boys and girls, children being used to get the cocoa pods from Africa and Ghana to America so Americans can have chocolate.

The rapes and beatings, the sodomizing of children including the possible murder of these children for trying to escape the Cocoa Plantations, it's no different than slavery on the cotton plantations and how it was enforced in America. From my research the Cocoa Plantations is the worst form of slavery of children and adults in the history of the world. These children are sold at the age of five years old, boys and girls. They are being raised by their slave masters, their oppressors. These children have no father and no mother to watch over them.

But there are laws in America called the International Labor Organization Convention 182 and ILO 29. These laws are not being enforced because to the American Senate and Congress the children being abused are not worth their time so of course the laws that are already in place to protect these children are not worth the Senate and Congress time to enforce.

Once again Senator Thomas Richard "Tom" Harkin and Congressman Eliot Engel are over the Cocoa Protocol they are aware of the child slavery, child abuse, child kidnapping and children being raped on the Ivory Coast of Africa and Ghana but have not done anything to stop the abuse of these children. The CRC, and other governmental officials are not enforcing laws set in place to combat this kind of treatment of children. Political figures are also aware along with the Chocolate Industry and the National Confectioners Association in Washington, DC.

No more chocolate America no more chocolate until the abuse of these children on the Ivory Coast of African and Ghana stops and renovations open to a new beginning. Things must change this is a great undertaking I need your support to stop the worst forms of child abuse ever. Ministers you also play a very big part in helping to correct the torture of these children. You have a voice behind the pulpit. I challenge you to announce in church that chocolate is not to be purchased any longer until these laws are enforced and renovations begin.

I am Elder Christian in Jesus name.

May God have Mercy on your soul? This is not the American way

"What Are You Subject Too"

You become a part of the decision you make

You listen and watch what is taking place throughout the world with children in not just Africa and Ghana but in many countries. Children are being mistreated they are forced to work in sweatshops to help with the family income, no education for them either. Yes it is all wrong and I am not oblivious to the nature of their suffering.

God placed it on my heart to write about the Cocoa Plantations because of the nature of the cruelty taking place in Africa and Ghana with 5 year old children being raped, sodomized, beaten with bike chains and possibly murdered, 5 year old children boys and girls working 100 hours a week.

This is a blood stained banner these children are not able to carry by themselves. They are taken from their parents on what I call an involuntary/voluntary need of survival sacrificed for the lesser of two evils. Thinking it is better that one child is sold into slavery than the whole family dying of starvation.

Former Senator Thomas Richard "Tom Harkin is said to be retiring in 2015. Who will be the next person in charge to come in under the presumption of more time delays will play a part before any help comes to these children and more investigations? They are all intentional delays. There was never any intention for change. It just looks good on paper.

Where is Senator Harkin's retirement going to leave the children on the Cocoa Plantations? Will the children suffer for another 100 years? No wages, no schools, no education, living in mud huts, continued rapes of 5 year old boys and girls oh did I leave out the abuse, poor health care and nutrition.

I know you did not know about the felons that are hired on the Cocoa Plantations to watch over these children. Do you really expect the felons to say anything they are just happy to have a job and all the young boys and girls they can get? And the pedophiles must most certainly think they are in paradise. All the children they can get.

I am Elder Christian in Jesus name.

Remember Americans IN GOD WE TRUST. Don't shred the MEMO

Copyrights Elder R. Christian all rights reserved ©

"You Support Raping and Abusing Children When you Buy Chocolate"

I am certain by now everyone is saying Elder Christian give us a break on the Cocoa Plantations we got it. What I want everyone to understand is the beatings and rapes, and sodomizing of these 5 year old children and murder of these children is something that has been over looked for years, at least since 1909 we are now in 2014.

Senator Thomas Richard "Tom" Harkin and Congressman Eliot Engel, politicians, government officials, National Confectioners Association and the Chocolate Industry have not moved to eradicate an ongoing problem. They have not moved or tried to show any intentions of giving these children some form of relief. And by passing a bill to put labels on products that come into America from other countries that have forced child labor is not enough.

Once these 5 year old boys and girls are no longer useful to the Cocoa Plantations how do they service the plantation owners? The

Cocoa Plantation owner usually desires the prettiest slave be it male or female. If the Cocoa Plantation owner is gay he may desire a five year old male slave. If these young children are going to stay on the Cocoa Plantations they have to earn their way daily in some way? Is sex trafficking next on the agenda for them?

Pay attention to these numbers there are 2 million children on the Cocoa Plantations. The Cocoa Plantations are spread throughout many regions and they are located in very distant and remote areas where the rapes and other things happening are not so easily detected.

When God is displeased with the wrong doings of mankind things begin to happen. Could "Ebola" be one of the plagues God is sending? Do you think it is strange that Ebola originated in Africa? Do I have your attention now? God said touch not my little ones.

I am Elder Christian in Jesus name.

Sodom and Gomorrah was only an example of God's displeasure concerning mankind. Stand up America and be a voice for these children

Copyrights Elder R. Christian all rights reserved ©

"What Changes Can You Make"

Many of you are looking forward to taking your children out for Halloween. Some of you are going to adult Halloween parties. What will the 5 year old children who are suffering on the Cocoa Plantations have for their enjoyment? Other than working 100 hours a week being raped, sodomized, beaten with bike chains and whips, locked up at night and watched by armed guards?

Many of you have said here he goes with this Cocoa Plantations stuff again. Well please let me interject and say if this was happening to your child I could never say enough until your child was safe. And it would not matter to you how redundant the subject matter just keep talking about it. (Heb 13v3) "Remember them that are in bonds, as bound with them; and them which suffer adversity as being yourselves also in the body." For this reason, and more (1Thes 5v17) says, "Pray without ceasing." Rendering all things unto God for the glory of his will and purpose knowing that you are a vessel for his use and it is for the purpose of serving him that you have been chosen.

Former Senator Thomas Richard "Tom" Harkin and Congressman Eliot Engel, politician's, government officials, National Confectioners Association, and Chocolate Industries, owners and distributors of Chocolate. And those of you in Washington, DC who are sitting on your hands how do you sleep at night? You must be in denial of what is taking place with these children?

These children need relief from the burdens of their oppressors Father God let the plagues come. I ask that you show your mercy to your children, if it is thy will Lord God please come quickly and let your mercy be shown to those who have shown mercy.

Saints of God beware of these man made holidays to promote CHOCOLATE, and say "No More Chocolate" to: Halloween, Thanksgiving, Christmas, New Year's Eve and Day, Easter, July 4th, Veterans Day, Columbus Day, Birthdays etc. the top chocolate foundation in America makes 60 billion and the second leading chocolate company makes 30 billion a year and just invested $300 million dollars in a new plant in Philadelphia in 2014. The money is there but the interest in helping to stop the worst forms of child slavery and forced child labor ever in the history of the world is not.

Join me in this greater undertaking. We joined together for the abolishment of slavery in America, the Bus Boycotts, and Civil Rights Movement. The cycle of slavery has resurfaced.

I am Elder Christian in Jesus name.

The purchase of your dollar goes a long way. Be cognizant on how you spend it

Copyrights Elder R. Christian all rights reserved ©

"Our Love for Christ Jesus"

Because of our love for Christ Jesus and doing what is righteous concerning the goodness in the examples Jesus left us with. It is by faith and only through our love for God and doing his will we fear no one. We are taught to only fear the one who can mutilate both body and soul, God.

The exposure of those who are suffering puts me on the battlefield for the Lord. Knowing their suffering and mine will not be in vain. Those of you who started with me may not finish the race. I say, do not let your fears overcome you. But overcome fear, God has not given us that spirit. Fear is only introduced by man. I pray one day you will reach that plateau where you will be strengthened to do what us righteous.

(Phil 1v21-27) "For to me to live is Christ, and to die is gain. (22) But if I live in the flesh this is the fruit of my labour: yet what I shall choose I wot not. (23) For I am in a strait betwixt two having a desire to depart, and to be with Christ; which is far better:(24) Nevertheless to abide in the flesh is more needful for you. (25) And having the confidence, I know that I shall abide and continue with you all for your furtherance and joy of faith. (26) That your rejoicing may be more abundant in Jesus Christ for me by my coming to you again. (27) Only let your conversation be as it becometh the gospel of Christ: that whether I come and see you, or else be absent, I may hear of your affairs, that ye stand in one, spirit with one mind striving together for the faith of the gospel."

I am Elder Christian in Jesus name.

(Phil 1v28-29) And in nothing terrified by your adversaries: which is to them an evident token of perdition, but to you of salvation and that of God. (29) For unto you it is given in the behalf of Christ, not only to believe on him, but also to suffer for his sake"

Jesus is on the thrown

A Heavy Price to Pay

Pt. 1"My Heart is Burdened but My Soul says, Yes Lord

They haven't any protection, no father or mother to see to their wounds or come to their relief.

It saddens me to say but our elected American politician's, government officials, NCA and chocolate industry owners have gotten into bed together. Our government which helped to create the laws against CHILD ABUSE and CHILD SLAVERY, and FORCED CHILD LABOR, has done nothing to help.

One of the president of the Chocolate Industry receives an $8 million dollar a year salary to make sure the number one Chocolate foundation makes it 60 Billion dollar a year sales but there are no renovations on the Cocoa Plantations to help these helpless children.

Former Senator Thomas Richard Harkin and Congressman Eliot Engel both who are Democrats have exemplified minute movement for change, since 2001 when the Harkin-Engel Protocol for the Cocoa Plantations was created. From 2001 to 2015 that is a lot of time for Senators, Congressmen and the National Confectioners Association (NCA) in America to say raping, sodomizing, beating and killing children is okay.

Know they want to wait another 5 years before they vote on the Harkin-Engel Protocol so the Senate and Congress can vote to push the dates up even further away from helping these children.

I am certain you are saying by now what is taking so long? Just think of these children who haven't any accountability on the Cocoa Plantations as being used for trafficking. Not just sex trafficking but the trafficking of organ sales. This is another big part of the Chocolate Industry. Many of these children are brought into America murdered and their body parts are sold for the purpose of saving someone else's life.

Since you are aware that human organs are expensive I wonder who are making these purchases. You guessed right the rich.

I am Elder Christian in Jesus name.

The adoption is a fake form of cross -border adoption. These children are never seen again

Pt. 2 "My Heart is Burdened but My Soul says, Yes Lord

My heart is burdened because this is America a county that frowns on the abuse of children. America is a nation that stands up for the rights of innocent children. So they may be able to live a full childhood and not have to worry about laboring in the work force.

Five year old boys and girls on the Ivory Coast of Africa and Ghana are not only just being sold into slavery on the Cocoa Plantations. They are also used in sex trafficking and organ trafficking. Organ trafficking is much worse. It is the sale of body parts, organs like heart replacement for the rich, kidneys for the rich, liver for the rich, etc. I say the rich because the poor cannot afford the immediate cost of a transplant.

Whatever part is needed off of the Adopted child from Africa that was purchased or illegally adopted and brought into the United States, of course, you know in order to get these organs the child is murdered. Where the body is disposed of I haven't any idea. Out of mere embarrassment it would seem like Senator Thomas Richard Harkin and Congressman Eliot Engel would began to implement positive corrections on the Cocoa Plantations and bring a halt to all of the abuse, rapes, sodomizing, beatings and possible murders taking place of these children there.

America is a nation of people who look out for the less fortunate for helpless little children who do not understand pain. America, what happened? These children's on the Cocoa Plantations blood has begun to fill the White House as we look at the connections of the Senators, Congressmen, the National Confectioners Association (NCA) and the Chocolate Industries. These children's blood cries out from the graves they are buried in. Help me father, help me mother, help me America.

I am Elder Christian in Jesus name.

False adoption papers on African children to cross the border for human parts and pieces of their body organs. So no to CHOCOLATE

"A Future without Hope for Change"

The last two days of information you have received should have devastated everyone. Just to think that Five year old children are being sold not only into slavery. But they are sold to American citizens through what is called false adoption papers. The false adoption papers are factual this is mentioned in Pope Francis speech. Also if you watched the true story of "Twelve Years A Slave" papers were change on him as well and his name was also changed. The name changing of a slave was common during slavery in America as well as slaves who worked on the Cotton Plantations. The Revolutionary Change as Pope Leo XIII spoke in 1878 began to make owners more aware of their so called human property. What is taking place with these children on the Ivory Coast of Africa and Ghana is considered to be worse than any form of slavery in the history of the world.

These children go from forced child labor to fake adoptions to having their heart, kidney, liver etc sold. So just a little FYI if a child's heart is needed or liver is needed that child will be murdered due to the fact that you cannot live without a heart or liver you only get one of those organs per body. What's sad is Senators, Congressmen, government officials and the National Confectioners Association all know what is taking place. They know of these crimes being committed and refuse to do anything to, help these children.

I am Elder Christian in Jesus name.

Former Senator Harkin and Congressman Engel I have lived my life doing what is right. Your positions allow for all the room you need to help. If you are not a part of the solution then you are a part of the problem. These children need our help America

"Have We Lost It America"

When we look at the past, present and future of our nation. A nation which has come such a long way, not living in the shadows of its past but moving forward to change, reflections of the past will haunt its natural meaning for which it stands. When we look at past history what do you see today, progress or recess? Remember this old saying; you don't know where you are going unless you know where you came from.

Justice is not served by overlooking some of the wrongs and calling it right. Justice is what's binding within the law across the board.

Just like scripture tells us that God will not accept you as being lukewarm or he will spew you out, it's either God or Satan. When we as Americans base these values of justice on (In God We Trust) what we as a country have to look at and question is our love for God as a nation not as individuals. We have to ask this question is justice being served across the board?

How is it that our desire to please our immediate needs over shadows its creation? America is a nation that believes in the freedoms of all children.

To sit back and accept the abuse of a child is unheard of in America. Has America became numb when we can allow our Senators, Congressmen, Chocolate Industries and the National Confectioners Association to overlook five year old children in Africa being raped, sodomized, beaten with whips and abused emotionally, verbally, physically and mentally for life. Then to allow false adoption papers of these children to be adopted out of Africa, possibly murdered and the child's organs sold to the highest bidder. All of this is being overlooked in order for the Chocolate Industry to make money and sale Chocolate in AMERICA. Where is our American compassion? Let's look a little closer at the Cocoa Plantations, Harkin-Engel Protocol Is it worth it.

I am Elder Christian in Jesus name.

We can never say too much or do enough when it comes to the safety of a child

Copyrights Elder R. Christian all rights reserved ©

Did You Leave Your Chains Behind
Black History or Black Imprisonment

Go to the river so you can drink. I did not say go to the Damascus River and dip seven times. Allow me spiritually feed your soul.

When you look at your place, your position in America what do you see. Do you see a people who have crossed over into the Promised Land? Or do you see a people who were already here in this land possessing ownership. In other words you cannot give me what is already mine. The bigger picture is you never realized the beauty you have inside of you so others began to dismantle you. Here is the breakdown so you can see for yourself.

There are 2 million people in America that are imprisoned. Out of the 2million imprisoned 909,000 are African American (Blacks). To break it down even further there are 841,000 Black men and 68,000 Black women, in Prison today.

For every 100,000 African American (Black) males today between the age of 19-24, 10,695 are incarcerated. For every 100,000 White males between the ages of 19-24, 1,685 are incarcerated.

There were 1hundred million Africans murdered during the Middle Passage, being brought over on slave ships to be sold in Europe.

In the true story Belle a Black woman born with royal blood. And to this day her sons born with Black royalty bloodline is still in England. The Zong Massacre was about 131 to 142 slaves handcuffed together and thrown overboard alive. Whites wanted to collect the insurance money off slaves they murdered and were denied. This was the beginning of the abolishment of slavery in 1781. The hearing would come later in England to establish slaves as humans and not animals.

Today we still have 2million children on the Ivory Coast of Africa and Ghana being raped, sodomized, murdered, organ trafficking, and sex trafficking. This is being orchestrated through the Cocoa Plantations, five year old children working 100 hours a week.

I am Elder Christian in Jesus name.

Who said Willie Lynch

They Just Keep Coming
"A Ram in the Bush"

God sends a special servant. Even with all of the hatred and bitterness in this world. With all of the envy, jealousy and strife, God is there. Although I gave you the scripture (Rom 15v1) which explains how the strong are to bare the infirmities of the weak. Who is God really talking to? He is talking to all of us because we are all weak in many different ways. In scripture he tells us when we are weak. "Let the weak say I am strong. It is so important to know how to call on the Lord. It is important to know you cannot do anything without your confession of your love for Christ Jesus.

If you are lost in the wilderness and trying to find your way back to the Lord. He needs to hear these words come out of your mouth. Your belief in Christ Jesus is the dividing sword.

God makes it plain as to what you must do in order to be saved. (Rom 10v9-10) "That if thou shalt confess with thy mouth the Lord Jesus, and shalt believe in thine heart that God hath raised him from the dead, thou shalt be saved. (10) For with the heart man believeth unto righteousness; and with the mouth confession is made unto salvation."

For those of you in HIGH PLACES doing evil God is not please. You cannot confess the love of Christ Jesus and turn your head to the diabolical mess you have created on this earth. Politicians, Senators and Congressmen and Congresswomen, government officials National Confectioners Association, Surgeons and affiliates, God is not blind to the wrongs you are doing. You cannot say you love your brother and murder his wife and children. You will hear these words in relations to your salvation "depart from me you that work iniquity I know you not."

I am Elder Christian in Jesus name.

You are not getting away in your creation of building a fortune for yourself. Remember the parable of the "Sour Grapes". And also that you have children. Look at their birth defects, do you wonder why

Author
Elder Raymond C. Christian C.O.G.I.C

Gods Eyes are Not Closed to the Truth

Prayer by Elder Christian

Let this book be a testimonial for a new coming a new change for all that is in need of taking place on the Ivory Coast of Africa and Ghana on the Cocoa Plantations. Let this book be the start of all the ground work that is in need of being broken in order that new earth is turned over. And the life and love of Christ Jesus (Yeshua), Adonia, begins to break ground and open up the darkness of this evil demon being used to haunt these little children on the Ivory Coast of Africa and Ghana.

You have said in scripture Father God in (Amos 3:3) "Can two walk together except they be agreed." There is so much contradiction taking place on the Cocoa Plantations, conflict of interest being used to blind the eyes of those who can see. But I thank you Father God for using me to reveal the ugly legions. Let the blood of these children not be wasted any longer Lord. I am asking in your Holy name (I Am that I Am). I know you are all Father, God and I trust in you. You have bid me to come and I came. I have set forth your directions Father, God I know you are all, the alpha and omega. I know you hung all the stars in the heavens, you carved out the foundation of the earth with your finger. And there isn't any life created on the face of this earth without your consent to have your breath of life in it. These are your children Father, God I beseech you to not let them suffer any longer.

You sent you're only begotten Son Jesus (Yeshua) to be born in a world full of sin and to give us a chance at salvation. To give everyone a chance to make it into heaven but there is no one at the gates to vouch for these children on the Ivory Coast of Africa and Ghana. What has an innocent child done to not have a chance at salvation? I know you are the creator of all life and there is more than abundance in the life only you can give. What kind of hatred is there in anyone who would want to consume the life of a child? When you have said in your word to touch not the little ones, let them pay the penalties for such disobedience. Do not let these legions of demon run ramped any longer Father, God do not let them have their way. The battleground has been set and the shackles of bondage need to be removed from the lives of these innocent children on the Cocoa Plantations.

I worship only you Lord G_D in my walk, I worship only you Father G_D in the journey of which I am being led to travel, I know my steps are ordered by you. The shackles of hatred runs deep in the pockets of those my eyes cannot see. But your eyes Lord G_D are everywhere so I trust in you to make this wrong, right. You are the restoration of life. You are the restoration of new life of new hope and of a new world to come, where old things are passed away.

The demons, Father, G_D they are consuming the flesh of your innocent little ones, I pray for your intersession and these demons who wonder without fear let them hear the name of Jesus. Give them no place to run, no place to hide as they have done these children for so many years cast them out Father, G_D as you did the swine into the water and let them drown in their struggle to be free. I believe in your word Father, G_D that you sent forth to change the course of the world. Be not far any longer from these children, they haven't any knowledge of your existence. They haven't any voice to call out to you help them Lord, G_D help them Yahweh. These children do not have a name to call and the demons are running ramped against these children through the fields of the Cocoa Plantations. The children haven't a name to call they do not even know of Jesus

(Yeshua). Because they are taught as trained animals to only seek after what they are told to do. Let you mercy be their blessing and let your name be glorified by their lips who know not your name.

You make the impossible, possible Lord, G_D and let this book you have given me to write edify your name in every city, state, and country let it reach to the four corners of the earth. Let this book be your vessel of change for these innocent children. In the book of (Hosea 4:6) you made it clear that "My people are destroyed for lack of knowledge: because thou has rejected knowledge I will also reject thee, that thou shalt be no priest to me: seeing thou hast forgotten the law of thy God, I will also forget thy children."

These people who are involved in the Chocolate Industry have profited greatly through the use of innocent children. Let their possessed souls be exposed and let their life be an open chapter to your warnings concerning the mistreatment of children. They glorify themselves Father, G_D and they haven't any shame in their unnatural use of these children on the Ivory Coast of Africa and Ghana. They haven't any mercy on a child who does not want to be whipped, raped, sodomized, used as a sex slave or for sex trafficking, a child who will succumb to the will of its oppressor to avoid the pains of life. But because these children have not been taught the way they have not been given the word, they know not the gift of personal sacrifice, they do not know who to call. But these children follow the voice of demons because they are under their authority. Hear their cries Father, G_D please hear them. (Matthew 8v9) "For I am a man under authority, having soldiers under me: and I say to this man, Go and he goeth; and to another, Come and he cometh; and to my servant, do this and he doeth it."

You are needed in this place Father, G_D where the shameless can see your power as their spirit becomes convict and brought to shame. Because their only interest is to please the flesh they have lost sight of what thus said the Lord thy G_D they only believe in themselves.

(Hosea 4v7) "As they were increased, so they sinned against me; therefore will I change their glory into shame?" What glory is the Lord, G_D talking about here? These people on the Cocoa Plantations who are having their way with these children believe they are living a good life as they will call it. They have enjoyed watching the pains and abuse of these children on the Cocoa Plantations and in other places. They keep forgetting about their children and their children\'s children which is their glory in the later years to come. This is what you will benefit from for making a mockery of G_D, for those who have sinned against the Lord, their children will be brought to shame as they become powerless over the things they once had and what use to bring them joy. Have your way Father, G_D, let the wicked feel your thunder and let the angels of the Lord bare witness. Let your mercy be as merciless as theirs and let your raft have rein over them for what they have done to the children throughout the countries of this world. In Jesus name I send this prayer to all four corners of the earth, Amen

Written by: Elder Raymond C. Christian

Pt. 1 "He Listens for Repentance"

When one is in observation of the earth, the world, the Milky Way, the Universe and beyond. One must be able to conceptualize the inner strength of one's gift, of ones power to wonder and bring to into ones belief the compassion of one's philosophical thinking.

This is not your typical every day sermon. Today I want you look deep inside of you and say these words to yourself "I don't want to get to comfortable". I want you to focus on the inner you of your being, your presence is not something that accidentally happened. Your life has purpose and meaning. Here is a quote by William Cullen Bryant, "Truth Crushed to Earth Shall Rise Again". But I am giving you knew hope not in an affirmation of thought. An original statement I want you to thrive and search you soul.

And see the realness within yourself of who made you, God. And who you belong to God and why those of us choose to stay on the battlefields of justice. Because we know and believe as a people the truth is being held back. You are being made to feel my Christian brothers and sisters you are fighting a worthless fight, not true.

The Holy Spirit gave me this, "The True Crust of the Earth Shall Rise Again". Meaning all is well with God, he has already told us the end of the story and there will be a wailing and gnashing of teeth. When the gates of heaven close it's too late to tell Jesus you are sorry you denied him. Your judgment is upon YOU, YOU, YOU. Those on the inside of the gate whom will hear the wailing going on by those on the outside let not your heart be troubled they made a decision on their own not to follow Christ Jesus.

I am Elder Christian in Jesus name.

Remember "The True Crust of the Earth Shall Rise Again, things are suppressed over a period of time for good reason. It's like compressing a precious gem; once it is discovered everyone wants a piece of it. The question is did they wait too late? The gates are closing

Where are the Children

There are so many issues of concern to consider when we began discussing the missing children in America. It should really make you wonder after reading this book about the Cocoa Plantations what is really happening to the children, in America and the rest of the world. Have you ever stopped to wonder how many children in America alone come up missing every year, the numbers will scare you? Or how about how many children that comes up missing per day? The numbers are quite frightening; if you allow me to I will give them to you as you, please keep reading. I am holding back this information because I want you to think about the missing children on the Ivory Coast of Africa and Ghana we know why they are there working as slaves. But what about the missing children in America, it would be to no surprise if they were found on the Cocoa Plantations working as well. The children in America are missing where are they and where have they been taken too? Unlike the children on the Ivory Coast of Africa and Ghana working on the Cocoa Plantations sold into slavery. They do not have a traceable history if they come up missing because they are so young when they are taken they are more than likely to not have a birth certificate to prove who they are, what their real name is or who their parents are? Once they are brought to the Cocoa Plantations to work their names are certain to be changed. There isn't any identification numbers to track these children since they are kidnapped or sold for as little as $30.00 United States dollars. They can be very easily written off for whatever reason as though they never existed should a question come up concerning their whereabouts; there is nothing to identify them. This is why their names are change and how they are able to go undetected as if they never existed.

There is an old cliché that says, "The pen is mightier than the sword." That would be true in this matter as it relates to child abductions, without a trace. Without a picture, a birth certificate or any other documents to prove the child on the Ivory Coast of Africa and Ghana was sold by their parents or either kidnapped the chances of this child ever being seen again is a very strong probable zero percent? Are these children lost forever that is a good question? Just think of the odds we face right here in America with all of our modern technology, the Amber Alert, and Imagery readings which helps tremendously if they are put into effect immediately. But even in America the first 48 hours remain to be crucial in finding the missing child. Now you can imagine with what is taking place here with the children in Africa and Ghana, without any restrictions on how the children are acquired and forced to work on the Cocoa Plantations, whether it is from kidnapping or purchasing a child. With them not having trained search teams on the Ivory Coast of Africa and Ghana and no Amber Alert or modern technology to reach out further to find these children. The chance of ever being found or seen again the percentage would be considered sub-zero.

The big question once again is where are the missing children? One of the children who worked slave labor on the Cocoa Plantations was able to escape. He was in Mali, Africa which is one of the poorest countries in the world. The young man said, "I might have gotten out but there are thousands of children still over there. If by your report, you can help free just one, you would be doing a good job."

What was also uncovered concerning these children working the Cocoa Plantations is the children who are being kidnapped are sold for $30.00 U.S. dollars. When I talk about the Cocoa Plantations what I have tried to get everyone to see is that there is not a specific single location of the cocoa to grow, it grows all over. This is why I titled the book the Cocoa Plantations because there are over 100,000 small farms where the children are taken to for work. Just like Nigeria have 36 states with 14 of its states involved in growing cocoa. Cocoa Plantations are not just in once specific area of Africa, Ghana, Indonesia, Cameroon, Brazil, Ecuador, Mexico, Dominican Republic or Peru. These are the top 10 produces of the Cocoa Bean in the world. These are the top 10 countries of which child abuse is prevalent, the abuse of these children are taking place. Once you look at all of the other countries from all over the world involved in the Cocoa Plantations. I want you to keep this in mind the Ivory Coast of Africa and Ghana is noted as having the **WORST FORM OF CHILD SLAVERY** in the world. Which also involves child sex slaves, child exploitation, child trafficking and child organ trafficking of five year old children working 100 hours a week? And five year old boys and girls being raped and sodomized etc. The Cocoa Plantations are found to be in secluded remote areas in places that are hard to find and get to because of the illegal activities taking place with the children. The extra added activities besides work that take place is when some of these children are left behind at small farm plantations and used as sex slaves and made to perform sexual acts of all kinds.

Further research findings states that when the police chief of Mali said, "It's definitely slavery over there", "The kids have to work so hard they get sick and some even die." Which also confirms what I have been stating throughout the book that children are dying and are possible murdered for trying to escape from the Cocoa Plantations. Once again I ask what is being done with the bodies of these children, how many die from heat exhaustion, heat stroke, and what is a five year old child doing working 100 hours a week. The deaths of these children go unquestioned because they haven't anyone to account for their whereabouts and nothing to trace them to a location. These children are driven like animals whether they are sick or not it does not make a difference they will work. Any condition a child five years of age would have to work under is considered to be too much for an America child to bear because a child should not have to work as a slave. These are the children who go unaccounted for, because they haven't a life to look for to and no future to dream about these children merely exist for the sake of working on the Cocoa Plantations. In life these children are considered by the Cocoa Plantation owners to be non-existent because they are slaves and in death they will they will not be missed because to the slave owner the only value a slave has is his or her ability to work and produce for their owners.

These children on the Ivory Coast of Africa and Ghana are sold and forgotten about such a tragic story and painful as it may seem American's continue to buy chocolate. There isn't an excuse and by the end of the commentary I will take you a little deeper and question, are American children in danger as well of having to suffer this kind of abuse in the future? This is a question that remains to be answered or could it possibly already be happening right under our very nose? Americans need to stop and think what they are buying. They should have a broader understanding of the issues concerning the missing children today. Which is now a fact that the abductions are just not coming from children missing overseas but now it is children missing in America as well? This is how it works with people when we formulate our thinking into believing that others do not count because they are inferior that is one cycle of evolution that hasn't any bearing on the purpose at hand which is to treat everyone the same as it is stated in scripture (Rom 2v11) "For there is no respect of persons with God." Unfortunately this is not the case with mankind who would much rather forget the creator. So my moralistic finding to this would be more so to give our children in this world today a fair chance where they can as a group of people without biases of which mankind meaning their parents have already contaminated in thought. Be allowed to work together and not be divided as people of past generations once were. When we as human beings are able to look beyond the realms of our passages and seek the true meaning of our experiences we can embellish the true crust of who we are without having to peel back any layers. Or look at others with a superior attitude of which only perpetuates disgust of one being to another. It stagnates grow and enhances the evolutionary concept of survival of the fittest when this theory of Charles Darwin goes against what scripture says which is, (Romans 15v1) "We then that are strong ought to bear the infirmities of the weak, and not to please ourselves." The children on the Ivory Coast of Africa and Ghana are sold and forgotten about. American need to stop and think about what we are supporting because we have the buying and spending power to make that determination which at this point would be a moral contribution towards mankind. There is still hope for this great nation and that is why the eternal flame continues to flicker. Our purchasing power as American shoppers control the market of corporate success in any business. American citizens determine how the cycle of supply and demand will flow in all businesses and will also determine their fall or rise to become successful. This will be a unified effort across the world nationally and internationally to make this scrupulous wrong against these innocent children right. We have the purchasing power America and it should be used wisely and not toward those who enslave children. Their blood is on the cocoa and the coffee that Americans drink. These five year old children sweat and blood is absorbed from carrying cocoa sacks which weighs 6kg. Converted to American pounds that is 13.2 U.S. pounds per sack. These five year old children are carrying this weight on their backs and shoulders and they have the wounds on their body to prove it. There isn't anyone to care enough to account for the children on the Ivory Coast of Africa and Ghana these children are usually taken off the streets. They are considered to be slum kids sold by their parents for just a few dollars. As far as seeing their parents or siblings again in life is most certainly out of the question. These slum children are taken out of their country to another country where they will work on the Cocoa Plantations as slaves. There will not be any questions ever asked about their whereabouts or their existence. I told you earlier there was a missing children's list in America and that the numbers would scare you. But there is also a missing children's list in Mali, Africa at the Sikasso police department. But there is no record of the recorded purchased of these child on the Ivory Coast of Africa and Ghana of their placement on the Cocoa Plantations. No record of their existence which makes it easier for the small farmers to get rid of the child if the child is killed or just dies from being overly exhausted. Is working a child until it dies from exhaustion considered murder? In matters as it relates to morals and common sense anyone who would work a five year old child 100 hours a week to the brink of that child's demise would be considered murder. A child five years of age hasn't any concept of time or of being tired which means they will work until they fall dead. The missing numbers will never match and we haven't a clue as to how many children have actually died on the Cocoa Plantations there isn't a history of records being kept concerning the child's existence.

Fortunately for American citizens whose children are kidnapped or come up missing documentation is filed and kept on record. They at least stand so form of a chance of getting their child back. I know that I promised you the numbers earlier and I am certain they amount of children that come up missing in America alone will make your even more aware that kidnapping is not just an international problem but it is a national problem as well. I must also state this is going to take a unified effort on everyone's part to bring this child abduction and child abuse to some form of closure. According to the National Center for Missing and Exploited Children, there are roughly 800,000 children reported to be missing in the United States a year. Which would be approximately 2,000 children per day that come up missing, although the United States has Amber Alert and modern technology to help track missing children so many still fall through the cracks and are never found.

With that being said I am certain you can now see the impact of what is taking place on the Cocoa Plantations without any regard toward the life or death of a child on the Cocoa Plantations, a slave hasn't any self-worth it only has a value of what it is able to produce for its owner. The children who are taken to work the Cocoa Plantations do not make the missing children's list in America but there is an International organizations developed to find missing children overseas. But I stand again to stipulate the facts that these children who are sold by their parents and kidnapped off the streets of the

Ivory Coast of Africa, Ghana and Mali do not have a trail of records following them. They do not have pictures and other documentation that would actually give them a chance of being found such as an America child would.

NATIONAL CENTER FOR MISSING CHILDREN/ INTERNATIONAL CENTER FOR MISSING CHILDREN NCMEC/ICMEC

Although this is true let's take a look at the (NCMEC) in 1998, the National Center for Missing and Exploited Children (NCMEC) Board of Directors approved the creation of a separate international organization, the International Center for Missing & Exploited Children (ICMEC). The two now act as sister organizations to combat child sexual exploitation, child pornography, and child abduction. The (ICEMC) held its first Board of Directors meeting in 1998. It was officially launched in April of 1999. Which means the International Center for Missing & Exploited Children was already in operation prior to the Harkin-Engle Protocol which was adopted in 2001 to help with the problems in existence with the children on the Cocoa Plantations. Of which Congress has **Congressional Authorization of which the NCMEC can perform the 22 specific tasks under (42 u.s.c. sos5773).** You can find the 22 task listed on the internet of what congress is able to provide internationally unfortunately I must say I and not sure if any of this was ever applied to findings that apply to what is currently taking place with children on the Cocoa Plantations. With both of the organizations working hand in hand the NCMEC and the ICMEC work nationally and internationally as sister organizations to combat the violations of these children together. They run a global missing children's network of twenty-two countries. ICMEC has trained law enforcement personnel from 121 countries, they work with law enforcement in over 100 countries and has worked with legislatures in 100 countries to adopt new laws combating child pornography. The ICMEC also encourages the creation of national operational enters built on a public –private partnership model, and leads global financial and industry coalition child sexual exploitation and child pornography. The Koons Family Institute on International Lay and Policy is the International Centre's research arm. There are many organizations that should have a hand in what is taking place on the Cocoa Plantations and if there are laws that need to be amended for the betterment of the conditions as well as the illegal use and forced slavery and exploitation of five year old children then modifications need to be made promptly. We are already fourteen years out of the window of doing anything on the Cocoa Plantations since the passing of the Harkin-Engel Protocol. The rapes, sodomy, beating, and abuse of the children on the Cocoa Plantations are still in existence. The ICMEC was granted "Special Consultative Status" by the United Nations Economic and Social Council (ECOSOC) to assist the UN with its expertise regarding child sexual exploitation and child abduction. The ICMEC also works with the intergovernmental organization INTERPOL, the inter-continental organization the Organization of American Status (the OAS) and the Hague Conference on Private International Law.

All of these organizations sound quite impressive and even the involvement of which congress is also tied in with the NCMEC to support what is needed on their part in aiding the NCMEC. But to no avail are has anything been corrected on the Cocoa Plantations. The children are still under aged, little boys and girls are not only being raped but also exploited. From further review of different reports the rapes, sodomy, abuse, beatings, child exploitations, child trafficking, child sex slaves and child organ trafficking are all still taking place today. What kind of immoral justice is this supposed to be that involves the torturing of innocent children of which there is no justifiable reasoning. With laws in place and organizations in place both nationally and internationally there isn't a format that should be needed once the words child abuse has been uttered. Every law of which the NCMEC and the ICMEC have been put into place since 1998 went in effect 1999 clearly shows on the Cocoa Plantations. The horrific reports from CNN New, ABC News, Journalist, Reporters, including this book reveals the monstrous situations the children are being made to live under. All of this is being allowed to happen to these children just to get the cocoa bean to America so the production of chocolate can continue to be produced and manufactured around the world. Remember the United States of America is the number one producer and manufacturer of chocolate in the world. Do you think there is a better way to get the cocoa bean to America without having children working 100 hours a week? I wonder just were does the moral arc of justice began to bend?

A Look at the Moral Arc of Justice

When I talk about my philosophical view of what I have depicted as **"the true crust of the earth rising again"** I am speaking about this world and how things are slowly changing and coming to pass in accordance with the will of God. It is evident now that even the justice system is in question of its scales being balanced properly as the judges send forth their ruling on African America (Black) men being murdered and the murderers which have been on the police force has gotten off on a technicality. The true crust of justice is being unveiled before the world. The wound is freshly open and the unbelievable lies coming out of it is beyond the arc that supposedly bends toward justice. The bend as stated I must say seems to have a longer curve to its angle when it comes to Blacks and other minorities in the system. I emphatically detest the issue of the curve in the justice system where there should not be any at all I find it to be impermissible. How can life be fair even as it once was with white schools getting books to read and minority schools getting books with pages torn out of them in order not to have the entire story as it is told in the book? This is the true crust of earth which is the same today. Haven't you all figured it out, why does a person cheat because they want to win, why does a person lie because they want someone, I did not say everyone but they want someone to believe they are telling the truth? Why would those in the educational field cheat the African American Children out of their proper reading material not because they truly hate them but because they would like for their white children to be considered brighter, wiser, smarter, a genius. But in all actuality they are the ones who feel they are inferior because they are the ones who cheated. You cannot give someone who already has an advantage an advantage because they will win every time. You can give someone who is at a disadvantage and advantage because they will then at least stand a chance of coming out ahead.

What do I mean when I say the "true crust of the earth shall rise again?" Consider the crust a layer of some sort depending on its thickness when it is opened up then and only then will its richer soil be exposed. It's like cultivating land when someone tills the land to plant new seed. The soil is turned over to expose the better dirt, its richness and its fresh minerals. While we watch what is taking place in the United States today another layer of hatred is being peeled back uncovered in the courts. I have said this before and I will say it again that although the court system shows the balanced scales of justice on the doors and bench of the courtroom. That would be only in speculation that one cannot say anymore that they received a just and a fair trial because of what is taking place today.

What do you visually see when we talk about Reverend Theodore Parker who state, **"The arc of the moral universe is long, but it bends at the elbow towards justice."** Having the vision of what justice should be like is not within the scales of what is supposed to be already balanced. When we look at the moral arc, the break in the straight line of justice that is not supposed to sway slightly on either scale? Because in our moral minds the scales are balanced and just and weighed the same and there is not a need for it to be calibrated. This is where the arc of moral servitude toward all mankind begins to sway. The bending of the elbow determines who will receive justice because it is at the elbow of justice until all evidence is heard. The elbow of the judge has to rule and it is at the bending of the elbow and the hand that controls the gavel as to whether you will hear a guilty or innocent finding. The scales of justice are no longer calibrated as they once were they are now color coded, and it depends on the amount of what is being given across the table that will determine the ruling. Yes! I must agree with Theodore Parker when he stated the arc of the moral universe, with moral being the key word. There isn't any bipartisanship to compare since we have left common sense in the courts of law today and have dwindled down to erased videos, taped cell phone conversations and words with rulings of justified murder.

Now let's look at the bending of the moral arc towards justice. What all does this incorporate in its bending there has to be some form of unevenness a change of course a swaying of the pendulum that confers to a course of what should have been a straight line but is now a bend. Why should one have to bend toward justice when there is no bend or is the curve in the elbow no longer presumed to be unbiased? To bend something means to bare down with pressure in order to get it to fit or be forced into something it was not designed to be fitted into. This is the oath that a judge takes and the intent of becoming a judge insights what kind of character they will later adopt as a judge. It is so important when we look at the justice system and the men and women we have seated in the highest court of the land call the United States Supreme Court. This is where the honored Justices look at not bending the laws to meet justice but more so understanding a change in time can also be deliberated without a case of precedence. But with mere morals and an honest elbow that bends toward justice, this is their moral arc which makes them constant in their legal ruling simply because a straight line never changes. Morals are upheld to be true and just not because they have the gavel in their hand but because justice will be swift and the courts of law will continue to uphold its findings and its rulings.

Giving Sight through Knowledge

"Opening Blind Eyes"

The trickery of this world is not hidden from us this is why we "Watch and pray" and we "Pray without ceasing". God lead his children out of Egypt lead us today. He has delivered his children out of the lion's den. He has shown us the devices the world will us to discredit his name. To have us not to believe in the blood Jesus shed. To cover and protects us from all harm and danger.

Being led by the Holy Spirit is a beautiful experience. Everything comes full circle and the cycle of it all is already in place because it was told to us we shall know the truth and the truth shall make you free.

God knows the trickery things the devil uses to attempt to get his children off course. Remember Satan took Jesus (Yeshua) to an exceedingly high mountain flashing kingdoms before Jesus in a matter of seconds. What will Satan tempt you with?

Understanding the devices of the devil is the discernment of power God continuously gives the saints. Knowledge is power and it is better for you to know than not know. I will continue to walk out on the water for you. (2Cor2v11) "Lest Satan should get an advantage of us: for we are not ignorant of his devices.

Mankind will continue to change out the bible and take away things of importance to hide the truth from us. Remember we serve a Father in heaven who is omniscient (all knowing) in the trickery of man and all other things to come. (Rom 8v27) "And he that searcheth the hearts knoweth what is the mind of the Spirit, because he maketh intercession for the saints according to the will of God."

Meaning when we pray God already knows what mankind has done to us by taking things out of the bible. God hears our prayers because he searches our heart.

I am Elder Christian in Jesus name.

Never be afraid to attain knowledge it is power (Hosea4v6) "My people are destroyed for lack of knowledge: because thou hast rejected knowledge, I will also reject thee..." Glory

Who Do You Call On

"Knowing the True History"

When we look at the name of Jesus we say it with meaning JESUS. During the translation of the bible in the Hebrew spelling the letter J had not come into existence so Jesus name is really enunciated as (Hesus). In the original translations of the Bible God's name which is Jehovah of which appears in the bible in seven different locations of the bible is not written as it should be (YHVH) which is enunciated (Yahweh) which does not appear in the KJV.

Please allow me to explain. The Hebrew tetragrammaton, YHVH is the way the name of God appears in the Hebrew Bible. The Hebrew language is a consonantal language, possessing no vowels. Vowels were pronounced as they spoke but never written. This is how a sentence would look in Hebrew, please follow me closely the language is written using no vowels. (EXAMPLE): THS S TH WY HBRW PPL WRT BCK THN translated=(this is the way Hebrew people wrote back then). Now you can get off into the comparison of names in the Bible and how they evolved.

The complete word Yahweh or (YHVH) is not in the KJV. Although in Hebrew it has always been YHVH (Yahweh) many are still uncertain of the complete spelling. Jews believe it is wrong to say the name God. Even today they won't even write the word "God" the Jews will write the word God like this G_D. That is misspelled by me so I will write it again for you Jews will not write God even today they write G_D.

I am Elder Christian in Jesus name.

I pray my teachings today were enlightening. Understand that mankind has had his way of keeping the truth from you. But all will be uncovered. Because my Brothers and Sisters in Christ Jesus you know the way. It is in your Christian spirit, your daily walk. Let not your heart be troubled but believe in the second coming of the Son of G_D. Pray without ceasing. (2Tim 2v15)" Study to show thyself approved unto God

Their Blessings for Illicit Use

"Their Blessings Shall Be Taken Away"

So many people talk about those who are blessed. Of which the blessings usually consist of those who have financial wealth and are able to attain the things in life that are pleasing to those who are not able (the on lookers). They usually want but cannot afford such luxuries.

What I am saying to you here is the Lord giveth and he taketh away. Because of the blessings he has allowed to be bestowed upon you. Because of the favor he has shown you many of you take the blessings and squander them without thought. And haven't any logical reasoning as to what gives credence into what you have done. By using your blessings to acquire or do things that are not pleasing to God. This is why you see so many people and not just the rich falling from grace. You see singers, actors; lottery winners end up with nothing because of Gods blessings being used for illicit reasons.

His financial blessings used for the purchase of

prostitutes, drugs, alcohol, behind the scene payoffs, under the table deals taking place. The blessing of being a beautiful woman and the wrongful use of her body etc, these are the things God is not pleased with.

He makes it known in (Hosea 4v7-9) "As they were increased, so they sinned against me: therefore will I change their glory into shame. (8) They eat up the sin of my people and they set their heart on their iniquity. (9) And there shall be like people, like priest: and I will punish them for their ways, and reward them theirs doings." Blessed be the name of the Lord.

I am Elder Christian in Jesus name.

God is not just talking about people and their wealth but also the wealth of a great nation America. Murders are being covered up, behind closed doors deals are being made, guilty people are being protected. God talks about the fall of a great nation. Have your way Father, God have your way

Do You Strive to Gain

"A Pinnacle of What Plateau"

People strive in life to be successful; some inspire to set goals and be an inspiration to others. Many who make it to that high point never look back. They feel as though they have arrived at their true existence of their calling.

There are many things that lurk about even in our private time when we feel all alone. Free from worldly strife, a letting go process is always within the grasp of what you so choose or choose not to hold onto. What determines you is not what makes you who you are. It is usually what others see on the outside of you.

I ask you to challenge yourself by asking yourself this question. Are my challenges in life being met in accordance to what I want to do or change? Or are you living a life based on others expectations of you? Has the inner you been released are your intellectual muses being powered by your peers or is it really you? Know there are different levels to life and the channeling process will only develop when you become you and stop hiding your strength.

Part of the pinnacle is a defining process of change, being you. Once that is defined within yourself it will challenge friendships and growth. My question to you is, are you really trying to reach your pinnacle of life by finding Gods true purpose for you? Or are you still trying to quote unquote "BE DOWN WITH EVERYONE IN YOUR CIRCLE". You'll never get there.

I am Elder Christian in Jesus name.

Change is inevitable and procrastination only brings more delay to you finding the beautiful person inside of you. Don't be afraid Jesus is there waiting with open arms

Tobacco Farms another Child Nightmare

You would think from reading this book that the problems I have discussed on the Cocoa Plantations concerning children are only happening on the Ivory Coast of Africa and Ghana. Well don't get to comfortable America we have a problem protecting our children here in America as well. We have not been paying attention to the children on the Tobacco Farms right here in America. They are not five years old like the children on the Ivory Coast of Africa and Ghana but they are very young. And it is happening right here in America a country where I am 100% percent certain that in America there are laws set up to protect children from working at the very young age of seven years old. They work on the Tobacco Farms for very little wages and put in twelve hours a day in health hazardous conditions that could lead to death.

Tobacco Farms are another area of interest Americans is going to have to keep a close eye on. When we talk about children and humanity we know for sure in America there is no way a child seven years of age would be engaged in any form of work. So many issues are being kept quiet as it relates to child labor, child sex trafficking, child slavery and child organ trafficking.

Just like the Cocoa Plantations there are laws already set in place to fight against such violations of human child rights such as forced child labor and child labor. On the Tobacco Farms parents who sign for their children who are twelve years old to work longer hours makes it legal for the twelve year old to work. A child seven years of age should not be working at all. Whereas a twelve year old can work unlimited hours with written permission from their parents unfortunately children on the Cocoa Plantations never see their parents again to say the least. The child workers on the Cocoa Plantations ages range from 5 to 14. On the Tobacco Farms these children age range from 7 to 14 years of age. It is such a tragedy concerning both situations but in the same sense it tells us how we as United States citizens have dropped the ball when it comes to taking care of our children.

I must honestly say the Cocoa Plantations and the Tobacco Farms are areas of interest that search teams and investigative teams need to be looking at concerning child abuse and child abduction. I am certain you would like to compare the differences and search for a better ending but there is nothing more explicit than what is taking place with these children while we sit and watch. Just like there isn't an accurate accountability for the children on the Cocoa Plantations we know well over 2 million children on the Ivory Coast of Africa and Ghana are working on the Cocoa Plantations.

What you did not know about the Tobacco Farms in America is out of the four states I have listed before you; North Carolina, Kentucky, Tennessee and Virginia is they produce 90% percent of the United States tobacco. Laws pertaining to child rights are being violated daily and law enforcement officials are not enforcing the law.

What are these law officials doing that would be the question that should be asked in the United States of America. If I may digress for a moment and remind you that the border patrol officers we investigated and fired for taking bribes to let Mexicans into America. Well if you would like to I would say just reverse the scenario with the Ivory Coast of Africa and Ghana. Also look at the Tobacco Farms. It does not take a rocket scientist to figure out why laws that have been ratified and passed into law are not being enforced by the law. There are laws that state children are not supposed to be working in an environment that would be considered to be hazardous to their help. Just like the Cocoa Plantations is noted as being the worst form of Child Slavery in the history of the world. Children who work on the Tobacco Farms right here in America, their life is also considered to be in danger daily. I will not go into the rapes and abuse taking place on the Tobacco Farms In America, I am certain you have heard enough of that since the beginning of this book. Of course I am being facetious because you should never have enough of hearing about child abuse, child slavery, sex trafficking, or organ trafficking at any time.

There are life threatening dangers on the Tobacco Farms and the children who work on the Tobacco Farms do suffer from acute nicotine poisoning of which is also call green tobacco sickness, or GTS. The children who work on the Tobacco Farms have the symptoms that fit the characteristics of acute nicotine poisoning. Many have reported vomiting problems, nausea, headaches, dizziness, skin rashes and burning eyes. How many more symptoms need to be presented to let others know their young and still growing bodies are being affected by working on these Tobacco Farms?

It is no secret that when these children work on the tobacco fields in the morning the tobacco is wet from the dew. When the children's clothing gets wet the nicotine from the tobacco is absorbed through their skin. When this tobacco is filtered in through their skin the children began to get sick every morning and some are so sick they cannot even work. Because their clothes is so wet the absorption of the nicotine through their skin is equivalent to each child smoking at least fifty cigarettes a day. We are fully aware of what the surgeon has put on each pack of cigarettes, "that nicotine can cause cancer" it is really smoke at your own risk. But remember these children do not have a choice their little life is just being put up for auction. Meaning they are being treated no different than a guinea pig, let's try this on you first and see if you are able to survive without getting cancer What are the risk factors involved? Have the children been monitored as to how many acquired cancer after working on the Tobacco Farms. The Human Rights Watch report stated that two-thirds of the children died in 2012 from occupational injuries were agricultural workers. The schematics for the children on the Tobacco Farms are similar to the children who work on the Cocoa Plantations. The children are not given any protective clothing; they are not given a safety class or safety gear. Children working the tobacco fields also climb heights of at least one story high to hang the tobacco so it can dry. These children can also fall and become seriously injured, maybe fatal. When you look at the tobacco fields in America and the children working them what is not being considered again is the laws being violated. United States law stipulates that children are not permitted to work until they are fourteen years old and there are strict limitations on the hours they can work and the jobs they can do. The legal limitations involved with the children who are working does not apply to children doing agricultural work, working on farms. Once consent is given by the parents a twelve year old child can legally be hired to work on a farm and the hours worked can be considered to be unlimited. There aren't any laws set to protect the children on the Tobacco Farms.

Due to the high demand for tobacco and the constant need for children to work the Tobacco Farms it is without sagacious thought that the children working the Tobacco Farms will not be worked equally as hard and just as long as the adult workers.

There isn't any respect here for the children on the Tobacco Farms and neither is there any respect for children on the Cocoa Plantations. There has to be a medium point somewhere because these children are in need of some form of refuge, they need a place to retreat to where someone will listen. There are laws set in place to help with the abuse of these children. Although we look at it logically and morally there are laws set for the people who run Tobacco Farms and Cocoa Plantations to abide by. Why they are not being enforced well as the old cliché goes it does not take a rocket scientist to figure it out. The United States Department of Labor Wages and Hour Division make it plain with this statement: Federal Child Labor Provisions, also known as the child labor laws, are authorized by the Fair Standards Act (FLSA) of 1938. These provisions were enacted to ensure that when young people work, the work is sage and does not jeopardize their health, well-being or educational opportunities. By knowing, understanding, and complying with these provisions, employers, parents, and teachers can help working teens enjoy those safe, positive, early work experiences that can be so important to their development. Well I have to say when does the Federal Child Labor Provisions (FLSA) begin to enforce what is written. The law says it is okay for children to work doing agricultural work in the Tobacco Farms with given written consent from the parents at the age of fourteen years old with unlimited hours. I have not read anywhere that it is permissible for children who are seven years of age to work any length of time on the Tobacco Farms even with the parents consent. These are children in America working at the ages of 7 to 17 years old and the hours they can work with the parent's written consent is unlimited. I see I am right back to my theory of Voluntary/Involuntary Conditioning with the parents who are also workers on the Tobacco Farms give written consent to sign their children over to officials on the farms giving them the authority to work their children unlimited hours. I am certain they are forced involuntarily to give the written consent if they want to keep their jobs. This would be the involuntary/voluntary action taking place here that shows no force but only the use of authority with the parents knowing that if they tell the officials no. They will more than likely be out of a job and have to find other means to support their family, when there isn't any.

These laws need to be amended that relate to the non-agricultural laws and the agricultural laws. Of which one permits and under aged child to work and the other does not. When these amendments are passed and become law it is still important for the laws that are passed to be enforceable. And from what I have read concerning the Cocoa Plantations the (ILO), (CRC) and the Conventions Laws nothing is being enforced. On the Tobacco Farms there were more than 1800 non-fatal injuries that happened to children under the age of 18. And not only is the nicotine from the tobacco affecting the children but the farmers spray nearby fields with pesticides while the children are working. The children on the Tobacco Farms working said they could smell, tastes and feel the pesticide spray on their bodies as the wind carried the mist through the fields. On the Tobacco Farms the numbers of injuries are accounted for. On the Cocoa Plantations on the Ivory Coast of Africa and Ghana there is no such list that I have been made aware of that shows fatal or non-fatal injuries. The world largest tobacco companies purchase tobacco grown in the United States. Here is a list of the top tobacco companies, Altria, British American Tobacco, China National Tobacco, Imperial Tobacco, Japan Tobacco, Lorillard, Phillip Morris International and Reynolds American. When it comes to having problems with breaking the law these companies appear to be somewhat caring but to no avail whatever precautions they are taking is not helping the child. With North Carolina, Kentucky, Tennessee and Virginia producing 90% of the tobacco it is only in recent years due to exposure concerning the abuse of these children in America that the venue for business concerning the Tobacco Farms has begun to change. As other countries get involved it becomes a more open issue on the Tobacco Farms, multinational tobacco corporations have begun their attempt to get away from the United States of America by getting other countries involved in Tobacco Farming. Nearly seventy-five percent of the tobacco farming is now being done in developing countries like Malawi, Tanzania, Zimbabwe, China, Brazil and India. The relocation to poorer countries gives less attention to the laws being violated due to their need for work. It is evident they are these Tobacco Farms even with the surgeon general's note on each pack of cigarettes warning everyone to stop smoking they continue to do so. People who run the Tobacco Industry haven't any intent to stop the production of cigarettes, cigars neither will they make an attempt to stop the use of under aged children, teenagers and adult workers who are having to work under such unsafe conditions. After reading the United States Department of Labor Wage and Hour Division Act it is clear the Tobacco Farms are in violation of unsafe working conditions, health hazardous conditions and the child's ability to function normally without showing the symptoms of acute nicotine poisoning better known as (green tobacco sickness) GTS.

Any child having to suffer under conditions of which are not normal would be considered to be tragic. There is no mild situation on either half of the this story a child suffering is a child in need of help. The Cocoa Plantations throughout the world of which the top ten are noted in this book. But out of the ten the five year old children on the Ivory Coast of Africa and Ghana produce 60% percent, the most cocoa beans produced in the world. These five year old children are being raped, sodomized, abused and beaten. These are children being used as sex slaves; they are unused in sex trafficking, and organ trafficking on the Ivory Coast of Africa and Ghana. They do not have a mother or father to return home to after a night of work. These children do not ever see their parents again and this is where the rubber does meet the road. When we look at the Tobacco Farms and the toxins these children have to work under daily, when I think about the poison that is seeping into their body daily it should raise a red flag that these children all over the world need to be helped. But we have to start somewhere America, my cry out is to my brothers and sisters that something has to be done. We are talking about children in a time civilization frowns on the thought of such things taking place. Yet we allow those we have put in office to not do anything about such crimes. We (American citizens) have given the inch and it has stretched out further than our imaginations here in America could ever perceive to think. Where do we start? Where does change need to occur the most? Just how much more damage are we willing to sit back and let happen? We can make a difference; we can make change occur by putting a stop to the WORST FORM OF CHILD SLAVERY IN THE WORLD on the Ivory Coast of Africa and Ghana. Please these are children who need our help.

Former Senator Thomas Richard "Tom" Harkin

Says Farwell

I want the readers to know that (Democrat) Senator Thomas Richard "Tom" Harkin is now a Former Senator of Iowa, he has retired. Although his name is mentioned many times in this book concerning the Cocoa Plantations he was once a major link in being able to make changes for these children in a big way and did not. His seat went to a woman Republican, Joni Kay (Culver) Ernst. Even with this being said I must still stipulate that Senator Thomas Richard "Tom" Harkin had plenty of time to make the appropriate changes for the children on the Cocoa Plantations. The Harkin-Engel Protocol was named after Senator Harkin of Iowa and Eliot Engel of New York. Considering the time involved with Former Senator "Tom Harkin" retiring in 2015 the Harkin-Engel Protocol went into effect in 2001of which allows Senator "Tom" Harkin over thirteen years to work on bringing relief to five year old boys and girls who are being forced to work as slaves on the Ivory Coast of Africa and Ghana. How can anyone retire with a clear conscious and not pursue the molestation of children, the raping of children, the sex trafficking of children, the organ trafficking of children, the sodomy, abuse and beatings of children and possible murder of these children. Laws being broken on the Cocoa Plantations are being committed daily and nothing is being done about it. The reports I have read speak for themselves and pinpoint the International Labor Organization laws, the Convention of the Rights of the Child, Conventions, 138,182 and 29, the National Confectioners Association who are supposed to take care of any concerns of policies and issues in relations to the Chocolate Industry. Yes, what I am saying here just from what I have reviewed from my notes the Harking-Engel Protocol with both Former Senator Thomas Richard "Tom" Harkin and Congressman Eliot Engel had enough legal documents to make many changes on the Cocoa Plantations but did nothing. The violations of these children's rights are clear of which is stipulated from the age, the purchasing of the child illegally, the kidnapping of many of the children, imprisonment of the children being locked in mud huts to sleep in, armed guards to make sure the children do not escape, not allowing the children to receive an education, unsanitary working conditions for the children, hazardous working conditions for the children etc. It's all the work of a disaster waiting to be corrected but the Harkin-Engel Protocol does not seem to be on anyone's protocol list no matter how serious the offense of child abuse that is being exposed. And I am quite certain we all would agree that child abuse of any kind is a crime itself.

Unfortunately for the five year old boy and girls the correcting of this problem of abuse, rape, sodomy, beatings, sex slaves, sex trafficking, and organ trafficking etc. The Harkin-Engel Protocol was not on the protocol list of things to be corrected after Former Democrat Senator Thomas Richard "Tom Harkin gave his retirement speech. The Former Senator better known as "Tom" Harkin said he would like to see these things taken care of after leaving office. These were the issues that needed to be adhered to, the four issues of importance to Former Senator Thomas Richard "Tom" Harkin are as follows:

1. **Close the growing inequality gap between the rich and the poor**
2. **Prevent the destruction of planet earth**
3. **Reverse the underemployment of people with disabilities**
4. **Pass the United Nations treaty for people with disabilities**

There is nothing mentioned concerning how the laws that protect these children who are being abused in these foreign countries should be enforced. Nothing mentioned about the Harkin-Engel Protocol as it relates to the Cocoa Plantations and how the children are being violated physically, emotionally, verbally and mentally. I have always seen political leaders speak up for the rights of children and how they need the laws that have been ratified enforce for their protection. Because of their innocence and inability to take care of their self these children look to America to do what is morally right and just. To ensure they are able to have a childhood in some way and if they were allowed to have a normal childhood they would grow to become better productive and hardworking citizens with morals and valued opinions just like other citizens.

The Former Senator Thomas Richard "Tom Harkin has now retired as stated I am not certain if the phone numbers will be the same but of course I will leave them just in case. I am certain the operator should be able to direct your calls to his protégé Republican Senator Joni Kay (Culver) Ernst. She took the seat January 3, 2015 as concerned citizens you should want to get an understanding of if she intends to pursue what is needed to correct the laws being violated with the illegal use of these children on the Cocoa Plantations, on the Ivory Coast of Africa and Ghana. Or will the Harkin-Engel Protocol be intentionally delayed once again, for further investigations to be made. I am certain that Republican Senator Joni Kay (Culver) Ernst is well informed on such an issue concerning little boys and girls being raped, sodomized, abused and used as sex slaves, sex trafficking, and organ trafficking. We are not interested in moving backward but only forward as it relates to the Cocoa Plantations of which strictly ties in with the Chocolate Industries in America and the National Confectioners Association whose headquarters is also in our nation's capital Washington, DC. The many years wasted for discovery, investigations and research on how to make things better for the children there continues to raise a brow with nothing to very little being done. I wonder will God have mercy on such neglect which appears to be more entertaining to others. What more can I say that I have not already said and that is to please do not allow this to continue any longer. I pray the new senator taking the place of Former Democrat Senator Thomas Richard "Tom" Harkin; his protégé is Republican Senator Joni Kay (Culver) Ernst. I pray the new seated senator Joni Kay (Culver) Ernst takes time to review the Harkin-Engel Protocol in order that the children on the Cocoa Plantations can receive the help they need. I ask that God Almighty has mercy on her as she pursues this mission that is long overdue and be a drum major for justice.

To Locate Former Senator Thomas Richard "Tom" Harkin offices

Former Senator Thomas Richard "Tom Harkin retired after his fifth term, he was chairman of the Senate Committee on Health, Education, Labor and Pensions. He is ranked as the most senior junior senator, as well as the 6th most senior Senator overall. Before retiring he had offices in Iowa Cedar Rapids, Iowa (319)365-4504, Davenport, Iowa (563)322-1338, Des Moines, Iowa (515)284-4574 just in case you good folks in the United States want to give the new seating Republican Senator Joni Kay (Culver) Ernst a call you should be able to reach her in her Washington, DC office. This is just a few of the offices Former Senator "Tom" Harkin had. Don't let me forget his Washington, D.C. phone listing (202)224-3254. Remember I did not say you had to call him. But just in case you cannot put down this book because of all of the disgusting things taking place with these children I just thought the right thing to do would be to save all of you a little time so you can just pick from the list I have provided and voice your concerns. If you would like to send a letter by mail to the new seated senator or make a call to her fulltime district offices this is how it is done:

To Locate Former Senator "Tom" Harkin replacement her information is listed:

The Honorable Joni Ernst
United States Senate
825 Hart Senate Office Building

Washington, DC 20510-1502
Phone 202-224-3254
Email: http://www.ernst.senate.gov/content/contact-joni
WWW Homepage: http://www.ernst.senate.gov/
Twitter: @senjoniernst

Fulltime District Offices:
Federal Building Room 733
210 Walnut Street
Des Moines, IA 50309 — Voice: 515-284-4574
111 Seventh Avenue SE, Suite 480 — Voice: 319-365-4504
Cedar Rapids, IA 52401-2101
1606 Brady Street Suite 323 — Voice: 563-322-0677
Davenport, IA 52803
19 Federal Building — Voice: 712-252-1550
320 6th Street
Sioux City, IA 51101

To Locate Congressman Eliot Engel

Here is **Congressman Eliot Engel** contact information, he works in the 17th district in New York he is over the **Cocoa Protocol** and his number is 914- 699-4100 in New York. If the line is busy call Bronx, New York 718-796-9700 if that line is busy call Rockland, New York 845-735-1000, his office in Washington number is 202-225-2464 the offices open at 9am and close at 5pm.

As I continued to do my research I was shocked to see there was a woman involved in such a horrific story of America's bitter sweet mess as it relates to the Cocoa Plantations and the rapes and abuse of the children. I found myself to be quite stunned to find out that a woman Susan Smith would have a leading role in the chocolate industry. A woman would have knowledge of the rapes and abuse of these little girls and boys and allow this kind of treatment of children to continue. What kind of a nurturing, loving, sincere, kind hearted and protective woman could stand back as though nothing is going on in the chocolate industry and not work even closer with Former Senator Thomas Richard "Tom Harkin and Congressman Eliot Engel, government officials and the National Confectioners Association to see that bills are ratified. To see that renovations take place and immediate changes began for the betterment of all on the Cocoa Plantations. Since I did not want to overlook anyone that might be of help I had to add Susan Smith to the list. With all of the new laws that have been ratified concerning the protection of children nationally and internationally it would appear to be that a woman aware of International Labor Organization, the Convention of the Rights of the Child, Convention 182, Convention 29, and Convention 183. The probability of Susan Smith not knowing what is taking place on the Cocoa Plantations would be almost to high of a percentage to calculate. For a woman to be aware of the rapes, abuse, sodomy and trafficking of these children and I will continue to add possible murders of these children taking place on the Cocoa Plantations. I would have to ask why she hasn't also contacted government official and politicians to inform them of the help these children need. Yes her name is Susan Smith a woman who happens to hold a very distinct position as it relates to this matter of chocolate.

Susan Smith

**Senior Vice President of Strategic Communication
For the National Confectioners Association (NCA)
Executive Director of Chocolate Confectionery & Policy Issues**

Susan Smith is the Senior Vice President of Strategic Communication for the National Confectioners Association (NCA). The Confectioners are also a part of the Nestles Chocolate of which the President of Nestles Chocolate & Confectioners Association USA is Bradley Alford.

Susan has been involved with Association management for the Confectionery Industry since 1984. Susan Smith was first hired by the Chocolate Manufacturers Association as director of legislative affairs. In 1992, Susan began working for the National Confectioners Association (NCA). She currently leads NCA communications efforts ensuring NCA strategically communicates candy specific information and concerns to NCA members, public policy opinion leaders, customers/trade and consumers/media. She also serves as issue spokesperson for the United States Chocolate and candy industry.

Prior to her tenure with the Associations, she was a Legislative Assistant in both the Senate and the House of Representatives, handling agriculture and environmental issues. **Susan Smith** belongs to the Chocolate Manufacturers Association.

This is a woman who plays a key part in what is taking place with the chocolate industry. Susan Smith is well educated and knowledgeable when it comes to the Chocolate Industry. As far as her being a spokesperson for the United States Chocolate and Candy Industry I would have to say she is also knowledgeable about the abuse and everything else taking place on the Ivory Coast of Africa and Ghana concerning the cruelty of these children. When anyone reaches such a high plateau in life such as Susan Smith prior to getting to the current positions held cannot say she was not privileged to the information I am putting forth in this book. To hold such positions and in order to be able to discuss commutatively and express her criteria for change she it would be imperative that she would have to be knowledgeable of what makes the chocolate industry run. Not only on the American side as it relates to the chocolate industry but she would have insight as to what is also taking place on the Ivory Coast of Africa and Ghana. Her job description should read that she must be able to inform Bradley Alford who is the President of Nestles Chocolate and the President of the Confectioners Association with any information concerning the Chocolate Industry and the Cocoa Plantations on any given moment's notice. The National Confectioners Association serves a key role as well into making sure policies and issues are handled adequately.

Susan Smith received an MBA from the Ohio State University and a Bachelors degree from Bowling Green State University.

With Susan Smith being a big part of the Chocolate Industry since 1984. The million dollar question is, does she have knowledge as to what is taking place with these children on the Ivory Coast of Africa and Ghana as it relates to chocolate and the Cocoa Plantations? In relations to her position over the Chocolate Industry **Susan Smith** would be just as guilty as **Former Senator Thomas Richard "Tom Harkin and Congressman Eliot Engel** concerning this issue of the Cocoa Plantations with the illegal use of the children concerning their age of the children being five to 14 years old, working 100 hours a week. The child sex slaves, sex trafficking, child abuse, sodomy, and organ trafficking of these children involves international laws of which fall under the jurisdiction of the United States of America. And into the lap of Former Senator Thomas Richard "Tom" Harkin, Congressman Eliot Engel and Susan Smith, of course, we want to look at the Chocolate Industry as a whole, as well as their Founders, Corporate leaders, and owners of the small cocoa farms, and the thousands of Cocoa Plantations through throughout the Ivory Coast of Africa and Ghana. These people have a lot of explaining to do?

Ratified Laws; bring no relief for the Children on the Cocoa Plantations

The Emancipation Proclamation signed by President Lincoln to abolish slavery in 1863 due the harsh and cruel treatment of Blacks in America should be the template used to abolish slavery all over the world. There is no excuse why any one of the three named individuals should not have called for corrections to be made on the Cocoa Plantations immediately at the Harkin-Engel Protocol went into effect in 2001.

The vein of chocolate runs deep within the core of so many countries and America is number one on the list for producing and manufacturing chocolate. There are so many children all over the world which are being forced to be a part of forced child labor. I want America and the rest of the world to know that with all of the children in other countries being violated. Many journalist and writers have stated that the Cocoa Plantations on the Ivory Coast of Africa and Ghana are the worst forms of child slavery and child abuse in the history of the world. Children all over the world need help. I have already listed the seven top largest cocoa producing countries in the world. I am certain you have forgotten so I will list them again Indonesia, Nigeria, Cameroon, Brazil, Ecuador, the Ivory Coast of Africa and Ghana of which the last two listed produces more than half of the global cocoa production 60 percent. My response to this continental spread of a problem concerning these children is that we have to start making the corrections somewhere. Two more reasons why I chose to write the book about the Cocoa Plantations. First of all because the Ivory Coast of Africa and Ghana are noted as having the worst forms of forced child labor and child slavery in the world. Secondly because these innocent children on the Ivory Coast of Africa and Ghana have to endure the rapes and abuse daily while their CRC rights are being violated and those who could have a major impact to begin to implement change are sitting on their hands.

Former Senator Thomas Richard Harkin, Eliot Engel, and **Susan Smith** all play a part on making these changes happen. The abuse on the cocoa plantations is the worst ever. I will not say since slavery was abolished because slavery was not abolished and the Cocoa Plantations are evident of it existence. Slavery is also being hidden behind the prison walls. And prison is an entire different subject matter, it most certainly would be another book, when I speak on prisons and "Mass Incarceration." The moral obligations set up to reestablish atonement with these children on the Ivory Coast of Africa and Ghana and not try to minimize their abuse because they are not in America is hideous. It will only suffice what drives the uncompassionate nature of the beast which is obviously driving this animal. When America politicians, government officials, National Confectioners Association and the Convention on the Rights of the Child (CRC) has the power to step in and stop what is taking place with these children of which is considered to be criminal. There are laws in place to protect these children, Convention 182, International Labor Organization. It's not right and it has got to change in order for the world of children to be able to progress and move forward. I must ask the question and I know I have asked you the reader a lot of questions in this book but what have these children done to be so overlooked and abused without thought? Without the government of the United States of America having a conscious mind to step in and stop the abuse of these children immediately. Let me clear this up on who's at fault by saying the United States of America is not the only country hyped on chocolate. I have already given you the top ten countries that produce and manufacture chocolate. I do not need to list the other nine but guess who is number one that's right the United States of America. There are international laws as I have stated that will allow America and other countries to intercede for the benefit of these children. This situation is not hopeless it is just there is a lot of time, money and renovations involved. But that is exactly what it is going to take in order for things to get better. Those who have been hired to protect these children rights need to step up to the plate and hit the home run, do something for these children.

The Good Old Boy

The one thing we must stop doing as Americans is stop playing the "good old boy" games and getting in bed with other countries just because everyone else is doing it. Everyone is trying to be in the know and get a piece of the pie. The problem gets a little more visual since everyone can see what is going on and pretend it's alight because they don't want to upset the wrong people. We also have to stop re-electing people to public office positions who are not doing their job. What we are finding out is there are hidden agendas when people are elected to office and other issues continue to arise but nothing seems to ever get resolved. Maybe the reason why is that it is not on the politicians important things to do list. Are we not tired of hearing the old put off game, "I'll get to it, I'm working on it, I'll give you a call, I got someone on it, call me later, sorry I have to cancel this appointment other things came up? This is exactly what I am saying here America, are you not tired of the same old put it off and let's see what happens routine. Those who are in the leadership positions are responsible for everything taking place within their range of control. We have created laws concerning forced child labor; the United States Department of Labor is well informed as to what is taking place. Unfortunately whatever movement if any is taking place to shut down the violators on the Cocoa Plantations and bring them to justice it would appear to be far from over. The progress made if any is so tiny that it would take a very powerful microscope to see if any advancement at all has been made concerning the changes that were agreed on to take place in 2001. We are now in the year 2015.

We are now waiting on changes in polices and amendments to take place fourteen years later.

When we look at politics we don't have to wonder why policies were changed neither do we really have to contemplate as to why delays were set into motion? The question that should be asked is when are you politicians, government official, and National Confectioners Association and Chocolate Industry owners going to do something to help these defenseless children. There is no way on God's green earth that every one of you seated in Washington, DC who has the power to change the conditions on the Cocoa Plantations can honestly go to bed at night. Without thinking of the children who are being raped, battered, sodomized, and possibly murdered and only God knows what else. You could not possibly be trying to clear your conscious and lie to yourself by saying these children to you would be considered to be in a better place. Could this be the case or are you saying, before you brought them to the Cocoa Plantations they were not promised a meal of corn mush a day and fresh water, at least they get that now.

People you should not be afraid to contact

Contact your church Bishop, the Pastor, the Elders, your Priests; contact everyone you know that has the power to make changes happen. And please remember I will not be buying any chocolate until this matter is resolved I am most certain after all of the information given you will not be purchasing chocolate.

You can also contact **David J. West** he is the CEO of Hershey Corporation.

"Is There Child Slavery in Your Chocolate"
By John Robbins

Feb 1, 2015

"improved supply-chain efficiencies." Such "efficiencies" allow David J. West, to make $8 million a year while unpaid children are forced to labor under vigilant working conditions on the Cocoa Plantations growing the company's cocoa." (please read the entire article)

Playing in the Devils Playhouse 666

I find it quite strange that our $8 million dollar man David J. West net of income a year has a little more significance to it than just a salary. What would a man who makes that kind of salary a year not want to do the righteous things by making the corrections that need to be made on the Ivory Coast of Africa and Ghana by making it more comfortable for the children there? Could it be that the wealthy CEO of the leading Chocolate Company really does not care about the children, I am not badgering, I am merely asking a legitimate question? Is David J. West putting up another smoke screen situation just like the Harkin-Engel Protocol where nothing is enforced but the laws being passed looks good on paper? This is what the Harkin-Engle Protocol exemplifies a smoke screen because nothing is being done to rectify the abusive, working conditions, living conditions, and rapes taking place on the Ivory Coast of Africa and Ghana. What you will be reading a little later in this book is what Pope Leo XIII, and Pope Francis has to say about the illegal use of workers concerning these factories and the illegal use of these five year old children on the Cocoa Plantations. I am quite certain that since I have made myself aware of the laws passed by the International Labor Organization, United States Senators and Congressmen, the Convention of the Rights of the Child and the National Confectioners Association that David J. West has the resources to remain well informed as to what is taking place nationally as well as internationally with the Chocolate Industry as a whole concerning its involvement as well as its connection with the Cocoa Plantations. When talking about what is known of the

Chocolate Industry please keep in mind there was a meeting that did take place in 2001 by six of the top leading Chocolate Industries. In 2001 six of the top Chocolate Industry leaders met with Senator Thomas Richard Harkin and Congressman Eliot Engel to create the Harkin-Engel Protocol. It was passed and it would be extremely hard for me to believe that David J. West was not fully aware of the violations of laws taking place on the Cocoa Plantations. As well as the trafficking of the children on the Cocoa Plantations organs along with the disguised adoption papers and the raping, sodomizing, and beatings taking place with these five year old boys and girls daily. It would be extremely hard for me to believe that David J. West the CEO of the leading Chocolate Company could be so irresponsible that a man of such high caliber, a man that is able to attain an $8 million dollar a year salary. Would not be informed of the laws set in place and not make it his primary interest of concern which involves the legalities of the Chocolate Industry empire. The leadership skills along with the intellectual abilities David J. West would have been able to exemplify to receive such a salary of $8 million dollars a year makes it very hard to believe any claim of his not knowing what is taking place on the Cocoa Plantations with these children. There are laws stipulating the age limitations of these children and the conditions under which they are able to work. You will see the **Convention on the rights of the Child (CRC)** again but for the purpose of proving to David J. West CEO, of the leading Chocolate Company in America that laws are being broken I present to you:

Article 34 Convention on the Rights of the Child (CRC)

States Parties undertake to protect the child from all forms of sexual exploitation and sexual abuse. For these purposes, States Parties shall in particular take all appropriate national, bilateral and multilateral measures to prevent:

a. **The inducement or coercion of a child to engage in any unlawful sexual activity;**
b. **The exploitative use of children in prostitution or other unlawful sexual practices;**

c. **The exploitative use of children in pornographic performances and materials.**

When I think about all that is being said in **Article 34** I have to look at what is being said in **Article 33** of which Article 33 stipulates (a) Provide for a minimum age or minimum ages for admission to employment. (b) Provide for appropriate regulation of the hours and conditions of employment; (c) Provide for appropriate penalties or other sanctions to ensure the effective enforcement of the present article.

Founders and CEO's make it personal with their supervisors and directors as to what they will accept concerning violations of the law in the work place. What kind of an Industry or Corporation will sit back and accepts little children being raped, sodomized, and beaten with whips and bike chains. Five year old children who are working 100 hours a week, every week what kind of a person would allow little children to be worked that hard for the purpose of padding his own pockets. What kind of a dark side is taking place on the Cocoa Plantations to allow such a horrific story such as this to be written about such ugliness involving one of the world's most beloved products, chocolate? What involvement is there in the higher levels of status structure of the Chocolate Industry? There are some things concerning the rights of the children that should question corporate leaders as well as their integrity? The other question I need to ask pertains to religion. Is David J. West a man of God a follower of Christ Jesus? I am asking this question because his $8 million dollars a year salary is equal to the mark of the beast. Making his monthly salary out to be what the Holy Bible says is the mark of the beast $666,666 per month if this is true it would explain why such harm is being allowed to come to these little innocent children. Is the dark side of the Cocoa Plantations tied in with hidden satanic secrets or is it a mere formality? Little children are sacrificed daily to appease the needs of those who have purchased them for a desired price. And what normal minded person would allow such organ trafficking of children to take place for the sale of child organs? The numbers 666 is the mark of the beast as it relates openly to the Holy Bible. As I stated throughout this book I will have some form of documentation as backup evidence to what is being said in this case I present to you the Holy Bible. If you will follow me to (Revelations 13 v 18): **"Here is wisdom. Let him that hath understanding count the number of the beast: for it is the number of a man; and his number is Six hundred threescore and six."**

Is David J. West a child of God? And if so why would he allow so much hatred to be channeled toward the lives of innocent children? Is money the main basis for opportunity, nothing at this point can be over looked and money usually turns out to be the primary factor? Hidden deep dark secrets in the emptiness of a wilderness where all echoes sound the same.

Echoes in the sense of children who are crying out in the midst of the day and in the hollowed forest areas of the Cocoa Plantations never to be seen again because they haven't any protection and they are a poor people no one seems to care. Could this be the one who is soon to be revealed to the world in the Holy Bible? Because the earth does tremble and is ready to erupt with the blood of these innocent children, yes they are the victims whose blood is oozing out of the ground. There will come a time when you cannot hide behind your success any longer. The time draws nigh David J. West when you will have to explain yourself and the reason why you have not done anything to correct the problems on the Cocoa Plantations and the 2 million children in slavery. Can Lucifer be so obvious, is the mark of the beast so evident that darkness dwells so deep in the souls of the corporate heads pockets. How could anyone allow such a mortifying situation to be connected to the Chocolate Industry and tie it in with the scandal taking place with little children. Or is it because you have been uncovered for who you are? I am certain a man receiving $8 million dollars a year $666,666 dollars a month must be intelligent enough to know you are doing the work of your father here on earth and that would be Satan, could that be you? The Holy Bible speaks of more than one devil. Please go to (James 2v 19) **"Thou believest**

that there is one God; thou doest well: the devils also believe and tremble."

For the love of money is the root to all evil, this too shall pass. God my Father in heaven said he shall reveal you to the world. Go to (Isaiah 14 v 16-17) **"They that see thee shall narrowly look upon thee, and consider thee, saying, Is this the man that made the earth to tremble, that did shake kingdoms; (17) That made the world as a wilderness, and destroyed the cities thereof; that opened not the house of his prisoners?"**

There are numerous violations of laws taking place on the Cocoa Plantations. Five year old children working 100 hours a week, the rapes, sodomy the beatings and sales of their organs on the black market is not something I just conjured up. My depiction is if you are a caring person, a husband to your wife and a father to your children than this could not possibly be you, could it? A reasonable man who has gotten quite wealthy off of the sales of slaves and the broken backs of children; this could not possibly be going on while you are the CEO of the Chocolate Industry Empire? No child deserves to have to live or work under such hazardous conditions of which the Cocoa Plantations exists. With the top company in the Chocolate Industry bringing in a profit of 60 billion dollars a year and the second bringing in 30 billion a year, I have not mentioned the profits of other companies within the Chocolate Industries throughout the United States. The Chocolate Industry is a trillion dollar industry of which almost five million tons of chocolate a year is produced this is a small part of its well kept secrets behind this chocolate mess. When trying to find the righteous thing to do it is a well-known fact that all we have is the leaders of the Chocolate Industry to look at for correction along with our political leaders, our government officials and other organizations involved in creating this melting chocolate mess. It is obvious the Cocoa Plantation Owners are not going to budge until America makes a move concerning the Chocolate Industries and force the Cocoa Plantations owners to stop enslaving children to work their plantations, pay these workers a reasonable wage, give them better housing conditions and build schools so these children can become educated so they can better themselves in exchange through education better their communities.

Readers you can also contact the National Confectioners Association (NAC) designed to correct any policy issues involving the chocolate industry below you will find their address:

National Confectioners Association
1101 30th Street NW Suite 200
Washington, DC 20007

The Red Record

I know it sounds a bit harsh but innocent black men and black women being hung in those days was like taking a casual walk in the park, nothing to get upset about, and who would care why they were hung, just hang them for the fun of it all. They were property they hadn't any value of life not to mention whether a crime was committed by the slave or not. Hanging a black man or his entire family was merely a form of entertainment to many whites.

I want to record for you a case I researched in a book titled "The Red Record". This book has recorded in it the names of alleged cases which involved the reasons as to why black men, women and children where either murdered, hung, shot to death or burned alive for crimes whites thought they may have committed. I will quote exact cases as to what took place straight from "The Red Record" book which explains to date why so many blacks live in fear of traveling the country side alone. Many blacks live with memories today of their loved one being taken from their home and never seen again. I want you to stay focused on what this book is about the Cocoa Plantations and the five year old children purchased or should I say sold into slavery. In the same sense I want you to hear what I am saying to you with this one particular case in "The Red Record" book

Here are a few cases quoted from **"The Red Record"** book

This case is titled: **LYNCHED BECAUSE THEY WERE SAUCY**

"At Moberly, Mo., February 18 and at Fort Madison, S.C., June 2, both in 1892, a record was made in the line of lynching which should certainly appeal to every humanitarian who has any regard for the sacredness of human life. John Hughes, of Moberly, and Isaac Lincoln, of Fort Madison, and Will Lewis in Tullahoma, Tenn., suffered death for no more serious charge than that they "were saucy to white people." In the days of slavery it was held to be a very serious matter for a colored person to fail to yield the sidewalk at the demand of a white person, and it will not be surprising to find some evidence of this intolerance existing in the days of freedom. But the most that could be expected as a penalty for acting or speaking saucily to a white person would be a slight physical chastisement to make the Negro "know his place" or an arrest and fine. But Missouri Tennessee and South Carolina chose to make precedents in their cases and as a result both men, after being charged with their offense and apprehended, were taken by a mob and lynched. The civil authorities, who in either case would have been very quick to satisfy the aggrieved white people had they complained and brought the prisoners to court, by imposing proper penalty upon them, did not feel it their duty to make any investigation after the Negroes were killed. They were dead and out of the way and no one would be called upon to render an account for their taking off, the matter was dismissed from the public mind."

This case is quoted from: **"The Red Record"** book

This case is titled: **LYNCHED AS A WARNING**

"John Peterson, near Denmark, S.C., was suspected of rape, but escaped, went to Columbia, and placed himself under Gov. Tillman's protection, declaring he too could prove an alibi by white witnesses. A white reporter hearing his declaration volunteered to find these witnesses, and telegraphed the governor that he would be in Columbia with them on Monday. In the meantime the mob at Denmark, learning Peterson's whereabouts, went to the governor and demanded the prisoner. Gov. Tillman, who had during his canvass for reelection the year before, declared that he would lead a mob to lynch a Negro that assaulted a white woman, gave Peterson up to the mob. He was taken back to Denmark, and the white girl in the case as positively declared that he was not the man. But the verdict of the mob was that "the crime had been committed and somebody had to hang for it, and if he, Peterson, was not guilty of that he was of some other crime," and he was hung, and his body riddled with 1,000 bullets."

Now that you see the truth of what is recorded in the "Red Book" the reality of what has taken place with slaves in America and the how they were treated is not a myth. It is an awakening to everyone who stands up to say "My country tis of thee sweet land of liberty of thee I sing." While you are standing up with your hand over your heart remember it comes with the respect of liberty and justice for all. The bigger question is how can you call yourself a Christian and then hang someone from a tree, or boil someone in oil, or skin someone alive just because you feel you were disrespected. This is how slaves in America were treated during slavery. I cannot begin to imagine how these five year old boys and girls on the Ivory Coast of Africa and Ghana are being treated. It is very disheartening to live in the United States of America knowing it is a nation divided. This has nothing to do with having a African American President in 2008. It was divided a long time before President Obama ever was elected into office. It was divided before it the media came up with the names of Blue and Red states. Try going back to the civil war when the North was fighting against the South. There will always be those who wanted slavery to not end but fortunately for African Americans slavery in the since of what it once was in America will never happen again, at least not in America. But for the two million children working the Cocoa Plantations on the Ivory Coast of Africa and Ghana slavery is very much alive.

Sex Trafficking and Murder
People in high places

This is what the Holy Bible speaks of when it says in Ephesians 6v 12, "to be aware of people in high places." It will be evident to you as to why you should be aware of people in high places because of the positions they have and things concerning the law they are able to get away with, sex trafficking as well as possible murder. Everyone is fully aware of sex trafficking and the different sex rings involved in kidnapping young girls and boys and making them sex slaves. These children on the Ivory Coast of Africa and Ghana who work on the Cocoa Plantations are victims to sex trafficking. It is big business and brings in a lot of extra money by making these children sex slaves. If I am getting to explicit than please turn the page but my position is to keep you informed as to what is taking place with these children on the Cocoa Plantations and that is what I intend to do. These children are purchased by some wealthy individual they are sold to the highest bidder and taken off to some remote area and made to have all kinds of illicit sex. These are five year old children boys and girls whose bodies are violated and the person who purchased the child due to their status will never be brought before any court of law.

These children are also used for the purpose of organ trafficking, yes their organs. Since nothing can really be validated as to the count of children being used on the Cocoa Plantations many of these children are never seen again. Once false adoption papers are set up and fake certifications are given for these children to be adopted once these African children are flown to their remote destinations they are never seen again.

The Holy Bible tells us about spiritual wickedness in high places. Yes, God is talking about heart surgeons and doctors who are able to remove the kidneys or the live or pancreas of the child. Please keep in mind that I am not trying to be funny but only stating a fact that you cannot live without a heart, a liver or pancreas. These are critical body organs that you are only given one of. When we talk about life threatening situations and look at the slaughtering of innocent children let it be known these people in high places will be held accountable. And please do not use (Ecclesiastes 3 v 3) "A time to kill". No it does not apply to freely being able to murder innocent children because someone's grandson or granddaughter, mother, father or whoever has a damaged organ and they want them to live, is just not right, murder is just what it is murder. Certain people have been blessed with money and others with certain talents like heart surgeons etc. the medical field becomes a very costly game. Because we began to wrestle against the rulers of the darkness of this world and the dark side of the world they serve is for self-preservation. They want more money, more riches and more wealth, better vacations, etc. and all of this can be purchased through the monies paid from trafficking organs of these children on the Ivory Coast of Africa and Ghana on the Cocoa Plantations.

Of course I am going to confirm what I am speaking on with scripture as I have done throughout this book. Please read with me (Ephesians 6v12) **"For we wrestle not against flesh and blood but against principalities, against powers, against rulers of the darkness of this world, against spiritual wickedness in high places."** These highly trained surgeons who are doing these implant removals and replacements have to operate with a team of people. There is a heart surgeon needed for this specialty which is the heart. Anesthesiologist is needed. And of course the surgeon's team of assistants is needed along with the medical equipment to perform such an operation. I will have to ask you the reader what actually happens to the bodies of these children are they dissolved by citric acid in a tub in someone's facility are the bodies carved up and fed to sharks in the ocean, or are they incinerated if you ask me it is all quite sickening. When you look at the bigger picture in the minds of those who are specially talented and gifted they deserve the best and to them this is what they went to school for to be able to take care of the sick not to becomed rich and wealthy at any cost. And they feel by any means they are going to have the best of life for their families and themselves. These are the people the bible speaks about in high places another perfect example of how the world takes care of its own. It would be impossible for these people who are obviously in darkness to ever be considered as Christians because it is also written "thou shalt not kill". Acts of evil such as murder are not a people who serve the one true God. They serve the world and because they serve the world they serve the father of the world which is Satan. Those who serve the world only want the things that please the father of this world. They are not interested in brotherly love and peace this is why they do not mind murdering innocent children because the dollar is their god.

(John 8v44) "Ye are of your father the devil, and the lusts of your father ye will do. He was a murderer from the beginning, and abode not in the truth, because there is no truth in him. When he speaketh a lie, he speaketh of his own for he is a liar, and the father of it."

The Pope Speaks
Pope Francis

The Pope speaks for all mankind to have compassion on others who are notably weaker than you. His first prayers for change in the world and headlines the newspapers on January 1, 2015 with: **"No longer slaves, but brothers and sisters" in his World Day of Peace statement.** Pope Francis speech was heartfelt and of course sincere as he expresses his personal feelings as well as biblical scripture given in his attempt to awaken mankind to a new way of thinking. **Pope Francis, "I pray for an end to wars, conflicts and the great suffering caused by human agency, by epidemics past and present, and by the devastation wrought by natural disasters, I pray especially that, on the basis of your common calling to cooperate with God and all people of good will for the advancement of harmony and peace in the world, we may resist the temptation to act in a manner unworthy of our humanity."**

(Authors Review)

Even with the Pope speaking and exposing the wrongs of the world in relations to slavery, prostitution, child exploitation and trafficking etc. They are different entities mentioned of which the dominant authority is based on those in power. Pope Francis prayers are for them to do what is right. And not use their power in a way of which it would be considered to be inhumane. Abuse of power is clear and concise as it relates to the Cocoa Plantations. It is known throughout the world that the children on the Cocoa Plantations on the Ivory Coast of Africa and Ghana suffer from being raped, sodomized, beaten, and worked worse than animals 100 hundred hours a week. Of which they don't receive any educational training, wages, and recreational fun to live their life as a child. Remember they have no father or mother to watch over them. With this being said: **Pope Francis speaks, "Since we are by nature relational beings, meant to find fulfillment through interpersonal relationships inspired by justice and love, it is fundamental for our human development that our dignity, freedom and autonomy be acknowledged and respected. Tragically, the growing scourge of man's exploitation by man gravely damages the life of communion and our calling to forge interpersonal relations marked by respect, justice and love. This abominable phenomenon which leads to contempt for the fundamental rights of others and to the suppression of their freedom and dignity, takes many forms. I would like briefly to consider these, so that, in the light of God's word, we can consider all men and women "no longer slaves, but brothers and sisters."**

(Authors Review)

With this being the case of everyone being seen as brothers and sisters as Pope Francis has stated it would be quite contradictory of the rest of the world to not have some form of compassion and do the righteous thing by making the corrections needed in many places. I mean we can start by looking at the job market, with employment for African Americans being the highest across the nation as it relates to the employment census. Well I guess we can also look at the prison system and how there is $185 billion dollars a year going toward building prisons. Of course we cannot tell the rich how to invest their money? If we are trying to build interpersonal relationships then we must be fair across the board. I have no other choice but to bring up the cruelty taking place with the 2 million children on the Cocoa Plantations, on the Ivory Coast of Africa and Ghana five year old boys and girls working 100 hours a week. I will not go into the exploitations trafficking of these children but if this world is to become a better place for everyone to live in than it all starts with taking care of our children first. Because it is just like

Pope Francis said we are all brothers and sisters. So if this is the case and we all are supposed to be brothers and sisters as stated in the bible "Am I my brother's keeper" Yes! Yes! Yes! I am. Therefore we are individually responsible for the wellbeing of one another. Can a man's heart be filled with the love of God and he does not know who to help? We are chastened by our own convictions to do right and to live right and to love God with all of our heart, our mind, our body and soul. Following in the way of righteousness in our willingness to want to be Christ like and do the will of the Father in heaven. We have a duty to not only show love to our brothers and sisters but to support them in their infirmities to intercede for them in their shortcomings.

(Romans 15v1) "We then that are strong ought to bear the infirmities of the weak, and not to please ourselves." I have written throughout this book the problems with those in power and their need to control which is usually due to fear. Not of the world but fear of themselves, not being safe with what is not known to them. I beg to differ but it would be prudent of me if I did not ask just what do all of these chocolate factory owners, and chocolate industries expect to do with these 2 million children who cannot read, write, spell their names or know how to care for themselves. Are they not the weak, the uneducated, do they not live in famine but those who are in charge out there have a tendency to continue with their oppression. This is exactly what Pope Francis was speaking about when he talked about those in power should act with a sense of humanity. Not to be over bearing in strength but serving with an acceptance of humility for those who do not understand why some have been blessed to have and others are not. Yet we still reflect back to those who choose the old ways. Those who look at these children on the Cocoa Plantations struggle and still do nothing. Even after attending church on Sunday and hearing the word of God they pretend as though these five year old children being raped and sodomized has nothing to do with their stress free life. These chocolate factories and industries have made trillions of dollars off of the backs of these children and those in charge refuse to do the righteous thing. Senators and Congressman have voted for amendments of the Harkin-Engel Protocol to delay renovations from taking place. Politician, government officials, and the National Confectioners Association seem to be enjoying their hidden little chocolate secret. And they all seem to not want to shake the mulberry bush afraid that too many issues will be uncovered at once. Greed over need, they haven't any mercy because they have not shown mercy. (Romans 5 v 19) "For as by one man's disobedience many were made sinners, so by the obedience of one shall many be made righteous."

I am asking everyone to thoroughly search within the physical realms of your inner self? Then ask yourself are you doing everything possible in order to bring to an end the suffering of these children. And if you search yourself deep enough you can also bring to an end the way in which they are suffering. Have you sat down and written one letter to your Senators, Congressmen, the President or any association that could possibly bring about a change to these innocent children's life? Are you still twiddling your fingers? There is so much you can do to help to make life better for children not just on the Ivory Coast of Africa and Ghana but children all over the world. The Children in Africa is just a start there is much work to be done to correct this chocolate mess and even more to do involving the abuse of these children all over the world. Have you told anyone about the horrific situations these five year old children live under daily? Have you ever set aside a little time out of your day to pray for them? God truly knows every little detail of what is taking place. And God knows the rest of the horrible treatment these children are receiving. This is why I love this particular scripture so when Jesus said, (Matthew 19v 14) **"Suffer little children, and forbid them not, to come unto me: for of such is the kingdom of heaven."** Not one child deserves to have to be burdened with such a hardship of laboring like a grown man who is trying to take care of his family? What person in their right mind would go out of their way and fly from America to Africa to fulfill their sexual desires with a child. Sex trafficking of children is against national and international laws that is spelled out for you in Article 34 of the Convention of the Rights of the Child. I have not read any laws that say the treatment of these children on the Ivory Coast of Africa and Ghana is appropriate and acceptable way to treat five year old boys and girls. With laws in place to combat such cruelty these children are still sold to the highest bidder for the desired amount of time needed to complete their sick minded fantasy. The children are damaged and left to pay the price of their body being violated. While the pervert is allowed to fly back to the United States and go home to his wife and children unscathed. Will we ever know what is literally taking place on the Cocoa Plantations concerning these children? A joint effort from the media, news reporters, newspapers, articles from journalist and documentaries are needed to uncover the story of the worse form of forced child labor and slavery in the history of the world. A joint effort from every one can bring positive changes to this melting mess and help the children on the Ivory Coast of Africa and Ghana to a different kind of life and a chance at having a better future. I will say once again this is a grave endeavor to take on but as God is the author and finisher of my life I must say to you I cannot see how anyone can overlook this kind of sex trafficking, slavery, organ trafficking and abuse of children that is taking place here and so many of you are willing to turn your head and look the other way for the taste of chocolate. Or is it being done for the money? (Ecclesiastes 10v 19) **"A feast is made for laughter, and wine maketh merry; but money answereth all things."** In your midnight hours of restless sleeps I pray that you hear the screaming and yelling of these children's pain. The relentless fear they have of no one to look to for their relief and no one to call on for help. These are children being made to go through an unbearable pain a pain that is beyond any of our imaginations. Yet for those of you involved in the chocolate industry you say to yourself all is well with you. If may appear to be that way but remember for the same dollar that gives you power will be the same dollar that weakens you. The same dollar that bought you all of the luxurious things in this world will not be able to reach the boundaries of what you will need in the days to come. Because if you call yourself a Christian and I of course doubt your confession of being one, a Christian that is. Please allow me to refresh your memory to these very precious words, Jesus said,

(Matthew 25 v 40) **"And the King shall answer and say unto them, verily I say unto you, Inasmuch as ye have done it unto one of the least of these my brethren, ye have done it unto me."** In your days to come you will understand the scriptures I have given you and you will understand why your pain will be even more unbearable then the suffering of these children. It is imperative to me that you do not have a clue as to the suffering of your very own families to take place in the future for what you have done and believe me the bible does not lie. Just a Pharaohs child was taken for the order of his god so shall it be by the order of my Father in heaven, the Father of Abraham, Isaac, and Jacob. I pray that you live to see the rapture of the anger he has sent out for you. The taking of a child's life to save your child's life is not sufficient with God. There is a penalty to pay for your disobedience and breaking the Lords commandments, and murder is one. Just like you think he is only your God I know better he is the God of us all the creator of all life. I will leave you with this scripture (Matthew 12 v 28-30) **"Come unto me, all ye that labor and are heavy laden, and I will give you rest. (29) Take my yoke upon you, and learn of me; for I am meek and lowly in heart; and ye shall find rest unto your souls. (30) For my yoke is easy and my burden is light."**

Slavery is not something that should be in question in the year 2015. It is amazing how Pope Leo XIII spoke on Capital and Labor in 1891. He discussed how the employer also had an obligation to treat their workers with some form of respect. Pope Leo XIII viewpoints are very similar to those of Pope Francis in 2015. Pope Francis, "The theme I have chosen for this year's message is drawn from Saint Paul's letter to Philemon, in which the Apostle asks his co-worker to welcome Onesimus, formerly Philemon's slave, now a Christian and, therefore, according to Paul, worthy of being considered a brother. The Apostle of the Gentiles writes: "Perhaps this is why he was parted from you for a while, that you might have him back forever, no longer as a lave but more than a slave, as a beloved brother" (15-16). Onesimus became Philemon's brother when he became a Christian. Conversion to Christ, the beginning of a life lived Christian discipleship, thus constitutes a new birth (cf. 2 Cor 5:17; 1Pet 1:3) which generates fraternity as the fundamental bond of family life and the basis of life in society.

Although the Pope speaks of the strong over powering the weak he makes it known that the world is not oblivious to the intent of those in power and that mankind's nature of subjugation has been in effect for many, many years. Pope Francis "From time immemorial, different societies have known the phenomenon of man's subjugation by man. There have been periods of human history in which the institution of slavery was generally accepted and regulated by law. This legislation dictated who was born free and who was born into slavery, as well as the conditions where by a freeborn person could lose his or her freedom or regain it. In other words, the law itself admitted that some people were able or required to be considered the property of other people, at their fee disposition. A slave could be bought and sold, given away or acquired, as if he or she were a commercial product. Today, as the result of a growth In our awareness, slavery, is seen as a crime against humanity, (4) has been formally abolished throughout the world. The right of each person not to be kept in a state of slavery or servitude has been recognized in international law as inviolable. Yet, even though the international community has adopted numerous agreements aimed at ending slavery in all its forms, and has launched various strategies to combat this phenomenon, millions of people today- children, women and men of all ages- are deprived of freedom and are forced to live in conditions akin to slavery.

I think of the many men and women laborers, including minors, subjugated in different sectors, whether formally or informally, in domestic or agricultural workplaces, or in the manufacturing or mining industry; whether in countries where labor regulations fail to comply with international norms and minimum standards, or, equally illegally, in countries which lack legal protection for workers' rights.

I think also of the living conditions of many migrants who, in their dramatic odyssey, experience hunger, are deprived of freedom, robbed of their possessions, or undergo physical and sexual abuse. In a particular way, I think of those among them who, upon arriving at their destination after a grueling journey marked by fear and insecurity, are detained in at times inhumane conditions. I think of those among them, who for different social, political and economic reasons, are forced to live clandestinely. My thoughts also turn to those who, in order to remain within the law, agree to disgraceful living and working conditions, especially in those cases where the laws of a nation create or permit a structural dependency of migrant workers on their employers, as, for example, when the legality of their residency is made dependent on their labour contract. Yes, I am thinking of "slave labor".

I think also of persons forced into prostitution, many of whom are minors, as well as male and female sex slaves.

I think of women forced into marriage, those sold for arranged marriages and those bequeathed to relatives of their deceased husbands, without any right to give or withhold their consent.

Nor can I fail to think of all those persons, minors and adult alike, who are made objects of trafficking for the sale of organs, for recruitment as soldiers, for begging, for illegal activities such as the production and sale of narcotics, or for disguised forms of cross-border adoption.

(**Author's comments**) *In the comments the Pope made about sale of organs that kind of exposure is hard for the rest of the world to understand. The rest of the world is not knowledgeable concerning the harsh treatment of the children on the Cocoa Plantations. They are not considered to be of any value to the owners of the chocolate industry these children haven't any self-worth to them other than the work they are required to do. These children are being adopted for their organs. Once it is determined what is needed from the child in relations to his or her organs. If a heart is needed, liver or pancreas etc. the child* will have to be murdered in some fashion in order for the organs to be taken out. I haven't any idea as to where or how the bodies are disposed of? There is not a lot of covering up to do in reference to the adopted child because no one will be concerned of its whereabouts. Mainly because the adoption is in accordance what Pope Francis said is, "disguised forms of cross-border adoption". The questions I would have to ask here is was there ever a real birth certificate, was the child ever given a real name by its parents or was the child's name changed which would be similar to what they did to slaves on the cotton plantations in America. And where is the accountability concerning these 2 million children on the Cocoa Plantations what census is being taken concerning their whereabouts?

"Finally, I think of all those kidnapped and held captive by terrorist groups, subjected to their purposes as combatants, or, above all in the case of young girls and women, to be used as sex slaves. Many of these disappear, while others are sold several times over, tortured, mutilated or killed."

(Author's Comment) In the comment here with the Pope saying these women are sold several times over and tortured. What is not being illustrated here is how these young African girls on the Cocoa Plantations are sold in sex trafficking. There are sold to the highest bidder and used as sex slaves for the rest of their life. They are used and sold over and over and over again until they no longer have any use this is when they are tortured and killed. This is not only happening to the young African girls but to the boys as well. Little boys are also used as sex slaves.

Laws to Protect Children
Convention on the Rights of the Child

From the understanding I have received from the research I have done involving this book on the Cocoa Plantations and the brutal treatment of these children and how it has surpassed any normal length of time in order for corrective measures to be taken it beyond my reason of conceptualizing what is truth. These are children five years of age little boys and girls who should be waking up and going to school. Having fun at a playground with other children, not children taught at the age of five to swing a machete. Once again there are laws in place to protect the children on the Cocoa Plantations.

What you are going to read below are the laws that apply to the rights of these children in international waters. I present to you some of the Preamble and what will follow will be the Articles to the Convention on the Rights of the Child. I am prayerful you will follow these articles which have been sanctioned by the General Assembly carefully and you can notate the uncountable violations of these children working on the Cocoa Plantations. Here is more legal documentation for you to apply in your letters to your Senators and your Congressmen and Congresswomen.

Convention on the Rights of the Child

Adopted and opened for signature, ratification and accession
by General Assembly resolution 44/25 of 20 November 1989
Entry into force 2 September 1990, in accordance with article 49

Parts of the (**Preamble**):

Recognizing that the child, for the full and harmonious development of his or her personality, should grow up in a family environment, in an atmosphere of happiness, love and understanding,

Considering that the child should be fully prepared to live an individual life in society, and brought up in the spirit of the ideals proclaimed in the Charter of the United Nations, and in particular in the spirit of peace, dignity, tolerance, freedom, equality and solidarity,

Bearing in mind that the need to extend particular care to the child has been stated in the Geneva Declaration of the Rights of the Child of 1924 and in the Declaration of the Rights of the Child adopted by the General Assembly on 20 November 1959 and recognized in the Universal Declaration of Human Rights, in the International Covenant on Civil and Political Rights (in particular in articles 23 and 24), in the International Covenant on Economic, Social and Cultural Rights in particular in article 10) and in the statues and relevant instruments of specialized agencies and international organizations concerned with the welfare of children,

Bearing in mind that, as indicated in the Declaration of the Rights of the Child, "the child, by reason of his physical and mental immaturity, needs special safeguards and care, including appropriate legal protection, before as well as after birth",

Although all of the articles listed are pertinent to the wellbeing of the child. I selected a few of which I felt were more prevalent to the violations of the child's rights. All of the articles listed below have been (Ratified).

Part 1

Article 1

1. For the purpose of the present Convention, a child means every human being below the age of eighteen years unless under the law applicable to the child, majority is attained earlier

Article 2

1. States Parties shall take all appropriate measures to ensure that the child is protected against all forms of discrimination or punishment on the basis of the status, activities, expressed opinions, or beliefs of the child's parents, legal guardians, or family members.

Article 3

1. In all actions concerning children, whether undertaken by public or private social welfare institutions, courts of law, administrative authorities or legislative bodies, the best interests of the child shall be a primary consideration.

Article 7

1. The child shall be registered immediately after birth and shall have the right from birth to a name, the right to acquire a nationality and as far as possible, the right to know and be cared for by his or her parents.

2. States Parties shall ensure the implementation of these rights in accordance with their national law and their obligations under the relevant international instruments in this field, in particular where the child would otherwise be stateless.

Article 8

1. States Parties undertake to respect the right of the child to preserve his or her identity; including nationality, name and family relations as recognized by law without unlawful interference.
2. Where a child is illegally deprived of some or all of the elements of his or her identity, States Parties shall provide appropriate assistance and protection, with a view to re-establish speedily his or her identity.

Article 9

1. Sates Parties shall ensure that a child shall not be separated from his or her parents against their will, except when competent authorities subject to judicial review determine, in accordance with applicable law and procedures, that such separation is necessary for the best interests of the child, such determination may be necessary in a particular case such as one involving abuse or neglect of the child by the parents, or one where the parents are living separately and a decision must be made as to the child's place of residence.
2. In any proceedings pursuant to paragraph 1 of the present article, all interested parties shall be given an opportunity to participate in the proceedings and make their views known.
3. States Parties shall respect the right of the child who is separated from one or both parents to maintain personal relations and direct contact with both parents on a regular basis, except if it is contrary to the child's best interests.
4. Where such separation results from any action initiated by a State Party, such as the detention, imprisonment, exile, deportation or death (including death arising from any cause

while the person is in the custody of the State) of one or both parents or of the child, that State Party shall, upon request, provide the parents, the child or, if appropriate another member of the family with the essential information concerning the whereabouts of the absent member(s) of the family unless the provision of the information would be detrimental to the well-being of the child. States Parties shall further ensure that the submission of such a request shall of itself entail no adverse consequences for the person(s) concerned.

Article 10

1. In accordance with the obligation of Sates Parties under article 9, paragraph 1, application by a child or his or her parents to enter or leave a State Party for the purpose of family reunification shall be dealt with by States Parties in a positive, humane and expeditious manner. States Parties shall further ensure that the submission of such a request shall entail no adverse consequences for the applicants and for the members of their family.

Article 13

1. The child shall have the right to freedom of expression; this right shall include freedom to seek, receive and impart information and ideas of all kinds, regardless of frontiers, either orally, in writing or in print, in the form of art, or through any other media of the child's choice.

Article 14

1. States Parties respect the right of the child to freedom of thought, conscience and religion.
2. States Parties shall respect the rights and duties of the parents and, when applicable, legal guardians, to provide

direction to the child in the exercise of his or her right in a manner consistent with the evolving capacities of the child.

3. Freedom to manifest one's religion or beliefs may be subject only to such limitations as are prescribed by law and ae necessary to protect public safety, order, health or morals, or the fundamental rights and freedoms of others.

Article 16

1. No child shall be subjected to arbitrary or unlawful interference with his or her privacy, family, or correspondence, nor to unlawful attacks on his or her honor and reputation.

2. The child has the right to the protection of the law against such interference or attacks.

Article 18

1. States Parties shall use their best efforts to ensure recognition of the principle that both parents have common responsibilities for the upbringing and development of the child. Parents or, as the case may be, legal guardians, have the primary responsibility for the upbringing and development of the child. The best interests of the child will be their basic concern.

2. For the purpose of guaranteeing and promoting the rights set forth in the present Convention, States Parties shall render appropriate assistance to parents and legal guardians in the performance of their child-rearing responsibilities and shall ensure the development of institutions, facilities and services for the care of children.

3. States parties shall take all appropriate measures to ensure that children of working parents have the right to benefit from child-care services and facilities for which they are eligible.

Article 20

1. A child temporarily or permanently deprived of his or her family environment, or in whose own best interests cannot be allowed to remain in that environment, shall be entitled to special protection and assistance provided by the State.
2. States Parties shall in accordance with their national laws ensure alternative care for such a child.
3. Such care could include, inter alia, foster placement, kafalah of Islamic law, adoption or if necessary placement in suitable institutions for the care of children. When considering solutions, due regard shall be paid to the desirability of continuity in a child's upbringing and to the child's ethnic, religious, cultural and linguistic background.

Article 22

1. States Parties shall take appropriate measures to ensure that a child who is seeking refugee status or who is considered a refugee in accordance with applicable international or domestic law and procedures shall, whether unaccompanied or accompanied by his or her parents or by any other person, receive appropriate protection and humanitarian assistance in the enjoyment of applicable rights set forth in the present Convention and in other international human rights or humanitarian instruments to which the said States are Parties.
2. For this purpose, States parties shall provide as they consider appropriate, co-operation in any efforts by the United Nations and other competent intergovernmental organizations or non-governmental organizations cooperating with the United Nations to protect and assist such a child and to trace the parents or other members of the family of any refugee child in order to obtain information necessary for reunification with his or her family. In cases where no parents or other members of the family can be found, the child shall be accorded the same protection as

any other child permanently or temporarily deprived of his or her family environment for any reason, as set forth in the present Convention.

Article 23

1. States Parties recognize that a mentally or physically disabled child should enjoy a full and decent life, in conditions which ensure dignity, promote self-reliance and facilitate the child's active participation in the community.

2. States Parties recognize the right of the disabled child to special care and shall encourage and ensure the extension, subject to available resources, to the eligible child and those responsible for his or her care, of assistance for which application is made and which is appropriate to the child's condition and to the circumstances of the parents or others caring for the child.

3. Recognizing the special needs of a disabled child, assistance extended in accordance with paragraph 2 of the present article shall be provided free of change, whenever possible, taking into account the financial resources of the parents or others caring for the child, and shall be designed to ensure that the disabled child has effective access to and receives education, training, health care services, rehabilitation services, preparation for employment and recreation opportunities in a manner conducive to the child's achieving the fullest possible social integration and individual development, including his or her cultural and spiritual development.

4. States Parties shall promote, in the spirit of international cooperation, the exchange of appropriate information in the field of preventive health care and of medical, psychological and function treatment of disabled children, including dissemination of and access to information concerning methods of rehabilitation, education and vocational services, with the aim of enabling States Parties to improve their

capabilities and skills and to widen their experience in these areas. In this regard, particular account shall be taken of the needs of developing countries.

Article 24

1. States Parties recognize the right of the child to the enjoyment of the highest attainable standard of health and to facilities for the treatment of illness and rehabilitation of health; States Parties shall strive to ensure that no child is deprived of his or her right of access to such health care services.

2. States Parties shall pursue full implementation of this right and, in particular, shall take appropriate measures:

a. To diminish infant and child mortality;

b. To ensure the provision of necessary medical assistance and health care to all children with emphasis on the development of primary health care.

c. To combat disease and malnutrition, including within the framework of primary health care, though, inter alia, the application of readily available technology and through the provision of adequate nutritious foods and clean drinking water, taking into consideration the dangers and risks of environmental pollution.

d. To ensure appropriate pre-natal and post-natal health care for mothers;

e. To ensure that all segments of society, in particular parents and children, are informed, have access to education to education and are supported in the use of basic knowledge of child health and nutrition, the advantages of breastfeeding, hygiene and environmental sanitation and the prevention of accidents.

f. To develop preventive health care, guidance for parents and family education and services.

3. States Parties shall all effective and appropriate measures with a view to abolishing traditional practices prejudicial to the health of children

4. States Parties undertake to promote and encourage international co-operation with a view to achieving progressively, the full realization of the right recognized in the present article. In this regard, particular account shall be taken of the needs of developing countries.

Article 29

1. No part of the present article 28 shall be construed so as to interfere with the liberty of individuals and bodies to establish and direct educational institutions, subject always to the observance of the principle set forth in paragraph 1 of the present article and to the requirements that the education given in such institutions shall conform minimum standards as may be laid down by the State.

Article 31

1. States Parties recognize the right of the child to rest and leisure, to engage in play and recreational activities appropriate to the age of the child and to participate freely in cultural life and the arts.

2. States Parties shall respect and promote the right of the child to participate fully in cultural and artistic life and shall encourage the provision of appropriate and equal opportunities for cultural, artistic, recreational and leisure activity.

Article 32

1. States Parties recognize the right of the child to be protected from economic exploitation and from performing any work that is likely to be hazardous or to interfere with the child's

education, or to be harmful to the child's health or physical mental, spiritual, moral or social development.

2. States Parties shall take legislative, administrative, social and educational measures to ensure the implementation of the present article. To this end, and having regard to the relevant provision of other international instruments, States Parties shall in particular:

a. Provide for a minimum age or minimum ages for admission to employment.
b. Provide for appropriate regulation of the hours and conditions of employment.
c. Provide for appropriate penalties or other sanctions to ensure the effective enforcement of the present article.

Article 34

States Parties undertake to protect the child from all forms of sexual exploitation

and sexual abuse. For these purposes, States Parties shall in particular take all

appropriate national, bilateral and multilateral measures to prevent.

a. The inducement or coercion of a child to engage in any unlawful sexual activity;
b. The exploitative use of children in prostitution or other unlawful sexual practices;
c. The exploitative use of children in pornographic performances and materials.

Article 35

States Parties shall take all appropriate national, bilateral and multilateral measures

Prevent the abduction of, the sale of or traffic in children for any purpose or in any form.

Article 36

States Parties shall protect the child against all other forms of exploitation prejudicial to any aspects of the child's welfare.

Article 37

States Parties shall ensure that:

a. No child shall be subjected to torture or other cruel, inhuman or degrading treatment or punishment. Neither capital punishment nor life imprisonment without possibility of release shall be imposed for offences committed by persons below eighteen years of age;

b. No child shall be deprived of his or her liberty unlawfully or arbitrarily. The arrest, detention or imprisonment of a child shall be in conformity with the law and shall be used only as a measure of last resort and for the shortest appropriate period of time;

c. Every child deprived of liberty shall be treated with humanity and respect for the inherent dignity of the human person, and in a manner which takes into account the needs of persons of his or her age. In particular, every child deprived of liberty shall be separated from adults unless it is considered in the child's best interest not to do so and shall have the right to maintain contact with his or her family through correspondence and visits, save in exceptional circumstances;

d. Every child deprived of his or her liberty shall have the right to prompt access to legal and other appropriate assistance, as well as the right to challenge the legality of the deprivation of his or her liberty before a court or other competent, independent and impartial authority, and to a prompt decision on any such action.

Article 40

1. States Parties recognize the right of every child alleged as, accused of, or recognized as having infringed the penal law to be treated in a manner consistent with the promotion of the child's sense of dignity and work, which reinforces the child's respect for the human rights and fundamental freedoms of others and which takes into account the child's age and the desirability of promoting the child's reintegration and the child's assuming a constructive role in society.

Part II

Article 42

States Parties undertake to make the principles and provisions of the Convention widely known, by appropriate and active means to adults and children alike.

Article 43

1. **For the purpose of examining the progress made by States Parties in achieving the realization of the obligations undertaken in the present Convention, there shall be established a Committee of on the Rights of the Child, which shall carry out the functions hereinafter provided**

2. **The Committee shall consist of eighteen experts of high moral standing and recognize competence in the field covered by this Convention. (1) The members of the Committee shall be elected by States Parties from among their nationals and shall serve in their personal capacity, consideration being given to equitable geographical distribution, as well as the principal legal system.**

The Flame of Justice is Still Burning Bright

Throughout this book I have listed the rights of the children. I am certain you have read them all and are able to assess facts that the International Labor Organization has justifiable laws set to bring sanctions on the Ivory Coast of Africa and Ghana to stop the murdering and abuse of these children. We are already aware the BLACK MARKET for purchasing organs is a big business. The other parts of the big business are those who are involved in falsifying the adoption papers made on these children. We also have to look at the heart surgeons and the medical teams throughout the world involved in such chaos? It would make a lot of sense in relations to their need for doctors, medical school can be quite costly and some people will do almost anything to live their dream life here on earth. Just keep in mind before a heart is implanted or a kidney is implanted or a liver is implanted etc. Certain medical characteristics have to match from the young child being adopted who would be considered to be an un-volunteered donor. Also certain characteristics are tested from the un-volunteered donor that has to match if the organ is going to be used. I am using the word un-volunteered because the child does not have the slightest clue it is being adopted for the organ or organs someone else needs. And if it is a major organ such as a heart or liver the child is basically being murdered. The children being tested do not have a clue as to why their blood and other x-rays are being run on their body. If you ever want to talk about a legal murder with no justification other than these well to do good folk feel they are doing these poor children a favor. By taking them out of their misery so they will not have to work on the Cocoa Plantations all of their life and suffer the abuse and beatings these children suffer with then they are most certainly WRONG!!!

I must say one might be a bit presumptuous in thinking that whatever is done for the children on the Cocoa Plantations no matter how little it may be, even a little help would be considered to be too much. I personally feel this Cocoa Plantations matter is a chocolate mess being made each day and very little is being done to clean it up. In review of the laws set forth to implement change which involves the decision makers in high places watching closely and saying to themselves, "will they ever figure it out?" I am here to tell you we have figured it out a long time ago. The final legality before bringing this book to and end is my being able to reveal to you laws that have been ratified in respect to what is now and has continued to be taking place on the Cocoa Plantations on the Ivory Coast of Africa and Ghana. Laws in support of abolishing the worst forms of child labor and child slavery in the world of which you will be reading about in the following pages. Laws that have been passed but are not being enforced some of them I have revealed to you in the early pages of this book. The International Labor Organization laws, the Convention on the Rights of the Child, and a few articles on the Convention involving child rights my reasoning for having the laws posted at the end of the book was because I did not want you to think this book was written because of what I humanely thought was wrong. No, that is not the case this book was written to bring awareness to the world because of the devastating insensitive and inhumane treatment these children are receiving. Finally it was written because of the laws being broken which relates to the rights of the child that are not being enforced. The politicians, government officials, political leaders, Former Senator Thomas Richard "Tom" Harkin and Congressman Eliot Engel who the Protocol was named after the Harkin-Engel Protocol, the National Confectioners Association and the Chocolate Industries all over the world there isn't anything being done to relieve these children of their suffering.

After careful review of some of the laws I have found referencing the children on the Cocoa Plantations and throughout the world. I have placed laws in this book for you to review I ask with all due respect that you review these laws carefully as they pertain to the rights of the children on the Ivory Coast of Africa and Ghana. Children whose rights are being violated and they are being forced to work under horrific conditions. When you review some of the laws I have posted below carefully what you will find is violation after violation of these children's rights. I have done my research and I continue to ask myself, why? Why are these children allowed to be treated worse than slaves and why is the United States of America allowing this to happen? ***"Laws are put in place to bring about social economical positive changes. When laws are not enforced by the lawmakers in***

position to enforce new laws set to bring about positive changes it is clear that the lawmakers do not want positive change to occur, not even for the betterment of all humanity."

The Flame of Life

Once again a justice long, long overdue, yet the flame of life continue to flicker in my heart and in my mind. This flame I am speaking of tells me there is a light burning bright, a light that shines beyond our spectra of common sense and rational reasoning. An internal flame that burns with a deep and compassionate desire for all of us to be free and to be able to do better with caring and being concerned about one another? A flame with a small light at the end of the tunnel that tells me there is still hope. There is still a chance a glimmer that maybe one day, someday we all will get a grasp of its meaning and have a better understanding of life and the freedoms of all humanity. A flame that shines in the face of justice and the scales are balanced equally. A flame that is too bright to see color too bright to see favoritism too bright to see, envy, hatred, and discontentment of any kind. A flame which encompasses the rainbow of life as it was promised to the world by Our Father in heaven that the earth would never be flooded with water again. A flame that features various colors and ethnicities of all the races of God's creation of life and continues to give us hope and reminds us we are not forgotten. One that sparkled before everyone many years ago and said I will take care of your hungry, your tired, your poor and deliver unto you all a new covenant of life. A flame that will lead us to a safe place without condemnation and shield us from the forces of evil into a land of hope and promise, a flame that will never die, let it remain forever in your heart as it encompasses your soul. With an understanding that God has a cup we can all drink from together and be proud of this flame of hope, of love, peace and charity he has placed in our heart. Let its burning desire to do the righteous thing give us all a second thought before we react toward the negative for he is a God of love. He is not a God of suffering or torment and his flame is ever lasting. In every smile you see, in every mouth you feed, in every opportunity you can let others see your love for Jesus. He told us in his word "with me you can do everything, without me you can do nothing. I am the way the truth and the life." What do you say fellow Christians with all the laws set before you why would you let these children on the Cocoa Plantations on the Ivory Coast of Africa and Ghana suffer such unmentionable treatment? We were all once lost and led out into the wilderness by a flame we followed and by a great leader who became a vessel for the Lord. Have you all forgotten to trust in the Lord thy God? There is a better way to do this work on the Cocoa Plantations other than through the use of five year old children. There is nothing too hard for God. That was proven as he became our flame and led us out of bondage have you forgotten these words "my sheep know my voice a strangers they will not follow." **(Exodus 14v 19-20) "And the angel of God which went before the camp of Israel, removed and went behind them: and the pillar of the cloud went from before their face, and stood behind them: (20) And it came between the camp of the Egyptians and the camp of Israel; and it was a cloud and darkness to them, but it gave light by night to these; so that the one came not near the other all the night."**

I believe you all have forgotten that God is in charge and you have forgotten how to trust in him. This book was placed on my heart to write and as an obedient servant I only want to do the will and work of my Father in heaven. Of course! we know obedience is better than sacrifice. A warning always comes before destruction. I ask you to please enforce the laws you have created and let God take care of the rest. I pray that some of himself of which he has placed in all of us be shown through and in the vessels that are willing and ready to do his will. I present to you some of the laws pertaining to the International Labor Organization and Conventions in reference to the **WORST FORMS OF Child SLAVERY AND Child ABUSE in the history of the world.**

My Final Appeal

My love for all humanity and my wanting for everyone to do well in life make us all venerable unless we all cross over together. When I think about the young children on the Cocoa Plantations being treated worse than slaves I become almost speechless because there is so much that should be done and said for these children. Every ounce of energy we as a nation of people have to help correct the worst forms of child slavery should have been put into action many years ago. It is very difficult for my mind to be able to phantom any child not being able to have a decent childhood let alone a childhood at all. Every child should have a childhood with memories of joy and happy moments locked in their minds forever, memories to help carry them through life.

There are so many different countries and governments involved in the chocolate industry that they have bought into the business of chocolate being so enriching only to their pockets and campaign funding. There isn't any concern for the children. The multitudes of countries and government officials involved is so phenomenal they have given focus only to the trillions of dollars they are able to make off of producing chocolate and the illegal use of these under aged and over worked children in Africa and Ghana. I would like for everyone in the world to take a close look at their self? For those of you who are running businesses which manufacture and produce chocolate it is clear you have lost sight of the Chocolate Industry founder's dream of how he wanted the chocolate industries to develop. You need to review your moral and ethical obligations as well as the legalities as it relates to small five year old children working 100 hours a week, is there anything right or righteous about this? All I can focus on concerning the Cocoa Plantations is the forced child slave labor, the under aged and the illegal use of these children on the Ivory Coast of Africa and Ghana. The most emotional part for me concerning this book is no one seems to care about the malicious ways these young children are being treated and misused. I can go into more detail but you have been hearing it throughout the book. Recently retired Former Senator Thomas Richard "Tom" Harkin,

Eliot Engel and those of you in the political field, government? Those of you who work for the chocolate industry and other chocolate organizations please do not offend me by trying to pretend like you are not aware of all of the havoc and problems these children face daily on the Cocoa Plantations. No one should have been allowed to retire as did Senator Thomas Harkin in January 2015 until this issue at hand the Harkin-Engel Protocol was resolved.

The majority of my life was dedicated to the service of my country and helping those who were less fortunate than I. During my military service in the United States of America where I served in the Afghanistan war. I had gone out on many missions outside the safety wire of protection of Camp Phoenix. I remember praying to God and asking him to please watch over me and all those around me who do not know God or know how to pray. Watch over the young soldiers who do not understand the need for prayer and for protection of the Holy Ghost. The convoys we traveled in were always in danger and all of us could have been killed by a sniper or suicide bomber at any time. God Almighty brought us back safely to the camp site. God has allowed many of us to return to the United States of America beaten but not broken. I continue to dedicate my life toward the betterment of all mankind even though the battles many times have appeared to be up hill and I was out numbered. I always keep this particular scripture in mind, "Do not fear the one who can mutilate the body but fear the one who can mutilate both body and soul." There are so many anointed men of God throughout the bible who were triumphant against great odds. The word of God is what I stand on and no one can refute his power. Moses was a great spiritual uplifting story, the story of Moses and the Ten Commandments showed Moses victory over great odds against Pharaoh and his kingdom. Don't forget about Gideon and the Midianites of which the Midianites were so many they were numbered like granules of sand, they were uncountable. Samson story and of course Jeremiah going up against five different kingdoms at one time etc. These men fought against great odds but they fought in Gods favor because God had already went before them.

Military Aide and Assistance in Afghanistan

The following pictures below describe perfectly what America has done for other countries starting with the Humanitarian Assistance Drops which is similar to a food drive for the hungry. Of which food and clothing is given away to help families that are having difficult times feeding and clothing their children. Below I will briefly describe each picture of which I was out on these missions to assist the Afghan people with food, medical assistance and school supplies needed for their children. My reason for adding these pictures is to inform you of the help being given. My question once again is since America is able to give these supplies to the Afghan people to feed and clothe their families. Give them jobs and free medical help why hasn't this hospitality been extended to the families and children on the Ivory Coast of Africa and Ghana to keep their families together. Instead of giving the Ivory Coast of Africa and Ghana families and children food and nutrition these families are made to sale their children so other children in the family won't starve. Instead of giving them medical assistance you give them home remedies. For food you give them corn mesh and for shelter you give the children of Africa and Ghana a mud hut with ventilation about the circumference of a baseball to breathe out of.

(Afghan women dressed in blue at Humanitarian Assistance)

What you do not see is what's enclosed in the blankets these women and children are carrying. The Humanitarian Assistance drops (HA) are missions of peace keeping during war time where the United States military go to different grid zones to give aide and assistance to many different provinces. These (HA) drops take a while to set up due to rebels and terrorists problems of which some in the past had been robbed for their medical supplies. Meetings have to be held and a grid zone set up for the meeting of the (HA) drop. Once we arrive the trucks are unloaded, perimeters are set up for protection and the citizens who are lined up depending on the province pick up their food which is rapped very carefully in a blanket for them to carry. Not all families receive a ticket and many are turned away due to the lack of supplies and the strenuous needs of the people. Each family that receives a ticket will receive, Humanitarian Assistance: Inside of each blanket is a 5lb bag of beans, a 5lb bag of rice, a 5lb bag of salt, a 5lb bag of sugar, a 5lb bag of flour, 1 gal of cooking oil, one outfit for a little girl, one outfit for a little boy, a pair of shoes for a girl, a pair of shoes for a boy, and a pair of sandals for the father and mother. There feet are never measured for the shoes and the clothing is not sized for the children; it's more of a pot luck situation because the military haven't the time or man power to make sure everything fits.

(Civilian Medical Assistance, Boy on crutches)

Because of the attacks involving certain locations given for the Civilian Medical Assistance visits (CMA). Once again grid zones have to be set up and meetings are held to synchronize the time and place with the head of the province needing the medical care. Once this is done perimeter are set and everyone soldier knows their job once we arrive at the designated sight. As you can see the picture of the little Afghan boy on crutches being escorted into the place designated for him and many other to receive their medical care. The danger levels at the Civilian Medical Assistance sites are heightened because of other provinces that also are in need for medical care. Due to the heightened dangers spot checks are given prior to anyone being able to go inside the facility to receive any assistance. As you can see in this picture many of these sites are accompanied with help from other countries below you see a mixture of American and Italian soldiers working together. This is an Italian soldier patting and Afghan man for weapons.

(Italian soldier patting down Afghan man for weapons)

When I think about the Humanitarian drops and Medical drops I went out on in Afghanistan and the dangers involved where so many soldiers never made it back. I know that my God, the Father of Abraham, Isaac and Jacob does not make mistakes; he brought me back home safely for many reasons. One of those reasons would be for the purpose of completing this book about the Cocoa Plantations. The purpose for the United States military for going into other countries is to protect the innocent people there. To make sure they are being taken care of and their government and laws which govern their people were properly being enforced. On our Military Peace Keeping Mission we gave food to the hungry, clothing to those who needed clothes. We provided fresh water wells to provinces that were drinking contaminated water.

**(Afghan schools made of tent tarp Major
Christian with the teacher)**

Although their schools are made of tent tarp there still seems to be a show of importance concerning the needs of these Afghan children to have an education. They on the other hand are not made to work 100 hours a week like the children on the Ivory Coast of Africa and Ghana. The tent tarp is out in the open and the children that are not seen in this picture are the little girls in school at a distance where their schools are held inside a hallow hold in the wall. Leaving all of these children subject to dirt and dust they are breathing in and the dry heat of the sun. There isn't any air conditioning or fans to keep these children focused on their work and their only stay in school a few hours a day.

We helped to supply their schools with pencils, paper and books for the children to learn. We gave the children of Afghanistan a chance to build on their childhood and we provided them with the opportunity to receive an education. That through reading, writing, arithmetic and other skills they will be given a fair chance in life.

I am showing these pictures I had taking while serving in one of my positions as a PAO (Officer) during the Afghanistan War. I am going to make my plea once again in case you did not get the memo the first time. If American soldiers can go into a third world country and help make positive changes there. American soldiers can most certainly be deployed to Africa and Ghana on a peace keeping mission. There placement there would be to help change the abuse that is taking place with these children on the Cocoa Plantations.

We have helped nations and countries in trouble could you please explain to me if I am wrong the distinct difference in the needs of a child. Aren't the fundamental needs of all children the same? To be able to receive food, shelter, clothing and love from both parents of which this is universal. A child is considered to be a child in any part of the world? Do the children on the Ivory Coast of Africa and Ghana deserve the same rights as other children all over the world? I should not have to ask that question and if they deserve the same chance in life and deserve the same treatment as other children please explain to me why is rape, sodomy, beatings, abuse, child sex slaves, child trafficking and child organ trafficking being allowed to take place right before the eyes of the world. It is not just the United States but other nations as well who are not enforcing the laws that have been put in place for the protection of these children. And if the laws were being enforced as they should we would not have a situation such as the worst forms of child slavery on the Ivory Coast of Africa and Ghana that would be in question today.

When I wore my uniform I put it on with pride, with integrity, honesty, fortitude, dignity and loyalty to my country. My military training taught me even more on how to go against greater odds. And my sword of life of which the Lord thy God has given me for protection makes me a heir to the throne. The abuse of these children in Africa and Ghana is not something the United States of America should be allowing to be over looked. The hatred contained in the heart of these men and women in government and in the chocolate industry who are aware of the torture and abuse of these children should also be in question concerning their position in public service and their judiciary duties to uphold the laws made to protect these children on the Ivory Coast of Africa and Ghana. They are not receiving any wages and they are not given an opportunity to have an education, or a healthy childhood, they have any father or mother to give them comfort. To rob these children of their life and act as though nothing is wrong breeds nothing more than contentment on the part of their oppressors of which are the politicians, government officials, the Chocolate Industries and the National Confectioners Association, my question to you once again is why? I have to as you political leaders and politicians, senators and congressmen does the greed in your hearts and in your pockets that you have lined them with in relations to the blood money you are in receipt of does it lessen the guilt of you turning your head another year to receive your filthy lucre. If you are of any form of human you should feel ashamed if not in the sight of yourself than in the sight of God Almighty in whom one day you will have to stand before. Not even a new born baby animal deserves to be treated in such a manner as these little children on the Cocoa Plantations. The disheartening thing about all of this child abuse is that it is just so all of you who love the taste of chocolate will have your chocolate at the expenditure of these little children. And you are willing to allow this type of tyranny to occur in the face of all Americans as other nations join in. I have on a different uniform now and I am on the battlefield for the Lord. I am not carrying an M204 any longer but I have a sword more powerful than any weapon mankind could ever make. It is called the Holy Bible, let our walk together be as one in understanding that change on the most part is inevitable and because it is inevitable change will occur. I ask in my final statement to all of you why, America why! How much longer will you turn your head?

I just wanted to end this Final Appeal on this day of Resurrection April 5, 2015 and close it out with the very same words my Lord and Saviour said before he gave up the Ghost "It is Finished."

Convention 138

Summarization by the Author

Convention 138 was created to regulated age limitations for child labor. Of which the International Labor Organization on June 26, 1973 as part of the General Conference legally documented the minimum working age for children and set it to 15 years of age.

Convention 138
Summarization by the Author

Adheres to the minimum working age to be 15 years of which depending on the severity of the work if there is no harm being questionable of child endangerment that a child can be as young as 13 years of age. As of June 19, 1976 the age limitations for dangerous work was set at 18 years of age. Once again depending on the hazardous conditions of the job an exception would be made for children as young as 16 years of age. For countries that are struggling there would be an exception made to allow children as young as 14 years of age to be admitted for employment.

Recommendation would fall under R146 to give members of the Convention some form of a guidance scale to adhere to.

Children's Rights are Ratified

Convention 138

The role of the convention 138 was to establish some playing field for the rights of children to be given a chance to have a proper childhood. Convention 138 expresses pertinent concerns of the development of the child, and how difficult it is for a child who is working to develop into a happy, high spirited child with a positive self-esteem. A child should be given the luxury of having the opportunity to develop properly in all areas of their childhood developmental stages.

To help the child to develop properly age limitations were set for the child to be allowed to work at the age of 15 years of age. At the age of 15 years of age the Convention members feel the child should have already met the criteria for its requirements as it relates to the child's developmental growth. At the age of 15 years of age the child should have also met all of its minimal basic educational needs.

Convention 138 is a legal binding document agreed upon by the members who ratified it. Thus pushing forth the group effort that all will abide by the laws which have been stipulated by the International Labor Organization members ratified by the Convention members and will be respected by all

Convention 138 Article 1

Summarization by the Author

This Convention 138 Article 1 is designed to ensure the abolishment of child labour and change the minimum working age of the child to make life less stressful. Each Member must put into effect a program and policy that will give children under their age stipulations an opportunity to develop both physically and mentally

Convention 182 (continued)

Earlier in the book I gave you some of Convention 182, Article1, Article 2 and Article 3 as I stated earlier to keep you better informed I will now give you Article 4, Article 5, Article 6 and Article 7 as it relates to protecting children.

Convention 182 Article 4

Summarization by the Author:

1. Talks about the how national laws and regulations in reference to Article 3(d). Stating that competent authority is to be adhered to by employers and worker. The just of this article as it relates to international standards and given consideration to be informed of the WORST FORMS of CHILD LABOUR when referring to Paragraphs 3 and 4

Summarization by the Author:

2. In order to bring about change and to show that these changes do exits the competency concerning the authoritative individuals to make such decisions must show the work as previously determined and employers and workers must be consulted to reach said changes.

Summarization by the Author:

3. There is a list of changes that are to take place of which is to be adhered to under this particular Article and there is

to be a periodic consultations of agreement concerning the changes with the employers and the workers

Convention 182 Article 5
Summarization by the Author

After the aforementioned parties have been informed the some form of a monitoring device should be established pursuant to what is to take effect as to what is referred to in the Convention. One again the employers and the workers shall be in consult with the Members.

Convention 182 Article 6
Summarization by the Author

1.   The Members were initially supposed to create programs that was to eliminate the Worst Forms of Child Labour

Summarization by the Author

2.   Once programs were created by the Members to be making the necessary changes to end the Worst Forms of Child Labour in the history of the word, government institutions and other groups of concern would get involved

Convention 182 Article 7
Summarization by the Author

1.   Due to new changes taking place the Members would also put into effect sanctions for those who may violate the new provisions of the Conventions and will suffer the consequences behind their actions should any violations occur.

Summarization by the Author

2.   In the process of eliminating child labour, the Members must take into account the importance of also establishing a

means of education for the children who have intentionally been deprived

Summarized by the Author

    a. The use of children must be prohibited as part of the worst forms of child labor;

Summarized by the Author

    b. The worst forms of child labor which once involved children is no longer acceptable and must be prevented;

Summarized by the Author

    c. The children who are taken off of the Cocoa Plantations once changes began to occur must be provided with some form of rehabilitation and social integration; this is necessary to move toward abolishing the worst forms of child labor in the world;

Summarized by the Author

    d. Although some of the training such as the vocational training may not be adequately ensured to all children it is understood that each child will be ensured access to fee basic education, as the process continues in the elimination of the worst forms of child labor;

Summarized by the Author

    e. The children who are at special risk there is a strong need to identify them in order that they receive adequate helped;

Summarized by the Author

    f. Because girls have been abused and violated special attention need to be provided.

Summarized by the Author

3. Concerning the Convention there must be competent authorities involved of which shall be designated by each Member

Convention 29

Ratified laws to protect the children
Forced Labour Convention

Article 1 of Convention 29

1. Each Member of the International Labour Organization which ratifies this Convention undertakes to suppress the use of forced or compulsory labour in all its forms within the shortest possible period.
2. With a view to this complete suppression, recourse to forced or compulsory labour may be had, during the transitional period, for public purposes only and as an exceptional measure, subject to the conditions and guarantees hereinafter provided.
3. At the expiration of a period of five years after the coming into force of this Convention and when the Governing Body of the International Labour Office prepares the report provided for in Article 31 below, the said Governing Body shall consider the possibility of the suppression of forced or compulsory labour in all its forms without a further transitional period and the desirability of placing this question on the agenda of the Conference.

Article 2 of Convention 29

1. For the purposes of this Convention the term forced or compulsory labour shall mean all work or service which is exacted from any person under the menace of any penalty

and for which the said person has not offered himself voluntarily.

Article 4 of Convention 29

1. The competent authority shall not impose or permit the imposition of forced or compulsory labour for the benefit of private individuals, companies or associations.

Article 5 of Convention 29

1. No concession granted to private individuals, companies or association shall involve any form of forced or compulsory labour for the production or the collection of products which such private individuals, companies or associations utilize or in which they trade.
2. Where concessions exists containing provisions involving such forced or compulsory labour, such provisions shall be rescinded as soon as possible, in order to comply with Article 1 of this Convention.

Article 10 of Convention 29

1. Forced or compulsory labour exacted as a tax and forced or compulsory labour to which recourse has had for the execution of public works by chiefs who exercise administrative functions shall be progressively abolished.
2. Meanwhile, where forced or compulsory labour is exacted as a tax, and where recourse is had to forced or compulsory labour for the execution of public works by chiefs who exercise administrative functions, the authority concerned shall first satisfy itself:

   d. That the work or service will not entail the removal of the workers from their place of habitual residence.

Article 11 of Convention 29

1. Only adult able-bodied males who are of an apparent age of not less than 18 and not more than 45 years may be called upon for forced or compulsory labour. Except in respect of the kinds of labour provided for in Article 10 of this Convention, the following limitations and conditions shall apply:

   a. Whenever possible prior determination by a medical officer appointed by the administration that the process concerned are not suffering from any infectious or contagious disease and that they are physically fit for the work required and for the conditions under which it is to be carried out;

   b. Respect for conjugal family ties.

2. For the purposes of subparagraph (c) of the preceding paragraph, the regulations provided for in Article 23 of this Convention shall fix the proportion of the resident adult able-bodies males who may be taken at any one time for forced or compulsory, provided always that this proportion shall in no case exceeds 25 percent. In fixing this proportion the competent authority shall take account of the density of the population, of its social and physical development, of the seasons, and of the work which must be done by the persons concerned on their own behalf in their locality, and, generally shall have regard to the economic and social necessities of the normal life of the community concerned.

Article 12 of Convention 29

1. The maximum period for which any person may be taken for forced or compulsory labour of all kinds in any one period of twelve months shall not exceed sixty days, including the time spent in going to and from the place of work.

2. **Every person from whom forced or compulsory labour is exacted shall be furnished with a certificate indicating the periods of such labour which he has completed.**

   I am going to end the recording of just some of the law which I feel were more specific when considering forced labour. I would advise you to read all of the Conventions thoroughly for your better understanding. It is important to know that laws have been put in place but. The laws put in place are not being enforced so I will end with Article 31 which is pertinent to all of the Articles written concerning Convention 29 Forced Labour:

Article 31 of Convention 29

At such times as it may consider necessary the Governing Body of the International Labour Office shall present to the General Conference a report on the working of this Convention and shall examine the desirability of placing on the agenda of the Conference the question of its revision in whole or in part.

(Authors review) Laws Not Enforced

With the aforementioned laws in place as they relate to the Conventions 138, 182 and 29 there is another article needed to help with the laws already ratified. The article that needs to be added to the Conventions should state that the laws already agreed upon to be enforced must be enforced by those who have implemented them for the betterment of change of which is the common ground agreed upon by all parties. As I have stated in this book the children on the Cocoa Plantations on the Ivory Coast of Africa and Ghana are not the only children in the world who are suffering. But the children on the Ivory Coast of Africa and Ghana are documented as being the worst of the children who are suffering. This is why I am trying to bring awareness to this matter in order that a course of action to be taken to help with the problems these children have to suffer with on the Cocoa Plantations.

The last organization I want to look at is the World Trade Organization and the role it plays in its involvement with what is taking place on the Ivory Coast of Africa and Ghana. As it relates to the worst form of child abuse, child slavery, child sex trafficking, child organ trafficking, abuse, sodomy, rape and murder of these children. I will share with you the position the World Trade Organization is taking in relations to this matter.

World Trade Organization ((WTO)

Before I get into the role the World Trade Organization is playing in relations to the Cocoa Plantations, I first want to explain who they are. Then I will explain the position they are taking in relations to all of the chaos of which does bind in with the trading taking place to get the cocoa bean or pod to America.

"There are a number of ways of looking at the World Trade Organization. It is an organization for trade opening. It is a forum for governments to negotiate trade agreements. It's a place for them to settle trade disputes. It operates a system of trade rules. Essentially, the WTO is a place where member governments try to sort out the trade problems they face with each other."

From reading about the World Trade Organization it should already make you wonder why the WTO have not stepped in to place some kind of sanctions on the illegal use of these children and the laws that are being broken not only in using them to work on the Cocoa Plantations but also the conditions under which they are being made to work. It would seem that since the World Trade Organization is the link that ties all of the different governments together in order for them to come up with an agreement. The World Trade Organization could exemplify a sterner method of rules that would make the different governments comply with the laws set aside in order for the children of which are being abused to receive some form of relief.

The World Trade Organization (WTO) was born out of negotiations, and everything the WTO does is the result of negotiations. The bulk of the WTO's current work comes from the 1986-94 negotiations called the Uruguay Round and earlier negotiations under the General Agreement on Tariffs and Trade (GATT). The World Trade Organ is currently the host to new negotiations, under the "DOHA Development Agenda" launched in 2001. Where countries have faced trade barriers and wanted them lowered, the negotiations have helped to open markets for trade. But the WTO is not just about opening markets, and in some circumstances its rules support maintaining trade barriers- for example, to protect consumers or prevent the spread of disease.

(Authors rebuttal) Since the WTO is able to support maintaining trade barriers due to protect the consumers. The WTO should also be able to control the possibility of disease being spread through blood and other foreign objects that get into the cocoa pods. Another reason for the WTO to step in would be to control the high probability of an "Ebola" contamination since the viruses origin is considered to be from Africa. When sanctions are set government agencies and others have a tendency to follow suit and abide by the regulations presented in order that they are able to continue to trade as well as make the monies necessary to keep them in business. The diseased cargo once again goes as far back as the late 1700 when slaves were considered to be cargo and not human. And diseased cargo was thrown off the ship to prevent further disease from spreading. The World Trade Organization could do a lot to help in support of the child rights. Although the WTO might instigate the fact that knowing what is done to the worker, the age of the worker, or how the worker is being treated is not the purpose the WTO serves many changes could occur if the WTO would get involved by making the law breakers live by what is stated in their bylaws to follow.

At its heart are the WTO agreements, negotiated and signed by the bulk of the world's trading nations. These documents provide the legal ground rules for international commerce. They are essentially contracts, binding governments to keep their trade policies within agreed limits. Although negotiated and signed by governments, the goal is to help producers of goods and services, exporters, and importers conduct their business, while allowing governments to meet social and environmental objectives.

(Authors rebuttal) Since the WTO is the mediating factor involved in the shipment of these products the government and other entities are trying to get transported to their places of business. It would seem like their powers would be more investigative as well as demanding on the part of those needing their transportation to transport their perishable and non-perishable products. An extra tax accessed to penalties that have been documented. The WTO can use certain percentages of the shipper's profits and taken them away for their failure to comply to the rules and regulations therefore set forth to complete their business transaction.

The system's overriding purpose is to help trade flow as freely as possible so long as there are no undesirable side effects because this is important for economic development and well-being. That partly means removing obstacles. It also means ensuring that individuals, companies and governments know what the trade rules are around the world, and giving them the confidence that there will be no sudden changes of policy. In other words, the rules have to be transparent and predictable.

(Authors rebuttal) The World Trade Organization purpose is to help trade flow and to make sure all parties involved know the rules of trading and they are not going to change. But there is always room for an amended regulation to be put in place. When giving consideration to the under aged children working on the Cocoa Plantations the countries involved with forced child labor could be given a heavier levy on their taxes for their embargo. Trading rules are one thing and employment regulations is something the World Trade Organization say they do not want to have to deal with. So what is being said by the World Trade Organization is the rapes, sodomy, abuse, along with the over working these children have nothing to do with their policies concerning trade and they really do not care. Because of the power the World Trade Organization has there are many changes that could be made to help control the abuse. To help bring about a better life for the children on the Ivory Coast of Africa and Ghana and to promote change not just on the Cocoa Plantations but throughout the world. How can the World Trade Organization look at one part of the regulation knowing children are being violated and not make new stipulations in the regulations to help the countries and employers on the Cocoa Plantations look for better options of employment.

Trade relations often involve conflicting interests. Agreements, including those painstakingly negotiated in the World Trade system, often need interpreting. The most harmonious way to settle these differences is through some neutral procedure based on an agreed legal foundation. That is the purpose behind the dispute settlement process written into the World Trade Organization agreements.

(**Authors rebuttal**) With all this being said in reference to the WTO agreements. Does the World Trade Organization really expect the different companies involved with forced child labor and abuse of these children on the Cocoa Plantations? To all of a sudden grow a conscious and say they will no longer be using children to work on the Cocoa Plantations. This is what I would call reaching for expectations that are not there and thinking these companies that are not paying these children any wages or giving them any health benefits. These Cocoa Plantation owners who are not allowing these children to receive any kind of education and are working these five year old boys and girls a minimum of 100 hours a week. Does the World Trade Organization expect the Cocoa Plantation owners and those who are purchasing the cocoa bean to produce chocolate think these people are just going to through their hands in the air and say let's do what's right before sanctions are levied against us for being a part of the WORST FORMS OF SLAVERY in the history of the world.

EPILOGUE

In closing out my final venue of the Cocoa Plantations I am closing out this book and being very prayerful. It is a start to new beginnings in relations to the Cocoa Plantations. The changes that need to be implemented immediately to show urgency to what is not acceptable in relations to the laws being violated concerning the condition of which the Cocoa Plantations are considered to be hazardous and the environment non-livable. The hypocrisy concerning the laws ratified and organizations being violated are hereby and forthwith because of their ratification are able to be enforced. The Cocoa Plantations is just a start to a worldwide abolishment of forced child labor. What is found out is the Cocoa Plantations are infested with slave labor of children who are not within the legal age limitations to officially be allowed to work and there are laws which stress the age limits. With chocolate industries having a vast amount of intelligence information as to what is taking place on the Cocoa Plantations as well as other affiliated associations being kept in the loop. It is pertinent information which brings awareness to the raping of these children on the Cocoa Plantations, the sodomy, abuse, working conditions and the sex trafficking and exploitation of these five year old children. While those in positon who can help look on as though it is not a problem. Their intentional delay in correcting such a horrific situation is just not acceptable at any level of the chain when it comes to child abuse and neither is child abuse acceptable in relations to any race. It just so happens to be that these children are on the Ivory Coast of Africa and Ghana. I explained earlier in this book there are five other countries involved in the major part of the cocoa bean sales. And I also stated I am starting with the Cocoa

Plantations in Africa and Ghana because it is noted as being the worse form of child slavery in the history of the world. Much worse than slavery as it was depicted during slavery on the time there were cotton plantations in America. Slaves in America did not have any rights because the laws of the land did not apply to them because they were considered to be property. The children on the Cocoa Plantations are in even worse conditions because they haven't any education, and the laws that apply to them are not being enforced by the (ILO), (NCA), and the Conventions that are ratified. I have to put forth this question, how does a child who does not know about their rights speak up to complain about any form of violations of the rights that has been made against them? That is impossible to do.

The Harkin-Engel Protocol is nothing more than a store front law set up by politicians in the United States of America to give them a form of leeway to say they are working on doing something about the monstrosity of a situation on the Cocoa Plantations of which is continuing to build. The Cocoa Plantations is nothing new to the itinerary it just seems to lack the importance of the support needed by the Senate and Congress to bring about change. I find it kind of strange that not one Senator or Congressman in Washington, DC wants to do anything for children who are being abused. I consider that to be a bit hideous when we have all of these laws against child abuse not only in America but also Internationally and as far as I know not one nation I have researched has sanctioned the abuse of children to be legal. I do not know of any significant changes Former Former Senator Thomas Richard "Tom Harkin or Congressman Eliot Engel has brought about since 2001 which is the year the Harkin-Engel Protocol passed into law. We are now fourteen years later in the year 2015 and without renovations to the Cocoa Plantations or help for these children on the Ivory Coast of Africa and Ghana. There are laws already ratified to help these children nationally and internationally Convention 138, Convention 182, Convention 29 and Convention on the Rights of the Child (CRC), there is also the International Labor Organization. The United States does have some rights of jurisdiction to step in and help these children yet our politicians and government officials do nothing. Government officials who partake in helping to make the policies and laws nationally and internationally must also be in question to their position as it concerns abuse of children and the lack of action taken to correct the abuse on the Cocoa Plantations expeditiously. The National Confectioners Association(NCA) also have a duty to make sure policies and issues as it relates to the (NCA) Association which is noted as being one of the oldest and most respected trade associations in the world. The National Confectioners Association appears to be very quiet when it comes to the Convention on the Rights of the Children (CRC) when referencing the children on the Cocoa Plantations. The National Confectioners Association is the major association representing the entire Confectionery industry, offering education and leadership in manufacturing, technical research, public relations, retailing practices, government relations and statistical analysis.

If in fact the National Confectioners Association (NCA) is involved in public relations, and government relations as stated. When were they made aware of the Harkin-Engel Protocol? What is the National Confectioners Association's intent on doing away with child slavery on the Cocoa Plantations? Has the (NCA) made arrangements with the government officials in relations to the policies and laws concerning the issues of rape, sodomy, hazardous working conditions, age limitations, and murder of these children who work on the Cocoa Plantations? In reality of the chocolate mess I must say that two million children in slavery are quite noticeable if they are doing their research and investigative reporting?

The solution to a better means is not getting rid of chocolate. This book is not being released to condemn chocolate. What I am trying to point out is these children, five year old girls and boys deserve to have a fair chance at life. In accordance to the laws set forth by the ILO, CRC, and the Conventions which are not being applied to the Cocoa Plantations five year old boys and girls should not be working at all but they are working 100 hours a week, every week. A child as stated by the Convention on the Rights of the Child is entitled to have a normal childhood. Under the conditions of which the Cocoa Plantations are operating normal is not even close to fairly feasible. There is a better future we can look forward to and the children on the Ivory Coast of Africa and Ghana should not be on the suffering end of the (Rerum Novarum) revolutionary change.